# THE ELEPHANT
# IN THE
# GREEK AND
# ROMAN WORLD

## H. H. Scullard

THAMES AND HUDSON

B.D.
et
W.A.D.
AMICIS
FIDELISSIMIS

WITHDRAWN

© 1974 THAMES AND HUDSON

PRINTED IN GREAT BRITAIN BY
THE UNIVERSITY PRINTING HOUSE, CAMBRIDGE
ISBN 0 500 40025 3

# CONTENTS

# LIST OF ILLUSTRATIONS

XIV   *a.* Taras with elephant on coin minted at Tarentum. *b.* Elephant on an Aes Signatum.★ *c.* Sow on reverse of *b.*

XV   *a.* Coin portrait of Ptolemy II and Arsinoe II.★ *b.* Coin portrait of Antiochus I. *c.* Alexander in elephant quadriga on a gold stater of Ptolemy I.★ *d.* Athene in elephant quadriga on a coin of Antiochus I.★ *e.* Coin portrait of Ptolemy III.★ *f.* Coin portrait of Seleucus II.★

XVI   *a.* Coin portrait of Diodotus of Bactria.★ *b.* Coin portrait of Antiochus III.★ *c.* Coin portrait of Philip V of Macedon.★ *d.* Coin portrait of Ptolemy IV.★ *e.* Elephant on coin of Antiochus III.★ *f.* Coin portrait of Euthydemus of Bactria.★ *g.* Coin portrait of Demetrius of Bactria. *h.* Coin portrait of Ptolemy V.★ *i.* Head of 'Africa' on coin of Agathocles.★

XVII   *a.* Lion fighting with an elephant. Mosaic in the Hormisdas Palace, Istanbul. *b.* Elephant fighting a bull. Mosaic from the Aventine. Museo della Civiltà Romana, Rome.

XVIII   Elephant depicted in mosaic in the Foro delle Corporazioni, Ostia.

XIX   *a.* Marble elephant from Lepcis Magna. *b.* Embarkation of an elephant. Scene from mosaic of the 'Great Hunt', Piazza Armerina, Sicily.

XX   *a.* Return of the god Dionysus from India on an elephant. Relief on a sarcophagus. Walters Art Gallery, Baltimore. *b.* Julian or possibly Antoninus Pius in an elephant quadriga. Ivory diptych.★ *c.* Venus in a boat drawn by four elephants. Wall-painting from the Via dell'Abbondanza, Pompeii.

XXI   *a.* Probable portrait of Hamilcar, on a Barcid coin.★ *b.* Elephant and rider on reverse of XXI*a.* *c.* Probable portrait of Hannibal, on a Barcid coin.★ *d.* Elephant on reverse of XXI*c.* *e.* Probable portrait of Hasdrubal Barca, on a Barcid coin.★ *f.* Elephant on reverse of XXI*e.* *g.* Masinissa on a bronze coin in Musée G. Mercier, Constantine, Algeria. *h.* Elephant on reverse of XXI*g.*

XXII   *a.* Elephant on bronze coin from Lascuta, Spain. *b.* Negro's head on coin from Etruria.★ *c.* Indian elephant on reverse of XXII*b.* *d.* Head of Hercules on a crude Aes Grave.★ *e.* Elephant on reverse of XXII*d.* *f.* African elephant on silver coin of Capua.★ *g.* African elephant on bronze coin of Atella.★ *h.* Elephant with tower on small silver coin, probably from Campania.★ *i.* Head of Heracles in same series as XX*h.*★ *j.* Elephant without tower on reverse of XXII*i.* *k.* Elephant on overstruck coin of Velecha. American Numismatic Society. *l.* Radiate head of Sol on obverse of XXII*k.* *m.* African elephant on bronze coin, probably from central Italy.

XXIII   *a.* Coin portrait of Seleucus IV.★ *b.* Coin portrait of Antiochus IV.★ *c.* Coin portrait of Demetrius and Laodice.★ *d.* New Style Athenian tetradrachm.★ *e.* Coin portrait of Juba I. *f.* Elephant on bronze coin of Juba I.★ *g.* Coin portrait of Juba II.★ *h.* Elephant on reverse of XXIII*g.* *i.* Elephant on coin of Juba II.★ *j.* Elephant on coin of Juba II.★

XXIV  *a*. Denarius of C. Caecilius Metellus.★ *b*. Elephant on coin of Q. Caecilius Metellus Pius.★ *c*. Elephant on coin of Q. Caecilius Metellus Pius Scipio.★ *d*. Elephant on denarius of Julius Caesar.★ *e*. Medallion of Gordian III, showing the Colosseum, with elephant fighting a bull.★ *f*. Deified Augustus in an elephant quadriga, on sestertius of Tiberius. *g*. Elephant quadriga on sestertius of Lucius Verus.★ *h*. Elephant quadriga. Gold medallion of Diocletian and Maximian. Staatliche Museum, Berlin.

*All subjects marked ★ are at the British Museum.*


## FIGURES

19  Map to illustrate battles and sieges in which elephants were involved.

20  Lamp in the form of an elephant from south Russia.

21  Figure of elephant from south Russia.

22  Head of bronze elephant wearing defensive armour.

23  Engraved gem of elephant with low platform and soldiers.

24  Circus procession shown on a sculptured sarcophagus.


## SOURCES OF PLATE ILLUSTRATIONS

# PREFACE

If the frequency with which elephants are used in modern advertising is any indication, a widespread interest in them exists, but no single book has been devoted to their activities in the classical world. The closest approach to a monograph is well over one hundred years old, namely Colonel P. Armandi's *Histoire militaire des éléphants* (Paris, 1843). This is an excellent and sensible work, but necessarily antiquated in many respects and covering only one, albeit the most important, aspect of their use. In this present book I have tried to present a general overall picture, but in view of Professor J. M. C. Toynbee's chapter in her recent *Animals in Roman Life and Art* (1973) in this series, I have not dealt so fully with the appearance of elephants in art as such. I have not aimed at complete documentation, but have tried to supply sufficient references for the classical reader (who will in any case know where to look further) without overloading the work for any more general reader who may be interested. I have also tried to bring the observations of the ancient writers into the light which modern zoologists have thrown upon the elephant's natural history, and for this aspect I am particularly indebted to the work of Dr Sylvia K. Sikes and others whose books are mentioned below.

The genesis of this book is that some twenty-five years ago I became interested in Hannibal's elephants, and this interest was further stimulated by a visit to the coin room of the British Museum where Dr (now Sir Edward) Robinson kindly directed my attention to some unduly neglected coins, and where I also met Sir William Gowers who had been drawn there on a similar quest; his intimate knowledge of elephants proved most helpful. The result was a couple of articles (one in collaboration with Gowers) and a few lectures. There the matter rested until quite recently I decided to turn to this topic again.

For translations of ancient authors I have gratefully made us of the Loeb Classical Library, with some minor adjustments, except for Aristotle where I have turned to the Oxford translation. I have not burdened any of my friends with the task of reading my manuscript, but I am most grateful to a few who have supplied me with various references; also to the staff of Thames & Hudson, especially Miss Jocelyn Selson, and to Mr Peter Clayton (now at the British Museum), for help with the illustrations.

Most of the coins here illustrated have been enlarged but since this is not primarily a book for numismatists it has seemed unnecessary to give the precise degrees of magnification.

H. H. Scullard

*London, 1974*

# CHAPTER I

# NATURAL HISTORY OF THE ELEPHANT

Herodotus, who can have had only a hazy idea of what an elephant looked like, found none during his visit to Egypt, and when he reached Lake Moeris some sixty miles south of modern Cairo he certainly had no idea at all that he was at the cradle of the elephant's earliest ancestor—and the graveyard of some of its representatives. But here at the beginning of the present century were discovered fossil bones of the earliest member of the order of Proboscidea which was appropriately named Moeritherium, the Wild Animal of Moeris. It was in fact a small creature, some 2 ft high, looking more like a diminutive hippopotamus than an elephant, but skeletal similarities proclaimed that it formed the earliest of the three suborders into which naturalists divide the Proboscidea. It made its debut on the world's stage some seventy million years ago at the beginning of the Eocene epoch of the Cenozoic era, but like the second later suborder (Deinotheridea) it was represented only by a single genus. The third suborder, named Elephantoidea, how-ever, developed three families and a large number of genera. This differentiation took place during a vast number of millennia as the early elephants spread out to become lords of creation in all the continents of the world except Australia and Antarctica. The dis-tribution centre appears to have been those parts of North Africa which were not at that time covered by the sea called Tethys; they consisted of fertile plains and swamps, where now stretch the arid wastes of the Sahara. Hence during the course of millions of years elephants spread to central and southern Africa, and to northern India, whence some returned to Africa; others made their way to Italy and north-western Europe, while yet others went through China and eastern Siberia over the land-bridge which preceded the Bering Strait to Alaska, to North and ultimately South

America. This vast explosion was caused partly by climatic changes and the need to seek fresh pastures, and in the process of adapting to new environments an immense number of new species was created, over 350 in all. We cannot here follow the emergence of this bewildering assortment of elephants of varied shapes and sizes, some extremely weird and wonderful, which evolved in the process of natural selection, but can only reflect with sadness that two species alone survive today.

Two other species, however, managed to survive until comparatively recently. The mastodons, who formed the second family of Elephantoidea, lived in North America until some 8,000 years ago when they must have been seen by early man there. The mammoths, who belong to the third and true family of elephants and appeared at the end of the Pliocene period, lived on to be hunted by Stone Age man who has left pictures of such hunts painted on the walls of his caves. Paradoxically, we know a great deal more about the mammoth than, for instance, about the elephants used by the Carthaginians in historical times, since frozen bodies of mammoths, with flesh still intact, have been found in the ice of Siberia.

One other genus of elephants may be mentioned parenthetically, since it is represented in an interesting discovery in our own country. In 1964 at Aveley in Essex the bones of a Woolly Mammoth were discovered in a clay-pit that was being worked commercially. A rescue excavation was mounted on August Bank holiday and in the process the remains of a second elephant were found a foot beneath those of the first. This proved to be a Straight-toothed elephant (*Palaeoloxodon antiquus*) which lived considerably earlier in one of the interglacial periods which alternated between the cold periods of the Ice Age to which the mammoth belonged. Thus we have specimens of a vast variety of prehistoric elephants, but no skeleton survives to reveal the structure of the elephants of the Atlas Mountains of classical times.

A diagram of the elephant's family tree may help to clarify this very condensed account:

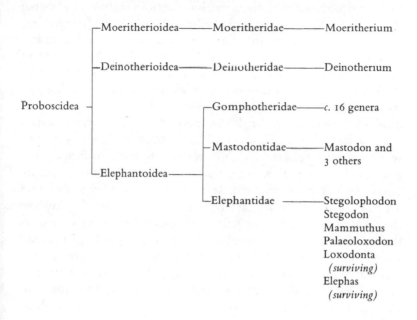

| SUBORDERS | FAMILIES | GENERA |
|---|---|---|
| Moeritherioidea | Moeritheridae | Moeritherium |
| Deinotherioidea | Deinotheridae | Deinotherium |
| Elephantoidea | Gomphotheridae | c. 16 genera |
| | Mastodontidae | Mastodon and 3 others |
| | Elephantidae | Stegolophodon Stegodon Mammuthus Palaeoloxodon Loxodonta (surviving) Elephas (surviving) |

Proboscidea

## THE ELEPHANT'S PHYSIOLOGY

The two living survivors of this widespread and richly diversified order of mammals are the Indian and African elephant, but before examining their minor differences we must consider their general characteristics. It is not proposed to attempt a description that would be appropriate to a book on natural history, but merely to emphasize some of their physical features, so that later we may consider in the light of present knowledge what Aristotle and others tell us about them. In what follows my debt to scientific books is naturally great and I would draw the reader's attention especially to two books (in addition to the standard work by H. F. Osborn, *Proboscidea*, 2 vols, 1936–42), namely an entertaining general account by R. Carrington, *Elephants* (1958), and a fuller more technical study, *The Natural History of the African Elephant* (1971) by Dr Sylvia K. Sikes.

Any general description of the elephant's body and its functioning might well start with the trunk or proboscis since this organ is

15

not only so unusual but is of the greatest importance to the animal itself. It is a muscular, prehensile elongation of the nose and upper lip, with nostrils at the end and one (in Indians) or two (in Africans) 'fingers' at the extreme tip. This tip is extremely sensitive and its nerves send detailed messages to the brain about the nature of objects touched or smelled; further, hairs on the trunk itself aid its sensitivity. In action the trunk is powerful, flexible and delicate. Its primary function is to act as a hand or arm to convey food and drink to the mouth; it can also be used for squirting water or sand over the body. The trunk also enables the beast to obtain food, even when attractive fruit or leaves are beyond its reach. In such a situation it will try to push a tree over with its forehead, but, if unsuccessful, will then curl its trunk around the tree and try to shake off the fruit, break off the whole tree or uproot it completely. Further, the trunk is used in part to help to produce the variety of sounds that an elephant makes: trumpeting, screams, squeals, groans and roars. With it the elephant disciplines or aids its young and caresses its mate. The Indian, but apparently not the African elephant, uses its trunk in collaboration with its forefeet to move objects, as logs, though the African does co-ordinate its use with its tusks in order to handle logs or even to carry very young calves. Elephants are essentially pacific, but can use the trunk either to throw an attacker in the air or crush him with forehead and rolled-up trunk (Africans may kneel on or gore an enemy with its tusks, but do not trample on him with the soles of their feet). The trunk is very vulnerable, and damage to it leads in the wild to 'roguish' behaviour through pain and often ultimately to starvation and death, while in warfare the trunk becomes a major target for the enemy. Lastly it may be of incidental interest to note that genuine examples are recorded of calves losing their trunk-tips to crocodiles, thus showing that Kipling's splendid story of how the Elephant's Child got its trunk was not entirely unrelated to the struggles of nature (in point of fact the evolutionary process can be traced with reasonable certainty).

The lower lip is thick and shortish, and the mouth too is small so that large branches must be broken before being inserted for mastication. The eyes also are relatively small and the eyesight is often said to be weak, but this applies to vision in bright sunlight: in forests the elephant can see keenly up to fifty yards. The ear is one of the chief marks of difference between African and Indian

I: *a*. African and *b*. Indian elephants. Note the contour of the back, the size of ear, and the carriage of the head (and the segmentation of the trunk in *a*).

II: *a.* Indian elephant pushing down a tree. *b.* Submerged elephants; on the left the trunk of one used as a snorkel.

III: *a.* Indian elephants being embarked on river barge in Burma. The gangway is camouflaged with grass. *b.* African elephants tethered in lines in camp.

IV: *a.* Young African elephant. *b.* Young Indian elephant.

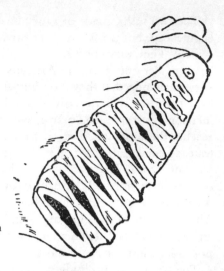

Fig. 1. Tooth, the sixth molar, of an African elephant (A. Jeannin, *L'Elephant d'Afrique*, p. 43)

elephants. The small ear of the latter contrasts with the great fan-like ear of the African, which helps to regulate the temperature by rhythmic flapping as well as appearing, when spread out at right angles, to increase the size of the beast in the eyes of an enemy.

The teeth, no less than the trunk, are both structurally very interesting and vital to the preservation of life. The elephant has no canines, and incisors only in the upper jaw; these, after the first growths or 'tushes' have fallen out like 'milk' teeth, grow into tusks. During its lifetime it is provided with twenty-four large molars, grinding teeth, each weighing eight or nine lb and attaining a foot or so in length; there are six, made up of a number of transverse plates of dentine covered with enamel and held together by cement, in each half jaw. The number of plates varies, Indians having more than twenty, Africans ten or less; in the African these wear down to a lozenge shape and have given this species its name of *Loxodonta* or Slanting-tooth. But in fact only four of the twenty-four molars are visible and available for use at any one time; as the grinding surface is worn down, they are replaced by four others. After six such changes the store of teeth is exhausted and the life-span of the elephant is reached; inability to masticate sufficient food is a contributory or at times a primary cause of death which comes between the sixtieth and eightieth year. Thus the elephant's expectation of life approximates closely to that of man.

17

The two tusks, made of ivory or dentine, at first have a conical enamel cap, but this soon wears away and the tip is covered with cement. They vary considerably in size and shape. Asiatic elephants have smaller ones than the Africans, while those of their cows are very small indeed, if they have any at all. In Africa the bull elephant has larger tusks than the cow, but today larger tuskers are becoming increasingly scarce, and a tusk weighing more than 130 lb rarely reaches the ivory auction; a weight of 116–220 lb and a length (outside curve) of 112–124 inches represent maxima for different parts of Africa. Tusks are not a reliable criterion for judging age, nor are they normally dropped by wild elephants. One tusk is usually more used than the other (cf. right- or left-handed men). Their uses are manifold: digging, moving branches, resting the trunk, offence and defence. They are also the elephant's deadliest possession: lust for ivory has threatened its very survival.

The skin of this pachyderm varies in different parts of the body, but in places reaches an inch in thickness; its creases give the beast one of its most obvious characteristics. A large number of tactile sensory nerve-endings on the skin can be used by riders or attendants to transmit orders. The tail is relatively short and mainly bare, but it ends in a tuft of long thick hairs, which today are commercially valuable for sale as bracelets or amulets. Between the eye and ear a small passage leads to a gland which has been connected with *musth*, a state of irritability and wildness which sometimes mysteriously falls on elephants; in particular it has been linked with periods of sexual activity, but this link is now generally discounted, since it occurs in females as well as in males while sexual behaviour often takes place when the animals are not on *musth*. Periods of aggression, however, do certainly take place, whatever their cause, more especially in the African elephant.

An elephant's skull has to be large in order to sustain the weight of the tusks, and indeed grows in proportion to this need. Its weight is reduced by the number of sinuses and cavities within. Minor differences of structure enable males to be distinguished from females, and Indians from Africans. The mechanism of the brain, which weighs between nine and twelve lb in an adult African bull, produces intelligence and bodily co-ordination which is surpassed only by the higher primates. The weight of the brain, however, relative to the body weight is much smaller than that found in man and apes. There is little to note about the vertebral column except that the back of the Indian elephant is convex or level, while that of the African is concave or 'saddle' shaped. The cylindrical pillar-like legs are well adapted to upholding the animal's weight; the thigh bone (femur) is proportionately longer than the shin bone (tibia) in elephants than in men or horses. The heel is slightly higher than the toes (half-way between plantigrade man and digitigrade horse) and the bones of the foot are embedded in a sponge-like cushion which acts as a shock-absorber. All elephants have five toes in each foot. The external hooves or toe-nails, however, vary; Africans have five in each forefoot and four in each hindfoot, but some tend to wear smaller or disappear completely. Though the elephant can move quickly, it cannot trot, gallop or jump. Though skilful in picking its way in mountainous country, even on narrow ledges of rock, it cannot come down by jumping from one foothold to another but has to slide down on its buttocks. Similarly its leg-formation prevents it crossing wide ditches with vertical sides, though it can *walk* down if they slope; a jump down would fracture its bones or wrench its shoulder. It can stand on its backlegs (in the wild as well as in the circus) in order to reach fruit high up in trees; it then often sinks back on its haunches and indeed sometimes sits on a log as if on a chair.

The so-called twin apexes of the heart have sometimes suggested that the elephant has two hearts, but this is really a bifurcation of a single apex and is much less pronounced in healthy wild elephants. The stomach is necessarily large in order to cope with the quantities of food and drink that are taken in. Twenty-two gallons of water may be consumed at one time and up to fifty in a day: thus African hunters in arid country have been known to kill elephants merely for the water in the stomach. As will be seen, when Aristotle says that the elephant appears to have four stomachs he is referring to the stomach, the caecum, the colon and the small intestine. He also reports, remarkably correctly, that there is no gall bladder. The sexual organs are peculiar in two main respects. The testicles are situated within the body of the male and are thus not visible; the penis lies externally in a sheath on the ventral surface of the body wall. Secondly, the vulva of the female is low down, well removed from the anus. The breasts lie behind the forelegs; they are thus more forward than in most quadrupeds, and they number only two.

The elephant impresses by its sheer bulk. It is exceeded in height only by the comparatively slim giraffe and in weight by no living land mammal. The largest recorded African elephant, now mounted in the Smithsonian Museum in the USA, stands 13 ft 2 in at shoulder height. As will be seen, Africans fall into two classes: the larger Bush elephant has an average herd shoulder height of more than 8 ft, while the smaller Forest elephant is under 8 ft. In general, Asiatic elephants are shorter at the shoulder than the larger Africans, but some tall heavy individuals, comparable with the Bush elephant, do occur. Five tons is a good average figure for the weight of an African bull, while some may reach six or seven; no rhinoceros or hippopotamus is known to weigh over four tons.

To support this bulk the intake is naturally great (though, in fact, weight for weight, it needs less food than a mouse). The elephant is herbivorous, delicately choosing the most succulent of berries and at the next moment overthrowing whole trees. A wild African elephant may consume 300–350 lb of vegetation a day, and may spend sixteen hours a day securing it; Indian elephants appear to eat only half or less of that amount. In captivity and inactivity they obviously need much less; 100 lb of hay, with a little supplementation of oats and vegetables, suffices. Such large quantities are needed because the elephant digests only 44 per cent of its hay which is much lower than the capacity of ruminants or horses. As we have seen, it can drink up to fifty gallons a day, taking up a trunkful of some two or three gallons at a time. When elephants come to water, be it river, lake, water-hole or marsh, they line up in an orderly fashion. After drinking, they bathe with great enjoyment; the babies are washed and the youngsters splash about like children, often squealing with fun. After coming out of the water they like to squirt mud or dust over their bodies; this skin treatment may help to reduce the irritation from flies. The elephant in fact likes water, both externally and internally. Elephants need much less sleep than human beings: some four hours a night suffices, lying down, though they may doze off for short periods in the day while standing. Puberty is reached at about ten–thirteen years of age; the reproductive mechanism does not differ between Africans and Indians; the method of copulation is that normally adopted by quadrupeds; gestation lasts about twenty-two months, and sexual activity continues in both bulls and cows into extreme old age. The life-span is between sixty and seventy or even eighty years, while it is possible that in some parts of the Congo some elephants may have reached a century.

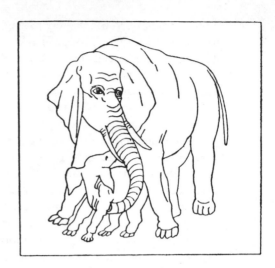

Fig. 2. Mother and calf. From a painting at Pompeii (S. Reinach, *Repertoire de pei.iture grecques* . . ., 1922, –. 357 no. 9)

## HABITS

After this sketch of the elephant's anatomy and physiology, we turn briefly to its habits and social behaviour. The social unit is a herd, but this larger group of some dozen to fifty individuals consists of three sub-units. First there is the family, comprising one cow and her offspring up to teenagers. Then a group of families join to form a clan under the leadership of the senior cow, with family units, each thought to be headed by one of her own daughters or sisters. Thus the system is essentially matriarchical. A herd is formed when joined by one sire bull who is often attended by one or more adult but inferior bulls. During mating periods bulls show considerable affection for the cows, but little interest in the calves when born. Twins are very rare. At a birth the female relatives often gather round and even assist the mother in her labour. When the herd is on the move the cows go first, led by the matriarch, while, unless danger threatens, the bull may lag far behind. Mothers show great maternal care for the calves, especially for the first two years, and female relatives also may help in their 'education'. The strong family bond is seen in the way injured or decrepit members are helped by the stronger. When an animal is dying the other members of the herd walk round it and then stand in a circle facing outwards; after it has died, they are reluctant to leave and often drop grass and branches on or around the corpse. On occasion herds may gather together and some regrouping takes place; this vast mustering of herds is an awe-inspiring sight, though seldom witnessed. Elephants are constantly on the move, foraging, and may undertake much longer migrations in response to the impact of wet and dry seasons. They move easily and can travel at some ten miles an hour. Rough terrain bothers them little, while they are good swimmers (the sinuses in their skulls help them to keep afloat). They have been seen swimming even in very deep rivers, such as the lower Zambesi, and the Nile and in Lake Chad, but when a river is not too deep they may prefer to walk across on its bed, using their trunks as snorkels, though the youngsters would have to swim and are placed on the upstream side. Indian elephants have been seen helping their calves to swim; no doubt Africans must be equally instructive. Ditches or ravines might seem a barrier in view of their inability to jump, but if faced with a vertical bank the elephant can wear it down with its forefeet and thus make a ramp to slide or walk down. Col. Williams (*Elephant Bill*, p. 44) records that when a party of wild elephants 'reached a muddy nullah with banks eight ft high, the leading elephants plunged their forefeet into the edge of the bank, broke it away, and, sitting on their haunches, made a toboggan slide for the herd following them.' In general the elephant shows great adaptability to changes of environment, including variations in temperature and altitude. Indeed it is said to be more adaptable than any other mammal, except man and the baboon. But though ready for change, when they are settled for a period in a district they appear (like many other creatures) to claim and mark out a 'territory'. Now that it seems that *musth* is not primarily a sexual activity, it is suggested that the temporal gland secretion, temporin, may be used to mark trees and thus delimit territory.

Within its habitat the elephant tends to live at peace, when not harassed by man. Bulls on occasion fight one another, but the rest of the animal world offers no serious challenge. The African elephant dislikes the black rhinoceros but takes little notice of lions apart from an occasional brush, although encounters between Indian elephants and tigers may be rather more serious. In the unnatural conditions of captivity, elephants may be frightened easily, even by the appearance of a mouse or a barking dog. Sometimes herds may panic in the wild (especially today when faced with 'unnatural' noises as low-flying aircraft); they have been seen fleeing, led by the senior cow, with the small calves running under their bellies and the older calves holding on to their mothers' tails with their trunks. In fact elephants show both nervousness and often extreme courage.

## INDIANS AND AFRICANS

We now return to the difference between the two surviving species of elephant, each the sole survivor of its genus: the Indian *Elephas maximus* and the African *Loxodonta africana*. Although superficially not very different, they have in fact a number of distinctive features which enable them to be distinguished at a glance.

The Indian (or Asiatic) elephant is indigenous to Asia and at the present day still enjoys a wide distribution, including India, Ceylon (Sri Lanka), Assam, Burma, Siam (Thailand) and Malaysia: it is adapted to a variety of natural habitats. The highest point of its body is the top of its head, which has twin domes, and its forehead is slightly indented. Its trunk has only one finger-like tip. The cows have very small tusks, or none at all, while the molars differ somewhat in structure from those of the African elephant. The back of the Indian is convex (or, at most, level, never concave). The skin, which is normally dark, sometimes becomes lighter in old age, but genuine albino specimens do occur and these 'white elephants' have generally been highly regarded in the East (though such gifts by Siamese kings have sometimes proved more burdensome than welcome to their recipients). In general they are shorter at the shoulder than Africans, but it must be remembered that just as among men, so among elephants, individuals vary and an occasional Indian might equal a large African specimen, although the average height is less.

The features which distinguish the African from the Indian are its greater height, its immense triangular ears (with the dorsal edge bending over medially), its concave back, and its trunk, which has two 'fingers' and is generally more strongly segmented than that of the Indian; the latter's hindquarters slope more sharply and at rest it carries its head lower. Thus the African species is quite distinct from the Indian, but individuals show so many minor variations that at one time the species was thought to include a large number of subspecies or races. It is now, however, customary to recognize only two, while the so-called 'pygmy' elephant is completely rejected (the 'myth' arose from inaccurate observation and the misidentification of young animals). These two are the larger Bush or Savannah elephant (*Loxodonta africana africana*) and the Forest elephant (*Loxodonta africana cyclotis*); the modern names are not very appropriate, since they do not correspond accurately with the habitat of the two races, but they are useful as labels. The main differences between the two are size (the average adult Bush is over 8 ft at the shoulder, the Forest under that figure) and the shape of the ears (the ears of the Forest race are smaller and rounded, hence the scientific name of *cyclotis*, while those of the Bush race are large and triangular with the apex lying more forward when at rest). The Bush elephant holds its head higher, emphasizing the concavity of its back, while the Forest holds its in a slightly forward-bent position which makes the back appear to be slightly less concave. The tusks of the Forest animal are usually straight, pointing downward and smaller, while those of the Bush are usually curved, carried forward and larger; the ivory of *cyclotis* is harder and denser than that of *africana*. A supposed variation in the number of hooves on the fore and hindfeet of the two races is no longer accepted, nor is *cyclotis* now regarded as essentially more 'temperamental' than his brother.

No ancient writer was able to observe all such distinctions, either within the African species or even as between Africans and Indians. However, as knowledge of the two species gradually increased, a general conclusion was reached that the Indian was larger than the African. The emergence and reliability of this belief will be better discussed later, after we have looked at what the early Greek writers have to say in general about elephants (see p. 6off.). And before that, the distribution of the animal in pre-classical and classical times must be considered.

DISTRIBUTION IN EARLY TIMES

At one time elephants roamed over the whole of Africa. Today they are confined to the area south of the Sahara in ever decreasing districts and numbers, and if it were not for the national parks, where, of course, conditions cannot completely reproduce those of the wild, they might be threatened with complete extinction. The Bush elephant is scattered in pockets throughout tropical and

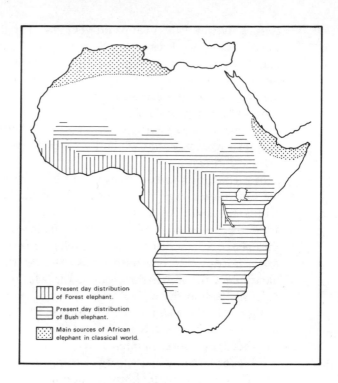

Fig. 3. Africa,
distribution map

southern Africa, but the Forest (*cyclotis*) is confined to a belt of
West and West-Central Africa, which includes Nigeria, Ghana,
Congo, and western Uganda. There is some overlapping and since
the two races will interbreed, intermediate types occur. The most
northerly of all surviving groups is found in modern Mauritania,
north of latitude 17° 10′ up to the heights of Tijelat. Reduced to
about a hundred head in 1947, they are short in height, due chiefly
no doubt to the poor vegetation around them and possibly partly
to excessive inbreeding through decreasing numbers.[2] There can
be little doubt that they belong to the *cyclotis* race and their significance far outweighs their numbers, since they almost certainly
represent the residue of the elephants which were spread over
north Africa before the desiccation of the Sahara and thus are survivors of the same race as that which in classical times lived north
of the Atlas Mountains and provided the Carthaginians with their
elephants. Further south beyond the Sahara were great herds of
of both Forest and Bush elephants. Those that lived in central and
southern Africa must have been largely beyond the horizon of the

25

classical world. One group, however, was within reach, namely those of Ethiopia, Eritrea and Somalia, which was exploited particularly by the Ptolemies (p. 126 ff.). These were probably Forest rather than Bush elephants (p. 62) and thus there is no reason to believe that to any significant extent they differed physically from those of North-west Africa.[3] In sum, in classical times there was one group in North-west Africa and a second known group around Ethiopia, with an unknown and untapped supply in the rest of the 'dark Continent'.

In prehistoric days the picture had been very different. During the Quaternary Age in Europe much of the Sahara was covered with trees and grass and was well watered by rivers, a habitat admirably suited to elephants, but as the ice-sheets retreated from Europe the Sahara dried up and the elephants were forced to withdraw northwards or southwards. Before this they had been plentiful in the north throughout the Megreb (i.e. roughly the Atlas massif and the coastal plain from Morocco to Tunisia) and in Egypt. In the Megreb the prehistoric *Elephas atlanticus* is found in all Palaeolithic levels until the full Upper Palaeolithic. It was succeeded by *Elephas africanus* which had probably appeared in pre-Neolithic times and survived from then on into the Christian era. These elephants are known not only from fossil bones, such as molars, but above all from representations in the cave-paintings of Neolithic man where they are depicted in considerable numbers. Their large ears and concave backs at once proclaim their African species.[4]

Further east the Nile valley ecologically constitutes a separate subdivision of North Africa. Here in Upper Egypt rock-drawings of the fourth or early third millennium BC show many pictures of elephants, sometimes with other animals and sometimes being hunted, though it would probably be premature to suppose that hunting led to capture and domestication (pl. VIa). Yet, there is a possibility that taming did take place in the pre-Dynastic (Naqada) and very early Dynastic periods. But between the First and Fourth Dynasties (during the first half of the third millennium) a temporary worsening of climatic conditions led to changes in the fauna: the elephant, together with the rhinoceros and the giraffe, disappeared from Egypt as aridity increased.[5] Thus future Pharaohs, who wanted to hunt elephants or obtain ivory, would have to go father afield, either south to Nubia or east to Syria.

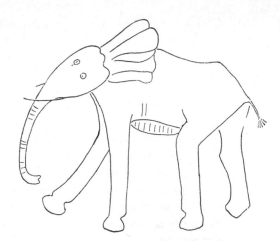

Fig. 4. Rock drawing of
elephant from Oued Djaret
(A. Jeannin, *L'Elephant
d'Afrique*, p. 224)

Although an elephant is mentioned in a fragmentary inscription which refers to an expedition by Sesostris I (Senusret I, reigned *c.* 1971–28) to Nubia, there is little to suggest that the Egyptian kings obtained live elephants from this source to any extent.[6] However, ivory was increasingly brought by trade down the Nile from the southern regions, especially during the New Kingdom (from *c.* 1580), while expeditions like that sent along the coast of the Red Sea by Queen Hatshepsut to Punt (Somalia) *c.* 1500 might bring back tusks. Yet this source was not adequate and had to be supplemented by imports from Asia. The expansionist policies of Thutmose I (1525–12) and his grandson Thutmose III (1504–1450) led them through Syria to the Euphrates and both took the opportunity to hunt elephants. The personal aspect of the exploit of Thutmose III is rather overshadowed by the fact that our knowledge of it derives not from a grandiloquent inscription of the king himself but from one set up by an officer named Amenemhab who steals the limelight: 'Again I beheld another excellent deed which the Lord of the Two Lands did in Niy. He hunted 120 elephants, for the sake of their tusks. I engaged the largest which was among them, which fought against his majesty; I cut off his hand [trunk] while he was alive before his majesty, while I stood in the water between two rocks. Then my lord rewarded me with gold.'[7] The development of the combat is not very clear: it has been suggested that Amenemhab was pursued by a (wounded?) elephant and took refuge between the rocks. This big game hunt had a happy sequel.

Like Alexander the Great and Napoleon, Thutmose III was not merely a conqueror but interested in the natural history of the lands he overran; at Egyptian Thebes he made a collection of all the interesting plants and animals which he came across in his travels. One of the Syrian elephants was presumably included: at any rate, in the tomb of his vizier Rekhmire, one of the most important monuments of the New Empire, is depicted an elephant, being led by a rope and with some form of covering on its neck. It is quite clearly an Indian, not an African, elephant.[8] (Fig. 5.)

India and elephants are closely linked in popular thought, but we cannot here attempt to trace the manifold uses in peace and war, in ceremonial and religion, to which the Indians put the elephant during ancient times, let alone in succeeding centuries. The elephant was known from earliest days and appears to have been tamed and domesticated during the so-called Indus civilization which flourished at centres such as Mohenjo-Daro and Harappa from about 2500 to 1700 BC. Here it is frequently depicted (pl. VIb) on numerous steatite seals, and since it is sometimes shown with a covering on its back, it was clearly being used by man; its use for riding and war became common in India in the first millennium.[9] This development is implied in the Vedas (c. 1500–1200 BC): in the earlier Rigveda the elephant is described as a wild beast (*mriga*) with a hand (*hastin*), but increasing familiarity led to the use of the word *hastin* alone. The slightly later Yaruveda texts refer to the keeping of tame elephants, though there is no suggestion that they were yet used for war.[10]. The Indian elephant (*elephas maximus*) was equally known and used in ancient China: during the Bronze Age in the second millennium it was tamed and kept in zoological gardens, while in the Yin and Chou Dynasties (c. 1750–c. 1123; 1122–256 BC) it was used for riding and as a beast of burden.[11]

The elephant does not appear to have played an important part in Mesopotamian civilization in early days. Elephant bones have been found in excavations at Babylon and Nuzi, belonging to the period of Hammurabi, while an elephant with rider is depicted on a relief from Digdiggeh in southern Mesopotamia, but this may have been imported from India, while ivory may have been brought from the Mohenjo-Daro civilization. In the fifteenth century elephants are attested near the Euphrates and in Syria by the hunting expeditions of Thutmose. At the end of the twelfth century we get further documentary evidence: the Assyrian king

Fig. 5. Painting of Syrian elephant in the tomb of the vizier Rekhmire.

Tiglath-pileser I in his fifth campaign drove the Ahlami to Carchemish and 'in the same region of Haran and of the river Habur I slaughtered ten mighty male elephants and took four alive. Their hides and their tusks, together with the live elephants, I brought to my city of Assur'. In the ninth century Assurnasirpal II wrote, 'I collected the herds of elephants in my city of Calah', where he seems to have established a zoo; he also killed thirty from an ambush. A more recently discovered stele of *c*. 879 adds further details about the king's prowess, 'I slew 450 mighty lions . . . I cut down 200 ostriches like caged birds, and 30 elephants I cast into the pit . . . 5 live wild elephants from the governor of Suhi and the governor of Lubda I received; they went along with me on my march.' The obelisk of Shalmaneser III in the ninth century (pl. VIc) depicts the tribute he received from Syrian and other rulers, among them Jehu of Israel; these gifts include an elephant from the land of Musri, which is probably to be sought in the region of the Persian Gulf and thus this elephant will have been of Indian origin. Other tribute might include tusks or hides. When the Hittite city of Carchemish was subjected to Assyria, the booty included elephant-hides, an item also contained in the tribute paid by Hezekiah under the terms he agreed with the Assyrian Sennacherib in 701 BC. Further, an elephant head with very large eyes comes from a temple of the second half of the second millennium at Beth-shan in Palestine.[12]

Elephants were clearly widespread in Syria in early times and their range may have reached a considerable way to the East. Thus some scholars speak of the 'Syrian' elephant, as distinct from the Indian and African. This term is more appropriate in a geographical

29

than in a physical sense, since there is no evidence that the Syrian differed in race from the Indian, although, of course, there may have been minor variations. The only Syrian of which a pictorial record survives is the one on the tomb of Rekhmire: its convex back and small ears proclaim its eastern origin. However, it is depicted as relatively small in comparison with a man nearby, but at the same time it has tusks: thus it is either a calf, with tusks wrongly added by artistic licence, or an adult which is drawn out of scale. At Alalakh in northern Syria, between Aleppo and the coast, elephant tusks have been found in a storeroom of the eighteenth-century palace, as also at Megiddo.[13] But just as much earlier the African elephant had died out in Egypt, so in Syria and Meso-potamia this 'Syrian' elephant disappeared in the first half of the first millennium and no wild ones were found there in later classical times. The cause may have been partly climatic but hunting must have been a major factor, and the reason behind this was not 'sport' as such but ivory. Amenemhab baldly stated that this was the motive which actuated Thutmose III, and, unfortunately for the elephant, ivory carving became a major art and the desire for ivory was widespread. Ivory was worked from a very early period in Egypt and Babylonia and, when the local supply failed in Egypt, the Pharaohs would tap eastern sources. Then too Minoans, Mycenaeans and Cypriots practised the art and needed raw material. If there was a slight lull in the troubled centuries around 1000 BC in the Aegean region, the demand was renewed from the ninth century onwards. An unrivalled series of carved ivories has been discovered at Samaria and in the Assyrian palaces at Nimrud and Khorsabad, and others have been found at Ephesus, Sparta, the Etruscan towns in Italy, at Carthage and in Spain. Phoenician and Syrian artists were the principal source and their work was widely exported and imitated, but their activity hastened the extinction of the Syrian elephant, after which ivory had to be sought from India, or Ethiopia or North-west Africa (p. 260 ff.).[14]

After the disappearance of the Syrian elephant the next to go was the North African one. Its distribution and duration are roughly known, but not in any detail. These animals were seen by the Carthaginian explorer Hanno in the Atlas Mountains region in the early fifth century BC (p. 30) and there is plenty of later evidence for their widespread existence in modern Morocco and Algeria, together probably with Tunisia. The Carthaginians drew heavily upon them for war purposes, and the fact that they were able to replace their losses in the First Punic War so quickly (p. 152 f.) demonstrates the number of elephants then available. The Romans later made even heavier inroads in order to stock their amphitheatres, while of course the demand for ivory continued. In the early third century AD they were common in Mauretania, according to Solinus (though he may just be repeating the remark of Pliny in the first century), while a mosaic at Piazza Armerina (pl. XIXb) shows that they were still shipped to Italy at the end of that century. But the supply gradually diminished, and in the fourth century Themistius said that there were no more in the country, while in the seventh century Isidore of Seville wrote of Mauretania Tingitana that 'it was once full of elephants; now only India produces them'. Some changes in climatic conditions *may* have helped the decline, but not necessarily: in modern times lions have become extinct in Algeria (not to mention elephants near the Cape of Good Hope) without this factor operating: man was the chief cause.[15]

# CHAPTER II

# GREEK KNOWLEDGE OF THE ELEPHANT

## THE EARLIEST WRITERS

The elephant was a somewhat late-comer on the stage of classical history. The word *elephas* (ἐλέφας) meant to Homer, as to the later poets Hesiod and Pindar, not the animal but ivory.[16] Gradually knowledge of the source of ivory must have become more widespread so that Hermippus, a comic poet writing at Athens about 430–420 BC, could say 'Libya supplies ivory in plenty for trade', but the animal itself is first mentioned in Greek literature by Herodotus (IV. 191), writing shortly before Hermippus. Herodotus visited Egypt and indeed went as far south as the settlement named after elephants, Elephantine, but he apparently never encountered an elephant, and so we lack a description to match his delightful portraits of the crocodile, hippopotamus and other Egyptian animals. All he knew was that the westwards parts of Libya were 'exceedingly hilly and wooded and full of wild beasts. In that country are huge snakes, lions, elephants, bears, asps, horned asses, and dogheaded men and headless men who have eyes in their breasts, at least as the Libyans say, and the wild men and wild women [gorillas or chimpanzees?], and many other creatures that are not fabulous'. Although the Greek is very slightly ambiguous, Herodotus by his remark 'as the Libyans say' is disclaiming responsibility only for the dogheaded and headless creatures (which may actually be monsters, though some would equate them with the dogheaded baboon and some ape which carried its head very low). Besides the North African elephant Herodotus knew, by inference, of the Ethiopian animal, since he records (III.97) that every third year the Ethiopians sent as tribute to the Persian court 'two choenixes (roughly quarts) of pure gold, two hundred blocks of ebony, five Ethiopian boys, and twenty great elephant tusks'; this tribute was still being paid in Herodotus' own day.

V: Large African elephant.

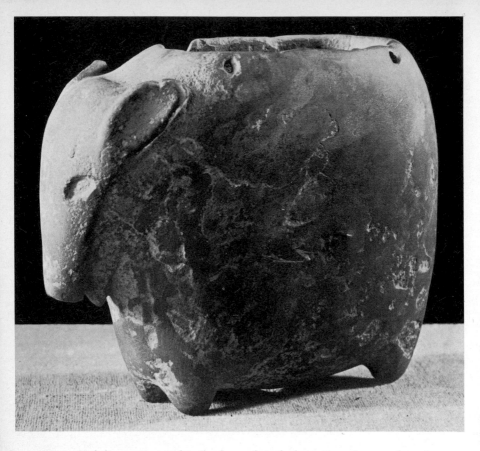

VI: *a.* Pink limestone vessel in the form of an elephant. Egyptian, pre-dynastic or of the 1st Dynasty. After this time elephants died out in Egypt. *b.* Steatite seal from Mohenjo-Daro, showing an elephant of the early 2nd millennium BC. *c.* Detail from black obelisk of the Assyrian King Shalmaneser III, after his victory over Hazael of Damascus, 841 BC.

VII: *a.* Painted dish from Capena in Campania, Italy, depicting a cow Indian elephant and her calf, 3rd century BC. It almost certainly represents one of Pyrrhus' elephants.
*b.* Terracotta statuette from Myrina in Asia Minor. The elephant is attacking a soldier, whose shield shows him to be a Celt. This probably commemorates the 'Elephant Victory' of Antiochus I over the Galatians.

VIII: *a.* Termination of a wall in the form of an elephant at Musaw-warat es-Sofra, Meroe, indicating the importance of the animal in this civilization. *b.* Painted frieze in a tomb of the late 3rd century BC at the Phoenician colony of Marissa in Judaea. The elephant is an African; a figure of an 'Aethiopian' standing by has been cut away.

We have, in fact, a slightly earlier reference than that of Herodotus, which records elephants in North Africa. It is a Greek translation of a report, written in Punic some time before 480 BC by a Carthaginian named Hanno who was sent out on an adventurous journey beyond the Pillars of Hercules to sail down the west coast of Africa, where he established a number of Punic settlements.[17] After passing Cape Soloeis (modern Cape Cantin) 'we arrived at a lagoon full of high and thick-grown cane. This was haunted by elephants and multitudes of other grazing beasts'. This lagoon was probably the marshes of the river Tensift, north of Mogador and at the foot of the Atlas Mountains. Incidentally, further on near Sierra Leone, Hanno found an island which was 'full of wild people. By far the greater number were women with hairy bodies. Our interpreters called them gorillas. We gave chase to the men, but could not catch any . . . we secured three women who bit and scratched and resisted their captors. But we killed and flayed them, and brought their hides to Carthage.' In fact the creatures are more likely to have been chimpanzees than gorillas.

The earliest surviving Greek writer who has much to tell us about elephants is Ctesias from Cnidus in south-west Asia Minor.[18] He was at the battle of Cunaxa in 401 BC where the rebellion of the younger Cyrus was crushed. Ctesias won the approval of the Persian king, Artaxerxes II, and especially of the queen mother Parysates, and served as court physician from 405 until at least 387. At Susa and elsewhere in the Persian empire he was in a unique position to see contemporary life and customs in the East and to learn about Eastern history; in fact he claims to have had access to Persian royal archives. Among other works, he wrote accounts of Persia (*Persica*) in twenty-four books and of India (*Indica*). Although unfortunately the text of these books is lost, we have some considerable extracts, summaries and quotations, especially a partial summary by the Patriarch Photius made in the ninth century AD. His works were widely read and were used by later writers such as Aristotle and Aelian (on matters of natural history), by Diodorus (on Persian history), and by Plutarch and others. Hence his importance was greater than the surviving fragments might suggest. His value as a historian has been variously assessed, since he deliberately set out to contradict Herodotus on many points and his narrative is full of many marvels and some inventions. However, he certainly did not lack some scientific interest, not least in

33

animals, and his life at the Persian court must have provided him with the opportunity of seeing elephants at first hand.

In fact he appears to have observed elephants very closely indeed, because he asserted that their semen hardened so much in drying that it became like amber. We owe this observation to Aristotle, who unfortunately does not quote the context of Ctesias' remark, but mentions the alleged fact only in order to deny its truth (*De Generat. Anim.* II.2; 736ᵃ5). However, Ctesias' statement, even if untrue, suggests that he may well have studied the behaviour of the animals at first hand, perhaps in some breeding stud (though it is not known that the Persian king kept a herd); at any rate, even if autopsy be ruled out, he will obviously have discussed elephants with men who knew them well. He probably gave some account of the elephant in his *Indica*, as he does of several other beasts, unless he considered it sufficiently well known as to be not worth mentioning beside some of the more bizarre products of that continent. He makes an incidental reference to elephants in a passage describing a mysterious man-eating beast called the martichora, which is probably to be identified with the tiger: 'to kill these beasts men ride on elephants and shoot down at them' (*Ind.* 7; Jacoby p. 491); he had already mentioned that the martichora could kill all animals it attacked except the elephant. He also discussed the use of the elephant in war, since Photius records (*Ind.* 3; Jacoby p. 487) that Ctesias wrote 'concerning elephants, demolishers of walls' (Περὶ τῶν τειχοκαταλύτων ἐλεφάντων). This remark is amplified by Aelian (XVII.29), who says that when the Indian king goes to war he is preceded by 100,000 elephants and followed by 3,000 of the largest and strongest who have been trained to overturn the enemies' walls by attacking them when the king orders; and they overturn them by the weight of their chests. 'Such', says Aelian, 'is the account given by Ctesias who writes that he heard this. But the same writer says that in Babylon he has seen date-palms completely uprooted by elephants in the same way, the animals falling against them with all their force. This they do if their Indian trainer so orders.' (Cf. pl. IIa.)

Ctesias supplies two accounts of elephants in battle, one more credible than the other. He relates that when Amoraius, king of the Derbikes (Scythians to the east of the Caspian), was attacked by the elder Cyrus of Persia, he placed some elephants in an ambush where they routed Cyrus' cavalry; the Derbikes, we are told, had received the elephants from Indians who were fighting on their side (*Persica* 6: Jacoby p. 457). The other splendid story hovers between legend and history. It concerns the campaign of the semi-mythical Semiramis, queen of Assyria, against India: it is recorded at length by Diodorus (II, 16 ff.) who closely followed Ctesias' account. The Indian king had many elephants, 'equipped in an extremely splendid fashion with things which would strike terror in war'. Diodorus adds that 'India has an unbelievable number of elephants, which both in courage and strength far surpass those of Libya'. (Since Ctesias himself presumably did not know African elephants, this remark must almost certainly be an addition by Diodorus, drawn either from his own knowledge or more probably from a written source, which will have been either Onesicritus or Megasthenes whose works are discussed later). Nonplussed at her own lack of elephants, Semiramis decided to make some dummies, hoping that these would frighten the Indians because of their belief that no elephants ever existed outside India. These models were made of ox-hide stuffed with straw, presumably round a light frame, and were moved by a camel and driver inside. In addition, according to the *Suda* (s.v. Semiramis, a passage which seems to go back to Ctesias, though it differs in details from Diodorus' account), two men ('Ethiopians') were placed on each animal's back. Further, Semiramis trained her horses to become used to these strange monsters. Though unaware of the secret weapon that was being prepared against him, the Indian king held a hunt of wild elephants in order to increase his force yet further, and 'thus when they advanced to the attack their multitude as well as the towers upon their backs made them appear irresistible'. Meantime deserters from Semiramis' army reported the true nature of her 'elephants' to the Indian king, who turned to face her in battle. Yet even so, not all went well for him; at first his cavalry, which was used to elephants, charged boldly, but when the horses got near the dummies and found their smell and other aspects unelephantine, they fell into confusion. However, when the king's own elephants advanced in front of his infantry, they smashed through Semiramis' ranks, 'trampling some under their feet, ripping up others and tossing many into the air with their trunks'. Thus King Strabrobates, who had gone into action riding on the most powerful of his beasts, was victorious and Semiramis had to withdraw to Bactria. What degree of truth lies behind all this is uncertain. In

35

Greek legend Semiramis was the daughter of a Syrian goddess and at death was changed into a dove, but behind the legend probably lies a historical figure, namely Sammuramat, regent of the Assyrian throne 810–805 BC after the death of her husband. The story of the battle may therefore reflect respectable history, but whether anything beside Ctesias' fertile imagination lies behind the weird dummy elephants can only be surmised. At least the episode has the use of demonstrating the value of elephants in war.

Thus well before 400 BC Herodotus and his readers knew that there were elephants in North Africa and by inference in Ethiopia, while some Carthaginians had publicly recorded the fact that Hanno had seen them on the west coast wallowing in the lagoons they loved. Then soon after the turn of the century Ctesias was able to provide some information about Indian elephants: their ability to uproot trees, their use in tiger hunting, and their employment in war, both to overthrow walls and in open battle, together with the fact that cavalry had to be trained to face them. But although the elephant had entered into the world of Ctesias it was still beyond the horizon of the average Greek. For more than half a century no Greek writers mention the animal, except Plato, who in the *Critias* (114e) records that in Atlantis there was an abundance of wild and tame animals, including the elephant, of which there was a very large number; pasture was sufficient for all, including this 'very large and very voracious animal'. There are two basic approaches to the perennial problem of Atlantis: it can be regarded either as a pure figment of Plato's imagination or as the residue of some tradition with a basis of fact behind it; proponents of the latter view then exercise their ingenuity in finding a suitable island, either Crete or Thera (Santorini), or in the Atlantic where Plato himself placed it. The passage in the *Critias* does not really help. If the island was imaginary, what more natural than to populate it with a rather strange beast about which Plato's average reader probably knew very little? On the other hand if we wish to move from wonderland to a more prosaic world, some might seek support for an island beyond the Pillars of Hercules in the fact, known to Hanno, that elephants did live there at the foot of the Atlas Mountains.

The break-through comes with Aristotle who knew and wrote much about elephants. Before discussing the sources of his knowledge, it will be well to collect his various references. This is the more necessary because he nowhere wrote a long description of the animal, since such treatment did not accord with his essential approach to zoology. Despite his analytical mind he did not write his Natural History on a taxonomical or classificatory basis; rather, he collected material together in order to discover the causes of the differences between animals. B. M. Balme in his introduction to the *De Partibus Animalium* writes that Aristotle 'is considering what natural principles and factors must be recognised in accounting for zoological phenomena . . . the whole discussion amounts to a philosophy of zoology: what are the causes operative in living nature and how they relate to each other'.[19] Thus we have to piece together for ourselves what Aristotle actually knew about the structure and habits of elephants. The main passages now follow, together with brief consideration of their reliability, where necessary, as seen in the light of what is known about elephants today.

*Trunk and Legs*

1  'In no animal is this part (i.e. the organ of smell) so peculiar as in the elephant, where it attains an extraordinary size and strength. For the elephant uses its nostril as a hand; this being the instrument with which it conveys food, fluid and solid alike, to its mouth. With it, too, it tears up trees, coiling it around their stems. In fact it applies it generally to the purposes of a hand. For the elephant has the double character, both of a land animal, and of one that lives in swamps. Seeing then that it has to get its food from the water, yet must necessarily breathe, inasmuch as it is a land animal and has blood; seeing, also, that its excessive weight prevents it from passing rapidly from water to land, as some other sangineous *vivipara* that breathe can do, it becomes necessary that it shall be suited alike for life in the water and for life on the dry land. Just then as divers are sometimes provided with instruments for respiration, through which they can draw air from above the water, and thus may remain for a long time under the sea, so also elephants have been furnished by nature with their lengthened nostril; and, whenever they have to tra-

verse the water, they lift this up above the surface and breathe through it. For the elephant's proboscis, as already said, is a nostril. Now it would have been impossible for this nostril to have the form of a proboscis, had it been hard and incapable of bending. For its very length would then have prevented the animal from supplying itself with food, being as great an impediment as the horns of certain oxen, that are said to be obliged to walk backwards while they are grazing [this comes from Herodotus, IV, 183]. It is, therefore, soft and flexible, and, being such, is made, in addition to its own proper functions, to serve the office of the forefeet; nature in this following her wonted plan of using one and the same part for several purposes. For in the polydactylous quadrupeds the forefeet are intended not merely to support the weight of the body, but to serve as hands. In elephants, however, though they must be reckoned polydactylous, as their foot has neither cloven nor solid hoof, the forefeet, owing to the great size and weight of the body, are reduced to the condition of mere supports; and indeed their slow motion and unfitness for bending, makes them useless for any other purpose. A nostril, then, is given to the elephant for respiration, as to every other animal that has a lung, and is lengthened out and endowed with its power of coiling because the animal has to remain for considerable periods of time in the water, and is unable to pass thence to dry ground with any rapidity. But as the feet are shorn of their full office, this same part is also, as already said, made by nature to supply their place, and give such help as otherwise would be rendered by them.' (*De Partibus Animalium*, II.16; 658$^b$ 30 f.)

*Trunk*

2 'For just as the organ of smell in elephants answers several uses, serving alike as a weapon and for purposes of nutrition, so does also the sting, when placed in connection with the tongue, as in some insects, answer more than one end' (*De Part. Animal.* IV. 6; 682$^b$35). Cf. *De Part. Animal.* II. 17; 661$^a$25.

3 'Such then in these animals (*sc.* gad-flies and cattle-flies) is the nature of the tongue, which is thus as it were the counterpart of the elephant's nostril. For as in the elephant the nostril is used as a weapon, so in these animals the tongue serves as a sting' (*De Part. Animal.* II. 17; 661$^a$26).

4 'The nostril (or nose) of the elephant is long and strong, and the animal uses it like a hand; for by means of this organ it draws objects towards it, and takes hold of them, and introduces its food into its mouth, whether liquid or dry food, and it is the only living creature that does so' (*Hist. Animal.* I. 11; 492$^b$17).

5 'The forelimbs then serve more or less the purpose of hands in quadrupeds, with the exception of the elephant. This latter animal has its toes somewhat indistinctly defined, and its front legs are much bigger than its hinder ones; it is five-toed, and has short ankles to its hind feet. But it has a nose such in properties and such in size as to allow its using the same as a hand. For it eats and drinks by lifting up its food with the aid of this organ into its mouth, and with the same organ it lifts up articles to the driver on its back; with this organ it can pluck up trees by the roots, and when walking through water it spouts the water up by means of it; and this organ is capable of being crooked or coiled at the tip, but not of flexing like a joint, for it is composed of gristle' (*Hist. Animal.* II. 1; 497$^b$23 f.).

Thus Aristotle appreciates that the trunk is a lengthened nostril and he understands its great value; at the end of (5) he seems to underestimate its flexibility, but perhaps he is primarily emphasizing by implication that it is boneless. He knows that the elephant can use it as a snorkel, though he wrongly implies that the elephant cannot swim; while recognizing its love of water, he appears to think that it got much of its food from water and spent more time in it than the animal normally would do.

*Legs*
6 'Animals have the flexions of their fore and hind limbs in directions opposite to one another, and in directions the reverse of those observed in the arms and legs of man; with the exception of the elephant. In other words, with the viviparous quadrupeds the front legs bend forwards and the hind ones backwards, and the concavities of the two pairs of limbs thus face one another. The elephant does not sleep standing, as some were wont to assert, but it bends its legs and settles down; only that in consequence of its weight it cannot bend its legs on both sides simultaneously, but falls into a recumbent position on one side or the other, and in this position it goes to sleep. And it bends

its hind legs, just as a man bends his legs' (*Hist. Animal.* II. 1; 498ᵃ 3 f.)

7 'It is indeed possible to move oneself even if the leg be not bent, in the way in which children crawl. This was the old though erroneous account of the movement of elephants' (*De Incessu Animal.* 9; 709ᵃ10).

8 Aristotle distinguishes two modes of flexion. That which he calls D (where the convexities of fore and hindlegs are turned towards one another and the concavities outwards) applies 'only to the elephant among quadrupeds and man if you consider his arms as well as his legs; for he bends his arms concavely and his legs convexly' (*De Incessu Animal.* 13; 712ᵃ10).

See also nos. (1) and (5) above.

*Feet*

9 'All animals have nails that have toes, and toes that have feet, except the elephant; and the elephant has toes undivided and slightly articulated but no nails whatsoever' (*Hist. Animal.* III. 9; 517ᵃ31) and cf. (1) above.

Aristotle advanced the idea that an elephant's forefeet are less useful than those of other animals which use them as hands as well as to support their weight (hence the elephant has a trunk which he can use as a hand: cf. (1) above). While it is true that the formation of the forefeet prevents an elephant from trotting or jumping, Aristotle exaggerates the lack of usefulness and of flexibility in the forefeet. However, he corrects the idea that it moved without bending its legs (does this 'old erroneous account' derive from Ctesias?). He also corrects the idea that it sleeps only when standing (it does, of course, doze off occasionally when standing), but he exaggerates the stiffness of the leg shown on lying down and wrongly believes that the elephant must fall one side or the other. He is not clear about the toes, not realizing that the real toes are internal and that what is visible consists of nails or hooves rather than toes. It is strange that he did not know the internal structure of the foot when he is so well informed about parts of the viscera.

*Teeth and Tusks*

10 'The elephant has four teeth on either side, by which it munches its food, grinding it like so much barley-meal, and, quite apart

from these, it has great teeth, or tusks, two in number. In the male these tusks are comparatively large and curve upwards; in the female they are comparatively small and point in the opposite direction; that is, they look downwards to the ground. The elephant is furnished with teeth at birth, but the tusks are not then visible' (*Hist. Animal.* II. 5; 501$^b$30).

Aristotle correctly refers to the four molars, but does not know about their successive replacement by 'molar progression'. He also appears to think that there were four molars on either side, i.e. eight in all. This idea could have arisen from inspecting a beast whose molars were in the process of changing when parts of the two might be visible in the four places. He is also right that the tusks of the male are larger than those of the female, but I have found no evidence that they point in different directions according to sex. They vary considerably in shape, with heritable traits, so that family likenesses have sometimes been traced in tusk characteristics.

*Tongue*
11 'The tongue of the elephant is exceedingly small, and situated far back in the mouth, so that it is difficult to get a sight of it' (*Hist. Animal.* II. 6; 502$^a$5).

Dr Sikes writes (p. 76): 'the mouth is relatively small, situated below and almost totally hidden by the base of the trunk. It is not capable of being opened very wide. . . . The tongue is large and mobile, but cannot be protruded beyond the lower lip'. Thus Aristotle may be excused for not having been able to examine its size in detail.

*Hair*
12 'The elephant, by the way, is the least hairy of all quadrupeds. With animals, as a general rule, the tail corresponds with the body as regards thickness or thinness of hair-coating' (*Hist. Animal.* II. 1; 499$^a$9).
13 'However, the thickest-skinned animals are not more so than other thick-skinned ones, as is shown by the class of swine compared to that of oxen and to the elephant and many others' (*De Gener. Animal.* V. 3; 782$^b$10).

This sentence is obscure, but Aristotle appears to say that the bristles of swine are thicker than those of elephants, though the elephant is the thicker-skinned of the two.

## Breasts

14 'In the elephant also there are but two mammae, which are placed under the axillae of the forelimbs. The mammae are not more than two because this animal has only a single young one at a birth; and they are not placed in the region of the thighs, because they never occupy that position in any polydactylous animals such as this. Lastly they are placed above, close to the axillae, because this is the position of the foremost dugs of all animals whose dugs are numerous, and the dugs so placed give the best milk. Evidence of this is furnished by the sow' (*De Part. Animal.* IV. 10; 688$^b$15).

15 'The elephant has two breasts in the region of the axillae; and the female elephant has two breasts insignificant in size and in no way proportionate to the bulk of the entire frame, so insignificant as to be invisible in a sideway view; the males also have breasts, like the females, exceedingly small' (*Hist. Animal.* II. 1; 500$^a$17).

16 'The elephant certainly has two breasts, not however in the chest, but near it' (*Hist. Animal.* II. 1; 489$^a$1).

Dr Sikes (p. 19) writes: 'The mammary glands and nipples at the time of the birth of the calf are about the size and weight of those of the average human African mother during lactation.' Aristotle might well consider them small when thinking of the bulk of an elephant and of a man.

## Gall

17 'With the elephant also the liver is unfurnished with a gall-bladder, but when the animal is cut in the region where the organ is found in animals furnished with it, there oozes out a fluid resembling gall, in greater or less quantities' (*Hist. Animal.* II. 15; 506$^b$1).

This correct reference to the absence of a gall-bladder implies knowledge based either on dissection or close investigation of a dead elephant.

*Intestines*

18 'The elephant has a gut constricted into chambers, so constructed that the animal appears to have four stomachs; in it the
food is found, but there is no distinct and separate receptacle.
Its viscera resemble those of a pig, only that the liver is four
times the size of that of the ox, and the other viscera in like proportion, while the spleen is comparatively small' (*Hist. Animal.*
II. 17; 507$^b$35).

The reference to four apparent stomachs applies to the stomach,
the caecum, the colon and the small intestines. The normal weight
of the liver is 80–100 lb in an adult cow, and 130–150 lb in an adult
bull; the spleen of an adult bull weighs some 21 lb.

*Genitals*

19 'The penis of the elephant resembles that of the horse; compared with the size of the animal it is disproportionately small;
the testicles are not visible, but are concealed inside in the vici-
nity of the kidneys (cf. 509$^b$11); and for this reason the male
speedily gives over in the act of intercourse. The genitals of the
female are situated where the udder in sheep is; when she is in
heat, she draws the organ back and exposes it externally, to
facilitate the act of intercourse for the male; the organ opens out
to a considerable extent . . . some animals discharge their urine
backwards . . . male animals differ from one another, as has been
said, in this particular, but all female animals are retromingent:
even the female elephant like other animals, though she has the
privy part below the thighs' (*Hist. Animal.* II.1; 500$^b$6).

So far from being comparatively small, the penis weighs over 60
lb and is proportionately long; this is necessary because of the anatomical position of the female's vagina. Aristotle's mistake may
have arisen from the fact that when at rest the penis lies in a dorsal
sheath under the body. He is correct in saying that the testes are
internal and implying that there is no scrotum. Copulation is said
not to exceed 120 seconds, but it may be repeated at intervals of
between ten and twenty minutes.

*Semen*

20 'What Ctesias the Cnidian has asserted of the semen of elephants
is manifestly untrue (cf. 523$^a$27); he says that it hardens so much

43

in drying that it becomes like amber. But this does not happen, though it is true that one semen must be more earthy than another, and especially so with animals that have so much earthy matter in them because of the bulk of their bodies' (*De Generat. Animal.* II.2; 736ª5).

*Breeding*
21 'Elephants copulate in lonely places, and especially by riversides in their usual haunts; the female squats down and straddles with her legs, and the male mounts and covers her' (*Hist. Animal.* v.2; 540ª20).
22 'The female elephant becomes sexually receptive when ten years old at the youngest, and fifteen at the oldest; and the male is sexually capable when five or six years old. The season for intercourse is spring. The male allows an interval of three years to elapse after intercourse with a female: and, after it has once impregnated a female, it has no intercourse with her again [cf. *Hist. Animal.* IX.46; 630ᵇ22]. The period of gestation with the female is two years [cf. *De Gener. Animal.* IV.10: 777ª10, where the length of gestation is attributed to the size of the offspring: 'for it is not easy for large masses to arrive at their perfection in a small time']; and only one young animal is produced at a time, in other words it is uniparous. And the embryo is the size of a calf two or three months old' (*Hist. Animal.* v.14; 546ᵇ7).
23 'The elephant of either sex is fitted for breeding before reaching the age of twenty. The female carries her young, according to some accounts, for two and a half years; according to others for three years; and the discrepancy in the assigned periods is due to the fact that there are never human eye-witnesses to the intercourse between the sexes. The female settles down on its rear to cast its young, and obviously suffers greatly during the process. The young one, immediately after birth, sucks the mother, not with its trunk but with its mouth: and can walk about and see distinctly the moment it is born' (*Hist. Animal.* VI.27; 578ª18).

For African elephants the age of puberty is placed between eight and thirteen years, but it is improbable that pregnancy often occurs before the age of ten in wild elephants, with the first calf appearing at twelve years. In this matter Aristotle is somewhat self-contradic-

44

tory, passage (22) being more accurate than (23). During copulation the female stands and does not squat, as Aristotle says, though the male seems to half-squat during part of the process. Since the usual time appears to be at sunset, during the night or at sunrise, no doubt it is seldom seen by man. For Indian elephants the mating period, when the female comes into season, is from December to February; in Africa it is throughout the dry season, and just before the onset of the rainy season the bulls move off to bull herds, to be followed later by the herds of cows and calves. Before mating both partners show much affection for each other and afterwards they may live closely together for some months (observers reach conclusions which differ from three to ten months); thereafter the cow is more concerned with her pregnancy and the bull later turns to another partner. Gestation lasts about twenty-two months. Parturition normally occurs with the mother standing on all fours (contrast Aristotle), but he is right in stating that she is virtually uniparous (twins are very rare) and that the young suck with their mouths, not with their trunks.

*Voice*
24 'The elephant makes a vocal sound of a wind-like sort by the mouth alone, unaided by the trunk, just like the sound of a man panting or sighing; but if it employs the trunk as well, the sound produced is like that of a hoarse trumpet' (*Hist. Animal.* IV.9; 536$^b$22).

The trunk is used by means of muscular movements to produce screams, squeals and trumpeting. When annoyed, elephants make a rumbling sound which is produced by the larynx; such roars and growls are very frightening. The Indian, but apparently not the African, elephant also makes a squeak of pleasure or greeting in the distal end of the trunk.

*Age*
25 'Man lives longer than any animal of which we have credible experience except the elephant' (*De Generat. Animal.* IV.10; 777$^b$5).
26 'Some say that the elephant lives for two hundred years; others, for one hundred and twenty; that the female lives nearly as long as the male; that they reach their prime about the age of sixty,

and that they are sensitive to inclement weather and frost' (*Hist. Animal.* IX.46; 630$^b$23. Pseudo-Aristotelian?).

27 'The elephant is said to live for about two hundred years; by others for three hundred' (*Hist. Animal.* VIII.9; 596$^a$9).

The age-span of the elephant, which roughly corresponds with that of man, is grossly exaggerated in these passages, while the elephant is not so delicate as is suggested.

### Diet

28 'The elephant at the most can eat 9 *medimni* of fodder at one meal; but so large an amount is unwholesome. As a general rule it can take 6 or 7 *medimni* of fodder, 5 *medimni* of wheat, and 5 *mareis* of wine, 6 *cotylae* going to the *maris*. An elephant has been known to drink right off 14 Macedonian *metretae* of water, and another 8 *metretae* later in the day' (*Hist. Animal.* VIII.9; 596$^a$3. Pseudo-Aristotelian?).

These figures are too large. Modern equivalents of ancient measures are difficult to assess accurately, since these varied locally, but on the Attic system (the Macedonian is uncertain) a *medimnus* = *c.* 104 lb: thus 9, 7, 6 and 5 *medimni* would equal 936, 728, 624 and 520 lb, respectively, whereas a modern African elephant is reckoned to consume between 300 and 350 lb a day. Five *mareis* of wine works out at about 14 pints. Of the figures for water 14 *metretae* = 118 gallons, and 8 *metretae* = 67 gallons. A modern elephant can drink some 22 gallons at a time, and some 50 a day. Thus in general terms Aristotle seems to have credited the elephant with about double or more than its actual daily intake.

### Disease

29 'The elephant, which is reputed to enjoy immunity from other illnesses, is occasionally subject to flatulence' (*Hist. Animal.* VIII.22; 604$^a$11. Pseudo-Aristotelian?).

30 'Elephants suffer from flatulence and when thus afflicted can void neither solid nor liquid residuum. If the elephant swallows earth-mould it suffers from relaxation; but if it goes on taking it steadily, it will experience no harm. From time to time it takes to swallowing stones. It suffers also from diarrhoea: in this

case they administer draughts of lukewarm water or dip its fodder in honey, and either one or other prescription will prove a costive. When elephants suffer from insomnia, they will be restored to health if their shoulders be rubbed with salt, olive-oil, and warm water; when they have aches in their shoulders they will derive great benefit from the application of roast pork. Some elephants like olive-oil, but others do not. If there is a bit of iron in the inside of an elephant it is said that it will pass out if the animal takes a drink of olive-oil; and if the animal refuses olive-oil, they soak a root in the oil and give it the root to swallow' (*Hist. Animal.* VIII; 605ª23. Pseudo-Aristotelian?).

Captive elephants do suffer from flatulence. Further, the idea of flatulence might be connected with a 'sound very familiar to hunters of African elephants . . . the so-called tummy-rumbling. This sound is heard when an elephant, or a herd of elephants, is browsing peacefully and completely undisturbed. Presumably the outsize liquid pop-pop-pop-pop sound is that of the stomach contents, after a long drink, undergoing peristaltic churning' (Dr Sikes, p. 115). Elephants also do swallow stones and small pebbles; these are perhaps eaten either accidentally or by design with the soil adhering to their food, while Indian elephants suffering from intestinal parasites are known to eat sand and gravel. Diarrhoea occurs in captive elephants but is rare in wild ones. It is normal procedure for Indian working elephants to be given oil both in their diet and applied externally to the skin.

### Size
31 'Excessive bulk, such as has been given . . . in still greater measure to elephants, is sufficient in itself to protect an animal from being destroyed by others' (*De Part. Animal.* III.2; 663ª5).

### Habitat
32 'The elephant is found by the banks of rivers, but he is not a river animal; he can make his way through water, as long as the tip of his trunk can be above the surface, for he blows with his trunk and breathes through it. The animal is a poor swimmer owing to the heavy weight of his body' (*Hist. Animal.* IX.46; 630ᵇ25. Pseudo-Aristotelian?).
See also no. (1) above.

*Temper*

33 'Other animals are easy-tempered and easily domesticated, as the elephant' (*Hist. Animal.* 1.1; 488$^b$23. Cf. 488$^a$28).

34 'Of all wild animals the most easily tamed and the gentlest is the elephant. It can be taught a number of tricks, the drift and meaning of which it understands; for instance, it can be taught to kneel in the presence of a king. It is very sensitive, and possessed of an intelligence superior to that of other animals' (*Hist. Animal.* IX.46; 630$^b$17. Pseudo-Aristotelian?).

35 'Elephants fight fiercely with one another, and stab one another with their tusks; of two combatants the beaten gets completely cowed, and dreads the sound of his conqueror's voice. These animals differ from one another to an extraordinary extent in the way of courage. Indians employ these animals for war purposes, irrespective of sex; the females, however, are less in size and much inferior in point of spirit. An elephant by pushing with his big tusks can batter down a wall, and will butt with his forehead at a palm until he brings it down, when he stamps on it and lays it in an orderly fashion on the ground. Men hunt the elephant in the following way: they mount tame elephants of approved spirit and proceed in quest of wild animals; when they come up with these they order the tame brutes to beat the wild ones until they tire the latter completely. Hereupon the driver mounts a wild brute and guides him with the application of his metal prong; after this the creature soon becomes tàme, and obeys guidance. Now when the driver is on their back they are all tractable, but after he has dismounted, some are tame and others vicious; in the case of these latter, they tie their frontlegs with ropes to keep them quiet. The animal is hunted whether young or full-grown' (*Hist. Animal.* IX.1; 610$^a$15. Pseudo-Aristotelian?).

Although the elephant is generally peaceable, fights do sometimes occur between senior bulls for leadership of a herd. They fight head on, by pushing or pulling in a tug-of-war with trunks interlocked. When one weakens, he is gored in the flank by a thrust of the tusks of the stronger animal. The account of hunting, given here by Aristotle, is much oversimplified, as will be seen by later accounts, as that by Megasthenes (p. 56), but he rightly says that tame elephants were used to overcome the wild ones.

IX: *a*. Rough stone carving of an African elephant (see the ear) at Alba Fucens in central Italy. It is probably connected with Hannibal's march past the city in 211 BC. *b*. Terracotta models of mother elephant and calf from the Sanctuary of Apollo at Veii. They look more African than Indian and so should be associated with Hannibal rather than Pyrrhus.

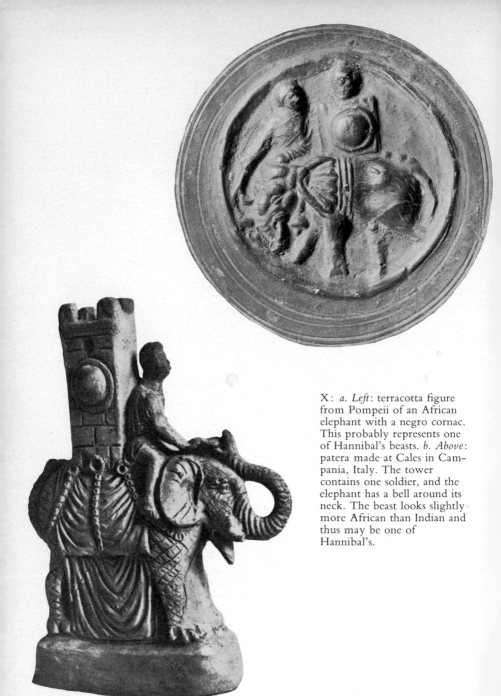

X: *a. Left*: terracotta figure from Pompeii of an African elephant with a negro cornac. This probably represents one of Hannibal's beasts. *b. Above*: patera made at Cales in Campania, Italy. The tower contains one soldier, and the elephant has a bell around its neck. The beast looks slightly more African than Indian and thus may be one of Hannibal's.

XI: Detail of carved relief of elephants on hunting expedition of the Sassanid period (*c.* AD 500?) from Taq-i-Bustan, Kurdistan.

XII: Silver phalera, showing an Indian elephant; its saddle-cloth is embroidered with a dragon. Now in the Hermitage, Leningrad.

36 Aristotle refers to those who believe 'that there is a continuity between the parts about the Pillars of Heracles and the parts about India . . . in further evidence in support of this they quote the case of elephants, a species occurring in each of these extreme regions, suggesting that the common characteristics of these extremes is explained by their continuity' (*De Caelo* ii.14; 298a).

Here Aristotle recognizes that there were elephants in both India and North Africa, but he is emphasizing similarity, and therefore he probably did not have any idea of any differences existing between the two species of elephants.

The sources of Aristotle's knowledge of natural history are closely bound up with the events of his life; the latter therefore need brief mention. His interest in physical science may well derive from his father who was personal physician to Amyntas, the king of Macedon. About 367 BC after his father's death Aristotle, then about seventeen years old, was sent to study in Plato's Academy at Athens where he remained for twenty years, researching and teaching. In 347 after Plato's death he went to the court of Hermias, the ruler of Assos and Atarneus in Mysia on the coast of Asia Minor, at the invitation of Hermias who had been a fellow student at the Academy. Two years later Hermias died and Aristotle moved to Mytilene in the island of Lesbos. It is to this period of his life that many of his zoological enquiries, especially in the field of marine biology, probably belong. In 343–342 he was invited by Philip, king of Macedon, to go to the Macedonian court at Pella to act as tutor to his young son Alexander. This interesting association did not last very long, but long enough perhaps for Aristotle to instil in Alexander an interest in the natural world, whether or not his influence extended to the realm of political ideas. In 340 Aristotle retired to his birth-place, Stagira, but after the death of Philip and the succession of Alexander 'the Great', Aristotle returned to Athens about 335. There he established a school of philosophy at the Lyceum for teaching and research. He collected a great library of manuscripts and maps, together with a museum of natural history. Alexander is said to have given him 800 talents for this purpose and to have instructed the fishermen, hunters and fowlers of the empire that he was conquering to report to Aristotle anything of zoological interest. Whatever truth lies behind the details of this story, it undoubtedly points to one of the main sources of Aristotle's increasing knowledge of the natural world and to the fact that a great deal more of the world was being opened up for Western eyes by exploration and scientific enquiry. On Alexander's death in 323, however, an outburst of anti-Macedonian feeling led Aristotle to leave Athens; he died in the following year.

Thus Alexander's expedition as far as North-west India was not confined to military conquest. As we shall see, his crucial battle against the elephants of the Indian king Porus opened up a new era in Hellenistic warfare, but doubtless his concern went beyond that of the military value of the elephant and he will have recalled Aristotle's keen interest in all creatures, great and small, just as by his exploration he was able to test and extend the ideas about geography which he had learnt from his teacher. In fact Alexander had taken with him many experts, not only technicians, as engineers and architects, but also geographers, surveyors, and botanists, as well as literary men. Although Aristotle himself did not accompany or later join the expedition, he sent his nephew Callisthenes with Alexander. Thus while Alexander's soldiers had met the elephant for the first time in a terrifying encounter, much of what was learnt about the nature, habits and handling of the animal must have reached Aristotle in Athens. This information must have come primarily from direct reports and letters from men on the expedition itself and no doubt later from talk with veterans. Many of the generals and specialists who accompanied Alexander later wrote accounts of his exploits and the new lands that were opened up: men such as Ptolemy, the future ruler of Egypt, Callisthenes, the nephew of Aristotle, Aristobulus, an engineer and architect, Onesicritus, seaman who steered Alexander's ship down the Jhelum, and Nearchus, commander of the fleet which he led along the coast from the Indus to the Tigris. Unfortunately the works of these 'Alexander-historians' survive only in fragments or in quotations in later authors who used their accounts. Problems abound regarding the dates and order in which they produced their literary works, and we shall shortly have to see what they tell us about elephants. Here we may note that although some at least of them must have contributed information to Aristotle either directly or indirectly, he probably could not make much use of their written works, which mostly will have been produced after his death.

It would be interesting if we could discover how much Aristotle knew about elephants before Alexander's conquests and how much he owed to this later source of information, but such an enquiry is obscured by the nature of his surviving writings and the difficulty of dating them. There is wide agreement that his *History of Animals* belongs essentially to the middle period of his life rather than the last phase, namely to the period he spent at Assos and Lesbos, since the distribution of place-names which he mentions in this work points to his residence in this part of the Greek world. Thus it might be thought that many of the references to elephants must predate the Alexander period. However, this is not so because of the nature of his writing. What we have is not a finished polished literary work, but rather the complete opposite of the beautiful Greek prose of his teacher Plato. Parts at any rate of Aristotle are rather like lecture notes or draft material, while some parts of the *History of Animals* as we have it (namely Book 10 and perhaps Books 7 and 9 and the last 10 chapters of Book 8) were written later (in the third century?) though some of the material may be Aristotelian. Further, we cannot be sure that some of the material in the genuine books was not added at a stage later than their original composition. Thus unfortunately it is unsafe to argue that any of the information about elephants must have been known to Aristotle before Alexander's expedition (though this also means that the *History of Animals* may still have been written earlier than Alexander: that is, one cannot legitimately use the references to elephants to argue that Aristotle cannot have known all this before Alexander and that therefore the work must have been composed in the later period of Aristotle's life).[20]

Aristotle's knowledge of the elephant is in general so good that one is bound to ask, though unable to answer, the question of the intimacy of his contacts: did he derive all from detailed reports by others who knew elephants or had he himself seen them at close quarters or indeed had he even dissected one? This last view, which is held by some (e.g. by M. Wellmann, *PW s.v.* Elefant, 2250), is based on the accuracy of his observation of the internal organs. Further, Wellmann adds, 'later dissections of elephants were not uncommon in Alexandria; on the ground of dissections the physician Mnesitheus (300 BC) reached the conviction that the elephant had no gall-bladder (Galen., 11.569).' Where then does Wellmann imagine that Aristotle saw a dissection: in Alexandria? Although the new city had been developing for some eight or nine years before Aristotle's death, there is no evidence that he ever visited it and its scientific centres. If Aristotle himself ever saw the inside of an elephant, it would seem more probable when he was in Asia Minor when he conceivably could have had the chance of investigating the guts of a dead beast. It seems generally to be assumed that Aristotle and Mnesitheus gained their knowledge about the absence of a gall-bladder independently of one another: at any rate the two passages are not brought into juxtaposition. In view, however, of the vagueness of our information about the date of Mnesitheus, there is no real hindrance to assuming that he was the source of Aristotle's knowledge. This Athenian physician seems to belong to the period after 350, but further precision is difficult. Aristotle might have read his works or met him in Athens. The source of Mnesitheus' knowledge must in turn remain obscure: he *could* have visited Alexandria in the brief period between its foundation and Aristotle's death, but were elephants (Indian or African?) really being dissected there as early as this? If not (and it should be noted that there is no direct statement by Galen that Mnesitheus had gained his knowledge by actual dissection, though the details given may suggest this), then we are left with the supposition that he had access to an elephant carcass elsewhere, e.g. in Asia Minor, or gained his information at second-hand.

## ONESICRITUS AND NEARCHUS

Surviving fragments of only two of the Alexander historians have much to tell about elephants. They are the two men to whom Alexander on his withdrawal from India entrusted the fleet on its hazardous voyage down the Indus and along the Arabian coast, namely the admiral Nearchus and the chief navigator Onesicritus.[21] The account written by Onesicritus preceded that by Nearchus, if it is true that the latter was partly designed to criticize the former (beside possible differences in the field of literature, the men certainly had a navigational dispute on the route to be taken in the Persian Gulf). A close dating of Onesicritus' work is not possible: one anecdote suggests that it had appeared before Alexander's death, another *might* imply that it belonged rather to the reign of Lysimachus (306–281 BC) to whom Onesicritus read his fourth book (cf. note 21). Nearchus' work will not have come far behind, but both probably appeared after the deaths of Alexander and Aristotle. Both men had seen many marvels in India, but Nearchus' work appears to have been the more sober and historically more reliable; Onesicritus, astounded by much that he saw, was more inclined to believe what he was told. The works of both men were widely used, especially for natural history, by later writers, Onesicritus by Strabo and Pliny, Nearchus by Strabo and Arrian. Aulus Gellius, writing under the Antonines, records that when he was returning from Greece and had reached Brundisium he 'saw some bundles of books exposed for sale . . . all these books were in Greek, filled with marvellous tales, unheard of and incredible things, but the writers were ancient and of no little authority'; they included Onesicritus and Ctesias.[22]

Onesicritus' contribution is as follows. He recorded, according to Pliny (*NH.* vi, 81; Jacoby, fr. 13), that the elephants in the island of Taprobane (i.e. Ceylon) 'are larger and better adapted for warfare than those of India'. He also said, according to Strabo (xv.1.43: Jacoby, fr. 14), that 'elephants live as long as 300 years and in rare cases even as long as 500; but that they are most powerful when about 200 years of age, and that females are pregnant for a period of about ten years. And both he and others state that they are larger and stronger than the Libyan elephants; at any rate, standing up on their hindfeet, they tear down battlements and pull up trees by the roots by means of their proboscis.'

Nearchus refers to the elephant's shrill cry (ὀξύ): he tells that when the Indian philosopher Calanus immolated himself on a pyre, Alexander showed his respect by ordering the whole army to raise the war-cry, while 'the elephants also chimed in with their shrill and warlike cry, in honour of Calanus' (Arrian, *Anab.* vii.3.6; Jacoby, fr. 4). Arrian (*Ind.* 15.1; Jacoby, fr. 7) writes, 'The Indians think the tiger is much mightier than the elephant. Nearchus says that he saw a tiger's skin, but not the tiger itself; but that the Indians assured him that it is as large as the largest horse, and that no other animal can compare with it in swiftness and strength. When the tiger comes into conflict with an elephant he leaps upon his head and easily strangles him.' From Strabo (xv.1.43; Jacoby, fr. 22) comes a further citation: 'Nearchus says that in the hunt for elephants foot-traps are also put at places where tracks meet, and that the wild elephants are driven together into these by the tamed ones, which are stronger and guided by riders; and that they are so easy to tame that they learn to throw stones at a mark and to use

53

weapons; and that they are excellent swimmers; and that a chariot drawn by elephants is considered a very great possession, and that they are driven under yoke like camels; and that a woman is highly honoured if she receives an elephant as a gift from her lover. But [adds Strabo] this statement is not in agreement with that of the man who said that horse and elephant were possessed by kings alone.' The value of elephants is stressed by Arrian (*Ind.* 17; Jacoby, fr. 11) in a passage which derives from Nearchus: 'Most of the Indians ride camels, horses and asses, and those who are well off, elephants. For among the Indians royal personages ride on elephants. . . . Their women, who are very chaste, can be seduced by no other gift, but yield themselves to anyone who gives an elephant; and the Indians think it no disgrace to yield thus on the gift of an elephant, but rather it seems honourable for a woman that her beauty should be valued at an elephant.'

Since what survives of Nearchus' account of elephants does not overlap in subject matter with the few remarks of Onesicritus, we cannot really compare their general accounts, and it is uncertain whether Nearchus deliberately sought to correct Onesicritus' account: if he had tried, would not Strabo probably have pointed this out?[23] What survives of Onesicritus does not inspire great confidence. He magnified still further the length both of life and of gestation, which Aristotle had already grossly overestimated.[24] His reference to the greater size of the elephant of Ceylon may derive simply from the idea that wonders increase the further east one goes, and his idea about African elephants may be part of his belief in the general superiority of India to Africa. On the other hand, his account of the uprooting of trees no doubt rests on autopsy; he had seen the war elephants of the Indian king Porus and may well have observed their activities off the battlefield.

Nearchus' remark about tigers is interesting. Although they do not normally attack adult elephants in the jungle and they cannot kill them, they may spring on their backs, causing severe wounds, in order to stampede a mother elephant and separate her from her calves; in fact the mortality of calves as the result of attacks by tigers in Burma is as high as 25 per cent, according to Colonel J. H. Williams.[25] Nearchus improves on Aristotle when he says that elephants are excellent swimmers and his account of hunting is reasonable. His remark about their being trained to throw stones and use weapons may be reliable, but a suspicion arises whether this might not be an additional observation made by Strabo himself who may have seen such tricks performed in a Roman circus. We must regret that so little of Nearchus, and indeed of Onesicritus, survives and in judging this we should remember that what we have comprises only summaries by other writers: if their own accounts survived in full, the picture might be somewhat different.

## MEGASTHENES AND AGATHARCHIDES

We now turn to another writer who knew more of India at first hand. An Ionian Greek, Megasthenes, who lived about 350–290 BC, was sent by Seleucus I more than once to the court of the Indian king, Chandragupta, at Pataliputra (Patna) on the Ganges.[26] He thus saw a great deal more of India than Alexander's companions had visited, although vast areas of the continent to the south still lay beyond the knowledge of the Greeks. He wrote an account of India in four books which became a standard work and was heavily drawn upon by later writers, as Strabo and Arrian, whose use of it provides us with the surviving fragments. Indeed, together with the Alexander historians, it long remained the chief source of knowledge of India for the Western world.

We have four short and one long quotation from Megasthenes. He refers to the greater size of Indians compared with Africans and offers an explanation: 'India also breeds elephants both in the greatest numbers and of the largest size, providing them with sustenance in abundance; and it is because of this food that the elephants of this land are much more powerful than those produced in Libya; consequently large numbers of them are made captive by the Indians and trained for warfare, and it is found that they play a great part in turning the scale to victory' (apud Diodor. II, 35.3; Jacoby, fr. 4). Referring to the military organization of the Indians, he says that one of six groups was devoted to the royal elephants: 'the elephant carries four persons, the driver and three bowmen, and these three shoot arrows from the elephant's back' (apud Strab. XV, 52; Jacoby 31). He also refers to hunting in a kind of 'Bacchic chase, when the king is surrounded by women; he hunts from an elephant, while the women ride either in chariots, or on horses or on elephants' (Strab. XV.55; Jacoby, fr. 32). Diodorus again (II.42; Jacoby, fr. 4) picks up Megasthenes' remark about the size of Indian elephants and adds some physiological details: 'Nor does this animal cover the female in a peculiar manner, as some say, but in the same way as horses and all other four-footed beasts; and their period of gestation is in some cases sixteen months at the least and in other cases eighteen months at the most. They bring forth like horses, but one young for the most part, and the females suckle their young for six years. The span of life for most of them is about that of men who attain the greatest age, though some which have reached the highest age have lived for two hundred years.'

The longest passage from Megasthenes comes from Arrian (*Ind.* 13 ff.; Jacoby, fr. 20): 'Most wild animals which the Greeks hunt the Indians hunt also, but these have a method of hunting elephants unlike all other kinds of hunting, just as these animals are unlike other animals. It is this: they choose a place that is level and open to the sun's heat, and dig a ditch in a circle wide enough for a great army to camp within it. They dig the ditch thirty feet broad and twenty-four deep. The earth which they throw out of the ditch they heap on either side of the ditch, and so use it as a wall. Then they make shelters for themselves, dug out of the wall on the outside of the ditch, and place small windows in them; through these the light comes in, and they watch the animals entering and charging into the enclosure. Then within the enclosure they leave some three or four of the tamest females, and leave only one entrance by the ditch, making a bridge over it; and here they heap much earth and grass so that the animals cannot distinguish the bridge, and so suspect any trick. The hunters then keep out of the way, hiding in the shelters dug under the ditch. Now wild elephants do not approach inhabited places by daylight, but at night they wander all around and feed in herds, following the largest and finest of their number, as cows do the bulls. And when they approach the ditch and hear the trumpeting of the females and perceive them by their scent, they rush to the walled enclosure; working round the outside edge of the ditch, they find the bridge and push across it into the enclosure. When the hunters see that the wild elephants have entered, some smartly remove the bridge, others hurrying to the neighbouring villages report that the elephants are caught in the enclosure. The inhabitants on hearing the news mount the most spirited, and at the same time most disciplined elephants, and then drive them towards the enclosure; when they have driven them thither they do not at once join battle, but allow the wild elephants to grow distressed by hunger and to be tamed by thirst. But when they think they are sufficiently distressed, then they erect the bridge again, and enter the enclosure; and at first there is a fierce battle between the tame elephants and the captives, and then, as one would expect, the wild elephants are tamed, distressed as they are by a sinking of their spirits and by hunger. Then the riders dismounting from the tame elephants tie together the feet of the now languid wild ones; then they order the tame elephants to punish the rest by repeated blows, till in their distress they fall to the earth; then they come near them, throw nooses round their necks, and climb on them as they lie there. That they may not toss their drivers nor do them any injury, they make an incision in their necks with a sharp knife, all round, and bind their noose round the wound, so that by reason of the sore they keep their heads and necks still. For were they to turn round to do mischief, the wound beneath the rope chafes them. And so they keep quiet, and, realizing that they are conquered, they are led off by the tame elephants by the rope.'

'Such elephants as are not yet full grown or from some defect are not worth acquiring, they allow to depart to their own haunts. Then they lead off their captives to the villages and first of all give them green shoots and grass to eat; but they, from want of heart, are not willing to eat anything; so the Indians range themselves about them and with songs and drums and cymbals, beating and singing, lull them to sleep. For if there is an intelligent animal, it is the elephant. Some of them have been known, when their drivers have been killed in battle, to have lifted them up and carried them to burial; others have stood over them and protected them. Others, when they have fallen, have actively fought for them; one, indeed, who in a passion slew his driver, died from remorse and grief.' [Here Arrian interposes some observations of his own, culled no doubt in the circuses of the Roman empire] 'I myself have seen an elephant clanging cymbals, and others dancing; two cymbals were fastened to the player's forelegs, and one on his trunk, and he rhythmically beat with his trunk the cymbal on either leg in turn; the dancers danced in a circle, and raising and bending their forelegs in turn moved rhythmically, as the player with the cymbals marked the time for them. Elephants mate in spring, as do oxen and horses, when certain pores about the temples of the females open and exhale; the female bears its offspring sixteen months at the least, eighteen at most; it has one calf; and this is suckled till its eighth year. The longest-lived elephants survive to two hundred years;

but many die before that by disease; but as far as mere age goes, they reach this age. If their eyes are affected, cow's milk injected cures them; for their other sicknesses a draught of dark wine, and for their wounds swine's flesh roast, and laid on the spot, are good. These are the Indian remedies for them.'

Strabo (xv.1.42–43; Jacoby, fr. 20b) gives a similar, but more succinct, summary of Megasthenes' account of the hunt. He adds that the elephants, after capture and before being fed, have their feet tied to one another and their necks to a firmly planted pillar, and thus are subdued by hunger. Further, at breeding-time in the spring the male 'is seized with frenzy and becomes ferocious; at that time *he* (contrast Arrian's application of this to the female, quoted above) discharges a kind of fatty matter through the breathing-hole which he has beside his temples.'

Thus Megasthenes provides much of interest. He carefully differentiates between Indians and Africans and offers an explanation. He corrects earlier views about copulation and rightly assigns mating to the spring. His account of *musth* has clearly not been reported accurately, since Arrian attributes it to males, and Strabo to females; could Megasthenes have in fact attributed it to both sexes and thus been in line with modern views? Unlike most writers, he under- rather than over- estimates the period of gestation. His idea that suckling continued until the eighth year is exaggerated, since two to three years is the normal period, but maternal care, if decreasing after weaning, is nevertheless maintained for a considerable time thereafter. Further, his estimate of the elephant's age as roughly that of man is good, and if his exceptional longevity of 200 years cannot be accepted, it is at least nearer the mark than some other ancient estimates. His fascinating account of hunting and capture of elephants seems essentially reasonable and can be paralleled in general by modern accounts.

A great variety of methods have been used both in ancient and modern times to trap elephants, some of which are described later: pits, falling spears, bamboo ring traps, trunk snares, ham-stringing or tendon-slashing, fire, poisoned arrows, the corral, and later, of course, gunfire. The corral method, which Megasthenes describes here, has been used widely in the East in more recent times. A full account of it is given by R. Carrington (*Elephants*, ch. 12), from which only a few points can be repeated here. Triangular or rectangular stockades, *keddars*, are made of tree-trunks, with an opening that can be closed by means of a rolled curtain of logs; within it is a pond or stream. A 1,000 or so men may be used as scouts and beaters, who over a period of weeks or even a couple of months very gradually round up a chosen herd, perhaps from twenty or thirty miles away. Eventually the elephants are herded into the enclosure. Tame elephants, mounted by their mahouts, then enter and separate out first one and then another from the mass, while another man, concealed under the tame elephant's belly, has the daunting task of slapping the wild beast's hindfoot and slipping over it a noose, of which the loose end is fixed to the tame elephant's collar. The captive is then led by the elephant to a nearby tree and tethered to it. Such resistance to these tactics may be shown that an obstreperous elephant may need three tame ones to control it. I have not come across any modern reference to female decoy elephants being used in a large-scale corral round-up, but one is sometimes tethered in an enclosure to entice a wild bull. It is possible that hunger as well as thirst is used as a bait in modern times, but it seems that a captive elephant, still tied to a tree, tends to refuse food through anger or fear; a tame elephant may be tied up nearby to give the wild one confidence until it quietens down and begins to accept its food. In the process of breaking-in, the skin of the elephant may be gently rubbed 'to the accompaniment of a monotonous and soothing chant . . . its effects are reinforced by the use of endearing epithets, such as "ho! my son" or "my father" or "my mother", according to the age or sex of the captive.' Such blandishments, however, often have to be supplemented with the use of the goad or ankus. This quotation, as much of the above account, derives from R. Carrington's description, to which the reader is directed for further detail. In sum, from such a comparison Megasthenes' does not come off at all badly.

An influential source of information about African elephants was Agatharchides of Cnidus, one of the most important Alexandrian writers in the mid-second century BC. He was primarily a geographer, whose works included a treatise *On the Red Sea*. This contained descriptions of the tribes that lived south of Egypt, their habits and the wild animals of their region; among them were the Elephantotherae and the Trogodytes. Agatharchides used many sources, such as personal enquiry from merchants and others, official documents, and the work of his fellow citizen Ctesias, and he quotes the elephant hunter Simmias (p. 135). Though his works are now lost, they were extensively used by Diodorus, who preserves for us a fairly close rendering of some passages: these include a graphic account of the hunting of the African elephant and the hazards of trying to ship the captured animals up the Red Sea coast: they are discussed later in their historical context (p. 127 ff.). Agatharchides' work had a considerable impact on other later writers beside Diodorus. These include Artemidorus of Ephesus who, in his eleven geographical books, turned to Agatharchides for his information on Ethiopia, and to Megasthenes and the Alexander historians for Indian matters.[27]

### 'INDIAN ELEPHANTS ARE BIGGER THAN AFRICAN'

Ancient writers are virtually unanimous in their opinion that Indian elephants were larger than Africans. This was the view of the earliest writers and it was reinforced by the authority of Polybius in his description of the one known battle in which Indians met Africans face to face, namely the encounter at Raphia in 217 BC between the 73 Africans of Ptolemy and the 102 Indians of Antiochus when the Africans, 'terrified I suppose by the great size and strength of the Indians, at once turned tail before they got near them'. This opinion continued to be the belief of the writers of the Roman empire: thus Pliny wrote: 'African elephants fear Indian, because the Indian is bigger.' We must now enquire when this idea first arose and how true it is.[28]

The first writer to voice this opinion may have been Ctesias. It occurs in a passage of Diodorus (II.16.4) in connection with Semiramis' Indian expedition, where the general context is derived from Ctesias (p. 35). The question is whether Diodorus' remarks about India and Indian elephants also derive from Ctesias or were added by himself either from his own knowledge or more probably from another source. If the latter, that source is likely to have been either Onesicritus or Megasthenes. At any rate if Ctesias be ruled out, though it is by no means certain that he should be, then the first reference to the superiority of the Indian comes from Onesicritus: Strabo reports that 'Onesicritus and others said that the Indian elephants were greater and stronger than the Libyan' (Jacoby, fr. 14). It would thus seem to have been the common opinion among the Alexander historians, while Megasthenes took it over and explained that India provided better fodder than did Africa.[29]

60

The belief of the ancient writers in the superiority of the Indian over the African was in fact generally accepted until towards the end of the last century. However, when the interior of Africa began to be opened up, doubts arose: the African elephant was now seen in his full stature and was clearly bigger than the Indian and so the ancients must be wrong. Early doubts were voiced in 1885 by Scharf in a work entitled *De natura et usu elephantorum apud veteres*. This new knowledge then led to an attack on Polybius in in particular and his account of the battle of Raphia; it was launched in 1900 by the military historian Delbrück. Soon these doubts became orthodox doctrine. The Hellenistic historian Edwyn Bevan pointed out that Indian elephants measure only up to 10 ft at the shoulder, whereas Africans often reach 12 ft. Sir William Tarn then lent his great authority to the view, and suggested that the alleged superior size of the Indians was just a silly mistake that had been made originally by Ctesias, who lied in order to flatter his Persian employer who owned Indian, not African, elephants.[30] Tarn based his opinion on two arguments: that Ptolemy's African elephants at Raphia did not belong to a smaller species now extinct nor were they immature animals. For the first point he relied on the weight of the 34 tusks which Ptolemy Auletes gave to the temple at Didyma, namely just over 24 talents: this is the equivalent of 31.7 lb per tusk, if the Ptolemaic talent was used, or 39.9 lb based on the Attic talent. Tarn was then led to believe that a current average weight for a tusk was about 20 lb and therefore not unnaturally came to the conclusion that Ptolemy's were 'a very fine average . . . the African elephants of the Ptolemies were then, at the very least, as good as those known today.' Tarn's second point that the elephants were not immature ones needs no further discussion, since there is no good reason to believe that those at Raphia were either youngsters or pygmies. He therefore concludes that Polybius was wrong and that Ctesias' silly mistake developed into a literary commonplace, a cliché that was thoughtlessly repeated by later writers, even by so good an historian as Polybius.

Tarn's view may be said to have held the field unquestioned for some twenty years until in 1948 it was challenged and demolished by Sir William Gowers, one-time governor of Uganda, who was a classical scholar and knew elephants at first hand.[31] He made clear that Tarn's main argument was based on a false premiss, namely that all African elephants belong to one race. This we have seen is not so, and the elephants which Ptolemy drew from the Eritrean area probably belonged to the smaller Forest (*cyclotis*) race which today has a wide range in a band across central Africa from the Atlantic to the Nile valley; this was probably larger 2,000 years ago and reached to the Red Sea and Gulf of Aden, where the very few surviving elephants are very small. No elephants now survive in the area in Eritrea behind Adulis where Ptolemy hunted, but one piece of evidence luckily survives to indicate their race. A zoologist who went on Napier's expedition to Magdala in 1868, which started from the site of Adulis, encountered and shot some elephants near the head-streams of the river Baraka: the cow measured 7 ft 8 in. at the shoulder, and the larger of two bulls 7 ft 4 in. As we have seen, Forest elephants on average stand at under 8 ft, Bush elephants at over 8 ft. Thus, since the evidence comes from a scientific observer and there is no good reason to question it, the elephants which the Ptolemies used at Raphia and elsewhere belonged to the smaller Forest race whose size is less than that of the Indian elephant. Slight support, if such is needed, is given to this conclusion by the fact that the Forest race is more easily trained than is the larger Bush, which in captivity is liable to become dangerous and less amenable for use in war. On the other hand the old idea that no African elephants could be adequately trained has long been exploded. The Belgians, for instance, have done it very successfully in the Congo, where youngsters of the Forest race (about 11 years old and 6 ft high) are captured and broken in in a matter of months by their cornacs, together with the help of older elephants who are trained as 'monitors'. When the Belgians started this enterprise in the Congo they secured Indian mahouts who soon taught the Azande natives to do the job very competently. Thus there is no reason why the smaller Forest animal should not have been trained and exploited for military purposes in the ancient world. As to Tarn's argument about the tusks, his figures for a modern estimate of an average weight seem too low. Dr Sikes writes of 1971 (p. 324) that 'tusks marketed today rarely exceed 100 lb each, the average being from 25 to 30 lb each.' But on the assumption that Ptolemy would send reasonably choice specimens to Apollo, an average weight of 30 or even 40 lb does not suggest the larger elephant. Sir William Gowers, who himself shot a 12-ft Bush elephant, remarks that 'a tusk of 40 lb is not regarded in East Africa as worth keeping as a trophy'. If therefore a 30 to 40 pounder was the best that Ptolemy could provide, this evidence would not support Tarn and the critics of Polybius but rather suggest that the tusks came from the Forest and not the Bush elephant and that therefore Ptolemy's elephants were in fact smaller than Indians. Thus if we may suppose that the ancients did not handle the massive African elephants, which were only revealed in the course of the last century, but drew upon the smaller animals from Eritrea and North-west Africa, then the *communis opinio* of antiquity that they were smaller than the Indian elephant may be once again accepted.[32]

After this probable vindication of the early classical writers on this specific point and before seeing what later writers have to tell us about elephants in general, we may turn to their accounts of the elephant in war during the period of Alexander and his Successors, for it was in this sphere that the elephant played its most important role.

# CHAPTER III

# ALEXANDER AND HIS
# SUCCESSORS

## ALEXANDER THE GREAT

In 331 Alexander overran Asia Minor, Palestine and Egypt and swept the Persian monarch Darius back beyond Mesopotamia. He then advanced over the Tigris for the final battle which led to the flight of the king and the collapse of the Persian empire. When Alexander first discerned Darius' line of battle at Gaugamela, his military skill was taxed to the utmost: he suddenly saw that this was to be no ordinary battle of heavy-armed infantry, but primarily a cavalry encounter. But in addition to the unusual preponderance of enemy cavalry, two other strange units were to be seen in front of the king's line: 15 elephants and a body of scythed-chariots. In the event neither gave him any serious trouble; he gave effective orders to deal with the chariots, while the elephants are not mentioned again and apparently took no part in the battle. Their 'disappearance' has perhaps not unnaturally led two of the historians who have most recently discussed the battle virtually to neglect them. However, Tarn rightly stressed their potential importance: he writes, 'Judiciously posted, the elephants might have prevented Alexander charging, as untrained horses will not face them: but probably they could not be put in line, the Persian horses not being trained to them either.'[33] This may well be so, since we know nothing of the earlier history and training of these elephants; all we are told is that Darius' army included 'not many elephants, but the Indians . . . had some fifteen' (Arrian, III, 8.6). Possibly they had not long joined Darius' forces and thus had not been properly trained to act with his cavalry, although it looks as if he hoped to make effective use of them since, according to the written disposition of his battle-line which fell into Greek hands after the engagement, the elephants were to be posted in front of the royal squadron, together with 50 chariots (11.6). After the battle, accord-

64

XIII: *a.* and *b.* Alexander the Great attacking Porus on an elephant, decadrachms minted in Babylon. *c.* Alexander the Great in elephant-scalp head-dress. *d.* Ptolemy I. *e.* Seleucus I. *f.* Demetrius Poliorcetes. *g.* and *h.* Elephants on coins of Seleucus I.

XIV: *a*. Coin of Tarentum, showing normal type of Taras on a dolphin, but with symbol of an Indian elephant, indicating the presence of Pyrrhus in the city. *b*. Aes Signatum of central Italy, depicting an Indian elephant, presumably one of Pyrrhus' beasts. *c*. Reverse of *b* showing a sow, a possible reference to the belief that in a battle with the Romans Pyrrhus' elephants were stampeded by some pigs.

XV: *a*. Ptolemy II and Arsinoe II. *b*. Antiochus I. *c*. Alexander in an elephant quadriga on a gold stater of Ptolemy I. *d*. Athene in an elephant quadriga on a coin of Antiochus I. *e*. Ptolemy III. *f*. Seleucus II.

XVI: *a*. Diodotus of Bactria. *b*. Antiochus III. *c*. Philip V of Macedon. *d*. Ptolemy IV. *e*. Elephant on coin of Antiochus III. *f*. Euthydemus of Bactria. *g*. Demetrius of Bactria. *h*. Ptolemy V. *i*. Head of 'Africa' on coin of Agathocles.

ing to Arrian, 'Parmenio captured the Persian camp with the baggage trains, elephants and camels', while they are also mentioned in a summary of Persian losses (15.4 and 6). This reference to them in connection with the camp might conceivably suggest that at some point before the battle a last-minute change took place and the elephants were kept back or withdrawn (because they were unruly?) and did not take any part in the fighting. This of course is speculation, but their inglorious role scarcely justifies the oblivion to which they are usually consigned. They might indeed have changed the course of history, or at least the development of the battle, but even apart from 'might-have-beens' they were presumably the first elephants that Alexander had seen in war, and their appearance, if not their performance, must have made him think, especially if he now contemplated an advance as far as India, the land of elephants. We do not know their fate. In view of future possibilities, it is not unlikely that he used this chance to familiarize himself with their behaviour and possibly employed them on transport duties. Did he even remember his tutor Aristotle and dispatch at least one of them to Greece? Such a journey would not seem difficult to the man who later in far-off Afghanistan chose the finest of 230,000 captured oxen 'which he wanted to send to Macedonia to work the land' (Arrian, IV, 25.4). But these 15 elephants were not Alexander's total haul: Curtius (V, 2.10) reports that when the conqueror was approaching Susa the local satrap sent presents which included swift dromedaries and '12 elephants that Darius had imported from India, no longer a terror to the Macedonians, as he had hoped, but a help, when Fortune transferred the wealth of the conquered to the conqueror'. Thus Alexander now had 27 elephants.

Gaugamela had opened up the whole Persian empire and the East to Alexander, who with incredible tenacity, speed and skill led his forces to Afghanistan and north-west India. After finally crossing the Hindu Kush and approaching the Indus he ordered Taxiles, the rajah of Taxila, and other Indians to meet him. They came with an escort of 25 elephants, which they promised to give to Alexander. But before he could reach the Indus much stiff fighting lay ahead, including the resistance of the Assacenians whose forces included 30 elephants (Arr. IV, 25.5). He captured a town named Ora, including a number of elephants that had been left there (27.9), and then achieved one of his most remarkable feats,

65

the storming of the rock-citadel of Aornus, which legend said even Heracles had failed to capture. He then turned to deal with the Assacenians, whose leader's brother, taking his elephants with him, had sought refuge in the hills. Alexander sent out a reconaissance force, since 'he was especially anxious to find out all about the elephants' (Arr. IV, 30.6). Learning from some captured tribesmen that Abisares, leader of the Indian highland tribes, had 'left his elephants at pasture near the river Indus, he ordered these men to lead him on the track of the elephants. Now many Indians hunt elephants, and Alexander was careful to keep such men in his following. With them he hunted the elephants, two of which threw themselves over the cliffs in the pursuit and died; the rest were captured and allowed riders to mount them and were taken into the army' (30.7–8). Diodorus (XVII, 86.2–3) refers to Alexander rounding up 15 elephants of an Indian ruler named Aphrices; this may well be a duplication of the story about Abisares. If the figure of 15 is accepted, with the loss of two, Alexander now had some 40 beasts, and in addition those captured at Ora, with the promise of still more from Taxiles. This herd was integrated with his army, although perhaps rather for purposes of transport or to impress the tribes through whose territory he advanced than for actual fighting. Further, having helped to round some up in person, he will have become more interested in this potential new arm.

Taxiles' promise was soon honoured: when Alexander reached the Indus he found there gifts which included 200 silver talents, 3,000 cattle and over 10,000 sheep, together with 30 elephants (Arr. V, 3.5). But when he arrived at Taxila itself, he was given 56 more elephants (Curtius, VIII, 12.11); his force now numbered more than 126. Apparently he wished for no more, because when soon afterwards a captured rebel leader of the Arachosii was brought to him with 30 elephants, he gave the beasts to Taxiles. Alexander was now ready for a final trial of strength with Porus who ruled the land between the Hydaspes (Jhelum) and the Acesines (Chenab) and would not treat with him. Porus was reported to have some 50,000 infantry, 3,000–4,000 cavalry, 300 war-chariots and 200 elephants. Despite this massive force of elephants Alexander, who (if he had kept the 30 Arachosians) could have mustered some 150 to face them, made no attempt to experiment in this new arm.[34] He clearly had not had time to co-ordinate all the various groups of elephants into a cohesive force, and still less had he trained his

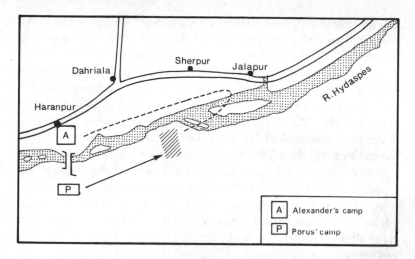

Fig. 6. Area of the Battle of the Hydaspes

horses to co-operate with them. He did, however, apparently begin to think out ways by which his men might try to cope with the enemy's elephants, as the subsequent battle was to show. This struggle is the first and classic example of a Greek army having to meet elephants face to face, but it is not always remembered how much Alexander already knew about this terrifying opponent.

Alexander delayed rather long at his base at Taxila, but when he knew that Porus would not submit he prepared to advance into the Punjab. One problem was that Porus was on the southern side of the great Hydaspes river which must be crossed; Alexander therefore ordered the pontoon-bridge which he had built over the Indus to be dismantled and transported by ox-cart for reassembling at the Hydaspes. Further, about the beginning of June (326 BC) the monsoon broke, and the river would be flooded. However, Alexander advanced, through torrential rains, to a point on the north bank where there was a ford (probably near Haranpur), but there he saw that the opposite bank was guarded by a very large enemy force which included 85 elephants (fig. 6). These beasts determined the course of the battle: Arrian emphasizes more than once that untrained horses simply will not face elephants. Thus even if Alexander could have got his cavalry across the swollen river, they would have been unable successfully to engage the enemy. He therefore had to try by many feints to lull Porus into thinking that he would wait until the river became less swollen, while in the meantime his cavalry began to probe the bank of the river upstream to the east. Here some seventeen miles from his main camp he found a large wooded island in a bend of the river, which formed a suitable stepping-stone across the river. Further, when he learned that Abisares, king of Kashmir, was coming to Porus' aid, he had to act quickly. While Alexander's main army remained in its camp under the command of Craterus, he himself proposed to attempt the crossing via the island by night with 5,000 cavalry and at least 10,000 infantry and then to advance westwards along the southern bank against Porus. Meantime three supporting divisions were to cover the northern bank and in succession to try to join him as he advanced westwards. Craterus was only to attempt to cross the river after Porus had moved eastwards to attack Alexander, and only then if no elephants had been left behind to defend the ford, or unless he was sure that Porus was in flight. Under cover of a stormy night Alexander then embarked his own force; in his own boat, which led the assault, were four of his future would-be 'successors', Ptolemy, Perdiccas, Lysimachus and Seleucus. Disaster nearly followed when he landed his force on what turned out to be another island, but eventually they reached the southern bank of the river. At first news of the landing Porus sent a force under his son with cavalry and chariots, but these were defeated, the boy being killed, while Alexander's horse Bucephalus received wounds which proved fatal. Porus then left a holding force with some elephants to prevent Craterus crossing and attacking him in the rear, and advanced against Alexander with his main force to fight the battle of the Hydaspes.[35]

Porus formed up his troops facing east on a sandy plain, with his left wing towards the river but not reaching it, apparently exposed to a possible encirclement, but in fact the swollen river and monsoon rains may have made this ground too treacherous in his view for any operations. First in the centre he placed his elephants in line, with gaps of perhaps 100 feet between each beast. Behind them came his main infantry line, with the units covering the intervals in the line of elephants in front. Other infantry detachments were posted on each wing, stretching even beyond the elephants. Next to the flanking detachments was the cavalry, with a cover of chariots.[36]

Alexander was faced with a tremendous, indeed an entirely novel problem: he could not use his cavalry against the enemy's

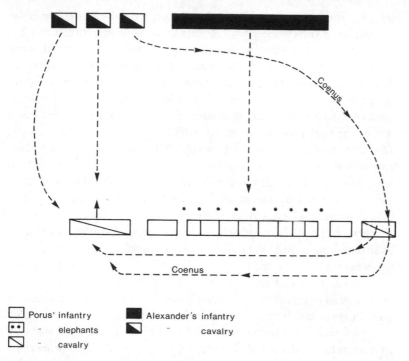

Porus' infantry      Alexander's infantry

   "    elephants      "    cavalry

   "    cavalry

Fig. 7. Battle of the Hydaspes

main line, since his horses just would not charge against, or between
the gaps in, the formidable row of elephants, while he would hesitate to send his phalanx against this untested opponent, since the
elephants might wreak an awful havoc against men inexperienced
in this new form of warfare. He therefore decided first to try by a
bold move to knock out Porus' cavalry and stationed all his own
cavalry on his right wing. As this wing appeared about to advance,
Porus seems to have felt that his own left would succumb to it, so
he ordered his right wing to come round to support it. Meanwhile
Alexander sent off part of his cavalry, under the command of
Coenus, to ride off to his left and make a turning movement against
the cavalry on the Indian right, either to deal with it on the spot or,
if Porus in fact switched it to support his other flank (as Alexander
may possibly have been hoping) then Coenus was to follow it
round. It is more probable that Porus' right wing and Coenus' pursuing column swept round *behind* the Indian infantry than that they
moved in front of it and the elephants. The cavalry on the Indian

left was thus supported by the horsemen from its right, but only to find itself surrounded by Coenus in its rear and threatened by Alexander in its front: Alexander had meantime advanced with two hipparchies, covered by 1000 mounted archers who successfully knocked out the chariots. While the Indian rear ranks had to wheel round to face Coenus, Alexander's charge against the front ranks was so demoralizing that they did not wait for it but 'fell back upon their elephants, as if to some friendly sheltering wall' (Arrian), that is, presumably between the line of elephants and that of the infantry. The elephants on the extreme left of their line then moved against Alexander's cavalry, as indeed did some Indian cavalry later, but by this time the main fighting had moved to the infantry; the cavalry was soon eliminated.

Alexander's phalanx, which so far had been held back, advanced against the main line of Porus' elephants with the infantry drawn up behind them. To the Macedonians the enemy line looked like a city wall, the elephants resembling towers jutting out from the curtain wall of infantry. This description is given by both Diodorus and Curtius, but it must not be allowed to suggest that the elephants themselves carried towers or howdahs. The evidence about towers, which is discussed elsewhere (p. 240 ff.), is virtually decisive against Porus' elephants carrying them: Porus himself, on the Greek coin which depicted his retreat, is shown riding bareback, so that it is unlikely that other riders were more protected (pl. XIIIa). Each elephant carried its mahout, riding on the neck, and possibly one soldier on the back, although the presence of a soldier is uncertain: the animal itself was the essential weapon. Alexander's men were ordered to try to encircle individual beasts: volleys of spears and javelins were to be launched against them, archers were to aim at the riders. Infantrymen with long pikes (sarissae) would not have to approach too close; others were to dash in and out, slashing their trunks with scimitars or hacking at their feet with axes; these curved swords, called copides, and the axes, had been made ready beforehand. However, the elephants wrought terrible havoc, crushing some men under foot, piercing others with their tusks, and seizing some with their trunks and dashing them on the ground (or, according to Curtius, sometimes passing them up to their riders to deal with). Gradually, however, the elephants were pushed back into a narrow space and started to do damage to their own troops, as they lost their mahouts and began to weaken from

70

wounds. Despite a final elephant charge by Porus in person, the beasts were beaten and 'still trumpeting only, they began to retreat like ships backing'. Alexander then tightened his ring of cavalry around the enemy and ordered his infantry to lock shields and to advance as a phalanx in the closest possible order. The battle was won and the surviving elephants were captured, to the number of 80 according to Diodorus.

After fighting to the end Porus rode off the field, refusing to surrender, until overcome with his many wounds he collapsed on his elephant and slipped to the ground. Curtius (VIII, 14.39–40) adds some pleasant, if unverifiable, details: when the king started to slide from the elephant, the mahout, thinking that he was merely beginning to dismount, ordered the beast to kneel; at this the rest of the animals followed suit, as they had been so trained, and so Porus and the rest were captured. However, when men were running up to strip the king's armour from his body, as he was thought to be dead, the elephant began to protect its master and to attack the spoilers, lifting the body on to its back; unfortunately it was then overwhelmed with weapons. Plutarch (*Alexander*, 60.7) has another version. When the elephant realized that its master was worn out with the multitude of missiles and wounds, fearing lest he might fall off, it knelt softly on the ground and with its trunk gently took each spear and drew it out of his body. The ultimate fate of Porus, heroic in spirit as in stature, is well known: he was 'treated like a king' by Alexander and restored to his kingdom.

A pleasant anecdote about one of the elephants is told by Philostratus (II, 12), who lived in the time of Septimius Severus: near Taxila, Apollonius, travelling with his friends, came upon an elephant which the natives anointed with myrrh and fillets. 'For, they said, this was one of those who fought for Porus against Alexander; and, as it had fought so gallantly, Alexander dedicated it to the Sun. And it had, they say, gold rings around its tusks, or horns, and an inscription was written on them in Greek, namely: 'Alexander the son of Zeus dedicates Ajax to the Sun.' For he had given this name to the elephant, thinking that so great an animal deserved a great name. The natives reckoned that 350 years had passed since the battle, without taking into account the age of the elephant when it went into battle.' It would be nice to think that Alexander's dedication was a fact, though not even a sacred Indian elephant is likely to have lived 100, let alone over 300, years.

Alexander next had to deal with tribes that bordered on Porus' kingdom. He received 40 elephants as a gift from Abisares and advanced eastwards. After crossing the river Acesines (Chenab) he sent Porus back to his own kingdom 'to pick out a body of his most warlike Indians and any elephants he had with him, and bring these to join him' (Arr. v, 21.2). This additional force reached him when he had advanced over yet another river to Sangala, which he was assailing. He now brought up his siege engines and captured the town by assault and then destroyed it; although Arrian does not mention them, the elephants could well have been of value in hauling the heavy machinery about, if they were not used in the actual assault itself. Alexander then pushed on to the Hyphasis (Beas), but that was the end.

For some time not all had been well with the troops. The terrible climatic conditions in which the campaign of the Hydaspes had been fought and the desperate nature of the battle itself with the crowning terror of the enemy elephants had dispirited the troops. Although Alexander resolved to press on to 'the end of India' he must have realized (probably for some time now) that India did not soon end at the river of the Ocean and that no physical 'end of the world' lay ahead. He tried to drive on his weary veterans, despite forests and poisonous snakes, but rumours began to circulate that twelve days beyond the Beas was a far greater river and beyond that a tribe with vast military resources which included 4,000 elephants. Whatever be thought about the number, the news about the elephants further east was not without foundation: those of the kingdom of Nanda (Ganges valley), not to mention those of Ceylon, were believed to be stronger than those of the Punjab which Alexander's men had met already. Megasthenes, as recorded by Aelian (XIII, 8), said that the largest elephants in India were called Prasian (the Prasii lived near Patna in the Ganges area) and that (XVI, 18) those of Taprobane (Ceylon) were greater still. This belief appears to be confirmed by Indian sources.[37] In a speech which Curtius puts into his mouth Alexander minimized the effectiveness of elephants in war, pointing out that he had not used in battle those that he had, and that the more numerous they were, the more likely they were to confuse each other and damage their own side (IX, 2.15 ff.). But the men who had fought against Porus knew better: and so did Arrian who does not include this nonsense in the speech which he attributed to Alexander. But words no

72

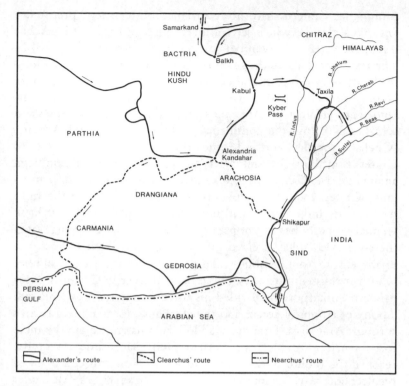

Fig. 8. Alexander in the East

longer sufficed. This was the last straw: the men mutinied and the Macedonian officers supported them; after a dignified interval Alexander capitulated. The eastern anabasis was over: they would turn south to the Indian Ocean and homewards. Thus one not inconsiderable factor which forced Alexander to break off his incredible march of conquest was the elephant: both those that had provided such a traumatic experience to the men who had tried to grapple with them on the Hydaspes, and the shadow cast by that innumerable force which barred the way to the Ocean.

The rest of the story is soon told. In the autumn of 326 Alexander marched back to the Hydaspes; *en route* he received 30 elephants from Abisares (although Arrian (v, 20.5) says that Abisares had already sent 40, these 30 appear to be in addition, but may possibly be part of the 40 already sent, but perhaps not yet handed over to Alexander in person: 29.4). When he reached the Hydaspes he found that Craterus had, in accordance with orders, prepared a vast naval flotilla, which set sail under the command of Nearchus down the river in November, carrying as many men as possible. The rest, who formed the main body of the army, marched along the banks: Craterus commanded the detachment on the right bank, Hephaestion advanced on the left with the main force which included 200 elephants.[38] After the fleet had weathered the rapids and whirlpools below the confluence of the Hydaspes and Acesines (Chenab), the elephants and some other troops were transferred to Craterus on the right bank (Arr. VI, 5.5), but after the campaign against the Malli in which Alexander was wounded, nearly mortally, Craterus and the elephants were ferried back to the right bank of the Indus which had now been reached, since that bank seemed easier for heavy troops (15.4). As he advanced further down the river Alexander received gifts of elephants from at least two rajahs (e.g. 30 from Sambus) and captured some more from another who had resisted him; these were handed over to Craterus. Near modern Shikarpore he divided his forces. Craterus was sent with a body of troops, veterans and the elephants, to march westwards through Arachosia, Drangiana and Carmania and rejoin the main force when it reached the Persian Gulf. Meantime Alexander reached the mouth of the Indus and while Nearchus commanded the fleet on a voyage along the coast of the Arabian Sea, Alexander led the army through Gedrosia. Despite terrible sufferings and deprivations the two arms of his service reached their goals; they made contact again in Carmania, and there at Galashkird (where Alexander founded another Alexandria) he was joined by Craterus and the elephants, which were soon handed over to Hephaestion to take with the greatest part of the army along the easy sea-coast to Persia. We meet them once again in Susa at the funeral of the Indian 'holy-man' Calanus, an incident recorded as we have seen by Nearchus among others (p. 53). At Babylon, which he planned to make his capital and where he was shortly to die, Alexander probably had a force of some 200 elephants since he had this number when he started on the long, long homeward journey and any elephants which fell by the way would be counterbalanced by the additional numbers he had received while marching along the Indus. It is of course possible that he could have left a few behind *en route* for guard duties in various provinces, but there is no direct evidence that he did.

Alexander is unlikely to have retained so large a force of elephants whose upkeep would be considerable, without demanding some return from them. They must surely have been employed on transport duties, along with mules, horses, asses and camels, since his vast lines of communication and supply needed all the support he could give them. Further, although he did not use his elephants in battle, they may well have performed some para-military duties, while even their appearance would inspire a certain respect among hostile tribes. When Alexander was back in Babylon, we know that he employed them for ceremonial purposes: Phylarchus (apud Athen. XII, 539 f.) describes the splendour of Alexander's pavilion with its golden throne and impressive ranks of Persian and Macedonian guards: 'outside the tent the elephant-corps (ἄγημα), fully equipped, was stationed in a circle'. The use of a military word, *agema*, shows that they were organized as part of the army. Before facing Porus, Alexander had been forced to work out a method of anti-elephant training by providing scimitars and axes. Thus, although his Successors were the first Greeks to use elephants offensively, they played no inconsiderable role in the background of Alexander's own life.

This is strikingly illustrated by the issue of some commemorative coins which he probably minted during his last period at Babylon; they were sent to Susa where he had agreed to settle arrears of pay and debts. They consisted of silver decadrachms, some of normal type, but others, which were perhaps intended for the officers, were of special significance (pl. XIIIa). If they were meant to sum up his achievement one might have expected the overthrow of the Persian empire to have been symbolically depicted: instead we find a heroic encounter between Alexander on his horse Bucephalus charging with his lance the great elephant on which sat Porus and his mahout. It was the defeat of India which he wished to celebrate. Unfortunately only three specimens of these coins survive, and the details are somewhat worn. The figure of Alexander is surprisingly small compared with that of Porus and the mahout. It is true that Porus was a giant of a man, but the mahout need not have been large. Perhaps the object was to emphasize the heroic struggle of a David against a Goliath. The mahout is riding normally on the elephant's neck with his legs tucked behind the ears, but he is turning round and threatens the attacker with a weapon in his right hand; this has been interpreted as his hooked goad (ankus), but since the hook is not easily detectable, it could be a javelin, especially as he holds two more in his left hand. Porus, riding bareback and astride, grips the animal with his bent knees and also turns back to defend himself against Alexander whose horse is rearing up. On the reverse of the coin stands the almost godlike figure of Alexander, the thunderbolt of Zeus in his right hand and a Victory flying to crown him with a wreath.[38A] The significance of this figure, which contrasts with the small figure on the horse on the obverse, need not be considered here, but one more monument must be mentioned. After his death a magnificent vehicle was constructed to carry Alexander's embalmed body to Macedon (though in fact it was diverted to Egypt). Its rich decorations included four paintings, one of which showed 'the elephants equipped for war, following the bodyguard. They carried Indian mahouts in front, with Macedonians fully armed in their regular equipment behind them'.[39] Since each elephant had only one mahout, the use of the plural here denotes only one soldier also for each elephant. Thus in death, as in life in his pavilion in Babylon, Alexander was escorted by elephants. An even closer link was forged when six years after his death Ptolemy, then ruling Egypt but as yet not having assumed the royal title, placed on the coinage of Alexandria the head of Alexander wearing a head-dress consisting of an elephant-scalp (pl. XIIIc). By this time the elephant was beginning to play a significant role in the warfare of the Successors: Ptolemy was not slow to indicate their hero's interest in this new weapon.

## PERDICCAS AND PTOLEMY

The death of Alexander initiated a new era in which his marshals, the Successors or Diadochoi, struggled among themselves for power: each attempted either to gain sole control of the empire or else to seize a portion of it for himself.[40] A very complicated political kaleidoscope developed and many battles, large and small, were fought. In these the contenders made increasing use of elephants and thus we shall have to consider several major set-piece battles; in order to appreciate how they came about we must look very briefly at the political background. This will be sketched in its barest outline only, with the omission of many developments of major importance; such over-simplification can be justified only because this is a book about elephants and not a history of the

Hellenistic world. Further, we must recall that although we have a reasonably good account of the decades after 323 BC in the work of Diodorus, which depends on a trustworthy historian of the time named Hieronymus of Cardia, nevertheless elephants must have figured large on many occasions of which we have no record. Thus, for example, their role in the quarrel between Perdiccas and Meleager, which is related below, is not mentioned by Diodorus, and we know of it only because a full account of the events immediately following the death of Alexander has been preserved by the Roman historian Curtius.

The interest of the struggles lies partly in the personalities and professionalism of the generals themselves: these were no upstart amateurs, but hard-bitten Macedonian nobles, born and trained to command, with years of hard fighting experience behind them. With the Grand Army at Babylon, the chief generals were Perdiccas, a proud and prickly man who was Alexander's second-in-command, and Ptolemy, whose portrait with its deepset eyes and hooked nose reveals his single-minded ambition to seize a part of the potential spoils rather than to sit alone on Alexander's throne. With them were other men who would soon make their mark: Lysimachus, one of Alexander's bodyguard; Seleucus, commander of the hypaspists and one of the most humane of the Successors and the one who best appreciated the military value of elephants; Eumenes, a civilian who was head of the imperial chancery and, unlike the others, a Greek from Cardia not a Macedonian, but who was to prove a very efficient soldier. In Cilicia was Craterus, an outstandingly competent soldier who had been greatly trusted by Alexander and who was very popular with the army. In the satrapy of Phrygia was Antigonus the One-eyed (Monophthalmus) whose daring and ruthless ambition gave him alone of the generals, a hope of reuniting Alexander's empire under his sole rule. In Macedon there remained old Antipater, who had once been the right-hand man to Alexander's father, Philip II of Macedon and still held the post of governor to which Alexander had appointed him in 334 when he himself left for the East. With so many ambitious leaders of men scattered around the empire, the prospects for a long-term settlement of the crisis which the sudden death of Alexander had precipitated, could not have seemed bright.

When Alexander died in June 323 the organization of his empire was far from complete, and he left neither will nor son to succeed him. Two possible successors were his half-brother, Arridaeus, an illegitimate son of Philip II, and his child, if it proved to be a boy, who would be born in August to his widow Roxane. But Arridaeus was mentally unfit to rule, while the child would long be an infant and, through his mother, half-Persian. While the Macedonian generals and the noble cavalry officers supported Arridaeus, the claims of the baby were upheld by the infantry which by custom was recognized as the Macedonian nation in arms with the right of approving any new ruler. Finally a compromise was reached by which both were recognized jointly as Philip III Arridaeus and Alexander IV, and a conflict of interest for establishing a single regent resulted in Perdiccas, who was on the spot in Babylon, gaining the chief authority. While risings against Macedonian control took place in Bactria and Greece (the latter being crushed by Antipater with help from Craterus), Perdiccas was engaged in a struggle of diamond-cut-diamond with Meleager, the commander of the infantry.

By withdrawing outside the city of Babylon with the cavalry and elephants, Perdiccas was able to exert pressure by controlling the food-supply. He then tricked Meleager by holding a ritual purification of the army according to Macedonian practice: after a limit to a plain had been marked out with the sacrifice of a dog, the army was drawn up within this area with the infantry on one side, the cavalry on the other. On this occasion, unlike the ceremony when performed in Macedon, there were also elephants present: they and the horsemen under King Philip Arridaeus stood facing the infantry which Meleager commanded. A clash seemed imminent when the king with a detachment of cavalry rode up to the infantry, acting at the instigation of Perdiccas, and demanded the punishment of Meleager's supporters: otherwise he would launch the cavalry and elephants against the infantry. Perdiccas thereupon managed to separate 30 ring-leaders and in the sight of the whole army threw them to the elephants. 'All were trampled to death by the feet of the beasts, while Philip neither prevented nor authorized it' (Curtius, x, 9.18). Meleager himself fled to the sanctuary of a temple, but in vain: he was murdered. This use of the elephants as executioners is interesting, since it suggests that they had been given training for war, while their presence with the cavalry had doubtless been a major factor in overawing the infantry.

Before long Perdiccas had to face the increasing hostility of Antipater, Craterus, Lysimachus, Antigonus and Ptolemy. An attempt to avoid war on two fronts and to hold off the rest while he led his main army against Ptolemy was successful. Eumenes, whom he sent to face an army which Craterus was leading from Europe to Asia Minor, won a battle in which Craterus was killed. (321) However, Perdiccas himself soon met with disaster in his struggle with Ptolemy, who had built up considerable forces in his satrapy of Egypt, not least by hiring mercenaries with money which he had appropriated there, while his prestige had been greatly increased by his skilful body-snatching of the corpse of Alexander which he proposed to bury with great splendour in Egypt. He allowed Perdiccas to advance without opposition to the Nile valley on which he based his defence (321 BC).

For details of the engagements that followed we depend solely on the narrative of Diodorus (XVIII, 33–36). Perdiccas approached the Nile near Pelusium and suffered his first set-back when the Nile overwhelmed the works he constructed in an attempt to clear out an old canal; many of his friends deserted to Ptolemy. Then by a night march he reached a fortified post called Camels' Fort on the other side of the Nile, but before he got all his men across Ptolemy managed to rush reinforcements into the post. At dawn Perdiccas launched an assault, led by his elephants, followed by the hypaspists and ladder-carriers, and then the rest of the assault party including picked cavalry. The hypaspists began to mount the assault ladders, while the elephants were tearing down the palisades and overthrowing the parapets (Diodorus says rather quaintly that this demolition was done by 'the men on the elephants', but they surely only directed their beasts). Ptolemy himself, standing on the top of an outwork and armed with his long Macedonian *sarissa*, put out the eyes of the leading elephant and wounded its mahout; his friends then rendered the next elephant in line useless by shooting its rider. After a daylong struggle Perdiccas called off the siege and retired.

He next tried to force the Nile near Memphis, where a large island divided the river. As his men attempted to cross to it, they were up to their chins in water and found the current too strong. Perdiccas now made a novel use of his elephants: he placed them in the river, upstream, to break the force of the water, while he put cavalry on the downstream side of his men to help those who were being swept away. However, there was an unforeseen result: after the first troops had got over, the river suddenly became deeper, owing to the elephants and horses stirring up the sand of the river-bed which the current then swept away. Perdiccas was compelled to recall those of his men who had already managed to reach the island. He had suffered heavy losses, since many men had been 'devoured by the animals in the river', namely the crocodiles. He could no longer command the loyalty of his officers and cavalry, and was stabbed to death in his tent. He had thus used his elephants to storm a strong-point in a way that had been normal since the time of Ctesias, while his less conventional, but sensible use of them as a breakwater had had unforeseen results. In due course, the two armies were reconciled and Ptolemy was offered Perdiccas' place, but he wisely decided to stay supreme in Egypt, where he was unchallenged, rather than to seek to step into Perdiccas' shoes or to oust the two nominal kings. The remains of Perdiccas' Grand Army was then allowed to withdraw to Syria.

Ptolemy is usually supposed to have had no elephants, and this is no doubt true in the sense that he could not put a large force into the field against any of the Successors with whom he clashed. But this is not to say that he had none. He certainly acquired some as the result of his victory over Demetrius at Gaza some years later in 312 (see p. 97), but his conflict with Perdiccas also may have yielded him some. At the Camels' Fort engagement Perdiccas' attacking force was on Ptolemy's side of the river, and although Perdiccas managed to withdraw it is very unlikely that he got all his elephants away; rather, Ptolemy will have rounded up some of them. Defeated armies probably seldom saved any but a very small fraction – if that – of their elephants. When a battle was lost the Indian mahouts would not mind giving themselves up with their beasts, nor often care very much which master they served; and beasts that had lost their riders could be rounded up. True, Perdiccas had withdrawn, but scarcely in such order as to be able to collect elephants which were wandering about without riders. In the attempted crossing of the Nile at Memphis we do not know how many, if any, elephants actually landed on the far bank, but a few of these too may have fallen to Ptolemy. After the murder of Perdiccas the remains of his army were well treated by Ptolemy and allowed to go back to Asia, but there is no reason to suppose that he handed back any elephants he had taken; indeed, for all we know he might have required the handing over of more. At any rate it is far from improbable that he began to acquire a small force of elephants as early as 321. And if he did not want them for purposes of war, he may well have had ceremony in mind. In Babylon he had seen the elephant-corps on guard outside Alexander's tent; he proposed to bury his body in Alexandria and knew that elephants decorated the bier which had conveyed the corpse to Egypt. What is more likely than that he would have liked a few elephants to celebrate his dead leader in Alexandria? Further, it is significant that, to recall his victory over Perdiccas' elephants, if not immediately at any rate within three or four years, he issued in Alexandria the coinage with the striking portrait of Alexander wearing an elephant-scalp head-dress (pl. XIIIc).

### ANTIGONUS AND EUMENES

When Perdiccas' defeated troops, who withdrew from Egypt, reached Triparadisus in Syria, they were joined by Antipater who had advanced with his forces from Europe into Asia Minor. They elected him guardian for the two kings. He decided to return to Macedonia and take the kings with him. He left to Antigonus the command of the Grand Army and the task of finishing off the war against Eumenes, who with others had supported Perdiccas' cause. Before leaving Asia Antipater divided his forces: he left to Antigonus 8,500 Macedonians, some cavalry and half of all the elephants – 70 in number – as a reinforcement for his war against Eumenes. With the rest of the Macedonians and the elephants he started off for Europe.[41] Thus apparently the elephant-corps, which under Alexander may have numbered at least 200 (p. 74), had dropped to 140 by 321 BC. Part of the difference must lie in the number of Perdiccas' elephants killed or captured by Ptolemy, but our inability to calculate accurately the original total number precludes a deduction that Perdiccas' losses were as high as 60: this seems rather too high, but the figures in general do suggest a heavy loss and do not make at all unlikely the possibility that Ptolemy retained a fair number.

Eumenes, whose earlier victory was now counterbalanced by the death of Perdiccas, tried to negotiate with some of Perdiccas' supporters who were still under arms, such as his brother Alcetas in Asia Minor and his brother-in-law Attalus who was on the coast, but they would not co-operate. Forced to face Antigonus alone, Eumenes withdrew to Cappadocia in 320 and faced his enemy at Orcynia. Antigonus at this point had only 10,000 infantry and 2,000 cavalry against Eumenes' 20,000 infantry and 5,000 cavalry, but he also had 30 elephants (Diodorus, XVIII, 40.7). If the figure of 70 elephants and 8,500 Macedonians which he received from Antipater (according to Arrian) is correct, he clearly did not take all his forces in his pursuit of the enemy (he detached some to watch Alcetas). At the very least he had 30 elephants and, although the details of the battle are not preserved, he doubtless owed his victory as much to them as to the fact that Eumenes' cavalry commander and his men deserted to the enemy at the height of the battle. Eumenes was forced to flee to a hill-fort called Nora where he succeeded in holding out against Antigonus' blockade during the winter (320/19); with him was the historian Hieronymus.

In 319 Antigonus turned his attention to Alcetas and Attalus. From Cappadocia he made a forced march (287 miles in seven days, it is said) to surprise Alcetas in Pisidia. When Alcetas suddenly found that the enemy was holding some rugged ridges above his position, he hastily drew up his phalanx and himself led a cavalry attack uphill against Antigonus, only to be cut off from his own phalanx by a counter-move by 6,000 horsemen led by Antigonus. Alcetas was forced to abandon his cavalry on the hill to the enemy and escaped to rejoin his phalanx. Antigonus then launched his elephants and his whole army down on the enemy who were inferior in number. This downhill charge by the elephants (we are not told how many there were; perhaps his full force of 70, less a few left behind to deal with Eumenes in Nora) must have been a terrifying sight. The elephants attacked from the front, the cavalry surrounded the phalanx, and the infantry was poised above them. Antigonus had won. Most of Alcetas' officers were captured; he himself fled but was later taken by treachery and killed while trying to hold out in Termessus. Only Eumenes remained for Antigonus to deal with. Soon news came that old Antipater had died, thus leaving to his friend Antigonus a path to still further power.[42]

Before we follow the fortunes of Antigonus in his continuing struggle with Eumenes, we must turn to the history of Antipater's elephants. At his death in 319 a very complex situation developed in Greece. His army followed his recommendation and elected as regent not his son Cassander but a man who had served under

Alexander without becoming one of the great marshals, namely Polyperchon. It was he who took over Antipater's army and the 70 elephants. Cassander quickly secured the support of Antigonus and Ptolemy and then entered upon a contest with Polyperchon for the control of Macedon. With naval and infantry support from Antigonus he sailed into the Piraeus. Polyperchon soon arrived with a large force which included 65 elephants (five of his original 70 seem to have dropped out by this time; Diod. xVIII, 68.2), but he soon abandoned any hope of a quick seizure of the Piraeus. Leaving his son Alexander in Attica with part of his army he led his main force to the Peloponnese where Megalopolis had declared for Cassander. Despite reports of the size of the royal army and the number of the elephants 'which were said to possess an irresistible fighting spirit and momentum of body', the Megalopolitans prepared for a siege (Diod. xVIII, 70–71). Polyperchon brought up siege-engines and breached the wall but the defenders managed to make good the loss by building an inner defence line. Next day he cleared the area of the breach in order to allow his elephants to attack through it, but the Megalopolitans had a trump card up their sleeves in the person of a certain Damis 'who had been in Asia with Alexander and knew by experience the nature and use of elephants, and by pitting his own intelligence against their brute force, he rendered their physical strength useless'. His plan was the equivalent of a primitive mine-field: he made a large number of frames which were studded with sharp nails and buried them in shallow trenches, with the projecting points concealed. He left this route into the city open, but posted javelin-throwers, archers and catapults flanking the lane. Polyperchon cleared the debris and sent his elephants charging down the lane, urged on by their mahouts who saw that there were no enemy troops in the way. As the spikes entered the elephants' feet, they became immobilized. Some of the mahouts were killed by the flanking troops, others were wounded and lost control of their animals, which began to rush hither and thither. 'Finally the most valiant and formidable elephant fell, and of the rest some became completely useless, while others brought death to many of their own side' (Diod. xVIII, 71.6). This suggests that they had a leading beast, whose loss, when realized, might result in a lowering of morale, as with the death of a human commander among his own men. Thus thwarted, Polyperchon left part of his army to continue the siege and returned to Macedon.

His elephants had not won him either the Piraeus or Megalopolis.

The pendulum was swinging in favour of Cassander. Many Greek cities, including Athens, went over to him, and in the spring of 317 he drove Polyperchon out of Macedon, capturing some of his elephants (the number is not given in an indirect reference to this episode by Diodorus, XIX, 34.7). Eurydice, wife of Philip Arridaeus, in her husband's name deposed Polyperchon as regent and named Cassander as Philip's minister. Leaving her to govern Macedon, Cassander marched successfully to the Peloponnese to win the whole of it from Polyperchon, but he was held up by the resistance of Tegea. Meantime Polyperchon in his desperation called on the help of Alexander the Great's mother, Olympias, who led a force from Epirus into Macedon, where in a blood-bath she murdered Arridaeus and forced suicide upon Eurydice. Cassander had to hurry north again and soon gained the upper hand: Olympias and her following, which included Roxane and her young son Alexander IV, were driven into Pydna. There, with the remainder of Polyperchon's elephants, she withstood a terrible siege: such was the famine that some of the mercenaries resorted to cannibalism, while the imprisoned elephants were fed on sawdust and died from lack of nourishment (Diod. XIX, 49.3). The city was finally forced into surrender (spr. 316). Cassander, who engineered the death of Olympias and imprisoned Roxane and her son, was now in control. He married Thessalonice, the half-sister of Alexander, and founded Thessalonica in her honour. He dominated central Greece where he refounded Thebes, but Polyperchon's son was still at large in the Peloponnese and held the isthmus. Cassander thereupon built some barges on which he transported his elephants to Epidaurus, while the rest of his army crossed in boats. He took Argos and other places, and before the end of 316 returned to Macedon; with both Greece and Macedon now in his power he might seem able to challenge Ptolemy and Antigonus for universal power, if that had been his aim. But although Polyperchon faded out as an effective opponent, Cassander's ambitions were more limited. In fact such was Antigonus' increased strength that Cassander decided to co-operate with Ptolemy and with Lysimachus in Thrace who had married his sister Nicaea. This new coalition then challenged Antigonus for the next four years (315–312): how Antigonus was in a position to face this war must be discussed after we have seen how he had dealt with Eumenes.

While Cassander's fortunes had been rising in Europe, Antigonus had to face Eumenes, who was under siege at Nora. Although he capitulated when Antigonus approached him through the agency of Hieronymus, he was soon won over to the cause of Polyperchon and the kings against the attempts of Cassander and Antigonus to overthrow the central power. Polyperchon gave him overriding powers in Asia (319/18) and sent him 500 talents and 3,000 Macedonian Silver Shields, a body of Alexander's veterans. To secure their loyalty and to underline his link with Alexander, Eumenes announced that all meetings of his staff would take place in a tent where they were to offer incense to Alexander, whose symbolic presence was embodied in a golden throne on which lay his diadem and other insignia. However, Antigonus moved swiftly and Eumenes was forced to withdraw from Phoenicia eastwards over the Euphrates. Despite the hostility of Seleucus in Babylon, he finally reached Susa (317) and built up a strong force. This he was enabled to do because a local civil war had caused all the other eastern Macedonian governors to concentrate their forces in order to crush one of their number. They now brought Eumenes 18,700 infantry and 4,000 horse, but most impressive of all was the contingent of Eudamus who came from India with a force that included 120 elephants; these he had secured when, left by Alexander as a Macedonian 'resident' with Taxiles, he had treacherously murdered Porus. Eumenes gave Eudamus 200 talents, nominally for the cost of maintaining the elephants, but actually to secure his loyalty, because, as Diodorus says (XIX, 15.5), 'Eudamus would tip the scales decisively in favour of any one of the rivals to whom he might attach himself, since the use of the beasts strikes terror.'

Antigonus, unable to prevent this concentration of enemy troops, wintered in Mesopotamia, where he recruited more men and was probably joined by his 70 elephants. In 317 he advanced against Eumenes, but had to negotiate two rivers; we are reminded of the practical difficulties involved when Diodorus (XIX, 17.3) refers to the depth of the Tigris (a mistake for the Rasitigris) as being 'about the height of an elephant'. Again we get a passing reference to the elephants, which must have been much used for baggage purposes, when Antigonus tried to reach Media by forcing his way through the mountainous country of the hostile Cossaean tribes where they, with his cavalry and infantry, had to face great hardship and death (Diod. 19.7). However, after much manoeuvring, in an effort to prevent Antigonus breaking through to the fertile area of Gabiene, Eumenes turned to fight and the two armies faced one another at Paraetacene, near modern Isaphan.

The ensuing battle was a set-piece between two large Hellenistic armies and the first in which a very considerable number of elephants was used on both sides. Further, we have a full account of it which goes back via Diodorus to an eye-witness, Hieronymus. The battle-order on both sides is described in great detail, with the composition, number and commanders of the various sub-units; there are a few minor discrepancies between the total figures given and those of the addition of the units, but these are trivial. After this promising beginning, the description of the battle itself is not too clear in some details (unfortunately including the actual fighting of the elephants), but the general tactical development can be followed. The numbers, apart from those of the elephants, need not be discussed here; they are merely set out schematically, together with the space occupied by the units, as calculated by Kromayer and Kahnes.[43]

ANTIGONUS

| Right Wing (734 metres) | Centre (1,750 m.) | Left Wing (1,090 m.) |
|---|---|---|
| 3,300 cavalry | Phalanx of 28,000 men | 4,900 cavalry |
| 30 elephants (the best) | 24 elephants (approx.) | 10 elephants (approx.) |

EUMENES

| Left Wing (712 m) | Centre (1,763 m) | Right Wing (634 m.) |
|---|---|---|
| 45 elephants | 40 elephants | 40 elephants |
| 3,200 cavalry | Phalanx of 17,000 men | 2,400 cavalry |

Several questions arise about the elephants. Antigonus had 64; he put the strongest 30 on his right, most of the rest in front of the phalanx, and a few on the left (how precisely the 34 were divided between centre and his left we are not told). Eumenes is said by Diodorus to have had 114, but the figures which he gives for the three units (45, 40 and 40) add up to 125: the latter which come from the detailed battle-order are more likely to be correct, and so we must assume that Eumenes had the 120 from Eudamus and may have picked up 5 more before the battle. Also it may be noted that on Kahnes' calculations there were 40 in front of Eumenes' right wing which was only 634 metres long, i.e. they were some 16 metres apart, while in the centre they would be 45 metres apart and on his left some 20 metres. Thus he had a strong right wing, where he also placed the best, though not a majority, of his cavalry. Lastly, whereas the two generals apparently drew up their elephants in a straight line in their centres and on one opposing wing, those facing each other on Antigonus' right and Eumenes' left were not in a straight line but ἐπικάμπιον and ἐν ἐπικαμπίῳ respectively; curved, bent, obliquely? What does this mean? On practical grounds the formation is hardly likely to have been either concave or convex. It is, of course, possible to envisage Eumenes using a wide concave trap into which he might hope to draw the enemy cavalry, but he would hardly use this against other elephants since the resultant melée would be too confined. A convex formation would have provided a useful shield but could perhaps have been disrupted by a charge in depth by the opposing elephants at its front central point. An oblique formation against outflanking and a consequential lengthening of the line would be feasible but for the fact that Diodorus stresses that the beasts were *in front of* their lines where an oblique order would seem inappropriate. The best solution is to suppose that the lines were partially bent: the greater part of each line in front of their troops would be straight, but they may have projected in a curve at the outside end. As Eumenes' left flank rested against a hill, it is perhaps more likely that the left end of his line would bend forwards. As to Antigonus' bend, it could be backwards in an attempt to cover his flank against the opposing projecting beasts, or forwards in an attempt to outflank them if they advanced. Between Eumenes' elephants were bowmen and slingers, between those of Antigonus picked light troops.

We may now turn briefly to the course of the battle. Antigonus, advancing over some hilly ground, halted on the ridges where he was seen by Eumenes who decided to fight. From this higher ground Antigonus could see how Eumenes was drawing up his troops and that on the latter's right wing the elephants were more thickly massed, while the standards and distinctive equipment of Eumenes' heavy cavalry would show that this too was on his right wing. Antigonus, therefore, could decide to send his lighter cavalry against Eumenes' right in a harassing move and mass his best cavalry on his own right for a knock-out blow against Eumenes' left. He himself took command of his right wing, with Pithon leading his left. Eumenes on the other hand may have hoped to deliver a decisive blow with his right wing.

The battle developed in three areas: these may be considered separately, although, of course, they partially overlapped in time. (a) Antigonus' Left Wing. Pithon led his cavalry including many mounted archers in an outflanking movement on the enemy's right wing; although he did not work his way to the front of the elephants, nevertheless from the flank he was able to wound many by direct attack or repeated flights of arrows; the beasts suffered much damage from this mobile foe since 'because of their weight they could neither pursue nor retire when the occasion required'. With his right wing thus hard-pressed, Eumenes hastily summoned Eudamus' squadron to ride round behind the lines from the left wing to the right. Thus reinforced, he pushed back Pithon's force and, with the help of the elephants, drove them to the foothills (presumably those from which they had started). (b) The Centre. This had meanwhile been engaged in a long bitter struggle in which casualties were heavy. Diodorus gives no detail of how the two lines of elephants acted; perhaps they became locked in single combats (as in the subsequent battle of Gabiene), while Eumenes' phalanx then advanced through their line. However that may be, a regular infantry struggle ensued in which the valour of the 3,000 Silver Shields, old veterans of Alexander all over sixty, gave Eumenes the victory: Antigonus' centre was pushed back to the nearer hills. (c) Antigonus' Right Wing. With his left wing in flight and his centre being driven back, Antigonus might have accepted defeat, but he saw an opportunity and brilliantly exploited it. Eumenes' centre had advanced so that a gap occurred on its left. Antigonus led his right-wing cavalry in a charge against his opponent's remaining cavalry and presumably the elephants on Eumenes' left, coming in on their exposed inner right flank; he may have swept right round behind them and pinned them against the hill. To help these left-wing troops of his, Eumenes recalled his victorious right wing, but too late to save the situation. Antigonus managed to rally his defeated troops and formed them all up in line on the foothills. It was now dusk and Eumenes too re-grouped his

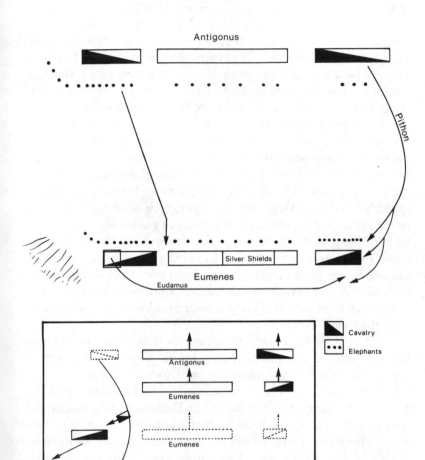

Antigonus

Pithon

Silver Shields

Eumenes

Eudamus

Antigonus

Eumenes

Eumenes

LAST STAGE OF BATTLE

Cavalry

Elephants

Fig. 9. Battle of Paraetacene

men, but the two lines which then stood facing one another once again were by midnight too exhausted to renew the battle. Eumenes withdrew his men to their camp; Antigonus, however, managed to force his men to hold the ground near the dead, and thus claimed a victory in an engagement in which in fact honours were fairly equal. Casualties had been heavy among the infantry (Antigonus lost 3,700 and over 4,000 wounded; Eumenes lost only 540), but very light among the cavalry (Antigonus lost 54, Eumenes very few) and among the elephants (in the following year at Gabiene Antiochus had 65, so he seems to have gained one (by capture?), while Eumenes had 114, i.e. the total which Diodorus had, probably wrongly, assigned him at Paraetacene; if there he had 125, he had apparently lost 11 in the battle. Diodorus' erroneous 114 for Paraetacene may well have arisen from a correct 114 for Gabiene). In view of the number of his casualties Antigonus' control of the dead offered only a hollow claim to victory and since he withdrew speedily to a part of Media where supplies were abundant, Eumenes remained the victor, although he could not pursue his enemy since he lacked supplies and real unity of command. He also soon withdrew, southwards into Gabiene. His 125 elephants, which had faced only 64 enemy beasts, had helped his right and centre to success but had failed to win him an overall victory. One thing, however, was now clear: both sides had trained their cavalry to co-operate well with their elephants.

Weakened by his casualties Antigonus determined to get in a blow before the full campaigning season of 316. He knew that Eumenes' troops were wintering in dispersed camps, some of which were six days' march from others. He would strike before they could concentrate. He set out in December 317, not by the regular route but through desert country in order to achieve surprise. His movements, however, were betrayed by camp fires which he was finally forced to allow, due to the intense cold. Eumenes managed to hold him up a little while by lighting camp fires which tricked him into believing that the enemy was close at hand. Eumenes was thus able to concentrate most of his army in one camp, but his elephants, which were slow in leaving their winter quarters, were vulnerable. Antigonus sent against them 2,000 Median lancers and 200 cavalrymen equipped with javelins (called Tarentines). When attacked, the commanders of the elephants drew them up in a square with the baggage in the centre and the rear protected by the only force they had, some 400 horsemen. This guard was easily swept away; the mahouts resisted but many were wounded and they could not counter-attack effectively. As they tried to advance a rescue force of 1,500 of Eumenes' strongest cavalry and 3,000 light infantry arrived just in time. With all his forces thus reunited Eumenes now prepared for another formal battle and camped at a distance of some four and a half miles from his enemy.

Hieronymus' account of this battle of Gabiene was no doubt as detailed as of Paraetacene, but Diodorus' résumé of it is unfortunately less full: thus he does not identify all the separate units or their strengths as he had for the earlier battle.[44] Nevertheless he makes its general course clear enough. Kromayer and Kahnes calculate the disposition and distances as follows:

ANTIGONUS

| Right Wing | Centre | Left Wing |
|---|---|---|
| *(890 metres)* | *(1,375 m.)* | *(1,112 m.)* |
| 4,000 cavalry | 22,000 infantry | 5,000 cavalry |

EUMENES

| Left Wing | Centre | Right Wing |
|---|---|---|
| *(780 m.)* | *(1,600 m.)* | *(556 m.)* |
| 3,500 cavalry | 17,000 infantry | 2,500 cavalry |

Antigonus had 65 elephants, which he distributed in front of his whole line, but since his main punch was to be on his right wing he may have placed some 30 of them there; the intervals between them were filled as usual with light troops. His right wing, where he himself fought, was commanded by his own son Demetrius, and his left by Pithon. Eumenes, who had 114 elephants, stationed 60 of the strongest in front of his left wing in a 'bent' formation; since he was outnumbered by enemy cavalry on this wing, perhaps the line of elephants bent backwards to guard the flank. He put other elephants in front of the infantry, and the weaker of his cavalry and of his elephants on his right wing. Philip, satrap of Bactriana, in command of the right wing, was ordered to avoid battle until he saw what was happening on the left wing where the main cavalry and elephant action was planned.

The engagement opened with the elephants joining battle, but no details of their prowess are given; then followed cavalry action. The open plain was dry and salty: hence it was soon enveloped in clouds of dust. Antigonus saw his chance and under the cover of this 'smoke-screen' he detached the Median cavalry and the so-called Tarentines from his left wing and sent them round Eumenes' right flank to the rear where they overran his baggage-train. Presumably Pithon with the rest of Antigonus' left wing took some distracting action but did not commit his cavalry in a full-scale attack. Meantime, Antigonus led an attack on his other wing with his cavalry and presumably his elephants. He had distributed the elephants in front of the whole of his line, but since on this wing he had to face 60 of Eumenes' beasts and was planning his major attack here, he may well have put more than an exact proportion of his strength on this wing, say 30 out of his 65. The cavalry was brilliantly successful; they put to flight Peucestas, satrap of Persia, together with 1,650 horsemen. Peucestas' precise position on the left wing is not stated, but since Eumenes himself held the extreme left, Peucestas is likely to have held the extreme right: if so, Antigonus will have repeated his manoeuvre from Paraetacene and hit the wing from its inside, separating it from the phalanx and threatening to outflank it. Despite the desertion by Peucestas, Eumenes held his ground and a fierce cavalry battle ensued, while the elephants fought it out among themselves until Eumenes' leading beast fell and Eumenes, being worsted, broke off and led his surviving cavalry round to the cavalry on his right wing under Philip who had not yet seriously joined battle. That he had been able to hold on so long may well have been due to his superiority in elephants since his left wing was weaker than that of his foe in cavalry even before the retreat of Peucestas.

Meanwhile the two phalanxes had been fighting it out in the centre; Antigonus' line was shattered and partly in retreat. Diodorus' account is short and unsatisfactory: he says that the Silver Shields, without the loss of a man, routed the whole line and killed over 5,000. He must here have falsely attributed the achievement of the whole phalanx to the Silver Shields whose exploits were no doubt spotlighted in Hieronymus' original account. Antigonus now must have brought his victorious cavalry across to his left

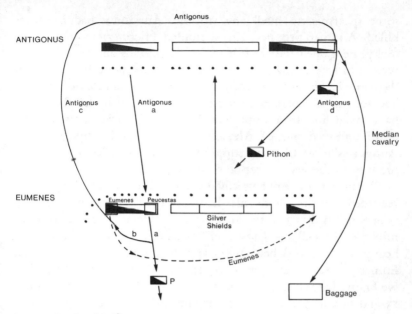

Fig. 10. Battle of Gabiene

wing, where he divided it: with one part he himself watched for Eumenes' next move, while he sent Pithon to the centre against the Silver Shields, who (presumably together with the rest of the phalanx) formed into a square and withdrew from the battlefield. The survivors of Antigonus' phalanx then presumably reached their camp in safety. Eumenes meanwhile had failed to rebuild his scattered cavalry into a fighting force, since Peucestas, so far from rejoining him, had fled further away and it was now dusk. Nevertheless, he wanted to fight on: the enemy phalanx had been broken and the cavalry on the two sides were about equal. Such arguments, however, could not convince his Macedonians whose baggage, wives, children and other relatives had been captured by Antigonus' brilliant stroke at the beginning of the battle. In order to recover their lost possessions they betrayed Eumenes, handed him over to Antigonus and enrolled in the victor's army. Antigonus is said to have wished to save Eumenes but could not trust him and so gave way to the wishes of the other officers. Despite some restlessness among some of the men, which according to Plutarch (*Eumenes*, 18.2) forced Antigonus to send ten of his strongest elephants with

93

some spearmen to quell any trouble, Antigonus had Eumenes killed. Another prisoner, the wounded Hieronymus, was more lucky; he gained the confidence of Antigonus and thus lived to write a history of the battle and of this whole period. Once again the battle had been a close-run affair: a preponderance of elephants had not gained Eumenes the victory, but those on his left flank may have saved him from complete defeat at a crucial moment. His death removed one of Alexander's most loyal supporters and Antigonus' most dangerous opponent: it also revealed more clearly the way to the vacant throne of Alexander.

The number of elephants killed at Paraetecene and Gabiene is not recorded, but since both sides had about the same number in 316 as they had had in 317, the losses at Paraetacene seem to have been minimal. At Gabiene, however, casualties appear to have been heavy. If there had been none and Antigonus had captured all Eumenes' beasts, Antigonus would have had 179 (65+114), but we know that when he attacked Egypt in 306 (p. 97) he took only 83 and that in 301 at Ipsus (p. 98) he had 75. At first glance this might suggest that 96 were lost at Gabiene. But between 316 and 306 there would have been a considerable natural wastage through old age of perhaps one-fifth, say 19 elephants: this would reduce to 77 the casualties of 316. Then, of course, Antigonus might have lost many in Egypt or not have taken his full force of elephants on the expedition, but neither supposition is probable: there was no set battle but operations largely revolved around the misfortunes of his accompanying fleet, while the fact that five years later he had only 75 at Ipsus where he would surely have mustered his entire force suggests that in 306 BC 83 is likely to have been the major part of his force. If we suppose that he left 12 behind and lost 5 on the expedition, this would reduce the hypothetical losses at Gabiene by 15 to 60. Then we do not know how many of Eumenes' elephants managed to avoid capture in and after the battle. Those whose mahouts were killed would most likely be rounded up by Antigonus, but others may have managed to escape, e.g. if one-quarter (28) escaped, the casualties would be reduced to 32. With so many imponderables speculation is not very profitable, but such evidence as there is suggests that Eumenes' losses at Gabiene must have been severe.

For the next fifteen years Antigonus struggled to reunite all Alexander's empire under his own rule against the 'separatist' generals who in consequence formed an alliance against him: Cassander in Macedon, Lysimachus in Thrace and Ptolemy in Egypt. Thus he had to face the threat of war on more than one front. In 314, anticipating that Cassander would try to win Asia and that Ptolemy would attack Syria, he left an army in Syria, which included 43 elephants (Diod. xix, 69.1), under the command of his loyal son Demetrius who had just won his spurs at Gabiene. In 312 the expected invasion came and Demetrius faced Ptolemy and Seleucus, who had fled to Egypt, at Gaza.[45] He was considerably weaker in heavy infantry (some 11,000 against Ptolemy's 18,000), about equal in light-armed troops, and slightly superior in cavalry; he had 43 elephants, while Ptolemy had none (or only a few; p. 80f.). He placed 30 of these in front of his left wing (with some advanced cavalry units), where he hoped to strike the decisive blow, and the other 13 in front of his phalanx. Between the intervals of his 30 elephants he placed light-armed men of whom 1,000 were javelin-throwers and archers and 500 were Persian slingers; the other 13 also had adequate light-armed support. His right wing, where he had no elephants, was ordered to act at first on the defensive.

Seeing this disposition in time Ptolemy, who had intended to strike on his own left, switched his greater strength to his right. But with no (or few) elephants to face the 30 in front of him, he had made preparation beforehand. Men rushed into position to stretch out some iron-spiked devices which were linked by chains. Their purpose was obviously the same as the nail-studded frames which Polyperchon had used at Megalopolis six years earlier (p. 83), but their construction appears to have been different. Diodorus (xix, 83.2) uses the word *charax* (χάραξ) which means a sharpened stake or a palisade made of stakes. In view of the need to put them in position rapidly, they can scarcely have been very complicated or heavy; perhaps we should think of iron spikes roped or chained together, but since it would not be easy to devise a method of keeping the spikes upright they could have been planks with nails driven through them and linked up by chains. Whatever their nature, they were to prove most effective. In front of the cavalry on his right wing Ptolemy stationed javelin-throwers and archers to shoot at the elephants and their riders, presumably as they began to advance into this 'mine-field'.

Diodorus' version of Hieronymus' account of this battle is less clear than are those of the two previous engagements because he concentrates on this right wing of Ptolemy and neglects events in the centre and his left. It opened with a cavalry action by the advance troops on the extreme wings in which Demetrius had the upper hand. Then the men under Ptolemy and Seleucus 'rode around the wing and charged with their cavalry drawn up in depth'; a severe engagement followed, at first with spears and then hand-to-hand with swords. The 'ride round' is not very clear, but since the 'elephant-trap' was partly in the way of a direct charge, the horsemen had to wheel round it on the outside. However, Demetrius' whole battle-line was shorter; hence the right-hand end of Ptolemy's cavalry may have projected beyond the 'trap', which may indeed have overlapped slightly with the extreme right of his own centre in order to cover the direct approach of all the 30 enemy beasts. Whatever may have been the precise situation during the cavalry battle Demetrius ordered his elephants forward but they soon fell into disarray when shot at by the light troops and on finding their feet pierced with the iron spikes. As Diodorus says, 'on smooth and yielding ground they display an irresistible strength in a direct attack, but on rough and difficult ground their might is useless because of the tenderness of their feet'. (In fact, the plated hooves of an elephant lie on the dorsal side of the foot, while the sole consists of cornified skin with distinctive fissures across it; there is also a shock-absorbing cushion of elastic fibres around the bones of the phalanges; this enables an elephant to walk silently over rough ground. But clearly parts of the sole are vulnerable, since the weight of the beast would drive in deep any spike which penetrated the outer skin). The result of the action was that after most of the mahouts had been shot down, 'all the elephants were captured'. If this was significant for the future, it was even more so for the outcome of the battle. Demetrius' cavalry panicked and fled. What happened elsewhere in the battle we are not told: presumably the cavalry on the other wing did not seriously engage, while Demetrius' centre soon collapsed, as is suggested by the fact that he lost 8,000 men by capture (some 500 were killed, the majority of them cavalry; the rest of the horsemen are likely to have got away). Thus Ptolemy, although without a force of elephants himself, nevertheless had learned how to deal with them, and the ultimate behaviour of the elephants had been the turning point in this battle at Gaza. Despite this disaster Demetrius retained his father's confidence and later won a series of victories for him both at sea and in Greece, gaining the name of Poliorcetes (Besieger).

Wars continued, but hardly any references to the part played by elephants in them survive. A peace was arranged in 311 but it only lasted a year; after this Antigonus tried to crush his opponents one by one: in 310–309 he turned against Seleucus who had occupied Babylon and the eastern satrapies and controlled the route to the source of elephants. In 306 he attacked Egypt with a force that included 83 elephants (Diod. xx, 73.2), but was beaten back partly through the flooding of the Nile. In 304–303 he was opposing Cassander in Greece. It was time for all his opponents to join forces: this they did in 301 in a concentration which faced Antigonus at Ipsus in Phrygia.

Diodorus' account unfortunately breaks off just on the eve of this decisive battle at Ipsus and the anecdotal chapters of Plutarch's *Demetrius* (28–29) are a poor substitute. Thus little is known about its course, although elephants clearly played an important role in it, both numerically and tactically. This came about through the adventures of Seleucus who had recently been acting independently of his allies; he had conquered many of the eastern provinces and then perhaps crossing the Indus, challenged an Indian rajah called Chandragupta who had consolidated India north of the Deccan into his Mauryan empire with its capital at Pataliputra (Patna). Seleucus could hardly expect to defeat a man with the vast resources of India behind him so he made peace by ceding the governments west of the Indus, together with the Cabul valley. In exchange for this concession of vast territories he accepted what he knew would be of vital value to him in his coming struggle in the west: a very large number of elephants. Our source for the treaty, the geographer Strabo, names 500 elephants (xv, 724; cf. xvi, 752); so also does Plutarch (*Alexander*, 62.2), who nevertheless attributes only 400 to him at the battle of Ipsus (*Demetrius*, 28.3). Diodorus (xx, 113) says that Seleucus had 480 when he joined Lysimachus before the battle. But 500 has seemed to many to be an incredibly large figure, while Tarn has shown that in Indian literature of the Hellenistic period the number 500 was in common use for any very large quantity of a wide variety of things, including elephants (e.g. King Ajasasattu visited Buddha accompanied by 500 concubines riding on 500 elephants, while Brahmadatta, king of Benares, possessed 500 elephants). Thus this Indian usage may have come into the Greek tradition via Megasthenes, but any attempt to try to assess the exact figure must be hazardous if not arbitrary (Tarn suggested that the figure in the treaty was 150, that in the battle 130). In any case, whatever their precise number, Seleucus brought to Ipsus a force of elephants numerically vastly in excess of the 75 which Antigonus could deploy.[46]

In the battle Antigonus had 70,000 infantry against the allies' 64,000; their cavalry was only very slightly stronger than his, and they had 120 chariots. All we know of the battle is that Demetrius led a cavalry charge which routed Seleucus' horsemen who were commanded by his son Antiochus, but he carried on the pursuit too far; Seleucus was able to use his elephants to cut off his return.[47] Thus Antigonus' infantry were exposed to harassing attacks by the enemy cavalry and men began to desert. Antigonus fought on until he was killed, his last words being, 'Demetrius will come and save me'. But his son could not come: the elephant corps had seen to that. With the death of Antigonus, who since 306 had claimed the title of king, an era ended: henceforth no one could hope to reunite under his own control the empire of Alexander. The victors shared the spoils, satisfied with separate kingdoms.

TWENTY YEARS ON

After the battle at Ipsus Ptolemy had at least 43 elephants (less any natural wastage), Cassander had some of Polyperchon's, say 40 in view of later developments (see p. 117), while Seleucus possessed a vast force which comprised an unknown number captured from the 75 of Antigonus and his own equally uncertain '500'.[48] Not without reason had Demetrius' drunken friends called Seleucus Master of the Elephants (ἐλεφαντάρχης: Plut. *Demetr.* 25), a role which he emphasized by issuing coins which depicted some of his fine beasts (pl. XIIIg, h). The new rulers held, and tried to snatch from one another, as much territory as they could. Seleucus controlled Syria and the East, Ptolemy Egypt, Lysimachus Thrace and parts of Asia Minor, and Pyrrhus Epirus; Cassander ruled Macedon until his death in 298/97, four years after which Demetrius managed to secure the throne. As time passed, many of the older men died, some first turning to their sons for co-operation in their struggles. Thus Demetrius' son Antigonus Gonatas was active after 287 and took the title of king on his father's death in 283 although he did not become the acknowledged king of Macedon until 276. In 292 Seleucus took his son Antiochus into partnership. Ptolemy in 285 appointed as joint-king his son Ptolemy Philadelphus who succeeded him in 283, thus thwarting the hopes of his half-brother Ptolemy Ceraunus (the Thunderbolt) who in consequence claimed Macedon (he was descended through his mother from Antipater). In 280 Ceraunus murdered Seleucus with his own hands, but he managed to hold Macedon for one year only since he was killed in resisting an incursion of Gallic tribes, the Galatae, who threw Greece and Asia Minor into disorder.

This confusing scene has been mentioned in order to emphasize that very many wars were fought in which elephants must have been used, although their participation is not recorded. The fate of the three main herds during the twenty years or so after Ipsus cannot be traced in detail: only a few hints survive. The efforts of the Ptolemies to maintain and increase their corps is discussed in the next chapter. A passing reference to Seleucus' elephants survives in the dramatic story of the downfall of Demetrius. In 287, driven out of Europe, he invaded Asia and for a moment seemed likely to win it from Seleucus, but by the next year he was hemmed in 'like a wild beast cornered'; even so, he fought his way out, defeating Seleucus in every engagement. However, he fell ill and his troops began to desert; desperately he engaged in a final battle in which he gained some success until Seleucus brought up eight elephants (thus Polyaenus IV, 9.3) and dismounting ran forward unhelmeted and begged Demetrius' mercenaries to surrender to avoid useless bloodshed. It was the end for Demetrius: after two years of honourable confinement (Seleucus indignantly rejected an offer of 2,000 talents from Lysimachus to have him murdered) he drank himself to death. The elephants, apart from their role in overawing the mercenaries, must have figured large in these and other engagements; as, for example, when Seleucus overran Asia Minor and defeated Lysimachus at Coropedium in the last great battles between Alexander's Successors (281), but their achievements there remain unsung. Then, as will be seen, this the greatest of all the Hellenistic elephant-corps mysteriously disappears from history.

The fate of the survivors of Cassander's elephants in Macedon receives a dim beam of illumination from one item of retrospective evidence: in 280 Pyrrhus had 20 elephants for his expedition to Italy. The sources from which he obtained these are contradictory: according to Pausanias (I, 12.3) he had captured them in a battle against Demetrius, while Justin says (XVII, 2.14) that 50 were lent to him by Ptolemy Ceraunus. The number 20 is almost certainly correct, but the version of either source is possible. The occasion for the capture would be 288 when Demetrius was at the height of his power and as king of Macedon had no doubt inherited Cassander's herd. His ambition to extend his realm to Asia and his preparation of a large fleet forced Ptolemy, Lysimachus and Seleucus into a coalition against him; they persuaded Pyrrhus to join in. While Ptolemy made a demonstration by sea,. Lysimachus and Pyrrhus invaded Macedon. Demetrius fled to Asia, where he met disaster and death, while they divided his realm between them, no doubt including his elephants (though they are not specifically mentioned in the brief accounts that survive). Lysimachus thus gained some of Cassander's herd, or all of it if Pyrrhus did not take his share. He gained sole control of Macedon in 284 but held it only until 281 when, as we have seen, he crossed to Asia Minor where he was defeated and killed by Seleucus; his throne and his elephants, which he is unlikely to have transported to Asia, will then have passed to Ceraunus whom the Macedonian army chose as king. Since Ceraunus would find Greece easier to control if Pyrrhus were absent, it is quite probable that it was he who lent him the 20 elephants, but since a reasonable historical background lies behind both accounts, it is difficult to choose between them. Finally, to look ahead: in 277 Demetrius' son, Antigonus Gonatas, succeeding to the Macedonian throne, presumably took over Ceraunus' herd (less any that the latter may have lent to Pyrrhus). But after Pyrrhus had returned from his Italian venture he defeated Gonatas who surrendered all his elephants. However, Gonatas got them back again after crushing Pyrrhus in 272 (p.117).[49]

# CHAPTER IV

# PYRRHUS

## ITALY AND HERACLEA

From infancy to death Pyrrhus, king of Epirus, was involved in the game of power politics.[50] By nature restless and impulsive he zestfully plunged into the troubled waters of his time, seeking to secure and extend his kingdom and also to win the throne of Macedon and perhaps even an empire in the western Mediterranean. Known to his own people as the Eagle, he was courageous and adventurous, and intensely interested in military affairs; thus his quest for power was backed by a professional soldier's concern in the means of attaining his goals. He wrote books on strategy and tactics, which no doubt included a discussion of the role of the elephant-corps. He was accounted one of the great captains of antiquity, and Hannibal is alleged to have said that Pyrrhus was the foremost of all generals in experience and ability, that Scipio was second and that he himself came third. Such an estimate, if made, must have rested on professional appreciation, since Pyrrhus could win battles but not wars, while some of his victories were so costly to his own forces that they became known as Pyrrhic victories. His ambitions were promoted by various marriages: he married the stepdaughter of Ptolemy, and the daughter of Agathocles, the tyrant of Syracuse, and he was a brother-in-law of Demetrius Poliorcetes: thus he looked both to Macedon and the West. His precise aims defy certain analysis. Did he hope by victories in Italy to smash the Confederacy which Rome had built up, then to win Sicily from the Carthaginians, and thence to cross over to Africa in order to defeat Carthage, as Agathocles had recently tried in vain to do; then, with the West behind him, to conquer Macedon and the East? If he had dreams on this scale, he would have to take into account the interests of the Ptolemies, and his relations with them have been differently interpreted. However, we should probably not attribute to him too much advanced planning: his aims were more probably short-termed and pragmatic, and he moved from one adventure to the next as circumstances allowed. In any case he seized the chance offered to intervene in Italy, where he hoped that his elephants might help to overawe opponents to whom they were unknown.

*If* the early Romans had produced ballad poetry, they might well have echoed the prophetic words which Macaulay attributed to Capys:

> The Greek shall come against thee,
>   The conqueror of the East;
> Beside him stalks to battle
>   The huge earth-shaking beast,
> The beast on whom the castle
>   With all its guards doth stand,
> The beast who hath between his eyes
>   The serpent for a hand.

A descendant of Achilles by claim and a relative of Alexander the Great in fact, Pyrrhus had many early adventures in securing un-divided control of Epirus. He later warred against Demetrius, as we have seen, and gained half Macedon, only to lose it shortly after to Lysimachus. Driven back into Epirus he could then, as Plutarch observes, have lived in peace enjoying what he had, but in 281 Tarentum, the largest Greek city in south Italy asked for his help against Rome. The situation in Italy was that by a mixture of statecraft and military power Rome had united most of the country into a Confederacy which comprised both citizens and allies of varied privilege. Certain of the Greek cities in the south, who were outside this Confederacy and were subject to harassment by the wild tribesmen of their hinterland, had been accustomed to turn to Tarentum for help and sometimes even to Greece itself. But now some looked to Rome instead. Tarentum objected and became involved in war with Rome, but not being strong enough to fight alone she requested the aid of Pyrrhus and his professional army. Pyrrhus, ever restless, accepted the call.

After the despatch of an advance force to Tarentum under Cineas, in the spring of 280 Pyrrhus launched his main force of some 25,000 men and 20 elephants. The actual distance across the

Straits of Otranto at the narrowest point is some forty miles; if he sailed from Aulon the distance to Brundisium would be about eighty, if from Epidamnus ninety miles. The Tarentines supplied a motley array of transports. Nothing is recorded about the passage of the elephants, but this could well be the longest sea journey yet experienced by these animals and the technical difficulties can only be imagined: not long after this the Ptolemies were to undertake the task of transporting African elephants on the Red Sea (p. 131). Unfortunately for the expedition it ran into a terrible storm: Pyrrhus had at the end to swim for the Messapian shore where he was joined by less than 2,000 infantrymen, a few horsemen and two elephants. However, the rest of his scattered fleet managed to get ashore and the force was reunited at Tarentum. There, his welcome was reflected in the coinage: the Tarentines issued a series of their coins marked with a symbol of Pyrrhus, a small Indian elephant, with convex back, placed beneath their own dolphin-rider (pl. XIVa). However, they soon found him a hard taskmaster, since he forced them to concentrate on the war.

In 280 the Romans had to send one of the consuls to beat out a smouldering revolt in Etruria, while the other, Valerius Laevinus, was sent post haste to the south to meet Pyrrhus before he was joined by Samnite and Lucanian tribesmen who had promised him aid. Pyrrhus chose a position in the plain between Heraclea and Pandosia in the extreme south of Italy, where his left flank was partially protected by the river Siris; there he awaited the Romans who slightly outnumbered him.[51] For the first time an amateur Roman legionary army had to face a professional Hellenistic phalanx, although not all Pyrrhus' Italian allies would be armed as full phalangists with the dreaded barrier of the heads of their long spears which projected in front of their line. However, not only did the Romans have to try to match with their short swords and *pila* Pyrrhus' central phalanx, but their weapons were not well adapted to deal with elephants (against the elephants of Porus the Macedonians of Alexander had at least had their 16-ft-long sarissas).

The course of the battle of Heraclea is described by Plutarch, whose account derives ultimately from Hieronymus and is enlivened with some anecdotal material from other sources. The Romans crossed the river and forced the withdrawal of a light guard stationed there. Pyrrhus deployed his infantry in battle-order and then charged with 3,000 horsemen before, as he hoped, the Romans could re-group in battle formation after crossing the river; but after a struggle in which he himself had his horse killed under him, he was forced to withdraw, and so he ordered his phalanx to engage. Here the battle swayed backwards and forwards seven times (presumably four attacks by Pyrrhus and three counter-attacks by Laevinus). He then threw in his elephants, and the Roman horses, untrained for such fighting, ran away with their riders; to complete the rout Pyrrhus sent in his reserve of Thessalian cavalry. Plutarch records that the Roman and Pyrrhic losses were, respectively, 7,000 and 4,000 according to Hieronymus, and 15,000 and 13,000 according to Dionysius.

This account, deriving from Hieronymus, appears quite reasonable, but some modern writers think that Pyrrhus would scarcely have thrown in his various troops in three separate moves (cavalry, infantry, elephants) and that the battle must have been on more conventional lines, with the cavalry and elephants on the wings of the phalanx and presumably a more concurrent engagement. Though no doubt the elephants must have been stationed on one or both of Pyrrhus' wings (they could hardly be behind the phalanx), it must be remembered that they numbered 20 or less and that he would want to deploy them to the best advantage. As a young man he had fought for Antigonus at Ipsus and thus had seen how useful elephants could be in cutting off enemy cavalry. So at Heraclea he might well have held them back until they could contribute to the final push which was to bring victory. The account of the battle preserved in Zonaras (VIII, 3), which perhaps depends on Roman sources, differs in certain respects: thus, Pyrrhus used his elephants to rout some Roman cavalry which Laevinus had put into an ambush beyond the battlefield. These beasts, reinforced by cavalry, would have completely annihilated their opponents, had not one elephant been wounded and thrown its fellows into confusion. This looks like a Roman attempt to minimize the importance of these 'Lucanian oxen', as the Romans called them after the district where they were first encountered. Zonaras adds a further important point: the elephants had towers with soldiers in them who contributed to the rout: 'some were killed by the men in the towers on the elephants' backs, and others by the beasts themselves, which destroyed many with their trunks and tusks (or teeth) and crushed and trampled under foot many more.' Is this reference to towers due to the imagination of later writers in the light of sub-sequent practice or were they used at Heraclea? It may well be the first known use of this device in Hellenistic armies (see p. 240 ff.); this view receives support from the well-known platter which depicts an Indian elephant and is usually attributed to Pyrrhus (pl. VIIa), although it is just possible that it showed an elephant on parade with a tower, rather than how the beast was actually equipped in battle. But since the use of towers soon became more common, perhaps Zonaras should here be given the benefit of the doubt. Thus Pyrrhus himself or one of his staff may have been responsible for this invention.

Pyrrhus, who was now joined by Lucanians, Samnites and some Greek cities in the south, followed up his victory by a dash towards Rome, hoping that Rome's allies would go over to him and per-haps that he might join hands with the Etruscans. But the large cities, such as Capua and Naples, shut their gates to him, the Latins remained loyal to Rome, the Roman armies hung on his heels, and so when within 40 miles of the city he was forced to return to the south for the winter. Realizing the strength of the Italian con-federacy he was now ready to treat; lengthy negotiations followed. The course of these is obscure in detail, but they were broken off when the blind old censor, Appius Claudius, rebuked the Senate for discussing terms while the enemy was still on Italian soil. They gave rise to many anecdotes, especially about the integrity of Fabricius, who could be neither bribed nor frightened. Plutarch tells how Fabricius was sent to negotiate, and, although poor, resisted Pyrrhus' offer of gold. Pyrrhus then tried fear: 'wishing to frighten a man who had not yet seen an elephant, he ordered the largest of his beasts to be stationed behind a hanging in front of which they were conversing together. At a given signal the hang-ing was drawn aside, and the animal suddenly raised its trunk, held it over Fabricius' head and emitted a frightening harsh cry. But Fabricius calmly turned and said to Pyrrhus with a smile: "Your gold did not move me yesterday, nor does your beast today".' But although cordial personal relations developed between the nego-tiators, terms were not reached, so that Pyrrhus once again must try the hazard of war.

In 279 two consular armies marched south to Apulia to face the enemy, whose forces, strengthened by contingents of Samnites and Lucanians, were about equal to their own. They met near Ausculum.[52] Three main accounts of the battle survive, those by Plutarch, Dionysius of Halicarnassus and Zonaras. Plutarch's rests on the reliable Hieronymus, but is very short. We must first see what he records, and then turn to the less reliable versions. In fact two engagements took place, on successive days. In the first, 'Pyrrhus was forced into an area where his cavalry could not operate and upon a river with a swift current and wooded banks, so that his elephants could not charge and engage the enemy phalanx' (note this primary function which is attributed to them). The Romans were able to withdraw and make some counter-moves (this is clear because Plutarch says that they were unable to repeat such moves the next day), but to no avail and so after a long tussle night ended the engagement.

'On the next day', wrote Plutarch, 'planning to fight the battle on level ground, and to bring his elephants to bear upon the ranks of the enemy, Pyrrhus early occupied the unfavourable parts of the field with a detachment of troops; then he put great numbers of slingers and archers in the spaces between the elephants and led his forces to the attack in close order and with a strong impetus. The Romans, having no opportunities for withdrawal and counter-movements, as on the previous day, had to engage on level ground and front to front; and being anxious to repulse the enemy hoplites before the elephants attacked, they fought fiercely with their swords against the Macedonian sarissas, not sparing themselves and thinking only of wounding and killing, caring nothing for what they suffered. After a long time, however, as we are told, they began to be driven back at the point where Pyrrhus himself was pressing hard upon his opponents; but the greatest havoc was done by the furious strength of the elephants, since the valour of the Romans was of no avail in fighting them, but they felt that they must yield before them as before an onrushing billow or a crashing earthquake, and not stand their ground only to die in vain, or suffer all that is most grievous without doing any good at all. After a short flight the Romans reached their camp with the loss of 6,000 men, according to Hieronymus, who also says that on the side of Pyrrhus, according to the king's own commentaries, 3,505 were killed.' Plutarch then refers to the version of Dionysius which recorded only one battle, the wounding of Pyrrhus and the plundering of his camp by Daunians, allies of the Romans. In Plutarch's own version there are obscurities (e.g. Pyrrhus' early occupation of some ground) and omissions (what happened to the cavalry?), but the general outline is clear: it was essentially a slogging-match between the legions and the phalanx, with the elephants held back and then thrown in at a late critical moment, as at Heraclea.

But what of the accounts by Dionysius and Zonaras? Only those of their variations that relate to elephants really concern us much here. Thus their confining the encounter to a single day, which will correspond to Plutarch's second day, is not here important since Plutarch makes clear that Pyrrhus could not use his beasts on the first day. However, we must note that Dionysius gives a very detailed account of the composition of Pyrrhus' battle-line, including the posting of the light-armed troops and the elephants, which numbered 19, in two groups behind both wings. (In passing it is interesting to see that detachments of his Italian allies were well distributed between sections of his own men, thus illustrating Polybius' remark (at XVIII, 28.10), that Pyrrhus 'placed units of his Italian forces and units composed of his own men from the phalanx in alternate order in his battles with the Romans'. Thus he apparently was imitating the Roman manipular system, perhaps now for the first time, since he had fewer Italian allies at Heraclea). Dionysius also gives the order of the four Roman legions and their relation to the various enemy units opposite them. Clearly the description of Pyrrhus' line derives from Hieronymus and perhaps from Pyrrhus himself. It is somewhat arbitrary to deny the validity of the description of the Roman order, as is done by some, on the ground that it must be from late Roman annalists: Pyrrhus was a professional soldier, and would surely have noted the disposition of his enemy, which would, of course, be made clear by their standards. If, then, this part of Dionysius' description of the battle rests on sound authority, we should be chary about rejecting all the rest *in toto* as bad annalistic; it may contain other sound elements, including perhaps some in regard to the elephants.

On the Roman side Dionysius introduces a new element. After mentioning the mixed Roman and allied cavalry on the wings he goes on, 'outside the line they stationed the light-armed troops and the 3,000 waggons which they had prepared for the battle against the elephants. These waggons had upright beams on which were mounted movable transverse poles that could be swung round as quick as thought in any direction one might wish, and on the ends of the poles there were either tridents or sword-like spikes or scythes all of iron; or again they had cranes that hurled down heavy grappling-irons. Many of the poles had attached to them and projecting in front of the waggons fire-bearing grapnels wrapped in tow that had been liberally daubed with pitch, which men standing on the waggons were to set alight as soon as they came near the elephants and then rain blows with them upon the trunks and faces of the beasts. Furthermore, standing on the waggons, which were four-wheeled, were many also of the light-armed troops: bowmen, hurlers of stones and slingers who threw iron caltrops; and on the ground beside the waggons there were still more men.' Zonaras refers to this device more briefly: 'The Romans, among other preparations, made ready, as a measure against the elephants, iron-pointed beams, mounted on waggons, and bristling in all directions. From these they intended to shoot fire and various missiles, in order to check the beasts.'

How effective in action are these machines said to have been? According to Dionysius, 'when the king has ordered the elephants to be led to that part of his line that was in difficulties, the Romans mounted on the pole-bearing waggons, on learning of the approach of the beasts, drove to meet them. At first they checked the onrush of the beasts, striking them with the machines and turning the fire-bearing grapnels into their eyes. Then, when the men stationed in the towers no longer drove their beasts forward, but hurled their spears down from above, and the light-armed troops cut through the wattled screens surrounding the waggons, and hamstrung the oxen, the men at the machines jumped down from their cars and fled to the nearest infantry and caused great confusion among them.' In Zonaras' account the role of these machines was even more of an anti-climax: the Roman infantry was beginning to push the Greeks back 'until Pyrrhus, bringing his elephants to bear, not opposite their waggons but at the other end of the line, routed their cavalry through fear of the beasts even before they engaged.' Now it is true that two contradictory versions of the fate of these machines in battle does not inspire confidence (except in so far as it demonstrates that their existence was recorded by two different strands of the tradition) and most modern commentators reject them entirely; thus, according to Lévêque, they were the result 'de l'imagination déchaînée d'un annaliste'. But why, in view of their unfortunate performance, should they have been invented? Presumably Roman annalists did not think up ways of showing the inefficiency or stupidity of the Romans. If due allowance is made for patriotic exaggeration, as for instance in the number or details of the machines, there appears to be no good reason to reject them entirely: the silence of Plutarch can easily be explained by his deliberate omission, in an already abbreviated account, of an aspect of the battle which was of little practical importance. Perhaps rather we should accept Zonaras' version that they did not go into action (the elephants presumably could move more quickly than the oxen drawing the waggons), and suppose that their ineffective fight was invented by later Roman annalists and taken over by Dionysius in order to attempt to save face to some extent. It might be objected that the Romans were an unimaginative people and would not try to think up counter-measures as the Hellenistic Greeks had done, for instance at Gaza (p. 95). They were, however, good engineers, and within twenty years of Ausculum they had invented the *corvus* which helped them to defeat the Carthaginian navy at Mylae. If Polybius had not described this machine in detail, perhaps some modern commentators would have been induced to believe that it was a figment of the imagination of later Roman annalists?

Whether or not these machines were employed in the battle, Pyrrhus' elephants certainly were, and with good effect. They were not apparently used in an initial charge to breach the Roman line, but held back for later use. After their own cavalry, originally stationed in front of them, had dealt with the enemy cavalry, they presumably advanced on the two flanks of the engaged infantry and fell on the two ends of the Roman line from the side and rear with great effect. Once again we get in the later tradition, in Dionysius, a reference to their towers and soldiers: this may be accepted somewhat cautiously. Dionysius further refers to Pyrrhus sending some elephants to counter the attack on his camp and also to some Romans taking refuge on a hill which was too steep for the elephants to climb, but the tradition is doubtful and anyway the episode is of little importance. Frontinus (I, 13.9) also contributes an anecdote: Gaius Numicius, a front-rank soldier (*hastatus*) of the

Fourth Legion, cut off the trunk of one of the elephants and thus 'showed that the beasts were mortal'. To many the detail will seem to have been invented for the sake of verisimilitude, but the name Numicius should give pause: it is an old Roman name and not common in later times. Thus the story may well be true and preserve a piece of family history.[53]

In view of his own losses and Rome's vast supplies of manpower, Pyrrhus had achieved little despite his two victories. At this point he was faced with two appeals, one from the Greek cities in Sicily to come to rescue them from the Carthaginians, the other from Greece where he learnt that Ptolemy Ceraunus had been killed in the Celtic invasion and that a way to the Macedonian throne might lie open to him. He chose the former: leaving about half his forces to hold southern Italy, he crossed with the rest to Sicily in 278. In the meantime Rome and Carthage had come to some agreement concerning their common enemy, but it had little practical effect. In Sicily Pyrrhus had to face a new situation, since the Carthaginians were not ready to face him in open battle but relied on their garrisoned cities. We are told that he had taken his elephants with him, and they are specifically mentioned again by Diodorus when he describes Pyrrhus setting out against the part of Sicily held by the Carthaginians: no doubt they would be useful in attacks upon strong points. Although he made good progress and ultimately confined the enemy to Lilybaeum, he could not achieve complete success and so decided to withdraw back to Italy. On the return voyage his fleet was badly mauled by the Punic navy and when he had landed he had to face a force of Mamertines who had crossed over from Messana; although he defeated them, he lost two elephants in the fighting.[54] Thus, although he had recruited many mercenaries and so strengthened his infantry, when he faced the Romans again he had 17 elephants (less any that he may have lost at Ausculum).

When the two consuls of 275 advanced separately southwards, Pyrrhus decided to strike before they joined forces. Dispatching a covering force against L. Cornelius in Lucania, Pyrrhus moved with his main force against Manius Curius who was camped near Beneventum (at this time called Malventum). Plutarch's account of the subsequent battle, although rather short, probably depends basically on Hieronymus, and may be followed. Pyrrhus was eager to force Curius to fight before Cornelius arrived, so he took his best men and the most warlike of his elephants on a night march through densely wooded ground in order to try to seize some hills which dominated the Roman camp, and from there to attempt an assault. But his men lost their way and when they ultimately reached the hills it was full day. In order to benefit from their disorder and weariness Curius led out his fresh troops in an attack which routed the enemy, who left behind some of their elephants which fell into the Romans' hands. Curius followed up this success by advancing on to the more level ground where at some points he routed the enemy, but at one he was overwhelmed by the surviving elephants and driven back towards his camp, whence he was obliged to summon his reserve troops. They came down and drove the elephants back on their own lines, causing confusion there. Pyrrhus withdrew to Tarentum before Cornelius could come up. His Italian adventure was over. He left some troops behind to encourage his Italian allies and then with the rest of his forces he set sail for Greece.[55]

The questions of numbers and of the reliability of a certain anecdote remain. According to Dionysius and Zonaras the Romans captured eight elephants (and two more were killed: Dionysius). Later in his triumph in 275 Curius displayed some of these beasts to the Roman people who thus saw elephants for the first time, as Pliny expressly says (*NH.* VIII, 16). According to Eutropius (II, 14.3) there were four of them in the triumph (had four died?), while Florus (I, 13.28) believes that they were carrying towers. Some historians (e.g. K. J. Beloch) have cast doubt on this occurrence on the ground that elsewhere Pliny (*NH.* VII, 139) wrote 'Metellus . . . qui primus elephantos in primo bello Punico duxit in triumpho': if Metellus was the first, then Curius cannot have been. But this interpretation is not certain: 'primus' may mean 'first during the Punic War' rather than 'for the first time in history' (while some would read *plurimos* in place of *primus*). It is perhaps better to try to explain Pliny's self-contradiction on these lines than to deny the truth of his first statement. No doubt Roman annalists did invent much to the greater glory of Rome, but some historians seem unduly suspicious when anything about elephants is recorded only in later writers. Thus, for instance, Lévêque, in reference to

Pyrrhus' advance by night to seize the heights at Beneventum, writes, 'Denys précise que les hoplites montaient par des sentiers de chèvre: y imagine-t-on les elephants?' The reply is obvious: anyone who has read Col. Williams' account of how a party of 45 elephants was brought safely over the precipitous mountain tracks from Burma to Assam in 1944 should have no difficulty at all in imagining Pyrrhus' movement.[56] That is not to say, of course, that it is necessarily historical but the episode does illustrate the undue readiness with which some scholars reject accounts of the activities of elephants. In the case of the numbers captured by the Romans at Beneventum, their reasonableness commends their probable historicity and they may well have been displayed later in Rome.

Next, the anecdote, which is related by Dionysius (xx, 12.14), Florus (i, 13.12) and Zonaras (viii, 6). During the battle a calf elephant was hit on the head by a missile and ran back screaming with pain; whereupon its mother caused confusion on her own side by rushing forward to rescue it. Since this is just what an elephant cow and calf would do, the story does not offend against natural history and it does not strike one as likely to be pure invention. Yet like other such episodes it attracts the sarcasm of some critics: thus Lévêque writes, 'de graves érudits discutent de l'âge de cette pauvre bête parcourant les rangs épirotes à la recherche de sa mère, mais ils ne prennent pas garde que l'épisode, touchant et sanglant à la fois, est controuvé.' When Orosius (iv, 2.5) records that the Romans had prepared hooked fire-darts which they hurled with effect at the animals' backs and at the towers, we get a comment of the same kind: 'curieux procédé, dont on a justement contesté l'efficacité'. The ground suggested for the rejection is that such devices are not known to have been used again. Now, it would obviously be rash to assert that the stories of the calf and of the fire-brands are assured historical fact, but it is surely hypercritical to reject them out of hand. If historical, where in the encounter does the incident fit? Dionysius' version rather suggests an early stage, i.e. the first battle, since he refers to Pyrrhus' troops and elephants 'ascending', presumably in their first move against the Roman camp. Florus on the other hand says that 'when the elephants were again moved forward into the front rank, a young one among them . . .'. This version favours the end of the later pitched battle, and perhaps should be preferred, since the consequent disturbance of a formal battle-line would probably lead to greater upheaval than similar trouble arising in what seems to have been the looser order of the first battle. The anecdote affords Florus the opportunity of summing up the results of Pyrrhus' three battles in Italy: 'thus the same beasts, which robbed the Romans of their first victory and equalized the second encounter, gave them undoubted victory in the third' (ac sic eaedem ferae, quae primam victoriam abstulerunt, secundam parem fecerunt, tertiam sine controversia tradiderunt. Florus, I, 13.13).

With the story of the calf should be considered the implications of the famous plate from Capena, now in the Villa Giulia Museum, which depicts a female Indian elephant, with a tower on its back, and its calf trotting behind.[57] (Pl. VIIa.) This is usually considered to be one of Pyrrhus' elephants, and there is no good reason to question the attribution. It is no objection that the elephant is a female, since others are known: thus Aelian (XI, 14) specifically mentions a female elephant named Nicaea which Antigonus Gonatas had with his war-elephants during his siege of Megara in c. 270 (p. 114). Her name, Victoria, suggests that she may well have seen action. The elephant on the plate has longish tusks, which is incorrect for an Indian beast, but the artist may have had in mind one of the males and not realized that a female should not be thus endowed. Sir John Beazley commented, 'The presence of the baby would be odd if the elephant were going into battle; this must be only a parade or march past.' But if a female elephant did go into battle, she would probably take her calf with her, since (I quote Sir William Gowers from our joint article), 'if the calf were taken away from the dam she would probably go on strike, and little elephants like this one easily keep up with the old ones and normally would give no trouble.' *If* there is any connection between the plate and the anecdote about the calf, then it is more likely that the plate commemorates the incident which, Florus says, saved the day for the Romans, than that a later Roman annalist would know the plate and invent a story to fit in with it.


ELEPHANTS AND PIGS

Another anecdote from one of Pyrrhus' battles raises some interesting problems which deserve airing although they evade any secure solution. Aelian (I, 38) says that 'the elephant has a terror of a horned ram and of the squealing of a pig. It was by these

113

means, they say, that the Romans turned to flight the elephants of Pyrrhus of Epirus and won a glorious victory.' The idea that elephants could be put to flight by small animals became a common idea (cf. Plut. *De Sollert. Animal.* 32, *Quaest. Conviv.* II, 7.3: Pliny, *NH.* VIII, 27) which is summed up by Seneca (*De Ira*, II, 11.5): 'elephantos porcina vox terret'. But besides being regarded as a natural phenomenon, it is quoted in at least two historical contexts: one by Procopius (*Bell. Goth.* IV, 14B533), which is rather remote from this period (p. 205), the other by Aelian (XVI, 36) and Polyaenus (IV, 6.3). The latter records that when the Megarians were being besieged by Antigonus Gonatas (Aelian carelessly calls him Antipater, but names him correctly in XI, 14) they successfully launched squealing pigs against the enemy. On this occasion the squealing was guaranteed since the unfortunate animals had been smeared with fat and set on fire. Aelian adds that 'the elephants broke ranks and were no longer tractable in spite of having been trained since they were small, either because elephants by some instinct hate and loathe pigs, or because they dread the shrill and discordant sound of their voices. In consequence those who train young elephants, being aware of this, keep pigs along with them, so it is said, in order that through herding together the elephants may get to fear them less.'

*If* there is any historical basis for either story, the Pyrrhus incident should take precedence, since it occurred first; it could well be that the Megarians knew of Pyrrhus' recent set-back and repeated the cause. If both incidents are rejected, presumably Pyrrhus' story will have been the prototype. But if it is to be considered at all seriously, to which of Pyrrhus' battles should it be assigned? Heraclea seems ruled out because of the success of the 'Lucanian oxen'. Though some scholars would assign it to Ausculum, it does not fit in very well with the elephants charging 'like an onrushing billow or a crashing earthquake'. In both engagements at Beneventum elephants were defeated. The first more irregular action might have given better opportunity for the use of pigs, but a set battle is not ruled out since the Romans could have brought up a number of pigs in carts on the wings and loosed them at the critical moment. At first thought the story hardly embodies an acceptable military manoeuvre and seems rather fantastic: but then so does Hannibal's famous ruse of oxen with lighted torches on their horns, an episode which is widely accepted as historical. As to the natural history aspect: *nihil obstat*. Although, in the wild, elephants are reasonably tolerant of smaller animals (p. 22), in captivity, writes Dr Sikes, 'elephants' fear of small animals sometimes results in what is, to us, a ludicrous reaction. Circus elephants have been known to panic because a mouse has run across the stable floor, or a dog has barked nearby' (p. 284). Perhaps battle may be considered closer to captivity, with its enforced obedience, than to wild life.[58]

Thus, apart from the silence of authors such as Plutarch, there seems no compelling reason to reject Aelian's story, and there is a piece of evidence which may be relevant to it, as it is certainly relevant to Pyrrhus, namely the large bronze 'brick' or piece of Aes Signatum as this early form of money is now called (pl. XIVb, c). It depicts an elephant on the obverse and a sow on the reverse. Other types found on these currency bars include a bull, a corn-ear, and a branch, which are natural for an agricultural community, and a sword, a scabbard, an anchor and a trident which are natural for a military people which was just beginning to take an interest in naval affairs. The one really surprising type is the elephant; it is so remarkable that it is generally connected with a historical event. Since it is an Indian elephant it cannot allude to the Carthaginian African elephants of the First Punic War (p. 148), and must almost certainly reflect Pyrrhus' beasts. It has no tower or harness, but does seem to have a bell around its neck, which would increase its terrifying impact on the enemy in battle. There the matter could rest if it were not for the reverse type, a sow. Is the juxtaposition pure chance? If so, could the legend have been invented very early on the basis of the bar? If not, what was the connection and should it be interpreted as representing a historical event in one of Pyrrhus' battles? In favour of a connection is the fact that the two faces of some other bars are linked together in the mind of the designer: thus there are a sword and scabbard, a branch and tendril, a shield seen from the inside and from the outside. Of course, the link could have arisen merely from a sense of humour, a deliberate contrasting of a large and small animal, but before some such a hypothesis is examined, we must digress briefly to consider another of these bars which depicts hens feeding and on the other side the beaks of ships.[59]

This second bar has often plausibly been connected with the naval action in 249 BC when P. Claudius Pulcher attacked the Carthaginian fleet at Drepana; his subsequent defeat was attributed by the pious to the fact that before the battle, when told that the sacred chickens would not eat, he had them thrown overboard, with the remark, 'Well, let them drink.' This anecdote, which is not given by Polybius, is naturally suspect. It could even have been invented on the basis of the bar, applied to Claudius and circulated by his political enemies, but if so it must have been invented early, since all the Aes Signatum went out of circulation soon after the First Punic War. Two objections arise against referring the bar to Drepana: on numismatic grounds a date as late as 249 is improbable, although not impossible, and secondly would the Romans have celebrated a naval defeat on their currency? One of our leading authorities on early Roman coinage, R. Thomsen, rejects the connection with Drepana because it was a defeat and because the sacred chickens seem on the bar to be eating, not refusing food; but he nevertheless thinks it has a historical application and represents the *pullaria auguria* being observed before *a* naval battle of the First Punic War, perhaps Mylae in 262. If any connection with Drepana is dropped, what then of the anecdote about Claudius? If it was early, it could have formed part of the accusation against him in his subsequent court-martial, while the circulation of this slightly earlier Aes Signatum would have emphasized in the popular mind the link between taking the auspices and naval actions.

To return from this necessary digression, what then are we to conclude? At very least we have two bars which refer in general terms to historical events: Pyrrhus' elephants and a naval battle. Each can be connected with an anecdote, but so to connect them leads to some difficulties of detail. If the elephant bar stood alone, coincidence would be easier to accept, but since there are two it might be wiser to suspend judgment and to leave open the possibility that Aelian's story might have a historical basis. At any rate we have a portrait of one of Pyrrhus' elephants, which now after Beneventum were reduced to a maximum of seven.

GREECE

Nothing daunted by his setbacks in Sicily and Italy, Pyrrhus returned to Greece to engage in a new series of adventures. The first was nothing less than an attempt to regain the throne of Macedon from Antigonus Gonatas. He quickly built up a new force, possibly with some help from Ptolemy; it may have included some of his few surviving elephants from Italy. In 274 he advanced into Macedon. Antigonus fell back and when caught in a mountain pass his elephants were hemmed in and their mahouts surrendered all their animals; his Macedonians refused to fight and he was deserted by everyone except his Gallic mercenaries. Though he held on to the eastern half of his kingdom, he thus lost the western half and all his elephants to Pyrrhus. These may have amounted to some 20, since he had apparently inherited Cassander's elephants which may have numbered about 40 (p. 100), less the 20 which Pyrrhus had taken to Italy. But shortly after this Pyrrhus had 24 (see below). This might suggest that he had brought back from Italy some or all of his surviving seven elephants. In view of our lack of detailed information, precise calculations are excluded, but the figures that survive tally quite reasonably well with each other, and we may suppose that on this occasion Pyrrhus acquired some 20 elephants from Gonatas. However, as usual, he failed to consolidate his conquests and by 273 Gonatas had rallied and driven him out of Macedon: Pyrrhus was more interested in another adventure in the Peloponnese which he hoped to win over from Gonatas.

He decided to help Cleonymus to seize Sparta where the latter's nephew, Areus, was ruling. He collected a force which included the remnants of his army recalled from Italy, and 24 elephants (Plut. *Pyrr.* 26.9). He advanced into Aetolia and crossed the Corinthian Gulf to the Peloponnese where he was generally welcomed. He then moved against Sparta but waited until the next day to attack the city: Areus and part of his army were away recruiting in Crete, and the city had no ring-wall and might seem an easy prey. But during the intervening night the women of Sparta, in order to allow their men to rest for the coming battle, dug a defensive line of trenches opposite to Pyrrhus' camp; at both ends they embedded a row of waggons up to their axles in the upcast soil 'in order to impede the advance of the elephants'. Plutarch gives a vivid picture of the siege but no further details about the elephants. However, when Areus returned and some mercenaries arrived, Pyrrhus finally called off the siege.

Pyrrhus next tried to seize Argos where one party had appealed for his help. He just slipped past the forces of Areus and those sent by Gonatas and reached the city, where his friends had planned to open a gate for him by night. Plutarch, in another very lively passage, describes what followed (*Pyrr.* 32 ff.): 'But the gate would not admit his elephants, and so the towers had to be taken off their backs and put on again when the animals were inside in darkness and confusion. This caused delay.' Thus the alarm was given and the Argives were alerted. When day broke, Pyrrhus had penetrated some way into the city, but in the confused street-fighting he feared that he might be cut off and so he sent a message to his son Helenus outside the city to tear down part of the wall. The message, however, was misunderstood and Helenus took the rest of the elephants and some picked troops and marched through the gate to help his father. But Pyrrhus was by now trying to withdraw along the narrow street and in the hubbub orders could not be heard, as some men tried to push their way out, others in. Confusion was worse confounded when the largest of the elephants fell across the gateway and lay there roaring. Another elephant, named Nicon, who was one of those that had originally entered the city, started a furious hunt for its wounded rider who had fallen from its back and thus blocked the way of the men trying to get out. 'Having found the body of its master, it lifted it up with its trunk and laid it across its two tusks [one is reminded of an Indian elephant carrying trunks of trees in more peaceful times] and, maddened, it overthrew and killed all who got in its way.' In the mêlée Pyrrhus himself was wounded, and then struck on the head by a tile hurled by a woman from a roof-top; one of Antigonus' men, seeing Pyrrhus lying in a doorway, drew his sword and hacked off his head. Whatever aid his elephants had given Pyrrhus in Italy – and initially they had certainly overawed the Romans – they had failed him at the end, or rather he had failed them: while they could usefully be used to help to demolish strongholds, it was a risky experiment to try to use them in the cramped conditions within a town, and it is strange to find a professional soldier of the stature of Pyrrhus failing to foresee the problem of getting them through the gates. He no doubt rightly judged that they needed the protection of towers against missiles launched from roof-top height, but it is extraordinary that he failed to ascertain from his Argive friends the height of the gate through which they must pass. His elephants fought bravely according to their kind, but, no more than camels, could they pass through the eye of a needle, as a later Rabbinic saying emphasized: their master had indeed failed them, but he had paid the price with his life.[60] Those that survived appear to have fallen into the hands of Gonatas, since when he occupied Megara, probably two years later, we are told by Polyaenus (IV, 6.3) that he had some elephants with him. There they had to face squealing pigs, as we have seen (p. 114), and panic triumphed. The ignominious death of the heroic Pyrrhus had a counterpart in this rout of his majestic elephants. They were, however, accorded an enduring memorial: when over 400 years later the traveller Pausanias visited Argos he saw in the market-place not only the sanctuary of Demeter in which lay the bones of Pyrrhus, with his bronze shield hanging over the doorway, but also Pyrrhus' elephants and other instruments of war carved in relief on a monument erected on the spot where his body had been burnt (II, 21.4).

# CHAPTER V

# SELEUCIDS AND PTOLEMIES

## ANTIOCHUS AND THE GALLIC INVASIONS

When Seleucus was killed by Ptolemy Ceraunus his field force passed over to his murderer, but there is no evidence that he had brought any of his elephants across the Hellespont into Europe for his attack on Lysimacheia. Loyalty to his cause did not collapse in Asia Minor, and his son Antiochus, who was far off in the East, sent troops to enforce his own authority in Asia Minor. Before long he reached an agreement with Ceraunus. Both kings were soon faced by a common danger in widespread incursions by Gallic tribes, but their personal fates were very different: Antiochus owed his victory over them to his elephants, while Ceraunus lost his life when his elephant was wounded in battle.

Bands of Celtic or Gallic tribes (or 'Galatians' as the Greeks called them) had long been moving about on the northern frontiers of the Balkans, and the storm broke in 279 when three war-bands invaded Macedon and Thrace, plundering the countryside and terrifying the inhabitants. Ceraunus, the Thunderbolt, did not wait to muster all his troops from their winter quarters but rushed to meet the invaders. The result was defeat. Memnon, a local historian of Heraclea, adds a vivid detail: 'Ceraunus was captured alive when the elephant on which he was riding was wounded and threw him.' Justin adds the grisly information that he was decapitated and the Gauls paraded his head on the point of a spear.[61] The Gauls continued to plunder far and wide, leaving Macedon without an effective king for the next two years. A second column was led by Brennus, who demanded danegeld from Gonatas. According to a story in Justin (xxv, 1), Gonatas entertained the envoys regally in order to impress them with his wealth and displayed his elephants in order to frighten them; however, the result was only to sharpen their lust for plunder. In the event, the Gauls penetrated as far south as Delphi, but were ultimately driven out of Greece.

A third Gallic band invaded Thrace and part of it crossed over into Asia Minor which had to endure widespread pillage that reached its peak in 277. But before he could check it, Antiochus, now king of Syria, had other troubles of his own to face. These included a revolt in the Seleucis, the heart of the Seleucid empire on the Orontes, where rebels seized Apamea.[62] This city, named after Seleucus' wife, was a military base where the Seleucids kept their elephants. As we have seen (p. 98 and n. 48), we really have no clear idea how many they may have had (true, Strabo, XVI, 10, says that Seleucus had 500 at Apamea, but this may derive from the tradition of his '500', and not from an independent source). If Seleucus had only 130 at Ipsus (Tarn's guess) and then captured some of Antigonus' 75 in the battle, a natural wastage (not to mention war casualties) might have reduced this total to less than 100 in the twenty-five years or so since the battle.[63] This is pure speculation, since if the '500' elephants which Seleucus had in 301 were anywhere near that figure, then the force that his son Antiochus had at Apamea must have been considerably larger. However, an extraordinary situation develops: this massive force simply disappears from history, since (as will be seen shortly) Antiochus had hastily to summon a mere 20 elephants from Babylon to help him against the Gauls. What happened to it can be only guess-work. The rebels at Apamea seem scarcely likely to have killed them all off. It is possible that in fact some were not at Apamea at all but had been withdrawn to Babylon. Later evidence for the herds of the Seleucids does not help much. Antiochus III had few: he used 10 against the rebel Molon and then apparently got more from India: he had 102 at Raphia in 217 BC (p. 139) and 150 during his eastern expedition, but by his day, some fifty years later, the elephants of Antiochus I would all have died in any case. Nevertheless, whatever the fate of the elephants from Ipsus, Antiochus soon managed to crush the rebellion and regained Seleucis. He then wintered in Sardes, doubtless hoping to deal with the Gauls in the next spring, but he first had to face another trouble: an invasion of Coele-Syria and Damascus by Ptolemy's troops in 276. Leaving his son Seleucus to try to protect Asia Minor, he crossed back over the Taurus mountains and successfully expelled the invaders. Then at last he could deal with the Gauls. A Babylonian Chronicle, which tells of his exploits, records that in the month of Adar (Feb.–Mar.) 275 he received supplies which he had ordered from his satrap in Babylon: these included 20 elephants.[64] He was now ready to recross the Taurus and face the Gauls.

Battle was joined at an unknown site. The only surviving source to provide any details of it is an unlikely one, the sophist Lucian (*Zeuxis*, 8–11), with the result that there is a tendency among some historians to depreciate his account. But in fact it may go back to a good source (possibly even to Hieronymus), since it contains an item whose authenticity is guaranteed by another reliable source: it records that Antiochus had 16 elephants in the battle, and this modest figure accords well with that given by the Babylonian Chronicle, allowing the loss of four perhaps from fatigue due to the long trek from Babylon. Thus, although not all Lucian's details may be acceptable, his outline of the battle may well have a good pedigree. On the flanks of a phalanx, which was hardly as professionally Macedonian-like as Lucian describes it, the Gauls placed their cavalry, while behind their centre they had a great force of chariots which included 80 scythed-vehicles. Against this Antiochus was lightly armed in view of his hasty preparations, but a skilled tactician, Theodotas of Rhodes, advised him on the placing of his 16 elephants: four on each wing were to engage the Gallic cavalry when it attacked, and the other eight were in front of the centre to deal with the chariots. Neither the Gauls nor, more important, their horses had ever seen elephants: terrified by their trumpeting, by their white tusks gleaming against their dark bodies, and by their trunks which towered over them like hooks, the Gauls and their horses fled even before getting within bowshot and many even tore into their own infantry ranks. The elephants pressed on, trampling, goring and tossing up all who stood in their way. Victory was complete and the Macedonians crowded round Antiochus, hailing him as Kallinikos, glorious in victory, but the king is said to have wept and called out, 'Shame, my men, whose salvation came through these sixteen beasts. If the novelty of their appearance had not struck the enemy with panic, where should we have been?' Antiochus then ordered that the trophy should be engraved with nothing but the figure of an elephant.

This 'elephant victory' as it is usually called did not completely end the Gallic menace in Asia Minor, but it was decisive enough for many cities to honour Antiochus as Saviour (Soter), a title which later became his cult name. It was celebrated in an epic composed by a certain Simonides of Magnesia (*Suda*, s.v.) which possibly had some influence on Lucian's account of the battle. The battle, and probably the trophy in particular, also furnished themes for sculpture. A well-known terra-cotta statuette from Myrina (pl. VIIb) shows an elephant, with a large mahout on its neck and an empty tower on its back, trampling on a warrior who has a sword in his hand and is recognizable as a Gaul from his oblong shield. An engraved stone, now in the Cabinet of France, shows a similar scene, though here the tower contains two men, while the elephant holds his victim in its trunk. Further, we hear (from Stephanus Byz, s.v. Boura) that an artist named Pytheas of Boura in Achaea painted an elephant on a mural at Pergamum which was later cut away and added to the picture gallery of the kings of Pergamum; this may well have had reference to the battle. Such were some of the smaller memorials to a victory which began to force the Gauls back into the centre of Phyrygia where later many settled and became known to us as the Galatians.[65]

### THE PTOLEMIES' INDIAN ELEPHANTS

By 275 BC the turmoil stirred up by attempts to win or partition Alexander's empire was dying down and more stable conditions might be expected with the emergence of the three great monarchies of Macedon, Syria and Egypt. The Ptolemies controlled Egypt, Palestine, Cyrene and Cyprus, while the Seleucids held northern Syria, much of Asia Minor, Mesopotamia and Persia, but one issue continued to keep them at loggerheads, namely control of southern Syria, or Coele-Syria, which was valuable for its maritime potentialities and for its position at the end of the great trade routes to the East. The legal claims of the two dynasts to it may have been fairly equal, and Seleucus and Ptolemy I managed to avoid open conflict on the issue, but on Seleucus' death Ptolemy II took advantage of the embarrassments of the new Syrian king, Antiochus, to extend his influence in Asia Minor and, as we have seen, to advance as far as Damascus, although he was soon driven back. This campaign was the first of a long series of Syrian Wars. Thus in 274 while Magas, Ptolemy's half-brother and viceroy of Cyrenaica, revolted against him, Antiochus took the chance to attack Coele-Syria, but was pushed back by attacks at different points by Ptolemy's fleet. In 272 he made a peace under which he kept Damascus but left all the Phoenician coast to Ptolemy.

It was against this background of wars with the Seleucids, present and to come, that Ptolemy II Philadelphus reviewed his military needs and he clearly gave elephants a high priority, since he began to send out hunting expeditions to the south to obtain beasts which he could use against the Indian elephants of the Seleucids. But before we turn to this theme, we should consider what elephants he already had and how he displayed them in a famous Procession (Pompe) in Alexandria in the 270s.

In 312 Ptolemy I had captured some 43 Indian elephants at Gaza (p. 95) and he conceivably might have increased his stock as a result of the bargaining that had followed Ipsus, but however that may be, he clearly had a moderate number of Indian elephants. This herd presumably declined, since political conditions may have prevented him from obtaining many more from the East to make up for natural losses. Contacts existed between his successor Philadelphus and Asoka, but Alexandrine trade with India was probably not very extensive,[66] and in any case the transport of elephants by land could have been controlled by the intervening powers. Ptolemy I's original captives may have contained a few females, so that breeding might have added a little to the declining herd, though not in sufficient numbers to make it of use for war purposes. If we allow for loss by death and a few replacements during thirty years, then Philadelphus will have inherited a small number of animals.

Elephants took part in the Procession of extraordinary splendour and wealth which Ptolemy II staged in Alexandria and which was described in detail by the Rhodian historian Callixeinus who wrote a work on Alexandria probably in the later part of the third century: a long extract from it on the Pompe is preserved by Athenaeus (v, 197–208). Often regarded as one of the early celebrations of the festival of the Ptolemaeia founded by Philadelphus in honour of his father, it may rather have been a special parade of the Alexandrian Pantheon, staged early in his reign.[67] Among a vast variety of items a representation of Dionysus returning from India was followed by a long line of various animals, led by 24 chariots drawn by elephants. Later on in the procession came a gold statue of Alexander, flanked by Victory and Athene, carried in a chariot drawn by 'real elephants (ἀληθινῶν)'. Are we to understand by this cryptic remark that the first group of elephants were models? (if so, their motive power could have been provided by concealed camels, as in the case of the story about Semiramis: see p. 35). Such a solution would be acceptable only if Ptolemy had virtually no elephants, but since he apparently did have some it would have been both ludicrous and unnecessary to put such models at the head of an imposing array of live animals (which included lions, leopards, panthers, camels, antelopes, wild asses, ostriches, a bear, a giraffe and a rhinoceros). The contrast made by the use of the word 'real', 'live', 'true' may be with the gold statue of Alexander which the elephants were drawing, or perhaps with the model of an elephant earlier in the procession: this was a figure on a cart on whose back reclined a figure of Dionysus which measured 18 ft and on whose neck sat a $7\frac{1}{2}$ ft Satyr (though Athenaeus does not specifically call this elephant a model, it can hardly have been a live one). Thus on balance the elephants drawing the 24 chariots are likely to have been living animals. But how many to each chariot? Two seems ruled out since the animals that followed are specifically described as being in pairs (συνωρίδες), e.g. eight pairs of ostriches. The answer, therefore, seems to be either one or four. One seems more probable in view of what we can surmise about Ptolemy's supply of elephants: if he had 96, he must have imported very many more than we suspect. Further, the statue of Alexander was drawn by elephants (in the plural) and a gold coin, minted in Cyrene between 305 and 285 by Ptolemy I, shows on its reverse a chariot drawn by four elephants, which are clearly Indian (pl. XVc). Thus in the Pompe the gold statue of Alexander was probably accorded the honour of a quadriga, while the 24 chariots had one animal apiece. Chronology suggests that these, like those on the slightly earlier coin, must have been Indians. As we shall see, Ptolemais Theron, the southern port for hunting African elephants, was probably not founded before 270 so that it is unlikely that any African elephants from there would have been available for the Procession. In any case it is perhaps unlikely that they could have been trained sufficiently, at any rate in a short time, to allow them with safety to be paraded through Alexandria. The more teachable Indian elephant must have been the beast used.[68]

Although the earlier Pharaohs had extended their influence far up the Nile valley, in the Ptolemaic period Egyptian power did not extend further south than around Aswan where lay the semi-Hellenized kingdom of Meroe. The Ptolemies began to cast their eyes towards this region which was rich in gold, iron and elephants. The elephant played an important part in the Meroitic kingdom, as is shown by the frequency with which it is portrayed in sculpture and reliefs. One relief from Musaw-warat es-Sofra shows a king. riding on an elephant and a servant kneeling down and apparently holding the end of its trunk; it is noteworthy that in relation to the two humans the figure of the elephant is reasonably small, which seems to confirm that these elephants were the smaller Forest race (see p. 62). At Musaw-warat there is a great complex of buildings, including a temple and colonnade and ramps; it has been suggested that the large enclosures were designed to herd elephants in and the ramps would be easier than steps for them to negotiate. This particular building may be somewhat later, but inscriptions in the adjacent Lion Temple suggest that the temple is early Ptolemaic in date. What matters here is the importance of the elephant in Meroitic culture and that we have representations of it.[69] (Pl. VIIIa.)

The Ptolemies began to investigate. Either Soter late in his reign or Philadelphus early in his sent an expedition under a man called Philon as far as Meroe. Philon wrote an account of his journey, as did many subsequent Ptolemaic explorers and these accounts survived, to be used by later writers such as Strabo and Pliny. Another source by which first-hand knowledge has survived was the work of Agatharchides *On the Red Sea* which is widely reflected in Diodorus and Strabo (p. 59). Thus we are well informed about many matters, but unfortunately we know no more than the bare fact, recorded by Diodorus (1, 37.5), that Philadelphus led a military expedition into Ethiopia; it probably resulted in his winning the gold mines of Lower Nubia. His interests also embraced the other coast of the Red Sea and trade with Arabia. On the African side, on the coast of the land of the Trogodytes, he established a number of settlements, harbours and stations. About 270 BC he sent Satyrus 'to investigate about hunting elephants' and to establish a settlement called Philotera about 100 miles south of Suez. Other foundations crept down to coast as far as Bab el-Mandeb (opposite Aden),

Fig. 11. Relief of a king riding on an elephant from Meroe
(Musaw-warat es-Sofra) (P. L. Shinnie, *Meroe*, 1967, fig. 27)

Fig. 12. Elephants engraved on a
bronze beaker from Meroe
(P. L. Shinnie, *Meroe*, 1967, fig. 48)

many bearing dynastic names: they include Arsinoe 'of the Trogodytes', Berenice, and especially Ptolemais 'of the Elephant Hunts'. This last was founded by a certain Eumedes: an inscription from Pithom records his progress down the Red Sea: 'he built a great city to the king with the illustrious name of the king . . . he made there fields and cultivated them with ploughs and cattle; no such thing took place there from the beginning. He caught elephants in great numbers for the king, and he brought them as marvels to the king, on his transports on the sea.' The leaders of other expeditions are reflected in the names of harbours, promontories and islands in the Red Sea, which are recorded by Strabo: the Harbours of Antiphilus, the Island of Straton, the Altars of Conon, the Look-out Post of Demetrius. We know from a papyrus of c. 255 BC that Demetrius, an official, was in charge of elephant expeditions, so that all these settlements may well be as early as the reign of Philadelphus. They bear vivid witness to the scale of the interest of the early Ptolemies in this area.[70]

Not only had expeditions to be planned and bases established, but elephants also had to be hunted and caught. Diodorus (Agatharchides) preserves a dramatic account of how the native Ethiopians, known as Elephant fighters (Elephantomachoi) went about their hunting. In thickly grown parts of the forest they watched from the tallest trees where the elephants were accustomed to gather and then picked out an isolated individual for a daring attack. When the beast passed under the tree in which the watcher was hiding, he 'seizes its tail with his hands and plants his feet against its left flank; he has hanging from his shoulders an axe, light enough so that a blow may be struck with one hand and yet very sharp, and grasping this in his right hand he hamstrings the elephant's right leg, raining blows upon it and maintaining the position of his own body with his left hand. They bring an astonishing swiftness to bear upon the task, since it is a contest between the two of them for their very lives.' The hamstrung beast then often collapsed on the spot, 'causing the death of the Ethiopian along with his own; sometimes squeezing the man against a rock or tree it crushes him with its weight until it kills him. Sometimes, however, the elephant in its extreme suffering, far from turning on its attacker, flees across the plain, until the man who has set his feet upon it, striking on the same place with his axe, has severed the tendons and paralyzed the beast. And as soon as the beast has fallen

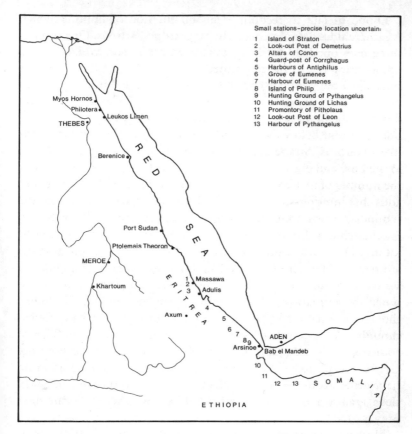

Fig. 13. Elephant hunting stations

they run together in companies, and cutting the flesh off the hindquarters of the elephant while it is still alive they hold a feast.' This
account of hamstringing is perfectly acceptable. Dr Sikes (*op. cit.*
p. 307) gives an account of a similar practice used in this area in
later times: 'Two or more horsemen armed with sabres would
separate an elephant from its herd, riding it off and annoying it. One
rider would distract it by attempting to slash off the tip of its trunk
while the most skilful of the group would ride to its rear, slip from
his horse (sometimes jumping on to the elephant's haunches, sliding
down the tail), quickly slashing the tendons of the hind legs. . . .
Variations of this technique have been described.'

Diodorus fails to recount a second method of hunting which Agatharchides describes, namely by poisoned arrows. Of a team of three men one held the bow, partly with his foot, while the two others drew the string and aimed at the middle of the elephant's side. The bow with one end resting on the ground must have been very large and powerful. The target is vague. Today the two main shots are the brain shot and the heart shot: the latter is aimed at the side at a point below the ear and near the top of the front leg. Unlike Diodorus, Strabo repeats this method, but assigns two men to the bow and one to the string. Pliny (*NH*. VIII, 8) is vague about the number of men to each bow which was fixed in the ground, but adds that hunting-spears were used instead of arrows and that the wounded beasts were then followed up by the tracks of blood. Agatharchides, Strabo and Diodorus all give a third method of killing, Diodorus at greatest length. Since it was thought that the animals could not lie down to sleep but rested against trees, hunters would note such trees and then nearly saw them through, so that when the animals next leant against them they would fall down; they could then easily kill their quarry since the elephant, it was thought, had a jointless leg and could not get up again. This of course is nonsense (Julius Caesar tells a similar story of how the Germans captured elks in the Hercynian forest), but it could easily have arisen from the fact that elephants often do rub, rest and even sleep against trees; thus hunters would know where to locate their prey.

However, what the Ptolemies wanted was not dead elephants but fighting-fit elephants, as Agatharchides points out when he says that 'Ptolemy urged the hunters to refrain from killing elephants in order that he might have them alive . . . not only did he not persuade them but they said that they would not change their way of life in exchange for the whole kingdom of Egypt': an early cry against the inroads of civilization. We must suppose, therefore, that Ptolemy had to organize his own hunting parties. He might have obtained expert help from the kingdom of Meroe, where the elephant was domesticated and hunting techniques must have been devised. Presumably the corral method of trapping must have been used, as in India and described in some detail by Megasthenes (p. 56). But capture must be followed by breaking in and training, and here we get a hint from a pleasant story in Aelian (XI, 25): 'Ptolemy II Philadelphus was presented with a young elephant; it was brought up where the Greek language was used, and understood those that spoke to it. Up to the time of this particular animal it was believed that elephants only understood the language used by Indians.' This anecdote strongly supports the view that Indian mahouts were imported to help in the training (the men could reach Egypt from India, even though it might be impossible to bring elephants all the way by sea thither). This idea is confirmed by the fact that riders in the course of time came to be called 'Indians', irrespective of origin, and the name remained even when the natives of Africa gained sufficient skill to replace any true Indians. Such a change in riders is shown by later evidence, e.g. a coin and a terracotta vase reveal that the Carthaginians were using some negro drivers in Hannibal's time (pl. XXIIb, & Xa; p. 172 f). The situation can be paralleled from modern times. At the beginning of their experiments to tame the African elephant the Belgians in the Congo obtained Indian mahouts, and the Azande natives learnt the job very competently from these professionals, including the sort of sing-song 'elephant talk' to which Aelian (XI, 14) makes reference.[71] As to the age of the quarry, the hunters may of course have gone first for young or immature animals, but if Ptolemy wanted a fighting force soon, some larger beasts would have to be included.

But even when the elephants had been caught and received basic training one more hazard remained: they had to be transported from Eritrea all the way to Alexandria. For this purpose special transport vessels must have been built. Diodorus (III, 40.3) describes how the sea is shallow and greenish from the masses of seaweed under the surface; this was all right for boats which were rowed, but 'the ships which carry the elephants, being of deep draft because of their weight and heavy by reason of their equipment, involve their crews in great and terrible dangers. Since they run under full sail and often are driven before the force of the winds during the night, sometimes they strike the rocks and are wrecked, at other times they run aground on slightly submerged spits. The sailors cannot go over the sides of the ships because the water is deeper than a man's height, and, when in their efforts to rescue their vessel by means of their punt-poles they accomplish nothing, they jettison everything except their provisions.' Thus perhaps some elephant bones were to be found among the carcases of the ships which Ptolemy specifically ordered should be left, like cenotaphs, as a

Fig. 14. Ornament of an elephant wearing a saddle-cloth from Ptolemaic Alexandria (Bienkowski, *Les Celtes dans les arts mineurs greco-romains*, 1928, fig. 217)

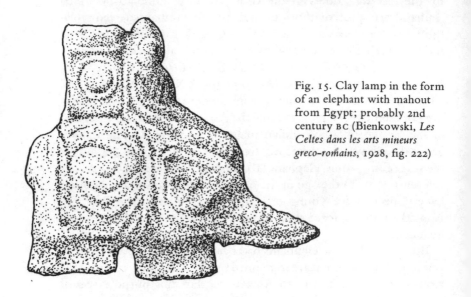

Fig. 15. Clay lamp in the form of an elephant with mahout from Egypt; probably 2nd century BC (Bienkowski, *Les Celtes dans les arts mineurs greco-romains*, 1928, fig. 222)

memorial to their crews and a warning to other sailors. The dangers are reflected in a letter of slightly later date (224 BC) which was sent by some Egyptians in Berenice to their fellows in a station further south.[72] It tells us that elephant-transports usually took on a return cargo of corn for the outlying stations. In this case the transport had sunk on its journey south, and the letter was written to reassure the men, reporting to them that a new elephant-transport was nearly completed in Berenice and would soon be on its way to them with supplies of corn.

Man and beast alike were no doubt relieved when the sea journey ended and they could land at 'Berenice of the Trogodytes' and then march through the Eastern Desert along the caravan route which Philadelphus developed to Coptos. Here perhaps 'the superintendent of the supply of elephants' took over, at any rate later on, as the organization grew. They were housed in a temporary depot in the Thebaid and had their chief stable at Memphis (*Pap. Petrie*, II, n. 20). Some will have been taken to Alexandria for display in the zoo which Philadelphus established. Not only was 'he passionately fond of the hunting of elephants . . . expending great sums of money on this . . . but he also brought to the knowledge of the Greeks other kinds of animal which had never been seen' (Diod. III, 36.3).

### THE ELEPHANTS OF PTOLEMY III AND SELEUCUS II

No detailed continuous narrative of either the Second Syrian War (260–255) or of the Third (246–241) survives: their stories have to be pieced together from scraps of information. The Second War was brought on by the accession of Antiochus II to the Syrian throne and was fought mainly in Asia Minor. With some help from Antigonus Gonatas and from Rhodes, he secured terms in 255 by which Ptolemy restored to him the Phoenician coast. We do not know how many, if any, elephants he used, nor how many Ptolemy opposed to him. In view of the strenuous efforts Ptolemy had been making to build up an elephant-corps, he is likely to have made some use of them in these campaigns, but the figures which survive for his total force inspire little confidence. St Jerome in a passage of his Commentary on the book of Daniel, which derives from the polymath Porphyry, attributes a force of 400 elephants to Philadelphus, while Appian (*Proem.* 10) assigns him 300. It would be interesting to know the earlier derivation of these figures, but they must clearly be rejected: Ptolemy's hunts cannot have been on *that* scale, though the figures testify to the belief that he had a strong corps.[73]

Fresh trouble broke out when two new kings succeeded to the two kingdoms in 246: Ptolemy III, later called Euergetes, and Seleucus II. It was provoked by the murderous intrigues of Laodice, the repudiated wife of Antiochus II. Ptolemy promptly led an army into Syria in a campaign which ended in one of the greatest military triumphs of his dynasty. This is referred to in Daniel (XI, 7–9): 'But out of a branch of her root [i.e. from the stock of the murdered Berenice of Egypt, who became queen of Syria] shall one stand up in his estate, which shall come with an army, and shall enter into the fortress of the king of the north [i.e. of Syria], and shall deal against them, and shall prevail: and shall also carry captives into Egypt their gods, with their princes, and their precious vessels of silver and of gold.' Neither Daniel nor Jerome, his commentator, who had previously referred to Philadelphus' alleged 400 beasts, mentions elephants on either side, but this omission is very adequately compensated for by a fascinating inscription which was set up at Adulis (some 30 miles south of Massawa) by one of the officers sent by Ptolemy on elephant-hunts in this area. The original is lost: what we have is the manuscript copy of a transcription made by the monk Cosmas in the sixth century AD. It runs: 'The Great King, Ptolemy . . . having inherited from his father the kingdom of Egypt and Libya and Syria [i.e. Coele-Syria] and Phoenicia and Cyprus and Lycia and Caria and the Cyclades, set out on a campaign into Asia with infantry and cavalry forces and a naval armament and elephants both Trogodyte and Ethiopic, which his father and he himself first captured from these places, and, bringing them to Egypt, trained them to military use. But having become master of all the country this side of the Euphrates and of Cilicia and Pamphylia and Ionia and the Hellespont and Thrace, and of all the military forces in these countries and of Indian elephants [i.e. of Seleucus], and having made the local dynasts in all these regions his vassals, he crossed the river Euphrates, and having brought under him Mesopotamia and Babylonia and Susiana and Persis and Media, and all the rest as far as Bactria, and having sought out whatever sacred things had been carried off by the Persians from Egypt, and having brought them back with the other treasure from these countries to Egypt, he sent forces through the canals . . .'. Here the inscription, as seen by Cosmas, broke off.[74]

The inscription exaggerates the extent of Ptolemy's territorial advances in the East: he probably advanced to Seleuceia on the Tigris and won the support of the eastern satrapies, but not to Bactria.[75] However, what is said about elephants is likely to be reliable: the fact that the inscription was set up in a town whose inhabitants must have known much about elephants would make falsification less probable. The distinction between Ptolemy's Trogodytic and Ethiopic elephants is interesting and emphasizes local involvement: the Ethiopic elephants presumably were from the inland area of Meroe, while the Trogodytic came from the country nearer the coast and Adulis. Unfortunately, no hint is given of the number of Seleucus' animals, nor how many Ptolemy got hold of, nor whether he won them by capture in battle, by surrender terms or even seized them in the royal stables at Apamea if any were still there. Two points, however, are very clear: Seleucus must have inherited a considerable force which his grandfather and father presumably had built up after the 'elephant-victory' over the Galatians (unless at that time a large herd had been kept back in Babylon) while Ptolemy, by obtaining them, henceforth had a mixed force of his own African and the acquired Indians.

Satisfied with his victory, or perhaps anxious about conditions in Egypt, Ptolemy hurried home, thus allowing Seleucus to counter-attack in 245 and expel the Egyptian garrisons that had been left behind. Thus Ptolemy's Asiatic empire crumbled and two years later Seleucus invaded Coele-Syria but only to meet defeat by land and sea. By 241 he was ready to accept a peace offer by which Ptolemy received the Syrian coast as far as Seleuceia-ad-Orontem. One long-term result of this war was that the Seleucids lost control of the Far East: Diodotus, the satrap of Bactria-Sogdiana asserted his independence, and Bactria became gradually a separate Hellenistic kingdom. Another independent power arose, that of the Parthians, whose era traditionally began in 247. These great movements had their repercussions on the future of elephant warfare: they lay athwart the land supply-lines to India, the source of supply for the Seleucid empire.

Despite the African and Indian elephants that he now possessed Ptolemy Euergetes was not satisfied but continued to send out further expeditions to the South. Diodorus (III, 18.4) expressly records that he was very keen on the hunts and that he sent one of his official Friends named Simmias to reconnoitre the land of the Ichthyophagoi (fish-eaters). Simmias perhaps founded Berenice Panchrysus. Other leaders left their names enshrined in The Island of Philip and The Elephant-hunting Ground (κυνήγιον) of Pythangelus, both well north of Bab el-Mandeb; also The Elephant-hunting Ground (θήρα) of Lichas, The Promontory of Peitholaus, the Look-out Post of Leon, and The Harbour of Pythangelus, all on the stretch of coast from Bab el-Mandeb to the tip at Ras Guardafui.[76] Peitholaus and Pythangelus appear to have been sent out under Euergetes, others by his son Philopator who succeeded him in 221; both Pythangelus and his son Ptolemaeus are mentioned as troop-commanders in a papyrus concerning hunts.

Philopator thus continued the policy of his father and grand-father, and it has recently been suggested that he introduced greater organization into a system which had been somewhat casual.[77] This he is thought to have done because of the elephants he lost in the battle of Raphia in 217, but as we shall see his losses there were not serious and he gained many of his opponent's Indian elephants (p. 142). Nevertheless he pressed on with his hunts which were now entrusted to officials who enjoyed the rank of general ($\sigma\tau\rho\alpha\tau\eta\gamma\acute{o}s$). Two of these receive mention. An Acarnanian named Lichas, who left his record in The Elephant-hunting Ground of Lichas and The Altars of Lichas, served at least twice, since in two dedications he refers to himself as 'sent out as general in charge of the elephant-hunts for the second time'. The dedications, which were offered between 215/214 and 209 B C, were made, one to Philopator and his wife Arsinoe and to Serapis and Isis (*OGIS*, 82), the second to the king and queen and to Dionysus and perhaps to Isis. A second commander was Charimortus, probably an Aetolian. Two of his subordinates are also known, one from a letter to an Aristoboulus named on an ostracon from the Thebaid; the second (dated after 209 B C; *OGIS*, 86) is a dedication on behalf of Philopator and Arsinoe and their son to Ares Nikephoros Euagros, the God of War, who gives victory and good hunting, by a man who was 'sent out as second-in-command to Charimortus, the general in charge of the elephant-hunt'. A few graffiti are found scratched on the statues at Abu Simbel by elephant-hunters, e.g. 'Craterus, son of Leucarus, came for elephant-hunting'. As a result of all this activity Philopator must by the end of his reign (203) have pos-sessed a very considerable herd of elephants indeed, but there is little evidence that his successors kept up this pursuit.

These hunters were soldiers, but their precise status is uncertain. Before the time of the battle of Raphia in 217 B C, the army in Egypt consisted of 'Macedonians' and mercenaries; a third class, com-prising native Egyptians, was added to meet the threat of Antiochus which culminated at Raphia (p. 139). The 'Macedonians' were the military settlers, the cleruchs, of Graeco-Macedonian origin, who had received grants of land in return for liability for military ser-vice when required. They formed the 'regular' army and the phal-anx in battle, but they were not adequate alone, especially after years of peace (241–221). They were supplemented by hiring mer-cenaries: thus at Raphia, where native Egyptians had been recruited to strengthen the phalanx, the mercenaries formed over one-quarter of the infantry and two-fifths of the cavalry.[78] Beside the permanent army stationed at Alexandria, garrisons were posted at important points throughout the empire, not least on the Red Sea coast; no doubt the further away from Alexandria they were, the greater would be the use of mercenaries. We have already met the Acarnanian Lichas and Charimortus who was probably an Aetolian. The latter makes a brief but lurid appearance in later history, as the friend and accomplice of the Aetolian Scopas who became very influential in Alexandria and 'aided by the savagery and drunken violence of Charimortus had utterly pillaged the kingdom' (Polybius, XVIII, 55.2). His career culminated in an unsuccessful *coup d'état* in 196 and it is interesting to note that when the king, Ptolemy V, arrested Scopas, he sent a force of 'soldiers and elephants' to surround his house. Was the duty assigned to the elephants to block the escape routes or perhaps even to batter open the house if need be?

Not all elephant-hunters, however, reached the fame of a Charimortus, who incidentally probably perished with his friend Scopas. We learn something of the lower ranks from a papyrus of 223 BC which refers to a Grammateus of the Kynegoi, a Quartermaster of the Hunters. The document records that the Royal Banker of the Apollonopolis nome (Edfus) had been ordered to transfer to the *grammateus* the wages of 231 huntsmen of the company of Andronicus who were going with Pitholaus to Eritrea, namely 2 talents, 1,860 drachmae for three months, or 4 silver obols per man per day. This is very good pay, equivalent to that of a high-grade scribe. It emphasizes the high cost of mounting these expeditions, since, as has been pointed out, the total of this three months' pay would not be covered by the net tax revenue received by the Royal Treasury from the sale of fish for half a year: from a papyrus of 235 BC we learn that the income from this source was a little over 11 talents, but the expenses were virtually 10 talents. And the pay of the hunters must have formed only a limited part of the whole expense involved in these expeditions.[79]


RAPHIA: AFRICANS VERSUS INDIANS

In the year of Philopator's accession, 221 BC, the history of Polybius begins and we have once more something like a connected

137

narrative of Hellenistic affairs. At this time there was a sudden change of rulers: the kings of the three great Hellenistic kingdoms died and were replaced by younger men. In 223 BC Antiochus III, later known as the Great and now aged about nineteen, succeeded to the Seleucid realm, while in 221 Ptolemy (IV Philopator), aged about twenty-three, and Philip V, at only seventeen, ascended the thrones of Egypt and Macedon respectively. Antiochus lost no time before reopening hostilities with Ptolemy: in 221 he advanced against the fortresses which barred the route into Coele-Syria. But the barrier did not give way at the first attack and when news reached Antiochus that Molon, his governor of Media, was in revolt he broke off the campaign. With Persia and Babylonia soon in Molon's hands, Antiochus hastened to the East in person, crossed the Tigris and brought the rebel to battle. The order on each side was normal, with cavalry on both wings and the main infantry line in the centre. But Antiochus had ten elephants, which he placed at intervals in front of the line. Molon apparently had no elephants, but he had scythed-chariots and these he placed in front of his line, hoping no doubt that the horses would stand up to the elephants opposite them or perhaps intending to send them in between the gaps against Antiochus' infantry line. But a general engagement was averted: although Molon's right wing vigorously engaged its opposite number, his left wing, which faced Antiochus, deserted him and he committed suicide.[80] It is noteworthy that Antiochus only used ten elephants, whereas three years later he had no less than 102. The reason for this great difference can only be surmised. He may have judged ten to be sufficient or they may have been all he had; if he had a larger force, perhaps part of it was in Syria and could not be brought to bear upon the enemy in time. His father, Seleucus II, had lost most of his elephants to Ptolemy in 246 (p. 134), but even if he had managed to retain a few, at least half of these would have died in the next twenty-five years. During this period he may have acquired some from India: if military demands were not pressing, the prestige and tradition of his house may well have required him to keep a certain number of elephants. If, however, Seleucus had been content to see his herd run down to only ten, then Antiochus must have done some brisk trading with India to raise his force to 102 within four years; in any case he must have acquired a considerable number in this short period; it is improbable that he can have had anything like it in reserve in 221 BC.

In 219 Antiochus returned to the attack on Egypt in the so-called Fourth Syrian War. He swept down the coast of Palestine as far as Tyre, but Ptolemy's forces managed to hold on to Sidon and some of the interior. Neither in this year nor the next did Antiochus attempt to advance on Egypt; instead he entered into futile negotiations which Ptolemy deliberately prolonged in order to gain time. This he used most effectively in a complete overhaul, reorganization and strengthening of his army, with the help of experts from Greece. Beside hiring numerous mercenaries he even incorporated a large number of *native* Egyptians into the phalanx, which then probably comprised 20,000 natives and 5,000 Graeco-Macedonians (this fresh move incidentally led to new social and political pressures). He now was able to put into the field a total force of some 50,000 infantry, 5,000 horse and 73 elephants (Polybius curiously does not mention the elephants when describing the organization of the army at v. 65, but only when they appear in the subsequent battle). Against this army Antiochus led out a force of 62,000 infantry, 6,000 horse and 102 elephants. After resting at Gaza he advanced to the frontier town of Raphia and here on 22 June 217 was fought the largest battle since Ipsus over eighty years earlier.

The disposition and battle-lines of the two sides is indicated in the accompanying diagram (fig. 16) and therefore details need not be repeated here.[81] Both Ptolemy, who was accompanied by his sister-wife Arsinoe, and Antiochus harangued their troops, especially their phalanxes because 'they placed their greatest hopes on them' and then took up positions facing each other, Ptolemy on his left wing and Antiochus on his right. The whole battle, in which Ptolemy's 73 elephants were heavily outnumbered by the 102 of Antiochus, must first be described before any comments are made. It falls into three distinct engagements, which largely succeeded each other in time. First came the fighting on Ptolemy's left wing, where the main struggle of the elephants took place. Antiochus opened the battle by ordering a charge of the 60 elephants on his right wing against the 40 on Ptolemy's left. Polybius writes: 'only some few of Ptolemy's elephants came to close quarters with their opponents, and the men in the towers on the back of these beasts made a gallant fight of it, lunging with their pikes (sarissas) at close quarters and striking each other, while the elephants themselves fought still more brilliantly, using all their strength in the encounter and pushing against each other, forehead to forehead. The way in which elephants fight is this. With their tusks firmly interlocked and entangled they push against each other with all their might, each trying to force the other to give ground, until the one who proves the strongest pushes aside the other's trunk, and then, when he has once made him turn, he gores him with his tusks as a bull does with his horns. Now most of Ptolemy's elephants were afraid to join battle, as is the habit of African elephants; for unable to stand the smell and the trumpeting of the Indian elephants, and terrified, I suppose, also by their great size and strength, they immediately run away from them before they get near them. This is what happened on the present occasion; and when Ptolemy's elephants were thus thrown into confusion and driven back on their own lines Ptolemy's Agema [a picked force of 2,000 peltasts] gave way under the pressure of the animals.' Meanwhile Antiochus led his cavalry in a sweeping movement outside the elephants and fell on the cavalry commanded by Polycrates on Ptolemy's left wing. At the same time Antiochus' Greek mercenaries, who had originally stood behind his elephants, charged Ptolemy's peltasts and drove them back since their ranks had already been thrown into confusion by the elephant charge. Thus the whole of Ptolemy's left wing began to retreat.

Ptolemy's right wing fared very differently. Here the commander, Echecrates, waited to see the result of the fighting on his left wing and then, when the Ptolemaic elephants were unwilling to attack those opposite them, he ordered the section of Greek mercenaries under Phoxidas between his own units and the Ptolemaic phalanx to attack the enemy in front of them (these would be Arabs, Cissians and Medes, and others). At the same time he himself advanced with his cavalry and the Gauls and Thracians who had been stationed immediately on his left; avoiding the onset of the elephants he led his men on the right round the enemy's left flank and quickly routed the cavalry opposite him, falling on its flank and rear. Meantime Phoxidas had put to flight the Arabs and Medes. Thus Ptolemy's right wing was successful while his left wing was routed. Unfortunately, the role of the elephants is far from clear since Polybius' writing is somewhat obscure. First, it is not obvious which elephants Echecrates saw were unwilling to attack the enemy beasts: were they those on the left wing or those in front of him on the right wing? If the former, then his own elephants may have made some advance and when Polybius says

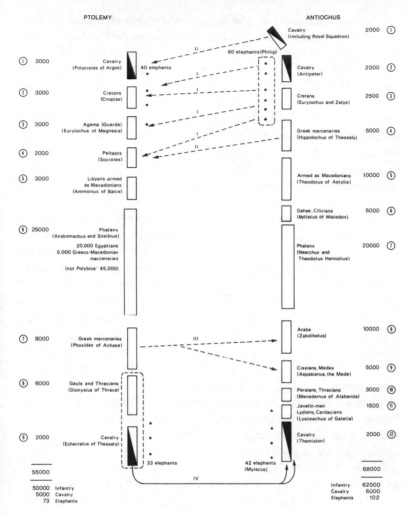

Fig. 16. Battle of Raphia

that his attacking force of cavalry got outside 'the onset ($\tau\tilde{\eta}\varsigma$ ἐφόδου) of the elephants', these would be his own as they advanced. On the other hand, the *ephodos* might mean the line of advance (if they *had* advanced), i.e. his cavalry swept clear to the right and thus avoided the risk of being in the path of either friendly or hostile elephants on this wing. The question is less important because in fact, in the absence of any hint to the contrary, we must suppose that the elephants on this wing did not in fact engage each other.

141

The two phalanxes in the centre were thus deprived of their wings, but Ptolemy himself, after he had been defeated on his left, had managed to get round to the back of his phalanx and now showed himself to them. Thus inspired his phalanx lowered their sarissas, charged and soon routed their opponents. Meantime, Antiochus in his youthful enthusiasm had been pursuing the defeated Ptolemaic left too far until his older officers pointed out to him that the cloud of dust from the phalanx was moving toward his camp. He tried in vain with his Royal Squadron to gallop back to the battlefield, but it was too late: his whole line was in retreat and he was forced to withdraw to Raphia. His casualties amounted to nearly 10,000 infantry, 300 cavalry and 4,000 prisoners. Ptolemy lost 1,500 infantry and 700 cavalry. The number of elephants lost presents some difficulty since Polybius records that Antiochus lost three in action and two by wounds, while Ptolemy had sixteen killed and most of the rest captured. This clearly does not make sense. Antiochus' defeated army could scarcely have captured nearly sixty, especially as the thirty-three on Ptolemy's right seem not to have gone into action. However, a trilingual inscription from Pithom records the precise opposite: it is a resolution of a synod of Egyptian priests at Memphis, passed in November 217 and commemorating the achievements of Ptolemy and his victory at Raphia, after which 'the king took as a prey much people, and all the elephants'. Thus Polybius must be corrected. One can assume that he misunderstood his source and attributed the losses to the wrong side or that the manuscript of Polybius is wrong, some copyist having accidentally transposed the clauses giving the figures (though admittedly such a transposition is not easily explicable).[82] In any case it is clear that Ptolemy had not only smashed the projected invasion of Egypt, but in the process he had collected a very large number of elephants, in fact the greater part of one hundred, to add to his own stock.

Polybius' description of the fighting of the elephants is vivid and may well reflect the account by an eye-witness. Further, it seems to be accurate, since it is very similar to a passage written by the great hunter Aloysius Horn: 'two bull elephants nearly full grown were having a fight on a sandbank. The two fighters did not charge each other but with head to head pressed each other back. There were great gaps in the sand caused by the weight and pressure of the fighters as they moved slowly in a circle. Now the younger one was forced head to ground and seemed fagged out and was bleeding from tusk wounds, and the larger elephant taking advantage of his position now forced his head up and jabbed him fiercely several times with his tusks.'[83] Polybius' is the best description in the ancient sources of what happened when elephant met elephant in battle, and it would appear that the tactics were for individuals to seek each other out and a series of duels ensued. At Raphia, however, there was an additional feature since the beasts were equipped with towers containing soldiers. As we have seen, there is no decisive evidence for the use of towers before the time of Pyrrhus. Thereafter Antiochus or one of his predecessors apparently adopted the idea. Ptolemy was forced to follow suit, whether or not his smaller African elephants were well adapted to carrying this extra load (on this see p. 243), simply because if he had not done so, his mahouts would have been skewered by the long sarissas of the enemy: he had to try to give his riders some protection. Since a sarissa was 16 ft long, we may imagine that before two beasts actually interlocked for their duel the men in each tower tried to spear the opposing mahout and soldiers in a kind of joust.

One final point remains: Africans versus Indians. If, as now seems established (p. 62), Ptolemy was using Forest elephants, which are smaller than Indians, then Polybius' statement that they were frightened by the greater bulk of the Indians need no longer be doubted. That they were frightened by their smell, however, is less probable; if hitherto unknown, it *might* have been off-putting, but in fact Ptolemy had some Indians as well as Africans and so the Africans are likely before the battle to have met their fellows in more peaceful surroundings and become accustomed to them (in the London zoo both races live happily in the same elephant-house). But not only is Polybius justified in general, but so are Ptolemy's elephants. It is not always remembered that they were heavily outnumbered: 40 against 60 on the left wing, and 33 against 42 on the right. Further, with towers on, height as well as bulk was important: the men on the taller Indians could strike down at those on the lower beasts. Thus the conduct of those that declined battle is understandable, if not praiseworthy. But some fought with great bravery. Though mere speculation, these could have been the Indians which Ptolemy had inherited from his father: they would then be facing their equals. However, perhaps one should not rob a few Africans of the glory which Polybius, who of course did not suspect that Ptolemy had any Indians, attributes to them.

After the battle a truce was soon arranged and later a treaty by which Ptolemy received Coele-Syria. Both kings were then concerned with their own affairs: Ptolemy with a 'native problem' in Alexandria, Antiochus with a rebel, Achaeus, in Asia Minor. After crushing Achaeus, Antiochus set off in 212 on an Eastern 'Anabasis' to restore his authority in his more distant provinces. He stormed through Armenia and Parthia, and for two years besieged Bactra (Balkh), the capital of Euthydemus' kingdom in Afghanistan. This war was then ended by mutual agreement: in view of threats from the nomads of the steppes Antiochus recognized Euthydemus as king, gave one of his own daughters to his son in marriage, and received his elephants. He then crossed the Hindu Kush into the Cabal valley where he made a treaty of friendship with the Indian rajah Sophagesenus, from whom he received more elephants, which brought his total to 150 (Polybius, XI, 34). He thus re-established his control in the East and returned home in 205; taking the title of 'Great King', he appeared to his subjects as a second Alexander the Great. He now possessed a new force of elephants which was half as large again as that which he had lost at Raphia. Once more, with good cause, he could place the elephant boldly on the Seleucid coinage (pl. XVIe), while Euthydemus probably replenished his own stock of elephants since later his son Demetrius I was depicted on his own coinage conspicuously wearing an elephant-scalp (pl. XVIg).

The death of Ptolemy IV in mysterious circumstances (probably in 204) led to an outburst of intrigue and murder in attempts to gain control over his successor, Ptolemy V Epiphanes, a young boy, while a native rising erupted in the Delta. At the same time Antiochus entered into a secret agreement with Philip V of Macedon to rob Egypt of its foreign possessions; as will be seen, when the Roman Senate ultimately got wind of this pact, its suspicions before long plunged Rome into Eastern affairs which henceforth became inextricably enmeshed with the Western world. Meanwhile, in 202–201 Antiochus started the Fifth Syrian War by a fresh invasion of Coele-Syria. After some fluctuations of fortune and a siege of Gaza he defeated the Ptolemaic army, led by the Aetolian Scopas, in a battle at Panium near the sources of the Jordan (probably in 200). Ptolemy V accepted defeat and ceded Coele-Syria to Antiochus. In these campaigns elephants played a part, but unfortunately Polybius' account is almost entirely lost. However, he does refer to the historical work of a contemporary, Zeno of Rhodes, which he criticizes very sharply; in fact he wrote to Zeno personally to point out some topographical errors (Pol. XVI, 14ff.). Another of Zeno's alleged failings was to sacrifice factual accuracy to ostentatious writing: Polybius demonstrates this by criticizing his account of the battle of Panium (XVI, 18f.) in which Antiochus put his elephants at intervals in front of his phalanx, with archers and slingers in the gaps. But later in the account the elephants are found behind the phalanx since they received the line when it retreated and then charged the enemy. Further, according to Zeno, the unaccustomed sight of the elephants threw Ptolemy's cavalry into panic, but Polybius asserts that Zeno's disposition of the cavalry did not allow them to face the elephants. It is impossible to try to reconstruct the battle from such pieces of criticism (whose validity we cannot judge), but clearly elephants played an important part, at least on Antiochus' side. The reference to Ptolemy's cavalry might suggest that there were no elephants on his side, but it would be strange if, when he himself had a large force, he did not send part of it against Antiochus' corps which was potentially 150 strong. At any rate the battle of Panium marked a decisive stage in Syro-Egyptian relations and hereafter the Seleucids retained Coele-Syria. After this if either monarch intended to use his elephants as an instrument of foreign policy, he would have to reckon with Rome: indeed within little more than ten years Antiochus was deploying his elephants against Roman legions.

# CHAPTER VI

# CARTHAGE

We now turn to the western Mediterranean in the period after the Romans had forced Pyrrhus to withdraw from Italy. Thereafter they controlled the whole of the peninsula through their hegemony in a Confederacy which they had skilfully built up around themselves during the previous two centuries. Thus united, Italy with its vast resources in men now became a potential world-power and an obvious rival to Carthage which controlled North Africa, Spain, Corsica, Sardinia and part of Sicily. Hitherto Rome and Carthage had maintained friendly relations, but Pyrrhus is said to have remarked as he left the shores of Sicily, 'What a cockpit we are now leaving for Carthaginian and Roman to fight in.' His alleged prophecy soon came true and the two powers were locked in a struggle which lasted nearly a quarter of a century (264–241 BC) and was fought largely in Sicily or at sea. In the land warfare elephants played a significant part on the Carthaginian side and, thanks to their experience in having had to meet the professional Hellenistic phalanx and elephants of Pyrrhus, the Romans were more prepared to face this new challenge.

The first attested use of elephants in war by the Carthaginians is in 262 BC, but when did they first start to develop this arm? Since a considerable number of years must be allowed for capturing and training a force of elephants, Carthaginian initiative must be put at least two or three decades earlier. But how much earlier? Elephants are not mentioned in the war of Carthage against Agathocles, the tyrant of Syracuse who invaded their territory in 310, though such negative evidence is not conclusive. Three small pieces of evidence might suggest a start before the third century: two coins and a story told by King Juba. One coin is very puzzling. It may be attributed to Panormus (Palermo in Sicily), which was essentially a Phoenician and Punic city, and has borrowed its reverse type of a swan from Camerina, but its obverse type is a female head wearing an elephant-skin, and on grounds of style numismatists would date it to the first half of the fourth century. It *might* suggest an early Carthaginian interest in elephants, though not necessarily in war-elephants, but in view of its uncertain date and origin it would be prudent not to build any theory on it. This type of the elephant-skin head-dress, which does not appear elsewhere until the time of Alexander the Great, brings us to a coin of Agathocles, issued probably during his invasion of Africa: the absence of the title of king shows that it was before 304 (pl. XVIi). The obverse has a young head with elephant-skin, the reverse a figure of Athene, winged and armed, with an owl at her feet. This coin, however, can scarcely suggest that Agathocles had a special interest in elephants or that he might have encountered them in the opposing forces of Carthage. The type is in fact probably borrowed from coins with the head of Alexander with elephant-skin which were minted at Alexandria by Ptolemy Soter (pl. XIIIc), with whom Agathocles soon made an alliance. Granted that his choice of an Alexander-type reflects his own ambition, the use of the elephant-skin head-dress rather than the common one of Alexander as Heracles might suggest that Agathocles had come to conquer a land of elephants, Africa, as Alexander had conquered another, India, the reference thus not being limited to Carthage itself. The reverse type is usually explained by a story that before a battle Agathocles let loose some owls, the bird of Athene, which settled on the shields and helmets of some of his men and appeared to them as an omen of victory. Finally, King Juba II of Mauretania, who lived in the time of Augustus and knew a great deal about elephants (p. 208), said that he himself had captured an elephant bearing a brand that was 400 years old. Whatever may be thought about his credulity and elephants' longevity, the story might imply that the learned Juba thought that the Carthaginians had branded elephants 400 years before his time, but it would be safer not to assume chronological accuracy despite his knowledge of elephants.[84]

Thus there is no reason to believe that the Carthaginians started to use elephants more than a very few decades before 262. Why did they start? We can only speculate. The invasion of Agathocles may have opened their eyes to the vulnerability of their country and thus they decided to strengthen their armed forces with this new weapon which was just beginning to show its value in the Hellenistic world. Although Carthage may not have feared any threat in the immediate future, she may well have wished to keep abreast of developments and to be as fully equipped as the new rulers in the East. That in building up an elephant-corps Carthage had Rome in mind is an idea which would commend itself only to those who can persuade themselves that her long-term policy was hostile to Rome, despite early and more recent treaties. A major factor was probably the elephants of Pyrrhus, which the Carthaginians themselves had faced in the war in Sicily (p. 110): they decided to follow the fashion. Having so decided they went about it on a generous scale: they had 50 or 60 by 263 B C. After losing these to the Romans they had another 100 in 256, and 140 in 255. Whatever may be thought of the figure of 200 attributed to Hasdrubal in Spain and of the stables allegedly for 300 elephants built in the walls of Carthage itself, the Carthaginians obviously, once they had adopted this new arm, decided to use it fully.[85] It is also noteworthy that with their adoption of elephants, the use of chariots was discontinued. These are attested in the war against Agathocles, but they disappear thereafter from the Carthaginian armed forces: they were replaced by elephants and by a greater use of cavalry.

Unlike the Seleucids, who had to seek elephants from far-off India, and the Ptolemies who had to go all the way to Eritrea, the Carthaginians had a more local source in Mauretania and Numidia. As we have seen (p. 62), these elephants were probably of the smaller Forest race and there can be no argument about their appearance since they are depicted in all their might on the Barcid coinage issued in Spain (pl. XXIb, d, f). But capturing and training elephants requires much skill, and the Carthaginians may well have imported Indian mahouts to help them out; whether they went further and even persuaded Ptolemy to allow them a few of his trained animals to act as 'monitors' must remain pure speculation, but commercial contacts with Egypt were not inconsiderable, especially under Ptolemy Philadelphus, since Egypt needed silver from Spain, which Carthage controlled, for her coinage, as well as such goods as horses, sulphur and tin, while Carthage even asked Philadelphus for a loan of 2,000 talents during her first war with Rome. As will be seen (p. 176) later on, Hannibal seems to have secured a very few Indian elephants (although of course his main force consisted of Africans): this could scarcely have been done without the approval of Egypt. Thus a possibility exists that Carthage was able to draw on some professional skill in training her force until natives of North Africa learned to do the job for themselves: as already mentioned, the mahouts continued to be called 'Indians', whatever their nationality.

### THE FIRST PUNIC AND MERCENARIES' WARS

The elephant corps was soon to be used in earnest. In 264 Carthage and Rome quarrelled over the control of the Straits of Messina and Rome sent an army to Sicily to challenge Carthaginian power there. After winning over the support of Hiero of Syracuse, the Romans advanced in 262 against the Punic headquarters at Agrigentum which they subjected to siege for five months. Carthage then sent out reinforcements which included their elephants, to the number of about 50. It is noteworthy that the Carthaginians had not only trained their elephants for war, but had been able to transport them by sea from Africa to Sicily, a passage that many a Roman navy was soon to learn could be anything but calm. When it had arrived in Sicily, after much skirmishing this new force ultimately decided to risk a pitched battle in order to try to relieve their comrades in Agrigentum. After a hard struggle the Romans forced the advanced line of Carthaginian mercenaries back on the elephants and the other divisions behind them, thus throwing them into confusion and gaining the victory. Roman legions, who had faced Pyrrhus' Indians in Italy, now for the first time had faced and defeated Punic African elephants. Polybius' account might suggest that the mercenaries had acted as a buffer and that the legionaries perhaps had only to deal with elephants which were already disordered and in retreat, but according to the pro-Carthaginian historian, Philinus, the elephants had originally numbered 60, of whom eight were killed and 33 wounded: this shows that they were in the thick of the battle and that the Romans had really got to grips with them. The victors managed to round up and capture most of the survivors and thus first gained possession of a considerable number of beasts.[86]

The Romans next encountered Punic elephants in Africa itself. Since they failed to drive the Carthaginians out of Sicily they built up a fleet with extraordinary energy, successfully challenged Carthaginian naval power and tried to end the war by sending an expeditionary force which landed in Africa in 256. The Carthaginians' best hope, according to Polybius, lay in their cavalry and elephants, but they foolishly took up a position on hilly ground, thus abandoning the plains where their elephants would have best served them. Realizing this, the Roman commander Regulus attacked at once and routed the enemy, though 'when they reached the level ground the elephants and cavalry made good their retreat without loss'. Thus Regulus gained Tunis and command of the open country.[87] Encouraged by his success, he refused to negotiate on terms which could be accepted by the Carthaginians, who spent the winter training their army under the guidance of a professional mercenary captain from Sparta, named Xanthippus. He urged reliance on the elephants and cavalry, and a battle in the plains. Since he now had 100 elephants, the Carthaginian hunters must have been very busy in the previous years in their efforts to make good the loss suffered at Agrigentum. In the battle Xanthippus drew them up in a single line in front of his whole army, which consisted of cavalry and mercenaries on the wings and a phalanx of Carthaginian citizen-soldiers in the centre: only in time of crisis did the citizens themselves take up arms. Fearing the elephants, the Romans placed light-armed troops in front of their main line which they made deeper and shorter than usual. Polybius curiously regards this as a correct method of facing elephants, but the result hardly confirms his view: Scipio Africanus was later to demonstrate the correct procedure at Zama (p. 168 f.). The Roman cavalry was on their wings. Xanthippus ordered his elephants to advance to break the Roman line, and his cavalry to outflank their opponents. The Roman line moved forward, but their cavalry was soon driven off by the superior numbers of the enemy. The left section (one legion?) of the Roman line advanced, inclining to the left to avoid the elephants, and fell on the mercenaries on the enemy right (those commanded by Xanthippus?) and routed them. The rest of the Roman line was less successful: the front ranks were mangled by the elephants, but of the rear ranks some were compelled to turn round to face the attack of the victorious Carthaginian cavalry, while others who forced their way through the line of the elephants were brought up face to face with the Carthaginian phalanx, which had not yet gone into action, and were destroyed. Many that survived were trampled by the beasts or shot down by the cavalry, while those that fled were caught on the level plain by horse or elephant. Few of the survivors, which included Regulus (soon to become a Roman legend), would have agreed that the Romans had solved the problem of how elephants should be faced in battle. On the other hand, the new Carthaginian emphasis on elephants and cavalry had proved strikingly effective.[88]

Encouraged by their expulsion of the Roman expeditionary force and by the subsequent wreck of a large Roman fleet in a storm, the Carthaginians pressed on with the war in Sicily, and sent Hasdrubal, son of Hanno, there with reinforcements which included 140 elephants. He got these across safely to Lilybaeum, where he busied himself drilling his elephants and other forces. Meantime, the Romans built another fleet and managed to capture Panormus. Their next task was to move against the towns that the Carthaginians still held in the western end of the island, but with reports of Regulus' disaster ringing in their ears they were reluctant to face the enemy on level ground 'so much did they dread a charge of the elephants'. Thus for two or three years something of a lull followed until Hasdrubal in 250 took the initiative by marching against Panormus and ravaging the fertile plain around it. The Roman consul, Caecilius Metellus, in the city lay low and enticed Hasdrubal over a river up to a trench which he had had dug near the city wall. In front of the trench Metellus stationed some light-armed troops with an extra supply of missiles to deal with the elephants. Another light-armed detachment advanced to harass the elephants, while he held some troops ready at the gate which faced the enemy's left. The riders on the elephants, eager to show their prowess, drove the enemy in front of them to the trench but here the elephants met with showers of missiles from the light-armed men at the trench and from archers on the wall. Maddened by their wounds, they soon turned back and threw their own lines into disorder. Metellus then launched a successful attack on the enemy's flank. Of the elephants he captured ten with their mahouts and after the battle he managed to round up all the rest which had thrown their riders. This he did, according to the Livian tradition, by promising freedom to any prisoners who brought them in. These included the mahouts (thus Zonaras) or Numidians (Eutropius), who may be one and the same, since native Numidians may well have learnt by now to become mahouts.[89]

Some twenty-five years earlier Curius had probably displayed a few of Pyrrhus' captured Indian elephants to the Roman people:

Metellus now intended to show them his much larger haul of Africans. Even though he had secured some of the mahouts, transport across the Straits of Messina presented difficulties. Since he lacked adequate shipping he constructed a raft, made up of large jars which were fastened in such a way that they could not break apart or clash; this framework was then covered with planks; earth and brushwood was placed on top, so that the raft looked like a farmyard. On this the elephants, not knowing they were on water, were ferried across; we are not told how many at a time. Pliny (NH. VIII, 17) gives different versions of their ultimate fate. According to an Augustan scholar, Verrius Flaccus, the Romans decided not to keep them or give them to any king (did Verrius have Hiero of Syracuse in mind?), and so they put them to fight in the Circus until they were killed by javelins. The annalist L. Piso, on the other hand, said that in order to encourage contempt for them, they were driven round the Circus by attendants carrying spears with a button on the point. Pliny adds that the authorities who did not think that they were killed, failed to say what was done with them. One thing is clear: the Romans apparently decided that they provided too double-edged a weapon for adoption in their own army. Thus the people of Rome became more familiar with the appearance of elephants, thanks to the victory of Metellus, whose descendants kept his exploit alive: many of the younger members of the gens Caecilia when they became mint-masters, placed an elephant on the coins that they issued, and the elephant became a kind of family badge (pl. XXIV, a–c).[90]

The war dragged on slowly while the Romans tried to take the two surviving Carthaginian strongholds in western Sicily. Hamilcar Barca infused some fresh life into the struggle when he was sent out in 247, but he is not said to have been given any elephants. Finally, by raising a new fleet and defeating the Punic navy, Rome emerged triumphant in 242. But the troubles of Carthage were far from over. A vast number of her mercenaries, whose pay was in arrears, broke into open revolt and this so-called Truceless War spread throughout Carthaginian territory. They advanced on Tunis and started to besiege Utica and Hippo Diarrhytus, thus cutting off Carthage from its hinterland. The Carthaginians entrusted the command to Hanno, the 'Great', who tried to relieve Utica with a force that included 100 elephants: after their loss of elephants in Sicily they had evidently been busy raising a fresh corps. His elephants stormed into the enemy's entrenched camp. The survivors fled to a strong hill position, and finding Hanno off guard they made a successful counter-attack which nullified the victory that his elephants had gained for him. Further ill-success led the Carthaginians to appoint Hamilcar Barca as commander-in-chief, with a force that included 70 elephants, although Hanno continued to operate separately. Hamilcar opened up communications again with the interior by forcing the river Bagradas which was held by the mercenary leader Spendius. Choosing a moment when a wind lowered the water, he managed by night to cross some marshy ground near the mouth of the river (here his elephants would be useful for transport) and marched down on the far side, with the elephants in front, then the cavalry and light-armed troops, and lastly the heavy infantry. By a feigned withdrawal he drew the enemy on and then swung his forces back into line (the manoeuvre is not quite plain in Polybius' account). He routed the enemy in a mêlée into which at one point his elephants charged. On the advice of his fellow-commander Mathos, Spendius now kept to higher ground to avoid the Carthaginian cavalry and elephants and managed to manoeuvre Hamilcar into a dangerous position. However, Hamilcar fought his way out in another battle, in which the elephants acquitted themselves well. The mercenaries had repeatedly shown appalling cruelty to all captives, and Hamilcar now replied in kind: men captured in battle were executed on the spot, while prisoners who were later brought in were thrown to the elephants to be trampled to death. After more bitter fighting Hamilcar managed to secure the persons of Spendius and some of his officers and to surround his force of 40,000 men with his own elephants and entire army, thus destroying them to a man. Mathos' defeat was not long delayed. This war, which according to Polybius 'far surpassed any that I ever heard of for cruelty and inhumanity', had been a life and death struggle for Carthage and not least among the factors that finally tilted the military balance in her favour was her possession of elephants, while the mercenaries had none. If both sides had been thus equipped the bitter struggle might have been more prolonged and the issue even more in doubt.

The troubles of Carthage were not ended with the Mercenaries' War, since in 238 in a moment of somewhat unpremeditated bullying the Romans seized control of Sardinia from her, thus embittering relations which seemed just to be healing after the First Punic War. Having lost both Sicily and Sardinia, the Carthaginians decided to regain control of Spain. Thither Hamilcar Barca was sent with his young son Hannibal in 237 with a force that apparently included 100 elephants. His purpose was to build up Carthaginian military and economic strength by conquest in order to compensate for their losses, but not necessarily at this stage with a view to a war of revenge against Rome: Carthage had been a great state and she naturally wished to remain one, with the mineral wealth and manpower of Spain in her hands. Hamilcar crossed over by the Straits of Gibraltar: if he had marched there from Carthage rather than sailed along the coast, the journey through Numidia and Mauretania would have been a long trudge for his elephants, unless he picked up some en route. In any case his progress should have impressed the natives of North Africa, but not sufficiently, since after he had started his campaigns in Spain he had to send his son-in-law Hasdrubal back to deal with trouble among the Numidians. An anecdote recorded by Frontinus (*Strat.* iv, 7.18) but undated, may refer to this episode: a certain Hasdrubal, finding the Numidians preparing to resist, tricked them by saying that he had come to capture elephants and promised to pay what they demanded; having thus misled them, he attacked and defeated them. As later Hamilcar's son-in-law had 200 elephants in Spain, the story may well apply to this man. Meantime, Hamilcar had conquered southern and south-eastern Spain and had built a dominating fortress named 'White Citadel' (Acra Leuce) at modern Alicante. In the winter of 229–228 he left his elephants and part of his army there while he besieged the town of Helice (=Elche), but when the chieftain of the Orissi (Oretani) came to its help, Hamilcar was routed and forced to flee: in crossing a large river he was drowned (Diodorus, xxv, 10–11).

He was succeeded not by one of his two sons, Hannibal or Hasdrubal, but by the other Hasdrubal, his son-in-law, who had arrived too late with more than 100 elephants in an attempt to save him. Hasdrubal now commanded an army of 50,000 infantry,

6,000 cavalry and, it is said, 200 elephants, but after defeating the Orissi he achieved more by diplomacy than force. He established a new base at New Carthage (modern Cartagena), and reached an agreement with the Romans, who showed interest as they saw the growing extent of his conquests: by this 'Ebro treaty' Hasdrubal agreed not to cross the Ebro with his armed forces, although the Roman side of the bargain is less clear. When in 221 he was assassinated by a Celt, he was succeeded by Hannibal, now twenty-five years old, who reverted to a more aggressive policy. He defeated the Olcades near the Upper Guadiana and in the next year attacked the Vaccaei and captured Salamanca, but on his return journey across central Spain he was attacked by hostile tribes near Toledo and faced what Polybius regarded as an extremely hazardous position. Forced to fight he crossed the Tagus and then swung back to face the enemy as they came over. With the help of the river and of his elephants, of which he had 40, he was victorious. As the Spaniards tried to cross, his cavalry caught some in the river itself, while his elephants patrolled the bank and dealt with others as they endeavoured to struggle out. He then crossed the river himself and routed the whole surviving force.[91] Thus all Spain south of the Ebro was now in his hands, except the city of Saguntum, which was Rome's ally. Nevertheless he besieged it and, since Rome sent protests but no physical help, Saguntum fell to him late in 219. This provoked the Second Punic War which was formally declared in the following spring, while Hannibal prepared his army for the long march against Rome.

Since Hannibal had been taken to Spain as a lad, he had now enjoyed close contact with an army which had included an elephant-corps for the better part of twenty years. Thus in deciding to take elephants with him on the long and arduous journey over the Alps he was clearly acting in the light of his knowledge of their behaviour. He may also have realized from his reading of Hellenistic history that elephants were most effective the first time they were hurled against troops that were unused to them, and he will have realized that most of the legionaries that would face him in Italy belonged to a younger generation than that which had faced Punic elephants in the First War. Polybius records that he left 21 with his brother Hasdrubal in Spain, while he apparently took with him 37; at any rate this was the number he had when he reached the Rhone. How the large herd of 200 which the other

Hasdrubal is said to have commanded some ten years earlier had diminished to this extent is unknown (the balance could have been included among the troops that he sent back to North Africa as a guard and a reserve, but this is not mentioned in any source). At any rate the role of the elephants had been widely advertised by the Barcids in Spain with the fine series of silver coins that depicted the beast (pls XXIb, d, f). The issue was possibly started by the earlier Hasdrubal, but more probably in 221 when Hannibal succeeded and a new regime commenced. The obverse bears the head of Melkart-Heracles, either bearded or unbearded, with his club, but it is a widely accepted conjecture that these two heads bear the likenesses of Hamilcar and Hannibal respectively. On the reverse of one is an elephant and rider, with cloak and goad; on the other the elephant is barebacked. Minted at New Carthage, this splendid series not only provides us with the best contemporary portrait of Hannibal's elephants (and indeed of the physical features of the smaller Forest elephant), but it also reminded his troops, for whose pay it was probably designed, that this arm of service was not the least. A second series has a slightly more aggressive elephant on the reverse, while the obverse shows a bare head, with laureate diadem. It is tempting to identify this portrait with Hasdrubal Barca, despite some difficulties of provenance; they are flatter and more Punic in appearance than the first series and were perhaps minted by him in Gades (Cadiz) later, or indeed immediately after the departure of his brother Hannibal in order to pay his troops and remind them that they still had elephants in Spain. An interesting aftermath comes from the little town of Lascuta which lay somewhere in the jurisdiction of Gades: it issued a bronze coinage, with the head of Heracles, this time with lionskin, and a crude elephant on the reverse (pl. XXIIa). Why one town thus commemorated the elephants can only be surmised: could it have been the base of Hasdrubal's elephant-corps?[92]

The epic story of Hannibal's march from New Carthage across the Rhone and over the Alps to northern Italy has often been told: here we are concerned mainly with two episodes, those at the Rhone and at the crucial Alpine pass, and even here we must leave on one side numerous problems, topographical and otherwise.[93] On reaching the Rhone Hannibal found his crossing contested by the Gauls on the further bank, but by sending a detachment to cross the river upstream secretly and then to sweep down on the unsuspecting enemy while he himself was trying to get his main forces across, he achieved a spectacular success. But he still had to transport the elephants across and this became urgent when he learnt that a Roman army was about to advance against him. This force was led by P. Scipio who, on the declaration of war, had been ordered to take an army to Spain to stop Hannibal there; however, he had been delayed and had landed in southern Gaul *en route* where he heard that Hannibal had in fact not only left Spain but was crossing the Rhone some three-days' march away to his north. Hannibal, equally surprised by Scipio's presence, made haste to send his main infantry off on their northward march along the river, while he stayed with his cavalry to get the elephants across. He had already been preparing for this by making a large number of rafts. Two, about 50 ft wide, were bound together and placed on the river bank; others were joined to these, projecting into the river at right angles and secured on their northern side by ropes tied to trees on the bank. At the end of this 200 ft projecting pier two specially well-made rafts were tied; they had tow-lines to several rowing boats which, when the ropes which moored the rafts to the pier were cut, could tow the rafts across the rest of the river. Deep soil was laid on all the rafts and the elephants were induced to walk along these by sending the females in the lead. But when they reached the two moored rafts, which were then towed off by the rowing boats, the elephants panicked: while some were too frightened to move, others threw themselves into the midst of the river and saved themselves by walking on the river bed and using their trunks to breath through; however, their mahouts were drowned. Thus all 37 elephants safely reached the further shore and Hannibal could now bring them and his cavalry to join the infantry which was marching north.

Such is Polybius' account. It is followed by Livy, with the slight variation that the elephants finally scrambled ashore rather than used the snorkel method; either is acceptable on physical grounds. Livy also records another version, although he is not inclined to accept it: when the elephants were assembled on the bank, a mahout deliberately annoyed his beast and then plunged into the water, followed by it and the rest of the herd; they were all swept across by the current. Despite the elaborateness of the method, Polybius' version must be accepted, since it is not likely to have been invented *ex nihilo*, and we may assume that Hannibal judged that the current would not have allowed the elephants just to swim or drift across. He must have valued his beasts highly to have expended so much effort in face of Scipio's imminent attack. Finally, it is interesting to note a modern parallel of transporting Burmese elephants across the Irrawaddy. Col. Williams writes (*Elephant Bill*, 126f.), 'In crossing a wide river, where the elephant has to swim a thousand yards or so, he may drift as much as four hundred yards downstream. He does not make strenuous effort to make the crossing where the river is narrowest, or to reach a particular point on the opposite bank. Although elephants are such good swimmers, they are not infrequently drowned, a fact which I can only put down to heart failure. . . . When elephants have to be moved long distances by water, they are frequently taken on rafts, or on river barges, which are towed alongside a paddle-steamer. Getting the elephants on to such flats needs endless patience. First one has to find a leader which the other beasts will follow, and then one has to camouflage the gangway with tall grasses, or palms, on either side of it to a height of ten or twelve feet.' Col. Williams provides a picture of such a gangway (pl. IIIa).

In the event, Hannibal got away just in time, and Scipio decided to leave him to his fate in the Alps and to send his own army on to Spain, as originally instructed by the Senate, in order to try to defeat the Carthaginian armies that were still there as well as to deny Hannibal the possibility of drawing supplies or reinforcements from the peninsula. Meantime, Hannibal marched up the Rhone valley and then swung along the Isère towards the Alps. Despite Polybius' discussions with survivors and a personal visit to verify the geography, his account has left the door wide open and provoked countless attempts to identify the pass by which Hannibal finally reached northern Italy. Wherever it was, his exploit has stirred the imagination of mankind.[94] His difficulties arose less from the actual route than from the extreme hostility of the Alpine tribes, combined with the fact that the descent was steeper than he had anticipated and was rendered even more perilous than usual by a fall of light snow on top of the existing packed snow which robbed man and beast of any secure foothold; to this was added a shortage of food and fodder. On the fate of the elephants we may turn to the sober, though graphic, account by Polybius, who first mentions them when the army was reaching the summit (III, 53.8): 'the elephants were of the greatest service to him; the enemy never dared to approach that part of the column where they were placed, being terrified at the strangeness of their appearance'. Near the beginning of the descent a landslide had made the path too narrow for the elephants or pack animals to pass. After three days of gruelling work a track was made and Hannibal got the elephants across 'though in a wretched condition from hunger'. On the whole the elephants seem to have been useful both as a deterrent and (we may guess) in helping to move rocks to clear the track, whereas the horses on one occasion proved very difficult: some wounded horses panicked and caused havoc both among the men and the pack-animals in the crowded pass with its precipitous sides. Nevertheless, despite all the suffering, Hannibal finally reached the plains of northern Italy: although his army was reduced after the terrible casualties to 26,000 men, not one of his 37 elephants is recorded as having been lost.

While Hannibal rested his exhausted troops the Romans hastily built up an army to challenge him: P. Scipio organized a force in Etruria, while his consular colleague, Ti. Sempronius, was hurriedly recalled from Sicily, where he had been planning for a possible attack against Carthage itself. After using the tributaries of the river Po to fight delaying actions, Scipio was joined by Sempronius and one late December day, in terrible conditions of cold and snow, they were provoked to face the enemy.[95] Hannibal, who was weaker in infantry, but stronger in cavalry, planned an ambush: he placed his younger brother Mago with a force of infantry and cavalry in a shrub-covered gulley which he hoped would be behind the Roman lines when battle was joined (fig. 17). Behind a covering of light-armed troops he drew up his infantry of Spaniards, Gauls and Africans in a single line (as opposed to the Romans who used their normal formation of three lines: *hastati, principes* and *triarii*, from front to rear), with his cavalry on the wings. He placed his elephants in front of the wings of his *infantry* (not in front of, or on the flank of, his cavalry).[96] The Romans had their cavalry on their wings.

Early one morning, before they had eaten, the Romans waded through the icy waters of the Trebia, a tributary of the Po, and battle was joined. Their cavalry was quickly beaten by the Carthaginian horse: thus the flanks of their infantry line was exposed to harassing attacks by Carthaginian light troops. Then the main infantry lines clashed, and the wings of the Roman line had to face

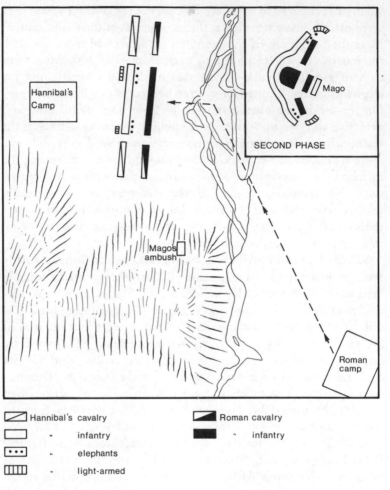

Fig. 17. Battle of the Trebia

not only the light troops but also the elephants and the infantry behind them. They were pushed back, only to find Mago in their rear: he had successfully eluded notice and now rushed out of concealment, while before very long the victorious Carthaginian cavalry returned from their pursuit of the Roman horse. Thus, while the rear ranks of the Roman line (the *triarii*) had to cope with attacks from behind, the central part of the two front lines (*hastati* and *principes*) managed to hack their way through the middle of the enemy line which comprised Celtic troops; then seeing their

160

XVII: *a.* Lion fighting with an elephant. Mosaic in the Hormisdas Palace, Istanbul.
*b.* Elephant fighting a bull. Mosaic from the Aventine, Rome.

XVIII: Mosaics paved the colonnade in the Foro delle Corporazioni at Ostia and illustrated the nature of the business pursued in each office. This African elephant indicates that the merchant traded in elephants or ivory.

XIX: *a*. This marble elephant stood on one of the main streets in Lepcis Magna in Tripolitania and illustrates the part played by the city in the export trade in elephants. *b*. Elephant being embarked for shipping to Italy. A scene from the 'Great Hunt' mosaic at Piazza Armerina in Sicily; the island formed a stepping-stone for the trade between Africa and Italy.

XX: *a*. Sculptured relief on a sarcophagus,
depicting the triumphant return of the god
Dionysus from India on an elephant. *b*. Ivory
diptych showing an emperor (Julian, or possibly
Antoninus Pius) in an elephant quadriga.
*c*. Wall-painting of Venus in a boat drawn by
four African elephants at the entrance of a shop
in the via dell'Abbondanza at Pompeii. The
shop-owner, Verecundus, was engaged in the
textile industry (a manufacturer of felt and a
tailor or draper) and advertised his devotion to
the city's patron-goddess.

own wings (i.e. the ends of the *infantry* line) were defeated, they pushed on to safety and ultimately reached the Latin colony of Placentia (Piacenza). Of the rest the greater part were killed by the elephants and cavalry, but some managed to escape and also reached Placentia. The loss of elephants, either in the battle or because of subsequent exposure to rain, snow and cold, is given variously. Polybius does not record any direct battle casualties, but says that all the elephants except one perished from cold, as did many men and horses. Livy, on the other hand, says that almost all (*prope omnes*) perished but later when Hannibal was crossing the Apennines in arctic conditions he lost the seven elephants which survived Trebia and that this left him with only one sole survivor.

In the spring of 217 Hannibal faced the task of crossing the barrier of the Apennines when the passes were free from snow. In marshes caused by the flooding of the Arno his troops suffered greatly, but he got them through in four days. He himself rode on the only surviving elephant, suffering intensely from opthalmia from which he lost the sight of one eye. The romantic figure of this great leader, mounted on his elephant and encouraging his men through extreme hardships, caught the imagination of later generations: 'cum Gaetula ducem portaret belua luscum' ('when the one-eyed leader was riding on a Gaetulian beast'; Juvenal, x, 158). Once across, Hannibal added the second and third great victories at Trasimene and Cannae to his first at the Trebia, but these he had to fight without elephants. In fact Trebia was the only set-piece battle in Italy in which he used them; although he received some reinforcements, they were not numerous, as we shall see, and in any case the Romans were then adopting Fabian tactics and did not allow him another formal engagement on the scale of his first three victories.

After the toll taken by the Alps and the losses suffered in three major battles, Hannibal badly needed reinforcements, but two barriers lay across their path. The sea-route from North Africa was blocked by the Roman navy which now dominated the western Mediterranean, and the Carthaginian forces that had been left in Spain found the land route to Italy controlled by the army of P. and Cn. Scipio who managed to hold the line of the Ebro. In Italy, when Hannibal found that his shattering victory at Cannae did not force the Romans to surrender, he had to fight on. The greatest by-product of his victory was the revolt of Capua, the second largest city in Italy, to his side; this was followed by some of the smaller cities in Campania, as Atella and Calatia. He now tried to win over the others, but as he could gain none of the ports, as Neapolis or Cumae, he could not receive any reinforcements from Carthage, even if they could dodge the Roman fleet. When his brother Mago arrived in Carthage to report the victory at Cannae, the Senate there decided to send reinforcements to him in Italy, including 40 elephants, but when in the next spring (215) Mago was about to try to take 20 elephants across to south Italy, they had to be diverted to Spain where the need was greater. However, later on, Bomilcar managed to land at Locri with some elephants (the number is not given) and after eluding the Roman commander, Appius Claudius, he joined Hanno among the Brutii. Meantime, Hannibal had besieged Casilinum (modern Capua) which he ultimately took, though not with the help of the elephants with which Livy credits him: this is an annalistic invention, since no reinforcements had reached Hannibal in 216. However, when the help did come, he moved against Nola, where he was challenged by Marcellus. The annalistic tradition describes an important battle in which the victorious Marcellus captured 2 and killed 4 of Hannibal's elephants. Since it was now Roman policy, as conceived by Fabius Maximus Cunctator, to avoid pitched battles, Marcellus' alleged success must be exaggerated if not entirely invented. On the other hand, sporadic fighting no doubt took place in which it is not impossible that six elephants were lost.[97]

As the war dragged on in Italy the Romans were able by 212 to try to reduce the rebel city of Capua. They surrounded it with a circle of earthworks, but since they feared an attack from Hannibal they also constructed an outward-facing ring to protect themselves. In 211, as the siege continued, Hannibal advanced in an attempt to relieve the city. Livy gives two accounts of the subsequent fighting: a large-scale battle, which he probably derived from the unreliable annalist Valerius Antias, and a second more sober account, which probably comes from the monograph on the Second Punic War written by Coelius Antipater. In the first account Hannibal arrived with 33 elephants; three of these with a cohort of Spaniards attacked the Roman *vallum*, but were killed by a Roman counterattack and their bodies, falling into the ditch, provided a bridge for the attackers. This, apart perhaps from the 33 elephants, does not seem unreasonable, but the casualty figures which Livy records are highly inflated. The second account, which Livy found 'in other authorities' (*apud alios*), describes a battle on a much smaller scale, but says that the elephants (not numbered) broke into the Roman camp, where they caused much confusion until driven out by the use of fire. Of the fighting at Capua we have a brief but fragmentary description by Polybius, but in it elephants are not mentioned at all. Because of this some modern historians, as G. De Sanctis, reject all that Livy has to say about elephants, although he admits that some of the details preserved by Livy and not recorded by Polybius may be reliable. But since the figure of three elephants is so modest and since (if it once admitted, as it is by De Sanctis, that Hannibal had received some fresh elephants) he would surely have tried to make some use of them sometime, it may not strain credulity to suppose that he used them in his desperate attempt to relieve his ally Capua.[98] But there is another piece of evidence to be thrown into the balance on the side of the elephants. While Capua and Atella were in a state of rebellion from Rome and in Hannibal's control, they issued coins bearing the figure of an African elephant, Capua in silver, Atella in bronze (pls XXIIf, g). Whether this was done at his suggestion or merely in his honour, the circulation of these pieces must have advertised and underlined the importance of his fresh supply of elephants. With hopes thus aroused, not to have used them at all would have been an anticlimax. Thus although Livy's sources may have exaggerated their role, elephants are likely to have figured in the struggle around the second greatest city in Italy.[99]

Since he could not break the Roman stranglehold on Capua by direct means Hannibal tried an indirect method; by a desperate throw he decided to march on Rome itself, thereby hoping to draw off the Roman armies from Capua. His gamble failed and after reaching the very gates of Rome he was forced to withdraw. The route he had taken to Rome was probably a wide sweeping advance through Samnium and the territory of Alba Fucens to Amiternum; thence westwards to Reate and then south to cross the Anio and reach Rome. A monument to this march may well survive at Alba, where recently two roughly carved stone elephants have been excavated; they are archaic-looking and of local manufacture, while their large ears proclaim them to be Africans and not Indians (pl. IXa). Thus they cannot have reference to Pyrrhus, but appear to be relevant to Hannibal's march on Rome and to suggest that he took some elephants with him. This may seem surprising in view of his need for speed and surprise (but then so also does the route he took), yet they might well add to the terror which his sudden appearance outside Rome would provoke.[100]

Left to its fate, Capua fell and Hannibal's grip on Italy increasingly contracted: soon he was virtually confined to the south where he fought essentially on the defensive. In 210 Marcellus had a successful skirmish with him at Numistro near Venusia, when Hannibal's 'elephants were driven into battle after the conflict had begun', while in the next year the two generals clashed again. Livy gives a long account of the fighting, which he derived from a late annalistic source, although what he says about the elephants might enshrine a reliable tradition. Again, as in 210, they were thrown into battle late and were causing much destruction when a military tribune, named Gaius Decimus Flavus, seized a standard and led the maniple to which it belonged close up to a crowd of elephants and showered them with javelins; the injured and uninjured alike quickly retreated against their own men, and in all five were killed. Plutarch gives an even more dramatic touch: Flavus struck the leading beast with the butt-end of the Roman standard. In 207 Hannibal faced the consul Claudius Nero near Grumentum in a disorderly battle in which he did not use his elephants, but the Romans managed to kill four and capture two.[101] Thus Hannibal's forces were gradually whittled down and no reinforcements had reached him for many years, though he had good reason to hope that the position would soon be changed: his brother Hasdrubal had at last managed to break through the Roman forces holding Spain and was now on his way to Italy. The brothers no doubt hoped to meet in central Italy, but as the engagement at Grumentum showed, Hannibal would find an advance difficult to achieve. Hasdrubal reached the Po valley by the late spring of 207 and advanced southwards. Then misfortune struck. His despatches to Hannibal fell into Roman hands and Claudius Nero took a momentous decision. Knowing that Hannibal had no accurate knowledge of Hasdrubal's immediate intentions, he decided to leave a covering force in the south, while he himself led the rest of his troops by a forced march up Italy to join his consular colleague, Livius Salinator, to face Hasdrubal in the north.

The two consuls met Hasdrubal in the valley of the Metaurus. His intentions and movements, much debated, need not concern us here. He was forced to fight: he drew up a deep and narrow line, with his Gauls on his left opposite Claudius Nero and the rest of his force deeply massed on his right with his ten elephants (Appian attributes 15 to him) in front. He was clearly risking everything on the success of his right which he himself led and which faced Livius Salinator. When battle had been joined, Nero found that the nature of the ground, as Hasdrubal had hoped, prevented him trying to outflank the enemy's left (or perhaps Polybius means that he could not outflank the left flank of the advancing enemy's right, i.e. strike in the gap between the Gauls on the left and Hasdrubal's own section). He therefore detached some men from the rear of his own right wing and led them behind the Roman lines to support Livius by attacking Hasdrubal's right flank. The elephants, tormented by missiles, affected both sides equally. Six had to be killed by their own riders, while the other four, who had broken through the Roman ranks and had lost their mahouts, were later captured. Livy records that the method of killing them when they got out of hand was to drive a chisel down between the ears with a mallet and that this practice had been introduced by Hasdrubal himself. Once again the unpredictability of elephants in battle had been demonstrated and these ten beasts which had marched all the long way from Spain, through the Pyrennees and Alps, deserved a better fate. They had not been able to save the day for their master, who himself was killed in battle and thus Hannibal's hopes of receiving help from his brother were shattered.[102]

While Hannibal had seen victory in Italy gradually slipping from his grasp as the years had gone by, the war had been fought in many other theatres as well: in Spain, Sicily, Sardinia, and Greece, but we hear of the use of elephants only in the first two areas. In Sicily the Romans had had to face the revolt of Syracuse in 215; a Carthaginian commander, Himilco, was sent in the next year to Sicily with a force that included 12 elephants. Syracuse had to stand a bitter siege by Marcellus and ultimately fell to the Romans in 212. Thereafter Marcellus defeated the Carthaginians near Agrigentum and captured eight elephants, which later graced his ovation procession, a minor form of triumph.[103] The elephants used by the Carthaginians in their struggle in Spain were more numerous. When Hannibal marched from Spain in 218 he had left 21 there with his brother Hasdrubal (p. 155), while Hanno had been sent with 30 more in 215 (p. 162). These Carthaginian forces had to face the armies of P. and Cn. Scipio who held the line of the river Ebro, which Hasdrubal made an all out attempt to force: this thrust was repelled at the battle of Ibera. The part played by the elephants in the fighting is not mentioned, but Livy records that when the Moorish and Numidian cavalry saw their own centre collapsing, they retreated driving the elephants in front of them. After this success the Scipios could advance south over the Ebro, where they rescued Iliturgi in Catalonia from a Carthaginian siege and in the process are said to have killed five and captured seven elephants. This account is not unreasonable, although it is embedded in some unreliable annalistic material in Livy's narrative. However, the alleged fighting around Munda, in which the Carthaginians are said to have lost first 39 elephants killed, and then three more with eight captured must be rejected.[104] But the successes of the Scipios were soon ended: in 211 both brothers were defeated and killed, and the Carthaginians again swept forward to the Ebro.

The fortunes of war in Spain again changed when the young Publius Scipio (later Africanus) was sent there and captured the main enemy base at New Carthage (209 BC). In the next year Hasdrubal decided once again to force his way out of Spain and join his brother Hannibal in Italy, while leaving two other Carthaginian armies to hold Spain. He met Scipio at Baecula, but had decided to break off the engagement if it began to go against him. This in fact happened: when by brilliant outflanking tactics Scipio was threatening to surround his force, Hasdrubal sacrificed some of his lesser troops and by a masterly withdrawal retired with half or three-quarters of his army, together with his money-chest and elephants. Polybius makes no reference to the elephants actually being involved in the battle, but implies that they were kept back for a possible withdrawal, as does Livy in one passage, though another suggests that they did see some action; he says that the Romans would never have advanced over such unfavourable ground 'if the ranks had stood unbroken with the elephants placed in front of the standards'. Since both writers go back to the same source, it is possible that Polybius has shortened his account or even that Hasdrubal divided his elephants, placing some in the battle-line and others in the rear. At any rate they seem to have had little effect on the result and he saved them to fight another day: that day proved to be the disastrous engagement on the Metaurus when at the last moment he failed to fight his way through to Hannibal.[105]

In the following year Hanno brought reinforcements to the armies left in Spain: these could have included some elephants, since in 206 the commander Hasdrubal, son of Gisgo, had 32. This Hasdrubal, who learnt of the death of Hasdrubal Barca at Metaurus, determined to risk all on a single battle and met Scipio at Ilipa, not very far from Seville. In this engagement Scipio used highly sophisticated outflanking tactics, but these and the general course of the fight cannot be described here. The elephants, placed in front of the two wings, when the Roman outflanking movement began, became frightened and stampeded, doing as much harm to their own side as to the Romans. They may well in fact provide the answer to one of the unsolved problems of the battle, namely what happened to the Carthaginian cavalry and why did it not try to prevent the Roman outflanking move? Polybius is silent, though when the elephants stampeded back they may have confused not only Hasdrubal's Spanish infantry in the centre but also the cavalry, which was thus thrown into confusion at the first shock, and thus the Roman cavalry in its outflanking movement had no difficulty in beating them off the field. If so, the elephants made a significant contribution to victory, but to the wrong side. Ilipa was decisive: Carthaginian power in Spain was shattered and the peninsula passed into the control of the Romans who were to dominate it for centuries.[106]

Thus the net was closing more tightly around Hannibal in Italy, but the Carthaginians made one final attempt to get help through to him. His brother Mago had managed to escape from the debacle in Spain and sailed to Liguria where he captured Genoa and built up a considerable force which was strengthened by the arrival of further help direct from Carthage: this included seven elephants (their long sea journey is likely to have been adventurous). However, he was not ready to invade Italy for two more years so that the Romans had time to prepare for this new attack by the third of the Barca brothers. He was finally defeated in a pitched battle in the Po valley. Of this Livy gives a detailed description, though as it derives from Valerius Antias, little faith can be placed in any detail. For what it is worth, Livy tells how Mago's elephants checked the attack of the Roman cavalry and prevented his line breaking, but later were driven back by the *hastati* of the Eleventh Legion who killed four of them; however, in the battle as a whole, the elephants had not done badly since they had trampled to death twenty-two sons of nobles serving in the cavalry (*equites illustres*). Mago was wounded and died soon afterwards (203).[107]

Before Mago's last desperate attempt to help Hannibal, the war had already moved to North Africa. Despite opposition from Fabius Maximus, Scipio had carried through his plan for an invasion of the Carthaginian homeland in order to force Hannibal to evacuate Italy and try to save Carthage. When news of Scipio's intention reached Carthage, Hasdrubal, the son of Gisgo, who had succeeded in returning home after Ilipa, was ordered to organize an elephant-hunt (thus incidentally showing that there were still plenty of wild elephants to be captured not so very far from Carthage).[108] In 204 Scipio's expeditionary force gained a footing in Africa not very far from Carthage itself and in the following spring he made a brilliant night attack on the joint camps of Hasdrubal and his Numidian ally, Syphax. The camps were burned, and according to Livy (Polybius' account breaks off just before the end) they lost eight elephants through fire and sword, while the Romans captured six more; these may well have included some of those that Hasdrubal had recently secured on his hunting expedition. Once again Scipio struck like lightning: while Hasdrubal was mustering a new force at the Great Plains (Campi Magni) in the interior of the country Scipio swooped on him and inflicted a decisive defeat, in which elephants do not appear to have played any part.

Carthage was desperate and Hannibal was recalled from Italy to try to save his homeland. Two of the greatest generals of antiquity soon met on the field of Zama. Despite the interest of a battle which determined world history, we must confine consideration to the role of the elephants, and this can be done the more easily since their part was limited to the early part of the encounter. Hannibal had 80 elephants and had posted them together with light-armed troops in front of his central infantry line, probably hoping to overwhelm the enemy by successive waves of attack: first the elephants, then his front line of mercenaries, next his second line of native Libyans and Carthaginians, and lastly, at a greater distance from the others, his third line comprising the Old Guard, his veterans from Italy. Scipio thwarted the first threat, that of the elephants, by a simple device. The normal Roman order of battle was that each of the three lines (the *hastati*, *principes* and *triarii*) were divided up into ten maniples of 120 men each (those of the

168

*triarii* had only 60 men). Between the maniples were intervals (perhaps as broad as the front of each maniple), and the three lines were so drawn up that the maniples of the second line covered the gaps of the first, and those of the third those of the second, i.e. a diamond-shaped formation. Scipio on this occasion drew up the maniples of each of the three lines directly behind each other, thus leaving large lanes running through the whole formation from front to rear. The intervals between the maniples of the first line, however, were filled with light-armed troops (*velites*). Scipio's friend Laelius commanded the cavalry on his left wing, his ally, the Numidian king Masinissa, commanded the cavalry on the right. The *velites* were ordered to start the battle and if they could not withstand the charge of the elephants, they were to retire quickly either down the lanes to the rear of the army or else to step aside into the lateral spaces between the lines of maniples. In the event, when the elephants charged, the noise of bugles frightened them: some turned back on the Numidian cavalry on Hannibal's left (which was also attacked by Masinissa's cavalry), while others charged the *velites* (who had advanced slightly), inflicting and suffering much loss until finally they were either driven down the lanes Scipio had prepared, leaving the maniples unharmed, or else were forced to the right where they met showers of weapons from the Italian cavalry under Laelius. Under cover of this confusion Laelius charged the Carthaginian cavalry and put it to flight. With the enemy elephants accounted for and the cavalry in flight, the struggle now developed into a long infantry battle of great complexity which was not decided until Scipio's victorious cavalry returned in the nick of time to fall on the enemy's rear. Hannibal was defeated, and it must be admitted that some of his elephants had been skilfully nullified while others had even contributed to his disaster by helping both Masinissa to drive back the cavalry on the Punic left and Laelius to deal with the cavalry on their right.[109]

Of Hannibal's 80 elephants, 11 according to Livy were killed; the rest were presumably captured. The Carthaginians were now forced to make peace and its terms included the clause that they must surrender all their elephants and agree not to train any in the future. Thus this weapon which they had wielded with varying success against the Romans since the time of the First Punic War was now snatched from their grasp. When some fifty years later the final clash between the two great Powers came, Carthage had no elephants with which to defend her territory during the Third Punic War. Meantime, in 202, the surviving elephants had been handed over to Scipio who gave some to Masinissa whose cavalry had served him so well at Zama. The greater number he took back with him to Rome. There they graced his triumphal procession. This must have been a moment of tremendous feeling for the Romans: Hannibal, who had defied them for so long and had come so near to overwhelming them, was at last humbled, and the elephants in the procession must have reminded them that the war had been completed in Africa and by the man who came to be called Africanus.[110]

ELEPHANTS AND THE HANNIBALIC COINAGE

After Hannibal's great victory at Cannae, many Campanian towns such as Capua and Atella had gone over to him and celebrated their revolt from Rome by issuing an independent coinage, which included the use of an elephant as a type in honour of Hannibal (p. 163). But these were not the only such towns: several other issues, which raise puzzling, but interesting, problems, must now be reviewed.

First, an issue of tiny silver coins[111] (pl. XXIIh–j). Three denominations are known, of 2, 1½ and 1 obols: the obverses bear the heads respectively of Hermes, Artemis and Hercules, bearded with fillet. The reverses all show an elephant; the first two carry towers with three heads showing above the coping, the third has a bare-backed elephant (perhaps because the coin is too small to allow a tower to be included). The first and third have respectively two and one pellets, while the second has the letter $\Gamma$ standing for *pente*, 5, thus showing that the system was decimal. They carry no ethnic or inscription, their provenance is unknown and they are exceedingly rare. Detailed numismatic argument would be out of place here, but all the evidence points to Campania and the late third century, and now that Sir Edward Robinson has lent his great authority to the view, they may confidently be assigned to the Hannibalic war. One strong argument in favour of this is that the bearded Hercules bears a considerable resemblance to that on the Barcid silver (pl. XXIa). Even more important are the elephants: are they African or Indian? There can be little doubt that they are Indian: the convexity of the back, the sharply sloping hindquarters (contrast those on the Barcid silver), the comparatively low carriage of the head, common in the Indian elephant when at rest, and the concavity in the profile of the forehead, all point to the Indian. True, the ear is somewhat large in the first two denominations, but not beyond the limits of inaccuracy allowed to themselves by ancient designers who often regard the ear as merely a decoration rather than an anatomical feature (e.g. on a sestertius of Tiberius the bodies of elephants drawing a quadriga are clearly Indian and they are ridden by turbaned mahouts, but the ears are quite wrongly shaped and much too large: pl. XXIVf). Even in the third denomination the ear is a little too long, but this is because the artist has attached it to the head too high up. True, also the convexity of the back is somewhat obscured in the two elephants with towers, but this is due to the 'dent' made by their weight. Thus on balance we are faced with Indian elephants in Italy at the time of Hannibal. To this we shall return shortly, after considering other coins with definitely African elephants.

Two specimens are known of a bronze coin with *obv.* winged bust of Victory and *rev.* African elephant with a bell hanging from its neck (pl. XXIIm).[112] These rather thick coins differ from other bronze coins of the revolt (e.g. they lack marks of value), but they seem to belong to this period, although perhaps minted not in Campania but in the hill country to which the next series belongs. This is the so-called MEL series of barbarous coarse Aes Grave (pl. XXIId, e) which has two elephant types: the triens has *obv.* a bearded Janus, and *rev.* an elephant with rider, while the sextans has *obv.* a bearded head of Hercules and two pellets, and *rev.* an elephant with rider. The elephants' large ears and concave backs show that they are Africans, not Indians, and therefore the earlier suggested connection with Pyrrhus must be abandoned. In fact, it is quite clear that the sextans is a debased copy of the fine Barcid silver coin with bearded head of Hercules (thus the club-head is visible behind the head between the two pellets): further, it is a mirror-copy. Thus this series must be later than the Barcid coinage in Spain, and, as it was minted in Italy, later than Hannibal's arrival in 218. This has great incidental value in determining the dating of early Roman coinage: the coins are of approximately the semi-libral standard which H. Mattingly and E. S. G. Robinson argued was current in 216. The implications of this are far-reaching but cannot be pursued here. To return to the series, the meaning of MEL is uncertain, but most probably it was an abbreviated place-name and the most likely place is Meles (Melae) in Samnium. Now Livy (XXVII, 1) luckily records that Meles was captured by Marcellus in 210: it had thus joined the rebels and had resisted for some years. Such an out-of-the-way stronghold might well have been a good place for a mint for that type of coinage to which the country-folk were accustomed, namely heavy Aes Grave as opposed to the finer struck coinage of the Campanian cities.

The MEL series links on to another group of coins with the legend VE or VELECHA. This comprises denominations of cast Aes Grave with *obv*. radiate head of Sun facing and *rev*. a horse's head, and also a cast coin with *obv*. Sun facing and *rev*. African elephant walking to right (pl. XXIIk, l). The link with the MEL series is provided by the MEL semuncia which also has facing Sun and horse's head. The VELECHA elephant also links with that of Atella which too has a facing Sun on its obverse. The VELECHA coins are found overstruck on other coins; one on a Mamertine coin, the other apparently on a Roman semi-libral uncia; they must therefore belong to this same period. Velecha is now generally identified with Volcei, a town in the Lucanian hill-country. It too had gone over to Hannibal and received a Punic garrison which was forced to surrender to the consul Fulvius in 209, one year after Meles had given in to Marcellus; these more remote towns had managed to hold out a little longer than the cities of Campania. But they were quite considerable strongholds and suitable places for mints: thus the Punic garrison at Meles, which surrendered to Marcellus, amounted to 3,000 men, while his booty included 240,000 modii of wheat and 111,000 of barley.[113] Thus it would appear that the arrival of Hannibal was advertised by the issue of elephant-coinage for both cities in Campania and towns of the mountainous interior, with much cruder and more primitive issues for the latter.

Finally there is a much better known, yet puzzling coinage, namely the bronze coins from Etruria which show *obv*. a negro's head, and *rev*. an elephant facing right, with a bell hanging from its neck and an Etruscan letter (mint-mark) under its belly (pl. XXIIb, c). These coins, which are much commoner than the very rare types that we have been considering, come from places in the Chiana (Clanis) valley, along or across which Hannibal marched in 217 on his way to Lake Trasimene. The elephant must be an Indian (the shape of its back and its drooping head make this clear), but

172

coins issued in this area so far north could have nothing to do with Pyrrhus. Must, therefore, the usual attribution to Hannibal stand, despite an Indian elephant? If they are Hannibalic, it could hardly be argued that the artist did not know what an African elephant looked like (and therefore designed something more like an Indian), because if he could not use a living model he could at least be supplied with a Barcid coin to copy. If Hannibalic, therefore, these coins must show that Hannibal had at least one Indian elephant, as already suggested by the tiny silver series. At first sight the negro's head is puzzling because even if the elephant *were* an African, the rider would normally be a Numidian Berber rather than a negro. The head might, of course, just be used as a label meaning 'African'; this need not have seemed inconsistent with an Indian elephant to the designer, who may not have known that no African elephants have bodies like this one; he knew the beast came from Africa, and it would not occur to him that it had not been born there. Alternatively, Hannibal might have had a negro slave as a personal attendant. But there is, in fact, some evidence which suggests that negroes did tend elephants, namely a terracotta that is described later (pl. Xa) and a reference by Seneca (*Epist.* 85.41) to a *minimus Aethiops* at whose bidding an elephant knelt down or walked on a rope. The alternative to such speculations is to dissociate the coin from Hannibal and to label it merely 'Etruscan' and to recall that Etruscan artists liked strange beasts and often depicted negroes. But such scepticism is unnecessary.

A new historical setting has recently been suggested for the coin by Sir Edward Robinson, who assigns the issue to Arretium at the head of the Clanis valley which was in a state of high tension with Rome in 209/8, though not of actual armed rebellion; he suggests that this dissentient city issued a provocative seditious type. This, of course, is possible, and one might go even further than Robinson by suggesting that the purpose of the issue was to herald the hoped-for arrival of Hasdrubal from Spain with his reinforcements and new elephants. However, despite the authority of the originator of this view, it may still be possible to cling to the older view that the coins belong to 217 and represent the propaganda of Hannibal's approach. But in either case the attribution to a Hannibalic context stands firm.[114]

One other important item of evidence remains to be mentioned. Pliny (*NH*. VIII, 11) tells us that the name of the elephant that fought most bravely in the Carthaginian battle-line was Surus, and that it had one tusk broken (off?). 'Surus' almost certainly means 'the Syrian', which again almost certainly points to an Indian rather than African elephant. This name would be most appropriate for any Indian beast that the Carthaginians had, since it would mark out the animal from the main bulk of Africans. True, Cato does not specify whether Surus belongs to the First or Second Punic War, but his personal interest and participation in the latter makes it by far the more probable. Further, Cato would expect his readers to understand that Surus meant a Syrian and this implies that the men who had themselves fought in the war did not think it impossible that Hannibal had an Indian elephant: the animal was doubtless a favourite topic of conversation in the Roman army at the time. Indeed it is not impossible that if Hannibal had any Indians, they may have survived the rigours of the Alps better than the main bulk of his Africans and that the sole surviving beast on which he rode through Etruria was an Indian. If so, we may know his name and even have his portrait on the negro-elephant coin.

Further, Surus seems to have appeared in Latin literature at the time. There is a desperately corrupt line of the poet Ennius which runs something like 'unus surum surus ferre, tamen defendere possent'; on it the Roman scholar Festus commented that 'Ennius seems to be joking'. Elsewhere I have suggested[115] in more detail that a solution may be found by turning to our friend Surus, who was no ordinary elephant: beside being the bravest of his fellows, he was conspicuously a One-Tusker ('altero dente mutilato', in Pliny's words). In these circumstances it would be strange if the Roman legionaries did not think of the Latin word *surus*, meaning 'a stake'. They carried their own stakes (*suri*) to build defensive palisades: the elephant had its one stake with which to defend the Punic troops. Or, since Festus says 'suri autem sunt fustes', the Romans may have thought of the cudgels with which military discipline was maintained: the elephant's tusk might be more formidable than a centurion's club. Such a natural transference of meaning is made all the more likely when we recall that the Romans, although in many ways a solemn people, had a weakness for puns. Thus canting 'types parlants' appear on Republican coinage, and it is also abundantly clear that the Roman legionaries did not differ from soldiers of all ages who have always delighted to find nicknames for their own or their enemies' weapons (cf. *aries, corvus, cuniculus, musculus, onager,* and *testudo*: note the tendency to turn to the animal world for names). And in this case they did not have to look far: the real name could become a Latin nickname, and the Syrian could be the Stake. Thus, depending on the restoration of Ennius' line, it could mean that Surus carried a stake, but nevertheless the Carthaginians could defend (their position or camp? – though they had no stakes with which to fortify it), or (better perhaps) that Surus could bring only one stake, yet could make a good defence.

Another reference to Surus has been detected, this time in comedy, in the *Pseudolus* of Plautus which was produced in Rome in 191 BC.[116] Here Pseudolus for dramatic reasons assumes the name Surus (1, 637), a suitable name for a slave since many slaves came from Syria; later when he appears in this false guise he is described as (1218ff.):

rufus quidem, ventriosus, crassis suris, subniger,
magno capite, acutis oculis, ore rubicundo, admodum
magnis pedibus.

'a red-headed chap, pot-bellied, with thick ankles, rather dark, with a big head, sharp eyes, and red mouth, and very big feet'. All but the first epithet would apply to an elephant, and even this could be relevant since the Indian elephant depicted on the Villa Giulia plate is in full battle-dress with a red saddle-cloth and a red shield painted on its tower. It is, therefore, not improbable that an audience in 191, helped no doubt by some clowning by the actor, would recognize the redoubtable Surus in these lines of Plautus. A possible objection is that the next line, by another speaker, says, 'You've destroyed me now that you have said "feet",' and earlier in the play (1176) there is a joke about 'ankles' (sura), which with the 'crassis suris' above might relate to the choice of the name Surus for the slave. But even a double pun is not excluded. The younger generation in the audience might only see the point about 'ankles', but veterans who had fought against Hannibal ten or more years before would well remember the elephant: a decade or so after 1918 a Music Hall audience might well respond to a joke about Big Bertha, the famous German gun of the First World War. Thus, while it would be hazardous to build upon the idea, at least there is a fair probability that Surus was well remembered when Plautus wrote his *Pseudolus* as when later Cato wrote his *Origines*.

But Surus was an Indian, and this brings us back to the numismatic evidence which, if it is granted that the die-engravers in any way approximated to accuracy, also suggests that Hannibal had at least one Indian elephant. If so, he presumably got them through Egypt which had a good supply, especially after Ptolemy captured a large number of Antiochus' beasts at Raphia in 217 (p. 142). Indeed it could be reports of how well these Indians had fought at Raphia that may have led Hannibal to wish to stiffen his African corps with a few Indians. As has been seen (p. 148), trade relations between Carthage and the Ptolemies were not bad, and during the First Punic War Carthage had not hesitated to ask Philadelphus for a loan of 2,000 talents. Thus, while it might be beneath the dignity of a Ptolemy to *sell* any elephants to Carthage, it is not unlikely that the king may have been persuaded to send her some as a royal gift, knowing that he would in fact receive a *quid pro quo*: Egypt needed silver and horses from Carthage. This, of course, is speculation, but it suggests that if the coins and the name of Surus require us to believe in Indian elephants among Hannibal's forces, then the political background does not seem to preclude the possibility.

Reference to two clay vessels must bring this survey of Hannibal's elephants to a conclusion. The first of these is a *phiale* from Cales in Campania, now in the Louvre (pl. Xb). It depicts an elephant carrying a tower with one man inside and with a driver on the beast's neck and a bell hanging from the neck. Although reproductions of the work are not very clear, on the whole the animal looks more like an African than an Indian; there is a suggestion of concavity about the back, the front of the head looks more African than Indian, and the ear, though quite unnaturalistic, seems too large to be Indian. This animal has often been connected with the 'Elephant Victory' of Antiochus I against the Galatians in 276 (p. 122), but the main reason appears to be its supposed resemblance to the terracotta from Myrina (pl. VIIb). Doubts, however, have been expressed, and it is not clear why this subject should be of particular interest in Campania, while if the species of elephant is in fact African any connection with Galatia must be ruled out. The pro-

176

XXI: *a*. Probable portrait of Hamilcar as Melkart-Heracles on double shekel of New Carthage. *b*. Reverse of (*a*). *c*. Probable portrait of Hannibal as Melkart-Heracles. *d*. Reverse of (*c*). *e*. Probable portrait of Hasdrubal Barca. *f*. Reverse of (*e*). *g*. Portrait of Masinissa on unique bronze coin. *h*. Reverse of (*g*) showing elephant and name of Masinissa.

XXII: *a.* Bronze coin of Lascuta in Spain. *b.* Head of negro on bronze coin of Etruria. *c.* Reverse of (*b*) showing Indian elephant. *d.* Head of Hercules on piece of crude Aes Grave from central Italy. *e.* Reverse of (*d*) showing elephant and rider, a crude imitation of the Barcid silver. *f.* African elephant on small silver coin of Capua, Hannibalic period. *g.* African elephant on bronze coin of Atella. *h.* Tiny silver coin, (greatly enlarged) probably from Campania, Italy. *i.* Head of Heracles on still smaller denomination in same series as (*h*). *j.* Reverse of (*i*). *k.* Elephant on an overstruck bronze coin of Velecha. *l.* Radiate Sol of obverse of (*k*). *m.* African elephant; victory on obverse. Bronze coin from central Italy?

XXIII: *a.* Seleucus IV. *b.* Antiochus IV Epiphanes. *c.* Demetrius I of Syria and Laodice. *d.* New Style Athenian tetradrachm; Indian elephant as Seleucid symbol. *e.* Juba I. *f.* Elephant on bronze coin of Juba I. *g.* Juba II. *h.* Reverse of (*g*). *i.* Coin of Juba II. *j.* Coin of Juba II celebrating victory over Tacfarinas.

a

b

c

d

XXIV: *a*. Denarius of C. Caecilius Metellus (consul of 113 BC?) celebrating victory of L. Metellus at Panormus in 251 BC. *b*. Coin of Q. Caecilius Metellus Pius, consul of 80 BC. *c*. Coin of Q. Caecilius Metellus Pius Scipio, consul of 52 BC, referring to his African campaign. *d*. Denarius of Julius Caesar, probably of 49 BC; elephant trampling on a dragon. *e*. Medallion of Gordian III; elephant fighting bull in the Colosseum, Rome. *f*. Deified Augustus in elephant quadriga on sestertius of Tiberius. *g*. Elephant quadriga on sestertius of L. Verus. *h*. Elephant quadriga on gold medallion of Diocletian and Maximian.

e

f

g

h

venance (Cales) is in favour of its being African and at the same time suggests that it may represent one of Hannibal's animals.

A terracotta figure from Pompeii, now in the Naples Museum, has an even stronger claim to be dissociated from the Galatian connection (pl. Xa). It is in the form of an elephant 'endorsed' with a tall but empty tower, with a driver on its neck who is placing something in its upturned trunk. The shape of the back and the large ear suggest that it is African, but in this example, if any degree of accuracy can be accorded to the artist, proof is provided: the tip of the trunk has two 'fingers' top and bottom. This is a distinctive characteristic of the Africans: Indians have only one 'finger' on the top. The two 'fingers' can be distinctly seen also on the Africans of the Barcid silver and on a Roman denarius of Metellus (pl. XXIVa). This feature would, of course, always provide an excellent criterion, but unfortunately it cannot always be distinguished on small coins, while ends of trunks tend to be broken on clay models. Here, however, together with strong segmentation of the trunk, it declares the model to be African, and in view of its Campanian provenance it may well depict one of Hannibal's animals. Further, the driver is a negro, so perhaps after all the Etruscan coin (pl. XXIb) does not stand alone: Hannibal may have had some negro drivers for both African and Indian elephants.[117]

# CHAPTER VII

# ROME

## ROME AND THE EAST

For more than fifty years after the Romans first met enemy elephants in the First Punic War they made no attempt to incorporate this weapon in their own armed forces. Though often not unwilling to adopt military ideas from their foes, in this case they decided not to use the animals they captured from the Carthaginians as the nucleus of an elephant-corps. Perhaps they trusted in the ability of their legionaries more than in the potential performance of elephants which they soon realized could be double-edged. However, after the end of the Hannibalic War they had some captured and surrendered elephants on their hands and they at last decided to use them in war, reinforced by others. Earlier the problem of obtaining elephants might have been serious, but now it presented no difficulty. They allowed their ally Masinissa and other Numidian rulers to keep elephants, and these client kings were only too ready· to offer some to their patron. Thus Masinissa sent ten to Flamininus for use against Philip, offered 20 against Antiochus, sent 22 against Perseus and ten to Nobilior in Spain at Numantia, and provided Scipio Aemilianus with some in the Third Punic War, during which Gulussa brought some to the Roman camp, while Micipsa sent ten to Fabius against Viriathus and twelve to Aemilianus at Numantia under Jugurtha. Jugurtha himself later had a considerable number. Thus Rome, if she had wished, could without difficulty have made a much greater use of elephants than in fact she did.[118]

No sooner had Rome defeated Hannibal than she became involved in wars against Philip of Macedon and later his ally Antiochus of Syria, whose earlier compact has already been mentioned (p. 144). Before this the Romans had already defeated Philip in the First Macedonian War when he had allied himself to Hannibal.

Then in answer to appeals from some of the victims of his aggression they again declared war on him in 200 BC from a very mixed variety of motives. A Roman expeditionary force was sent to Greece, commanded by Sulpicius Galba; it included some elephants. As Livy (XXXI, 36.4) records, this was the first time for the Romans to use elephants, and the reason he gives is merely that they had some which they had captured in the Punic War. The number employed is not known, but they did not seek to increase it by requesting more from Masinissa, who supplied them with cavalry only; perhaps they were testing out this new arm on a relatively small scale. Sulpicius used them first in 199 when he met Philip in Lyncestis and placed his elephants as a cover for his own front, but he failed to tempt the king out of his camp to face a large-scale battle. Nevertheless, the Romans apparently thought well of the elephants, since in 198 they allowed Masinissa to send ten to Greece where Flamininus had succeeded to the command. We are not told how he used them at first, but they were probably valuable in the attacks he made on various walled towns in Greece. In 197 he faced Philip in the decisive battle at Cynoscephalae. Unlike his Antigonid ancestors, Philip had no elephants (though curiously one of his commanders, Nicanor, was nicknamed the Elephant – because of his bulk?), while Flamininus deployed his elephants in front of his right wing. Despite its historical consequences, we need not here follow the battle in detail. It was fought on rough and hilly ground that told against the Macedonian phalanx. The right wing of each army was successful, the left was retreating, and victory was in the balance when the Romans skilfully transferred some troops from their victorious right to their hard-pressed left. Suffice it to note that the elephants played a most valuable part in the success of Flamininus' right. Philip was beaten; although allowed to retain his throne, he was confined to his kingdom of Macedon and had to abandon all his conquests.[119]

After a few years of deteriorating diplomatic exchanges with Rome, Antiochus the Great of Syria determined to intervene in Greece in response to an appeal from the Aetolians, although he knew this would mean war with Rome. So once again the Romans sent a force to Greece (late in 192), to face an opponent who this time had elephants in his army. He had six when he landed, but may of course have received some reinforcements later. He made use of them in an attack on Larissa, when he placed them in front of his troops which advanced behind them in a hollow square. The Romans too had some elephants: Masinissa promised to send 20 to the Roman commander, Acilius Glabrio, in Greece, who arrived there with 15 (part of Masinissa's promised 20, or 15 others?), but curiously we do not hear of them taking any part in the subsequent campaign. Soon Antiochus was forced to fall back on Thermopylae which he tried to hold against the Romans coming from the north. He strengthened his position in the famous Pass by a rampart and wall, while detachments of his Aetolian allies held various strongpoints on the hills above. He placed his elephants 'with their usual guard' (perhaps a screen of light-armed troops?) on the marshy ground between the right-hand end of his fortifications and the sea. A frontal attack in the narrow pass by Acilius Glabrio failed to break through, but a night attack led by Cato dislodged the Aetolians on Mt Callidromus above the Pass. Cato swept down on the rear of Antiochus and his army broke and fled. The king skilfully used his elephants to cover his retreat, and in the narrow valley they prevented the Roman cavalry from getting through and delayed the advance of the infantry. But his army was in flight and his elephants were either killed or captured by the Romans. His invasion of Greece had failed disastrously and he hurried back to Asia.[120]

Late in the year 190 a Roman army crossed over the Hellespont into Asia for the first time in history, led by the consul Lucius Cornelius Scipio, who had his brother, the great Africanus, serving with him.[121] After a long advance they came up with the vast army of Antiochus, who had some 75,000 men against their 30,000. The king stood and fought at Magnesia. The Romans adopted their usual battle-order, with their left flank somewhat protected by a river; their weak spot was their exposed right wing in the south which faced Antiochus' scythed chariots, dromedary corps and cavalry amongst others. They also had 16 African elephants, but they wisely kept them as a reserve behind their battle-line: the reason was that Antiochus had 54 Indians. These were protected with head-pieces and crests and carried towers in each of which were four soldiers, besides the rider. To have opposed the smaller African elephants, which probably did not have towers, against this vastly superior force of Indians would have invited trouble. Antiochus put 22 in his front line, two between each of its ten sections; they would guard the flanks of each detachment and protect the front, while if driven back, they could withdraw in the space behind them which could then easily be filled by infantry-men since Antiochus had drawn his phalanx up to the unusual depth of 32 men. Sixteen other elephants were placed on the extreme left wing, while the remaining 16 were on the right, apparently between the infantry and cavalry and drawn up in close formation (Livy calls them a *grex*, a herd). Antiochus' battle-line was to say the least impressive, and when it was revealed to the Romans as an early morning mist dispersed, it might well appear as an impregnable city wall with the elephants as towers at regular intervals in the central line. The king was on the right flank, his son Seleucus and his nephew Antipater on the left, while one of the three commanders of the centre was Philip, *magister elephantorum*. The king must surely have given a passing thought to his ancestors and the great days of elephant warfare. Lucius Scipio determined to strike hardest at the king's left. Here after archers and slingers had scattered the Syrian scythe-chariots, his ally, Eumenes of Pergamum, charged home and thrust the king's armoured horse in confusion on their own centre. Meanwhile, Antiochus himself had led a charge of his Iranian horse on his right and driven back the Roman left wing, but he repeated the error that he had made at Raphia, by carrying on the pursuit instead of wheeling to sup-port his centre or broken left. At first his centre resisted, but accord-ing to Livy the Roman soldiers were by now accustomed from their campaigning in Africa to avoid the charges of elephants and to attack them with *pila* from the side or, if they could get nearer, to hamstring them with their swords. Any way the result would sug-gest that the legions had lost some of their earlier fear of the beasts. But with its flanks exposed and other threats Antiochus' centre gave way and there was a disordered flight of confused men, ele-phants, dromedaries and chariots. Losses were enormous, including the capture of 15 elephants and riders. At one blow the Romans had thrust Antiochus from Greece, now by a second from Asia Minor. Under the terms that he was finally granted, he was confined to his kingdom of Syria and had to surrender many armaments, including all his elephants with the injunction not to have any in the future. When he handed over his beasts to the ten Roman commissioners, they passed them on to Eumenes as a gift, by no means his only reward for his help at Magnesia. When Lucius Scipio triumphed at Rome, no elephants are recorded in his procession, but among the heaps of treasure carried along were no less than 1,231 ivory tusks: clearly Antiochus' store-chambers had been forced to yield much accumulated treasure of the Seleucid kings.[122]

For many years Rome's relations with Macedonia remained reasonably friendly, even after Philip had been succeeded by his son Perseus in 179, but suspicions of the other's intentions hardened on both sides. These increased, fanned by the intrigues of Eumenes, until in 171 the Romans declared war on Perseus on the ground that he had attacked some of their allies. A Roman army was once again sent to Greece, commanded by P. Licinius Crassus, who had some 37,000 men, many of them recruits, against Perseus' 43,000 men, of whom half formed the phalanx (a force larger than that with which Alexander the Great had crossed to Asia). Perseus chose to defend his kingdom in the south in a strong defensive position based on the Mt Olympus range, whence he could take the offensive in the plains of Thessaly. The Roman forces included some elephants. In order to secure them and some Numidian cavalry which Masinissa had promised, the Romans sent a special triumviral commission to the king to arrange this; 22 elephants were placed under his son Misagenes. The Roman forces met Perseus in Thessaly, suffered a setback in a cavalry engagement and then near Phalanna fought another battle which the Roman annalists magnified into a great victory, in which the elephants are recorded to have contributed their share.[123]

No decisive action took place in 170, but the Romans apparently thought additional elephants would be useful, since Masinissa promised them twelve more. Further, if Polyaenus (iv, 21) is to be believed, in addition to these African elephants the Romans received some Indians from King Antiochus of Syria: unless this is some misunderstanding of those that Antiochus III surrendered after Magnesia, his successor Antiochus IV will have supplied some and the Romans would then have a mixed force of Africans and Indians. In any case the Romans must have had at least 34 Africans in Greece after the arrival of Masinissa's extra twelve. These soon took part in a spectacular exploit. In 169 the consul Q. Marcius Philippus decided to try to force his way past Mt Olympus and reach the Macedonian coast. Perseus divided his forces to guard the three main passes, while Philippus advanced over the pass of Lake Ascaris (Nezero) where he swept the defending force aside. The descent from the summit was exceedingly steep, but he could not turn back. Baggage animals and their loads suffered terribly, and the elephants panicked and threw off their mahouts and scared the horses. Philippus' engineers then devised a method of descent which would allow the beasts, which physically cannot bend their knees sufficiently to walk down steep slopes (pp. 19, 22), to slide down. Needless to say, Livy's account of this has been rejected by the sceptics, but it was essentially perhaps not much more complicated than other feats of transport (e.g. that of Hannibal's elephants over the Rhone) that are undoubtedly historical. Further, Livy here depends on Polybius who not only liked describing technical military devices, but was personally involved in the general course of events: when Philippus had succeeded a short time later in occupying Heracleum, Polybius, who was hipparch (second officer) of the Achaean League, was sent with other ambassadors to Philippus to report that the League had decided to co-operate with the Romans; when his colleagues returned, Polybius stayed on with Philippus and took part in the campaign. Thus he probably heard the exciting story of the passage over the mountains from Philippus himself, and while Livy may have misunderstood some details of Polybius' description of the episode, his general account may be accepted. He describes how, where the track ceased, the Romans marked off stretches on the steep hillside; at the lower end of each stretch two posts were set up, slightly further apart than the width of an elephant. They were joined by cross-beams and on them rested the bottom end of platforms, each some 30 ft long. These platforms, or bridges, were covered with earth. An elephant was driven from the firm ground on to the first of these platforms, the posts were then cut, the platform began to tilt downwards and the animal began to slide down to the head of the next runway, where the process was continued until more level ground was reached. Some of the elephants slid standing upright, others squatting on their haunches. If the picture presented is slightly comic, nevertheless in the act itself both men and beasts must have had a strenuous time, but Roman ingenuity triumphed and Hannibal was not alone in getting elephants over mountains. Thus the Romans had turned the Olympus range and reached the sea. Perseus is said to have received the surprising news while in his bath: leaping out he cried that he had been beaten without a battle. However, the Romans lost some of their advantage because they ran short of supplies through the inadequate co-operation of their fleet, and so Perseus was able to dig in at a strong point near Dium.[124]

In 168 Rome sent out reinforcements and a new commander, L. Aemilius Paullus, who brought Perseus to his last battle near Pydna. He posted his elephants in front of the Italian allied infantry on his right wing over against some of Perseus' auxiliary troops, with his cavalry on his left wing, a somewhat unusual formation. The battle began on the Roman right where the elephants charged, followed up by the Latin allies, and routed Perseus' left wing. In the centre a grim struggle occurred between the legions and phalanx: later Paullus often confessed to his friends that he had never seen anything more terrible than the Macedonian phalanx at Pydna, though he had fought in many a battle. The Romans at last carried the day and Perseus fled, soon to be captured and deposed from his kingdom. Thus the Roman victory was due in part to the elephants who had started the rout. They were also useful in the mopping-up operations: some of the men who escaped from the battle fled to the sea and swam out to some small boats which they mistakenly thought to be friendly. Those that were not picked off by the men in the boats, swam back to the shore where the elephants, guided by their mahouts, trampled them as they tried to scramble ashore. Livy adds an interesting item of information: 'elephantomachae nomen tantum sine usu fuerunt' (the elephant-fighters were a mere name without practical effect). This implies that Perseus had trained a special corps to deal with the elephants, while Zonaras says that they were hoplites whose shields and helmets were studded with sharp iron nails. This is reasonable enough, but some doubt may arise when he adds that Perseus had trained his horses to face elephants by making model elephants, smeared with an evil-smelling ointment and equipped to emit loud roars (by a man with a trumpet inside, adds Poly-aenus). However, although slightly ridiculous, this method of training may have been tried (how *would* an ancient commander, who had no live elephants to use for the purpose, train his horses to meet the threat and smell of elephants?), but if it was tried, it proved ineffective in practice. After his victory Paullus triumphed during the next year for three days: in the procession were 2,000 tusks, three cubits in length, from Perseus' Treasure (some perhaps the relics of earlier herds of the Antigonid kings, others perhaps the result of trade). Further, at the Games which he gave to the Roman people he threw foreign deserters from his army to be trampled to death by elephants, a grim adoption by a Roman of a Carthaginian custom.[125]

Thus the Roman use of elephants in these wars in Greece, though modest, had made no small contribution to two of their victories: they had helped Flamininus' right wing to success at Cynoscephalae, and Paullus' right wing at Pydna. Thus, unlike the Carthaginians, the Romans had not discovered to their cost the potential danger the animals could prove to their own side. Perhaps the explanation lies in the fact that they used only small numbers, which may have been trained more intensively and become less subject to panic. It is strange that this promising beginning did not lead to their employment on a larger scale, but doubtless the Romans still believed that the essential way to win a battle was to rely on the legionary.

SELEUCIDS, JEWS AND PTOLEMIES

While Rome was concentrating on the Macedonian war both Egypt and Syria seized the opportunity to renew their struggles. The king of Syria, now Antiochus IV Epiphanes (pl. XXIIIb), forestalled an Egyptian attack on Coele-Syria by advancing into Egypt, where he crashed through the frontier defences, took Pelusium and threatened Alexandria, thus succeeding where Perdiccas, Antigonus and his own father, Antiochus the Great, had failed (169 B C). Civil war in Egypt between the two brothers, who later ruled in a period of destructive mutual hostility, made his task easier, as did Rome's preoccupation with Perseus. After the battle of Pydna the Romans intervened and Popillius was sent to order Antiochus out of Egypt: the king meekly obeyed. Not much detail is preserved about the composition of the army which Antiochus had led against Egypt, but 1 *Maccabees* (1.17) records that he advanced 'with chariots, and elephants, and horsemen, together with a great fleet'. At first sight this appears unacceptable, since his father had been forbidden to keep any elephants or a fleet, but there is other evidence to show that he had both. Clearly, therefore, the Romans must have turned a blind eye for some time to this rearming by Syria. The confirmatory evidence is found in a reliable source, namely Polybius, who tells how Aemilius Paullus held splendid games at Amphipolis to celebrate the victory of Pydna, to which all Greeks were invited.

Antiochus, not to be outdone, held a magnificent pageant at Daphne, a suburb of Antioch, with festivities lasting a month. In the procession marched gorgeously equipped troops; while statues and gold and silver vessels were carried aloft. Behind the horse-chariots came 'a chariot drawn by four elephants, and another by two; and then 36 elephants in single file wearing their equipment'. Thus Antiochus had got together over 40 elephants in defiance of the treaty his father had signed with the Romans, who presumably thought that the king, who would respond instantly to an order from Popillius in a major issue, might be allowed a few foibles to suit his ostentatious and Bohemian character. Where he got them from is a problem, since the growth of the Parthian kingdom is generally thought to have cut off the supply from India for the Seleucids, but apparently he had succeeded in getting round the Parthians, physically or metaphorically.[126]

Thus Antiochus, who had won a military victory and suffered a political defeat, was able to hide the past in a cloud of glorious celebrations, and he had at least held Coele-Syria. But here too trouble developed from Antiochus' quarrel with the Jews which resulted in a nationalist uprising led by the Hasmonean family. He decided to force upon all the Jews the Hellenizing policy which some of them were adopting; this he did in an attempt to unify his kingdom, but he reckoned without the loyalty of many of the Jews to the strict faith of their ancestors. The result was his occupation of Jerusalem and the transferring of the Temple of Jehovah to Zeus Olympius, the 'Abomination of Desolation', with pigs sacrificed on a Greek altar. Mattathias, followed by his son Judas Maccabaeus, led the resistance. Antiochus himself left Syria for a campaign in the East, and entrusted the Jewish revolt to Lysias, whom he left as regent 'with half his forces and the elephants' (I Maccab. 3.34) together with the care of his young son Antiochus (the future king, Antiochus V). In 164 Lysias, with an army that included 80 elephants according to II Maccabees (11.5), engaged the forces of Judas near Bethsuron and met with a defeat. Then news came of the death of the king Antiochus. Lysias made peace and reversed the policy of persecution: the Temple was restored to Jehovah. But this arrangement soon broke down and in 162 Lysias, accompanied by the boy-king Antiochus V Eupator, advanced on Palestine from the south: his elephant-corps consisted of 32 beasts. According to II Maccabees, which attributes only 22 elephants to

186

Lysias, Judas made a preliminary night attack on the royal pavilion with a picked force of young men; these killed 2,000 men and stabbed to death the chief elephant and its mahout. This episode, which is not recorded in I *Maccabees*, might be a misunderstanding of an incident told in the latter work about Eleazar's attack on the leading elephant. At any rate I *Maccabees* gives a full account of the subsequent battle. 'The elephants were roused for battle with the juice of grapes and mulberries. The great beasts were distributed among the· phalanxes; by each were stationed a thousand men, equipped with coats of chain-mail and bronze helmets. Five hundred picked horsemen were also assigned to each animal. These had been stationed beforehand where the beast was; and wherever it went, they went with it, never leaving it. Each animal had a strong wooden turret fastened on its back with a special harness, by way of protection, and carried four fighting men as well as an Indian driver. The rest of the cavalry Lysias stationed on either flank of the army, to harass the enemy while themselves protected by the phalanxes.' A dramatic moment occurred in the battle when Judas' brother, Eleazar, 'seeing that one of the elephants wore royal armour and stood out above all the rest, thought that the king was riding on it. So he gave his life to save his people, and win everlasting renown for himself. He ran boldly towards it, into the middle of the phalanx, dealing death right and left, while they fell back on either side before him. He got in underneath the elephant, and thrust at it from below and killed it. It fell to the ground on top of him, and there he died'.[127] Eleazar thus did acquire an everlasting name, but unfortunately he did not save his people since the battle went against them. Further, famine weakened the Jews' chances of prolonged resistance, but they were saved when a rival claimant to Lysias' position forced the latter to make peace with them, which allowed Judas to hold Jerusalem, but as the king's governor (*strategos*).

The elephants were roused for battle by the use of wine, but where the Authorized translation gives 'they showed the elephants the blood of grapes and mulberries', the *New English Bible* suggests that the beasts drank the mixture: 'the elephants were roused for battle with the juice of grapes and of mulberries'. This latter view is almost certainly right, since III *Maccabees*, 5, describes how Ptolemy IV intended to let drunken elephants trample Jews to death in the hippodrome of Alexandria. Further, Aelian (*Nat. Hist.*

XIII, 8) says that for war an elephant drinks wine, not, however, that made from grapes since men prepare a wine from rice or cane. The grouping of a large squadron of cavalry with each beast, which presupposes careful training of the horses, is interesting, while it should be noted that the number of the men in each tower is uncertain. The reading of '32' is clearly impossible; emendations include 'two or three' and 'picked warriors', but that adopted by the *New English Bible* is given above in the extract from that version.

This same year, 162 B C, saw the intervention of Rome, who sent out a triumviral commission to disarm Syria: dynastic problems were arising from the succession of a boy-king and the claims of Demetrius, grandson of Antiochus the Great, who was in Rome as a hostage and was trying to persuade the Senate to agree to his claim to the Syrian throne. When the commissioners reached Laodicea they proceeded to enforce some of the terms of the Peace of Apamea by burning the warships and hamstringing the elephants. This dismal sight provoked the people to attack the commissioners and the senior man, Cn. Octavius, a former consul, was killed. Thus the official ban on the Seleucids retaining an elephant-corps, which had been overlooked for over twenty-five years, was implemented. The Romans were not provoked to retaliate, but in 161 the Senate made a treaty of friendship with the Jews which would enable them to interfere more easily in Syria, where Demetrius, who had escaped from Rome with the help of his friend Polybius, had arranged for the murder of his boy-king cousin and seized the throne.

The Maccabeean revolt smouldered on, and Nicanor, 'commander of the elephant corps' who was now, it might be thought, deprived of his specialist duties, was sent by Demetrius to deal with it. In March 160 a formal battle was fought by Judas with what forces he could muster; victory was his, and Nicanor was killed (his head later hung from the citadel in Jerusalem, and the 13th day of the month Adar, Nicanor's Day, became an annual festival). If II *Maccabees* (15.21) is to be believed, Nicanor had deployed some elephants in his battle-line, but since it is difficult to see where he could have obtained any, this alleged addition to his forces must be highly suspect.

On the other hand we find that some later Seleucid kings had elephants, but that came about through the Ptolemies, and they were African, not Indian, beasts. Ten years after Nicanor's Day in 150 Demetrius was defeated in battle and killed by Alexander Balas, who claimed to be a son of Antiochus IV Epiphanes. This victory, which gave him the Syrian throne, Balas owed to the support of Ptolemy Philometor who gave him his daughter, Cleopatra Thea, in marriage, but at the price of Egyptian dominance. In 147 the young son of Demetrius tried to regain his father's kingdom, which he attacked with a force of Cretan mercenaries. Ptolemy then intervened, with an eye to gaining Coele-Syria for himself. He invaded Syria with an army which, as subsequent events showed, included elephants: thus he must have kept up some of the hunting expeditions to Ethiopia, like his ancestors. He entered Antioch in support of young Demetrius and was tempted to accept the offer of the kingdom of Syria, but this was too risky: the Romans, who had just sacked Carthage and Corinth, would not welcome the extension of his power. So with Demetrius, now declared Demetrius II, he advanced against Balas who was defeated on the river Oenoparus. But the noise of an elephant caused Ptolemy's horse to shy and throw the king, who five days later died of a fractured skull. This left his troops leaderless in Syria, and Demetrius promptly turned against them, massacring those who did not escape. However, he kept Ptolemy's elephants, and thus gained a herd of Africans.[128] However, he did not keep them for long. In 143 a former supporter of Balas, a man from Apamea named both Diodotus and Tryphon, raised a revolt in favour of Balas' young son; he seized the province of Apamea, which was the military centre of the kingdom, and thus won the royal arsenals and the elephants: it was the centre where elephants had been kept since the days of the early Seleucids (p. 121).[129] He entered Antioch and the boy was proclaimed as Antiochus VI Dionysus. After Tryphon had murdered the boy and usurped the throne he was later expelled by a brother of Demetrius II, who became Antiochus VII Sidetes. Sidetes presumably took over any of the elephants which survived, but as they gradually became too old for fighting, the later Seleucid rulers must have conducted their quarrels without such help.

A son of Demetrius II, who became king of Syria in 121 as Antiochus VIII Grypus, has perhaps left a final memorial to the Seleucid elephants. One of the so-called New Style Athenian coins shows an owl standing on an amphora and, in the field, a small Indian elephant (pl. XXIIId). The dating of this series is very controversial and the coin, which obviously commemorates the presence of one of the Seleucids in Athens, has also been variously assigned, for instance to the future Antiochus Epiphanes, who spent some time there about 175 BC, or to Antiochus VII in exile c. 148. A recent suggestion points to the future Antiochus VIII who was sent there by his mother Cleopatra in 130/29. If this is correct, it is interesting to note that the elephant is an Indian, the mainstay of the Seleucids for so long, and not an African such as they had recently taken over from Ptolemy Philometor.[130]

During the first half of the second century when the Romans were making intermittent use of elephants in their wars in the East, they apparently did not employ them in their early struggles against the Celtiberians in Spain: neither Cato nor the elder Gracchus is recorded as having any. However, the modest but valuable contribution made by the elephants to their eastern victories seems to have stimulated their use in the west from 153 BC onwards. In that year the Celtiberians made a bid for freedom. Q. Fulvius Nobilior led an army against their capital of Numantia and suffered a serious defeat when marching through a defile to the south of the town. However, he rallied his forces and encamped on a hill some four miles to the east of Numantia where substantial remains of his well-built stone camp still survive. He had with his forces ten elephants which Masinissa had sent him, and they were probably stabled in a large building just outside the west wall of the camp which faces towards Numantia. Another record of their presence may be the drawing of a turreted elephant on a clay loom-weight which was found not far away at Azaila (fig. 18). In his attack Nobilior kept his elephants behind his troops which suddenly opened ranks and allowed the elephants to charge through them. It must have been a terrifying sight for the Celtiberians; neither they nor their horses, as Appian says, had ever seen an elephant in war before: presumably they must have actually seen them before the charge, since it would hardly have been possible for the Romans to have hidden them completely, while Celtiberian scouts must have seen them as they watched the army advancing on Numantia. At any rate the Celtiberians fled back to the protection of their town, and Nobilior led his army forward to storm it. All went well until one of the

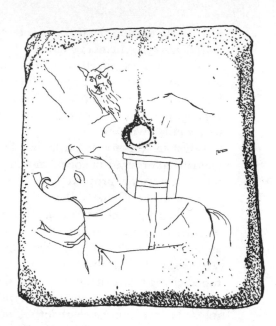

Fig. 18. Clay loom-weight from Azaila near Numantia in Spain (A. Schulten, *Numantia*, IV, 90)

elephants was hit by a large falling stone, when it went wild and caused its fellows to panic: 'some people call them "the common enemy" on account of their fickleness' is Appian's comment, perhaps echoing Polybius whose account of the episode he was using. The Celtiberians rallied, routed the Romans and killed three of the elephants.[131]

The performance of the elephants at Numantia did not dampen the enthusiasm of the Roman commanders for them. In 151 or 150 young Scipio Aemilianus, who was serving on the staff of L. Licinius Lucullus, was sent by him from Spain to Africa to get some more from Masinissa, a mission which was successfully carried out. Fighting continued in Spain and was intensified with the guerilla campaign of the Lusitanians, led by Viriathus in the west. A somewhat improbable anecdote tells how in 142 Q. Metellus Macedonicus deliberately starved his elephants in order that, by this as well as other methods, he might hand over a weaker army to his successor, and personal enemy, Q. Pompeius; at any rate it testifies to the fact that the elephants were still being used. Indeed in the following year Q. Fabius Maximus Maximus Servilianus, who was campaigning in Further Spain, wrote to Micipsa, Masinissa's successor, asking for some elephants as quickly as possible: they were duly

sent. Lastly, during the final siege of Numantia by Scipio Aemilianus (134–33), Micipsa's nephew, Jugurtha, arrived to help with
twelve elephants, 'together with the archers and slingers that were
usually brigaded with them'. Thus in Spain, as in the East, the
Romans had kept their use of elephants to small numbers, but
apparently had found them useful, probably not least in attacks on
native hill-towns.[132]

When in response to an appeal from Massilia (Marseilles) the
Romans intervened in southern Gaul against the tribes of the interior, they soon provoked the hostility of the Allobroges and
Arverni in the Rhone valley, and they thought that these Celtic
tribes, like the Celtiberians in Spain, might find the impact of
elephants alarming. Thus in 121 Cn. Domitius Ahenobarbus, with
an army that included some elephants, defeated the Allobroges at
Vindalium. Q. Fabius Maximus arrived with fresh troops and
together the two generals defeated the Arverni, though their elephants are not mentioned in this battle. No details of these engagements survive, but the elephants obviously had a frightening effect
on barbarian tribes meeting them for the first time, and thus they
made their contribution to Rome's first step in her conquest of
Gaul. Southern Gaul soon became a Roman province, *the* province,
Provence. Domitius is said to have celebrated his victory by riding
on an elephant through the province with a military escort, as if
holding a triumph.[133]

At the siege of Numantia the Romans had been helped by the
young prince Jugurtha, who had been accustomed to hunt lions
and other wild animals (including the elephant?) in his native
Numidia, but when by murder and intrigue he had seized the
Numidian throne, the Romans were gradually forced into hostilities with him. At first they tried to avoid too deep a commitment:
thus, even after war was declared in 111 BC, the consul Calpurnius
Bestia persuaded Jugurtha to make a formal surrender in return
for retaining the throne; *inter alia* Jugurtha handed over 30 elephants (though he may have kept others: he later had at least 44).
However, after a visit by Jugurtha to Rome the war was renewed
and a Roman army under Aulus Albinus was humiliated near
Suthul. In Rome a tribune named Mamilius demanded an enquiry
into many scandals connected with the conduct of the war, including the handing back of his elephants to Jugurtha; apparently this
had been done under terms reached locally by Albinus. At last

Rome was committed to full-scale warfare under an efficient commander, Q. Caecilius Metellus. As in the days of the Punic Wars Rome now faced an enemy who had war-elephants, while she had none of her own in Africa. The first major clash came on the river Muthul: while Metellus engaged Jugurtha's main force, which caught him in an awkward position, he sent Rutilius with a lighter force to occupy a good and well-watered position for a camp. Bomilcar, who had been put in command of the elephants and part of the infantry, thrust between the two Roman detachments, and while the main battle was raging, he attacked Rutilius' camp. As long as they felt protected by their elephants the Numidians pressed on, but when they saw their elephants entangled in the branches of some trees and separated from one another, they fled: the area was dusty scrub-land, with bushes and trees. The Romans captured four of the elephants and killed 40. However, Jugurtha still had some others, since in the course of subsequent negotiations he handed over 'all his elephants', but in vain, since he later decided to continue fighting.[134] Although he raised fresh forces, these do not appear to have included any elephants, nor do we hear that his new ally, Bocchus the Moor, provided him with any. Marius, Metellus' successor, had to face a long struggle before Jugurtha was finally defeated, but he did not have to cope with elephants.

When Sulla had gained supreme power in Italy he sent young Pompey to crush the supporters of Marius who were still holding out in Sicily and Africa. Pompey landed in Africa in 81 BC and within forty days he had defeated Cn. Domitius Ahenobarbus and the Numidian usurper, Iarbas, who was helping Domitius. Since Plutarch records that he took back to Rome 'many elephants which he had captured from the kings', Iarbus must have put some into the field, while the use of 'kings' suggests that Hiempsal, to whom Pompey restored Numidia, had presented him with more. After his victory Pompey spent some time in Numidia, hunting lions and elephants; if he captured any elephants alive, these would not be broken in in time for him to take home with him. In Rome a ridiculous incident occurred. Dreaming no doubt of Alexander the Great, young Pompey, who though not yet a senator had forced Sulla grudgingly to grant him a triumph, decided to enter the city in a chariot drawn by four elephants. However, the gate of the city was too narrow and he had to change over to horses. One may imagine that the scurillous verses that soldiers chanted at their general's triumph might contain sarcastic references to this episode, especially as they were disgruntled at the amount of booty they had received.[135]

In his *Gallic Wars* Julius Caesar presents a vivid picture of how he forced a passage across the river Thames against fierce opposition during his second invasion of Britain in 54 BC, but he has not a word about elephants. However, Polyaenus, writing in the mid-second century AD records that Caesar had one large elephant, which was equipped with armour and carried archers and slingers in its tower. When this unknown creature entered the river the Britons and their horses fled and the Roman army crossed over. Most historians reject this anecdote out of respect for Caesar's silence, but an attempt has been made by C. E. Stevens to save it on the ground that it might have been recorded in the annual despatch that he sent to the Senate at Rome and not in his written Commentaries, and thus have reached Polyaenus, perhaps by way of Livy. Stevens goes further and suggests a motive for Caesar's use of an elephant and for his omission of the episode: he will have been rivalling the conduct of Domitius Ahenobarbus who used to ride about on an elephant after his Gallic victory (p. 192) and who was the grandfather of Caesar's bitter political opponent in the mid-fifties. Since Caesar failed to conquer a province whereas the elder Domitius had succeeded, Caesar's action was rather foolish and so he did not call attention to it in his Commentaries. This ingenious explanation seems rather far-fetched, nor can it confidently be supported by another argument on which Stevens based it. A silver denarius of about this time bears the name 'Caesar' and shows an African elephant (note the two 'fingers' of the trunk), trampling on a dragon which Stevens takes as a symbol for Ocean (pl. XXIVd). Unfortunately the coin evades precise dating: it has been assigned to 54, which would fit this theory very neatly, but the evidence of coin-hoards suggests 49. An obvious date would be 46 after Caesar's victory at Thapsus in Africa, where he defeated the elephants of Juba (p. 197), but if the hoards compel an earlier date, then perhaps the elephant might refer to the belief that 'Caesar' was the Moorish word for 'elephant'. In sum, it seems hazardous to accept Polyaenus against Caesar.[136]

In 49 BC civil war broke out between Caesar and Pompey, and Caesar sent a force under Curio to secure Africa which was held by a former governor of the province, named Varus. The latter had the support of Juba, king of Numidia, whose father owed his throne to Pompey; Juba hated both Caesar who in a quarrel in Rome had once pulled his beard, and Curio who as tribune had proposed that the kingdom should be annexed to the Roman province of Africa. In line with Roman policy of allowing native rulers in Africa to keep elephants, Juba had a large number. He was proud of the fact which he advertised on his bronze coinage (pl. XXIIIe, f). After some initial success Curio met with disaster in a final engagement to which Juba contributed 60 elephants. Thus Africa remained in Pompeian hands.[137]

After Pompey had been finally defeated by Caesar at Pharsalus the surviving Pompeian forces concentrated in Africa to fight on to the tune of ten legions while Juba brought four more and a number of elephants which rumour raised to 120 but which from the subsequent fighting seem to have amounted to some 60 or 70. The Roman forces were commanded by Pompey's father-in-law, Q. Metellus Scipio. Though he had no elephants of his own he issued a coinage for the pay of his troops, and one issue depicted an elephant (pl. XXIVc). This was particularly appropriate since it showed his men the value of Juba's contribution, while the elephant had become the family badge of the Metelli (p. 152) into which he had been adopted. As soon as he was free to leave Italy, Caesar sailed for Africa and landed on the east coast of Tunisia (winter 47/6) where he mustered eight legions.[138]

The campaign that followed has been described by a participant and eyewitness, not Caesar himself but an unknown soldier, perhaps a centurion, in the *Bellum Africum*. While Caesar was operating around Ruspina, Juba had to return to his own kingdom which was being attacked by Bocchus, king of Mauretania, and a Roman adventurer, named Sittius, but he left 30 elephants with Scipio. These elephants needed some training, which is described in *Bellum Africum*: to represent the enemy Scipio drew up a line of slingers opposite the elephants, and his own battle-line behind them. The slingers bombarded the elephants with small stones and when they wheeled back on their own side they received another volley from them and thus turned again to face the 'enemy'. This method worked, although it was slow, 'since elephants are rough creatures, and it is difficult to get them fully trained even with many years of training; and if they are led out to battle they are equally dangerous to both sides'. Thus thought the writer, but he does not explain why they needed this training. The explanation may perhaps be found in Florus (II, 13.67) who says that Juba's elephants were unaccustomed to war and had only recently been brought from the forests. Thus probably before the events of this war Juba had had little occasion to use them in battle and he appears to have increased his number as a result of Caesar's invasion: the fact that he left untrained elephants with Scipio and perhaps took the better trained ones back to protect Numidia is in line with the off-hand way in which he treated Scipio in some other respects. Each day Scipio tried to entice Caesar into a pitched battle, by drawing up his line with 30 turreted elephants in front of it, but Caesar was not ready. Scipio even sent spies to see if Caesar had made any elephant-traps in front of his camp or at the gates of his ramparts. The theatre of operations then shifted a few miles away to Uzitta, where again Scipio challenged his opponent; this time his elephants are described as turreted and armoured and were interspersed between squadrons of cavalry on the wings. When Juba returned with 30 elephants Scipio on the very next day offered battle with his entire forces which now included 60 elephants, but again Caesar bided his time. The author of *Bellum Africum* describes – yet another time – the battle-line with the elephants on both wings at regular intervals, supported in their rear by light-armed troops and Numidian auxiliaries. Caesar became increasingly concerned about the influence of the elephants on the morale of his troops and found an answer to this worry by sending to Italy for some elephants which he intended to use for training-purposes and not for actual fighting. Where they were obtained from we are not told: perhaps from the amphitheatres where they were used for public spectacles (there is no direct evidence that any were kept by the State at this time, as they were under the Empire). When they arrived in Africa his troops were shown the vulnerable parts of their bodies and also what parts were still left exposed when they were accoutred and armoured (*ornatus ac loricatus*). The horses also were trained to become accustomed to their scent, trumpeting and appearance. Thus the troops lost their fear by handling the beasts and recognized that they were slow (*tarditatem*); the cavalry hurled dummy javelins at them, and the horses realized their docility (*patientia*) and became used to them.

The scene was now set for the final encounter when Caesar moved towards Thapsus. We need not follow the manoeuverings around the lagoon near the town which led to the choice of the battle-field. Caesar detached the ten cohorts of the Fifth Legion from the main line and stationed five on each wing against the enemy's elephants. Through the impetuosity of his troops battle was joined sooner than Caesar wished, but all went well: on his right wing the slingers and archers drove back the elephants on to their own supporting troops and rushed to the uncompleted gates of their rampart. The legionaries, having routed the enemy left, rolled up his line, and stormed the camp. The elephants on Scipio's right no doubt tried to cover the retreat of that wing, and it was probably here that an episode occurred which displayed the courage and resourcefulness of a veteran of the Fifth: a wounded elephant was crushing a sutler underfoot when the veteran distracted the beast which then lifted him in the air with its trunk; whereupon the soldier kept hacking at the trunk with his sword until pain caused the beast to drop him. After the victory Caesar led 64 captured elephants, armed with their turrets and gear, against Thapsus. At first unawed by this massive spectacle, the city soon had to surrender. Thus both Caesar's men and horses had withstood the onset of Scipio's elephants and he had managed to roll up his enemy's line: if the elephants on Scipio's left had stood their ground, the result might well have been very different. In the event, victory gave Caesar control of Africa, and with it of virtually the Roman world. Cato's suicide after the battle symbolized the death of the Roman Republic, and the way was open for Caesar's brief dictatorship. The Romans had fought their last battle with elephants for some 300 years.[139]

In 46 BC Caesar celebrated in Rome a fourfold triumph, the last day being for his African victory. Though he had better reason, he made no attempt, as Pompey had done, to ride on or be drawn by elephants in this the most magnificent triumph yet seen at Rome. However, after the celebration he was escorted home by a vast crowd with 40 elephants on his right and left carrying torches in their trunks. In the Games which he then arranged a battle was staged between two groups of 500 infantry, 20 elephants and 30 horsemen on each side, also a fight between men mounted on elephants, 40 in number. These elephants, or at any rate many of them, were probably Juba's animals which Caesar had brought back. Whether any or all were killed is not recorded, but a later chance reference suggests that casualties may have been light. Early in 43 BC Cicero was urging the Senate to oppose M. Antony, who was besieging Decimus Brutus in Mutina in northern Italy, and in his *Fifth Philippic* he records how Gaius Caesar (i.e. young Octavian, later Augustus) had set out with an army to relieve Gaul and had brought cavalry, archers and elephants under the authority of himself and that of the Roman People. This had come about soon after the murder of Julius Caesar when Octavian had managed to win over from Antony many of Julius' old troops. 'He also captured', wrote Dio, 'all the elephants of Antony which he happened to meet as they were being driven along.' This appears to have been near Brundisium where Julius had been mustering forces for his projected Parthian campaign: thus, despite his experience of the behaviour of Juba's elephants at Thapsus, Caesar seems to have intended to take some to the East. Instead, they came into the hands of Octavian, and Cicero implies that he intended to take them to northern Italy to help relieve the siege of Mutina. Thereafter they disappear from history.[140]

## THE ROMAN AND SASSANIAN EMPIRES

Imperial ceremonial and public spectacle were the spheres in which elephants were seen during the Roman Empire. The Romans had abandoned their use in war, and they had not been found in the armies of Rome's enemies in the East in the later Republic: neither Mithridates of Pontus, nor Tigranes of Armenia, nor indeed Pompey on the Roman side, had used them. The Parthians, who could easily have obtained elephants from India, preferred to rely on their cavalry, the Romans on their legionaries, and neither empire was attracted by this weapon whose value had so often proved ambiguous. It is noteworthy that Arrian, writing his *Tactica* in the second century AD, says (ch. 22) that it would be a waste of time to detail the units and organization, together with their names, of the corps of chariots and elephants, because these had long since ceased to be used (while the Romans themselves had never used chariots).

One early superficial exception is the emperor Claudius, whose troops in AD 43 invaded Britain, fought their way to the Thames and then waited for their emperor to come to share in the glorious culmination of the first campaign, the capture of Camulodunum (Colchester). Dio Cassius (LX, 21.2) records that Claudius had already got together 'much equipment, including elephants' for this expedition, and he duly arrived in Britain with detachments of the Praetorian Guard and part of legion VIII. Dio does not specifically mention that the elephants were actually taken to Britain, and so some scholars have questioned their presence, but he clearly implies it and there is no good reason to doubt it. His purpose will have been to overawe the natives and also perhaps to make a more impressive progress through the province, though probably not as a mount for himself: as shown on the coinage, the arch which he erected in Rome to celebrate his British triumph was topped by the figure of the emperor riding a horse.

More than a century later another attempt was made to use elephants. In AD 193 the short-lived emperor Didius Julianus, facing the invasion of Italy and Rome by Septimius Severus, turned to the animals which were used in ceremonial processions, the *pompe*, and tried to train them to carry turrets and men on their backs, hoping that they would frighten Severus' Illyrian cavalry. But in vain: the beasts would not submit and threw off their riders and turrets. Some twenty years later another emperor brought elephants to public notice: Caracalla, who regarded himself as a second Alexander the Great and was obsessed with his memory, established a phalanx of Macedonians; it was only natural, therefore, for him to take about with him many elephants 'that he might seem to be imitating Alexander, or rather, perhaps, Dionysus', as Dio comments, referring to the god's traditional journey back from India.[141]

From the days of the early Empire an official supply of elephants had been maintained. This imperial herd was administered by an official named the *procurator ad elephantos* at Laurentum, near Ardea and not far to the south of Rome. This herd (*Caesaris armentum*) is mentioned by Juvenal who perhaps wrongly implies that it was maintained solely by import since he thought that elephants could not breed in Italy, although in fact Aelian records, in connection with a show that Germanicus was staging, that there were several adult elephants, both male and female, and calves born of them in Italy. Nevertheless Juvenal's lines deserve quotation:

> quatenus hic non sunt nec venales elephanti,
> nec Latio aut usquam sub nostro sidere talis
> belua concipitur, sed furva gente petita
> arboribus Rutulis et Turni pascitur agro;

Caesaris armentum nulli servire paratum
privato, siquidem Tyrio parere solebant
Hannibali et nostris ducibus regique Molosso
horum maiores ac dorso ferre cohortis
partem aliquam belli, et euntem in proelia turrem.

('since elephants are not for sale, and that beast does not breed in Latium or anywhere else beneath our skies, but is brought from the dark man's land to be fed in the Rutulian forest and the domains of Turnus. The herd is Caesar's and will serve no private master, since their forebears were wont to obey the Tyrian Hannibal and our generals and the Molossian king [i.e. Pyrrhus] and to carry cohorts on their backs, a considerable part of war, towers going into battle').[142]

The possession of elephants appears to have been an imperial prerogative, although just before the establishment of the Empire we hear of a private individual apparently owning one. L. Cornificius, a friend of Octavian, during the civil war had in 36 BC managed to extricate three legions from a dangerous position in Sicily and led them safely to join Agrippa's forces. He used to commemorate his achievement by riding on an elephant whenever he dined out. Later, elephants could be used as marks of imperial favour: thus Hadrian gave an elephant among other gifts to Pharasmanes, king of the Iberians in the Caucasus, while Aurelian, before he became emperor, was sent on an embassy to the Persians and received the present of an exceptionally large elephant which he then donated to the emperor (Valerian) but which apparently he was allowed to keep, since the *Historia Augusta* records that he was the only private citizen who ever owned an elephant.[143]

For over two centuries the Roman Empire faced few serious threats to its existence but during the third century AD external pressure began to build up to a critical point: barbarian tribes in the West and the Persians in the East were no longer content to remain beyond the frontiers that Rome had established. We are concerned here only with the East, since elephants were not used in the West, but after a lapse of centuries they made their appearance once again in eastern armies in the service of the new Sassanid kings of Persia. The Parthian empire had collapsed, largely through internal dissensions, and was replaced by a new power, the dynasty of Sasan, whose grandson, Ardashir (Artaxerxes) had been king of

Persis and a vassal of the Arsacid king of Parthia. Ardashir gained control of the central Parthian empire and then extended his conquests eastwards to Afghanistan and Baluchistan. He organized his empire on much the same administrative lines as that of the superseded Parthian empire, but with stronger central control. His army too was organized and equipped much as that of the Parthians, but with one addition: he apparently revived the idea of an elephant corps.

Rome was thus faced by the challenge of a new power which sought to revive the great Persian empire of the days of Darius and Xerxes. In 230 Ardashir began to move westwards and besieged Nisibis. Rome reacted quickly and the emperor Severus Alexander led a large force against him. However, a three-pronged attack led to an indecisive action, followed by a cessation of hostilities. This battle was magnified in the *Historia Augusta* into a glorious Roman victory, but Herodian's more sober account reveals that in fact it was a Roman reverse after which Severus left the East. Further, the *Historia Augusta* asserts that Ardashir had 700 elephants, with towers and archers, and that Severus in his report to the Senate claimed to have killed 200, captured 300 and sent 18 to Rome, while at his triumph four elephants drew his chariot. The figures for elephants, as also those given for the Persian cavalry, are clearly nonsense and could well be divided by ten. The elephants are not mentioned at all by Herodian and so they might be thought to be inventions designed to portray Severus as a second Alexander the Great who had faced the elephants of Porus. Or it could be argued that, *if* the *Historia Augusta* was composed in the time of Julian or later in the fourth century when elephants were well known to have formed part of the Persian army, then they were naturally presupposed to have been there in an earlier period. But Herodian's account is fairly brief and gives no detail about the composition or numbers of the forces on either side, while it is certain that the Sassanids did adopt the use of elephants: a century later Ammianus Marcellinus met them face to face in battle, and did not find it an agreeable experience. Thus behind the exaggerations of the *Historia Augusta* may lie an element of truth.[144]

Ardashir's son, Shapur (Sapor) who succeeded to the throne in 242, renewed the offensive and advanced into Syria but was thrown back by Gordian III in a victory at Rasaina and soon afterwards made peace with Philip, now emperor. Gordian is said in the *His-*

*toria Augusta* to have sent 12 (or 22) captured elephants to Rome, while the Senate decreed chariots of four elephants to draw his chariot for a Persian triumph. However, while he was still in the East Gordian was murdered with the connivance of Philip, who in 248 celebrated Games in honour of Rome's millennium: at these he showed and killed a vast number of animals which Gordian had collected at Rome, including 32 elephants.[145]

Hostilities with Persia dragged on intermittently, reaching their lowest point with the capture of the Roman emperor Valerian, but notices are scanty and to get details of military actions we have to wait until the mid-fourth century when fortunately a large part of the work of one of the major historians has survived for this period, namely the History of Ammianus Marcellinus, who himself fought in the Persian campaigns. In 337 Shapur II took advantage of the troubles that followed the death of Constantine the Great to invade Mesopotamia, where for two months he vainly besieged the fortified city of Nisibis. The defence was led by its bishop St James, whose help was efficacious, even if he did not, as is reported by Theodoret, miraculously send a swarm of gnats to sting the trunks of the Persians' elephants. Constantius II, who became ruler of the East on the death of his father Constantine, hurried to the East and reached an agreement with Shapur which lasted until the latter in 344 crossed the Tigris and fought an indecisive battle against Constantius near Singara; the Romans were gradually getting used to facing elephants once again. After a brief and abortive siege of Nisibis again in 346, Shapur returned to the assault for the third time in 350, and of this siege Julian in his second oration in honour of Constantius (64 ff.) provides some details. First, the besieged made a sally against the heavily-armed Persian cavalry and drove them back into a bog, where they floundered. Then the elephants were sent in: Julian thinks that the Persians must have been mad, because 'an elephant is heavier than a horse since it carries the load, not of two horses or several, but what would, I suppose require many waggons, I mean archers and javelin-men and the iron towers besides'. The elephants at equal distances from each other were stationed in the phalanx; thus the line advanced to overawe rather than to give battle, but it was provoked into hostilities and was driven back; some of the elephants being wounded by the fire from the walls sank into the mud and perished; the others were led back. An attempt to divert the local river, the Mygdonius, from its course was no more successful and so the siege was abandoned.[146]

In 359 Shapur again invaded Mesopotamia and laid siege to the fortified town of Amida on the upper Tigis. Ammianus, who for some years had been attached to the staff of Ursicinus, the commander-in-chief in the East, was among the besieged: he has left a vivid account of the town's gallant resistance. As Shapur advanced on the city, at the first gleam of dawn the next day Ammianus looked out: 'everywhere as far as the eye could reach shone with glittering arms, and mail-clad cavalry filled plain and hill'. Outside the west gate 'slowly marched lines of elephants, terrifying with their wrinkled bodies and loaded with armed men, a hideous sight, dreadful beyond every form of horror, as I have often repeated' (XIX, 1.2; 2.3). After describing the frightfulness of many days of siege Ammianus refers to the worst moment when the enemy's artillery (*ballistae*), mounted on iron-clad towers, was causing great carnage, while formidable bodies of Persians attacked along with companies (*agminibus*) of elephants: 'the human mind can conceive nothing more terrible than their noise and huge bodies'. Nevertheless, stones shot by Roman engines known as scorpions shattered the joints of some of the towers and brought them down, while the elephants were attacked on all sides by means of fire-brands, and turned tail as soon as these touched their bodies (7, 6–7). But that was the end: after seventy-three days the city fell. Ammianus managed to escape in the darkness and after many adventures joined Ursicinus at Melitene. Although Shapur had suffered great losses, he was able in the next year to capture Singara and other towns.

After becoming emperor Julian in 363 led a major expedition against Persia, with which Ammianus again served. Marching along the Euphrates, together with his fleet, he stormed many towns and then met and defeated a Persian army in front of Ctesiphon. Although Shapur had not yet arrived, it is noteworthy that elephants were employed: thus they were a regular arm of the service and not merely a royal force to be used by the king himself. This time they seemed to Ammianus like 'walking hills'. Anticipating Shapur's arrival, Julian decided to withdraw and literally burn his boats behind him. All the way his retreat was harassed by constant enemy attacks; these included elephants, which were thus apparently able to keep up with the speed of the Romans. Once

Ammianus spoke of the terror inflicted by their gaping mouths, their trumpeting and their odour on both men and horses; one might have thought that these aspects would have lost some of their sting for the legionaries, but Ammianus was there and knew better. He also adds that the riders carried knives bound to their right hands, remembering what had happened at Nisibis, and that they could kill unruly beasts by a blow where the head joins the neck; he interestingly adds a reference to the similar procedure adopted by Hasdrubal Barca at Metaurus (p. 185). After this engagement near Maranga the Romans later turned and stood to fight again, and their light-armed troops attacked the legs and backs (hamstrung?) of the elephants as they turned to withdraw; this time Ammianus mentions the frightening crests that they wore. In the battle Julian received a fatal wound, and was succeeded as emperor by Jovian who during the continued retreat had to fight at least one more engagement. Recoiling from the initial shock of the attack, the legionaries named Joviani and Herculiani rallied and killed a few of the animals; then, supported by the Jovii and Victores, they killed two more. This episode is mentioned not only by Ammianus but also in the briefer account by Zosimus who, writing at the end of the century, had not bothered to refer to elephants in his shorter account of Julian's campaign: but then he had not faced them in battle. Jovian now decided to reach terms with Shapur, who learnt of the various set-backs to his armies and 'a greater loss of elephants than he had ever known in his reign'. The terms which Jovian accepted, including the abandonment of much of Mesopotamia and allowing Armenia to revert to Shapur, were generally denounced as shameful, but they gave a kind of peace for the thirty years of their duration. Thus Julian's major campaign had ended in near disaster, and to this Shapur's elephants had made a very considerable contribution if Ammianus is to be followed.[147]

Jovian's peace allowed Shapur a free hand with Armenia, on which he launched a three-pronged attack. On this occasion, as in other Persian-Armenian struggles, Faustus of Byzantium records the use of elephants. He tells a story in this campaign which recalls Eleazar the Jew. The Armenian general Pacas in command of one of the three armies saw a magnificent elephant, caparisoned with royal banners, and erroneously thought the king Shapur was riding it. He rushed in and hamstrung the animal, which fell on him, and both died. Apart from use in actual battle Shapur at times used his elephants to trample prisoners to death. In regard to Rome Persia remained at peace for a very long time and Roman armies did not have to face elephants, but memories of them remained alive in the West, as witness the remarks of St Ambrose some twenty or thirty years perhaps after Jovian's peace: 'their line advances as if hedged in with walking towers. Who dare approach them, when he is easily pierced by missiles from above and trampled on by the advancing elephants below? . . . Elephants rush against their foe with a force that cannot be withstood so that they are held up by no line of soldiers, by no body of warriors, by no fence of shields; in battle they behave like moving mountains.' Finally, the Romans were reminded of the appearance of elephants since the orator Pacatus, acclaiming at Rome the arrival of the emperor in 389, refers to a Persian embassy which brought gifts of gems, silks, and elephants.[148]

During most of the fifth century hostilities had ceased between Rome and Persia, but they broke out again in the reign of Anastasius in 502. The Persians were still using elephants and we may glance at a few episodes, though without considering the later period in any detail. In 502 the Persian Kawad (Cobades) invaded Roman Armenia and captured Amida after a tough siege. He entered the city riding on an elephant. His successor, Chosroes, was at war with the Empire during most of Justinian's reign. In 544 he besieged Edessa, where one of his elephants came towering above the wall and the 'large number of soldiers on it' (Procopius) rained down missiles on the defenders. However, the besieged were not baffled: they held a squealing pig over the wall, which so angered the elephant that it got out of control and retreated. One is reminded of the pigs that the elephants of Pyrrhus had to face (p. 114). Chosroes was next involved against the Lazi, a people who lived in ancient Colchis on the eastern shores of the Black Sea, an area which served the Romans as a barrier against the barbarians north of the Caucasus and also against a Persian attack through Iberia. Elephants are mentioned, but Procopius' account of the Persian Wars does not suggest that they were used in very great numbers. At the siege of Archaeopolis eight elephants are mentioned: great efforts had been made to open up a smooth road through rough country for them and the horses. At the siege they moved in close to the wall, together with the battering-rams, but, as so often, one was wounded or over-excited, got out of control and broke up the formation of its fellows (551). A little later some elephants were placed in the river Phasis on either side, as far in as they could stand, behind a barrier of stockades and boats in order to help the passage of the Persians against the current.[149]

War was resumed under Justin II, and Chosroes, now over eighty years old, himself took command of the siege of Dara, where elephants contributed to his success (573). Two years later the Romans defeated the Persians in battle at Melitene and captured much booty which included elephants; old Chosroes managed to escape across the Euphrates on the back of his elephant which swam over safely. Twenty-four captured beasts were sent to Constantinople. In 582, the emperor Maurice sent an elephant on request to the Khagan of the Avars at Sirmium; the Khagan had never seen one and when he did he reacted unfavourably: he refused it 'whether from fear or in order to snub the Romans, I cannot say,' wrote Theophylactus. Maurice later supported the exiled Chosroes II against Bahram in an engagement at Sargana, where elephants apparently fought on both sides: if so the Roman Narses must have used some captured in previous wars. Bahram was defeated and his elephants were given to Chosroes who threw his prisoners to them (591). Further wars followed when the Persians swept over much of the Roman East, and Jerusalem fell in 614. Thereafter in 622 Heraclius during the next six years forced the Persians back. In 628 he captured Dastagerd where the Great King had a great pleasure park, full of animals, including, it was said, 960 elephants. At any rate after losing this, Chosroes raised another army which included 200 elephants. Heraclius entered Constantinople in a chariot drawn by four elephants, and many were exhibited in circus and hippodrome. But both peoples were now exhausted and dominion in the East was to pass into other hands with the rise and conquests of the Arabs.[150] The Muslims, however, did not forget the elephant, but long honoured the Year of the Elephant, AD 570, when an Abyssinian army with elephants had attacked Mecca and was routed by the grandfather of the Prophet.

In taking leave of the Indian elephant in the East, we should see him in all his glory on the reliefs carved in a cave at Taq-i-Bustan (pl. XI). These have been dated to the late fifth century or even more than a hundred years later, namely to the reign of Chosroes II. They depict royal hunts in a 'paradise' like that at Dastagerd and various episodes are shown. Amid swarms of wild boars the king, standing

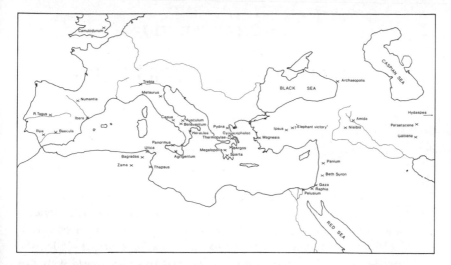

Fig. 19. Map to illustrate battles and sieges in which elephants were involved

in a boat in which he is being rowed across a swamp, is shooting with his bow. On either side, in panels, the dead animals are being loaded on to elephants, 'whose realistic renderings rank among the finest achievements of Oriental art'. Nor should we forget the African elephant in this later period; if he appears less in war and more in the arena, his numbers were well maintained, since Nonnosus, Justinian's envoy to the ruler of the Axumite kingdom of Ethiopia, reported that at one place on the road between Adulis and Axum he had seen nearly 5,000 elephants which were feeding on the countryside and which could not easily be approached by the natives or driven from their pastures.[151]

# CHAPTER VIII

# THE LATER WRITERS

## JUBA AND PLINY

We saw earlier what the first Greek writers had to say about elephants and then surveyed the elephant in action from the Hellenistic to the Roman period. We now come to the later writers, such as Pliny and Aelian, who relied to a great extent on their Hellenistic predecessors. The elephants of their contemporary world were not the war-elephants of earlier days but rather the animals used in circus and ceremonial. A link between these two periods is provided by a man who knew elephants at first hand and also wrote about them, namely Juba II, the son of Juba of Numidia whose elephants had faced Julius Caesar at Thapsus (p. 197). The younger Juba was brought up in Italy and returned to Africa c. 25 BC; he married Cleopatra Selene, the daughter of Antony and Cleopatra, and died c. AD 23. Near the end of his reign an insurrection broke out in North Africa, led by Tacfarinas. This was crushed by Roman armies; doubtless Juba lent help, which may well have included some elephants. At any rate he issued coins which showed a turreted elephant holding a crown in its trunk; they bear a regnal date, the equivalent of AD 21/22, and probably commemorate successes against Tacfarinas who was finally defeated and killed in 24 (pl. XXIIIj). Juba was a man of culture and learning and wrote many books in Greek on a variety of subjects, including geography, natural history and mythology. Despite a scientific interest, he appears on occasion to have been somewhat over-credulous. He was particularly interested in elephants, and both Pliny and Aelian in their books on natural history drew from him material which will be considered further later. Here it may be noted that Juba is known to have discussed the following topics: tusks were horns, not teeth; the shedding of tusks; voice; longevity; methods of capture; memory; intelligence; sense of justice; affection for some women; delicacy; and piety. The loss of his works has clearly robbed us of a first-class source of information about the elephant of North-west Africa.[152]

Pliny the Elder (AD 23–79) was a man of affairs who was in command of the Roman fleet at Misenum when scientific curiosity led him to approach too far into the danger zone when Vesuvius was erupting and thus to lose his life. His major literary work was his *Natural History*, of which zoology forms only one section. For its composition he read extremely widely and showed incredible industry and application, but though he was a careful writer and extremely interested in what he wrote, he was not an original thinker and his work is essentially a compilation from the writings of others and lacks judgement in sifting the false from the true. It contains much entertaining and anecdotal as well as scientific information. In Aristotle, and to a lesser extent in Aelian, the material relating to animals is largely scattered throughout their works. Pliny on the other hand gives thirteen consecutive chapters (VIII, 1–13) on the elephant: since this is the longest passage on this subject in the ancient authors, we may look at the substance of it, even though some is more amusing than scientific (with a few brief comments in square brackets).

'The largest land animal,' Pliny wrote (VIII, 1), 'is the elephant, and it is the nearest to man in intelligence: it understands the language of its country and obeys orders, remembers duties that it has been taught, is pleased by affection and by marks of honour, nay more it possesses virtues rare even in man, honesty, wisdom, justice, also respect for the stars and reverence for sun and moon. Authorities state that in the forests of Mauretania, when the new moon is shining, herds of elephants go down to a river named Amilo, and there perform a ritual of purification, sprinkling themselves with water, and after thus paying their respects to the moon return to the woods carrying before them those of their calves that are tired' [this might well refer to one of the periodical gatherings and regroupings of herds, which has only seldom been witnessed by modern man (p. 22). The females in a herd often aid a youngster by pushing it up a bank or helping it out of a mudhole or river-bed, and even carry them at need. Col. Williams writes (*Elephant Bill*, 44): 'I believe that, if she is disturbed, the mother elephant will carry her calf, during its first month, holding it wrapped in her trunk. I have seen a mother pick up her calf in this way.'] 'They are

209

also believed to understand the obligations of another's religion in so far as to refuse to embark on board ships when going overseas before they are lured on by the mahout's sworn promise in regard to their return. And they have been seen when exhausted by suffering ... to lie on their backs and throw grass up to heaven as though deputing the earth to support their prayers.' [Could this be a misunderstanding of the normal process of squirting themselves with dust, etc., after a bathe?] 'Indeed so far as concerns docility, they do homage to their king by kneeling before him and proffering garlands. The Indians employ the smaller breed, which they call the bastard elephant, for ploughing.'

After describing some of their circus tricks, which are mentioned later (p. 253), Pliny continues (6), 'Mucianus, who was three times consul, states that one elephant actually learnt the shape of the Greek letters and used to write out in words of that language: "I myself wrote this and dedicated these spoils won from the Celts;" and also that he personally had seen elephants that, when having been brought by sea to Puteoli they were made to walk off the ship, were frightened by the length of the gangway stretching a long way from the land and turned round and went backwards, so as to cheat themselves in their estimate of the distance' [Mucianus, a contemporary of Pliny, wrote a book of geographical *mirabilia*. This anecdote seems to show that the 'elephant victory' over the Galatians in 275 BC (p. 122) was still remembered. The disembarkation difficulty recalls Hannibal's trouble in getting his elephants to walk on to the pontoons in the Rhone (p. 157)].

(7). 'They themselves know that the only thing in them that makes desirable plunder is in their weapons which Juba calls "horns", but which the author so greatly his senior, Herodotus, and also common usage better term "teeth"; consequently when these fall off owing to some accident or to age they bury them in the ground. The tusk alone is of ivory; otherwise even in these animals too the skeleton forming the framework of the body is common bone; albeit recently owing to our poverty even the bones have begun to be cut into layers, inasmuch as an ample supply of tusks is now rarely obtained except from India, all the rest in our world having succumbed to luxury. A young elephant is known by the whiteness of its tusks. The beasts take the greatest care of them; they spare the point of one so that it may not be blunt for fighting and use the other as an implement for digging roots and thrusting massive objects forward; and when surrounded by a party of hunters they post those with the smallest tusks in front, so that it may be thought not worth while to fight them, and afterwards when exhausted they break their tusks by dashing them against a tree and ransom themselves at the price of the desired booty.' [One tusk is usually used more than the other (p. 18). When a unit is attacked, the matriarch takes up the advance position, with her own calves close, behind or even under their mother, while her younger daughters with their calves bunch around. Perhaps this grouping of the youngsters has given the impression that those with the smallest tusks were in front].

(9). 'It is remarkable in the case of most animals that they know why they are hunted, but also that almost all know what they must beware of. It is said that when an elephant accidentally meets a human being who is merely wandering across his track in a solitary place it is good-tempered and peaceful and will actually show the way; but that when on the other hand it notices a man's footprint before it sees the man himself it begins to tremble in fear of an ambush, stops to sniff the scent, gazes round, trumpets angrily, and avoids treading on the footprint but digs it up and passes it to the next elephant, and that one to the following, and on to the last of all with a similar message, and then the column wheels round and retires and a battle-line is formed; since the smell in question lasts to be scented by them all, though in the majority of cases it is not even the smell of bare feet. . . . It is certain that such forests are very little frequented. Granted that no doubt the elephants may be surprised by the mere rarity of the print; but how do they know that it is something to be afraid of? Indeed, why should they dread even the sight of man himself when they excel him so greatly in strength, size and speed? Doubtless it is Nature's law and shows her power, that the fiercest and largest wild beasts may never have seen a thing that they ought to fear and yet understand immediately when they have to fear it.'

(11). 'Elephants always travel in a herd; the oldest leads the column and the next oldest brings up the rear. When going to ford a river they put the smallest in front, so that the bottom may not be worn away by the tread of the larger ones, thus increasing the depths of the water. Antipater states that two elephants employed for military purposes by King Antiochus were known to the public even by name: indeed they know their own names. It is a fact that

Cato, although he has removed the names of military commanders from his *Annals*, has recorded that the elephant in the Carthaginian army that was the bravest in battle was called Surus, and that it had one broken tusk (cf. p. 174). When Antiochus was trying to ford a river his elephant Ajax refused, though on other occasions it always led the line; thereupon Antiochus issued an announcement that the elephant that crossed should have the leading place and he rewarded Patroclus, who made the venture, with the gift of silver harness, an elephant's greatest delight, and with every other mark of leadership. The one disgraced preferred death by starvation to humiliation; for the elephant has a remarkable sense of shame, and when defeated shrinks from the voice of its conqueror, and offers him earth and foliage. Owing to their modesty, elephants never mate except in secret, the male at the age of five, and the female at ten' [cf. Aristotle quoted above, p. 44 and comments]; 'the mating takes place for two years, on five days it is said, of each year and not more; and on the sixth day they give themselves a shower-bath in a river, not returning to the herd before. Adultery is unknown among them, or any of the fighting for females that is so disastrous to the other animals.' [A herd usually has a senior herd bull, the sire bull, but he may be accompanied by one or two lesser, but mature, bulls who will sometimes mate with the herd cows. Apparently younger bulls trying to copulate with a cow will give way to the senior bull without much ado if he disapproves, though cases of fighting are recorded.] They do not fight, 'though not because they are devoid of strong affection, for it is reported that one elephant in Egypt fell in love with a girl who was selling flowers, and (that nobody may think it was a vulgar choice) who was a remarkable favourite of the very celebrated scholar Aristophanes; and another elephant is said to have fallen in love with a young soldier in Ptolemy's army, a Syracusan named Menander, and whenever it did not see him to have shown its longing for him by refusing food. Also Juba records a girl selling scent who was loved by an elephant. In all these cases the animals showed their affection by their delight at the sight of the object and their clumsy gestures of endearment, and by keeping the branches given to them by the public and showering them in the loved one's lap. Nor is it surprising that animals possessing memory are also capable of affection. For the same writer records a case of an elephant's recognizing many years later in old age a man who had been its mahout in its youth, and also an instance of a sort of insight into justice, when King Bocchus tied to stakes thirty elephants which he intended to punish and exposed them to a herd of the same number, men running out among them to provoke them to the attack, and it proved impossible to make them perform the service of ministering to another's cruelty.'

Pliny next (16) records the first appearance of elephants in Italy, namely the Lucanian oxen of Pyrrhus and those captured by Metellus at Panormus, and the transport of the latter to Rome, together with their fate in the Circus (see pp. 111 f., 152). He then refers (18) to 'a famous story of one of the Romans fighting single-handed against an elephant, on the occasion when Hannibal had compelled his prisoners from our army to fight duels with one another. For he pitted one survivor against an elephant, and this man, having secured a promise of his freedom if he killed the animal, met it single-handed in the arena and much to the chagrin of the Carthaginians dispatched it. Hannibal realized that reports of this encounter would bring the animals into contempt, so he sent horsemen to kill the man as he was departing. Experiences in our battles with Pyrrhus made it clear that it was very easy to lop off an elephant's trunk'. Pliny then states, on the authority of Fenestella, that an elephant first fought in the Circus at Rome in 99 BC, and was first pitted against bulls twenty years later; he quotes other fights, which are mentioned later (p. 250 ff.).

After these grim episodes Pliny turns (23) to the gentleness of elephants. 'A story is told that the animals' natural gentleness towards those not so strong as itself is so great that if it gets among a flock of sheep it will remove with its trunk those that get in its way, so as not unwittingly to crush one. Also they never do any harm unless provoked, even though they go about in herds, being of all animals the least solitary in habit. When surrounded by horsemen they withdraw the weak ones or those that are exhausted or wounded into the middle of their column, and advance into the fighting line in relays as if by command or strategy' [Dr Sikes writes (p. 261) about a herd which is threatened: 'The herd matriarch cautiously steps towards the source of the sound . . . the others only accompany her if she screams or growls to them. More usually they remain stationary, but poised and alert, with the calves beside and under them'].

(24). 'When captured they are quickly tamed by means of barley juice. The method of capturing them in India is for a mahout riding one of the domesticated elephants to find a wild elephant alone or detach it from the herd and to flog it, and when it is tired out he climbs across on to it and manages it as he did his previous mount' [It is strange that Pliny makes only this short remark about the capture of Indian elephants, when he has much more to say about Africans: apart from this brief reference to the use of tamed 'monitors', he has not recorded the detailed account of the corral method of capture of which Megasthenes has given a vivid description: see p. 56 ff. above]. 'Africa captures elephants by means of pit-falls; when an elephant straying from the herd falls into one of these all the rest at once collect branches of trees and roll down rocks and construct ramps in an attempt to get it out' [Again, Dr Sikes (p. 272): 'If a member of the clan is injured by a falling tree, falls into a pit or is injured in a fight or by a weapon, the others cluster round it and attempt to assist it to its feet using their foreheads, trunks and tusks. There was a time when the recounting of this behaviour by old hands in Africa, of an evening, brought cynical if patient smiles to the faces of the hearers. Nowadays, however, this behaviour has been witnessed frequently and consistently by reliable observers and groups of observers. . . .' This kind of comment by a modern naturalist should put one on guard against a too ready sceptical rejection of some of the stories told about elephants by the ancient writers.] 'Previously for the purpose of taming them the kings used to round them up with horsemen into a trench made by hand so as to deceive them by its length, and when they were enclosed within its banks and ditches they were starved into submission; the proof of this would be if when a man held out a branch to them they took it gently from him' [cf. the corral and hunger method used by the *Indians*, as described by Megasthenes: above p. 56 f.]. 'At the present day hunters for the sake of their tusks shoot them with javelins in the foot, which in fact is extremely soft.' Pliny then describes Trogodyte hunting, both by hamstringing (he says of *both* legs) and by shooting with the big bow fixed in the ground; the account of both methods goes back ultimately to Agatharchides (p. 60).

Pliny next turns to training (27). 'The females of the genus elephant are much more timid than the males. Mad elephants can be tamed by hunger and blows, other elephants being brought up to the one that is unmanageable to restrain it with chains. Besides this

214

they get very wild when in heat and overthrow the stables of the Indians with their tusks. Consequently the latter prevent them from coupling, and keep the herds of females separate, in just the same way as droves of cattle are kept. Male elephants when broken in serve in battle and carry castles manned with armed warriors on their backs; they are the most important factor in eastern warfare, scattering the ranks before them and trampling armed soldiers underfoot' [not in Pliny's day!]. 'Nevertheless they are scared by the smallest squeal of a pig; and when wounded and frightened they always give ground, doing as much damage to their own side as to the enemy. African elephants are afraid of an Indian elephant, and do not dare to look at it, as Indian elephants are indeed of a larger size' [see p. 60 ff.].

(28). 'Their period of gestation is commonly supposed to be ten years, but Aristotle puts it at two years, and says that they never bear more than one at a time, and that they live 200 and in some cases 300 years. Their adult life begins at sixty' [but see above p. 45]. 'They take the greatest pleasure in rivers and roam in the neighbourhood of streams, although at the same time they are unable to swim because of the size of their bodies, and also as they are incapable of enduring cold: this is their greatest infirmity; they are also liable to flatulence and diarrhoea, but not to other kinds of disease. I find it stated that missiles sticking in their body fall out when they drink oil, but that perspiration makes it easier for them to keep their hold. It also causes them disease to eat earth unless they chew it repeatedly; but they devour even stones [cf. Aristotle: p. 46 above], consider trunks of trees a great delicacy, and bend down the loftier palm trees by butting against them with their foreheads and when thus prostrate consume their fruit. They eat with the mouth, but they breathe and drink and smell with the organ not unsuitably called their hand. They hate the mouse worst of living creatures, and if they see one merely touch the fodder placed in their stall they refuse it with disgust. They are liable to extreme torture if in drinking they swallow a leech; when this attaches itself in the actual breathing passage it causes intolerable pain.'

(30). 'The hide of the back is extremely hard, but that of the belly is soft; it has no covering of bristles, not even on the tail as a guard for driving away the annoyance of flies (for even that great bulk is sensitive to this), but the skin is creased, and is inviting to this kind of creature owing to its smell; consequently they stretch the creases open and let the swarms in, and then crush them to death by suddenly contracting the creases into wrinkles. This serves them instead of tail, mane and fleece.' [Elephants, of course, do have hairs at the end of their tails; Dr Sikes observes (p. 31) 'how mobile and sensitive the flank skin of a healthy elephant may be, and how it may be perceptibly flicked to and fro in an attempt to shift an irritating fly in a similar manner to that used by a horse. Only rarely has one seen this habit in very elderly elephants or in those with dry, heavily calloused skin.' She discusses the flies and parasites that attack elephants, pp. 185–200].

(31). 'The tusks fetch a vast price, and supply a very elegant material for images of the gods. Luxury has also discovered another thing that recommends the elephant, the flavour in the hard skin of the trunk, sought after, I believe, for no other reason than because the epicure feels that he is munching actual ivory. Exceptionally large specimens of trunks can indeed be seen in temples, but nevertheless Polybius has recorded on the authority of the chieftain Gulussa [Masinissa's son] that in the outlying parts of the province of Africa where it marches with Ethiopia elephants' tusks serve instead of doorposts in the houses, and partitions in these buildings and in stabling for cattle are made by using elephants' tusks for poles.'

(32). 'Elephants are produced by Africa beyond the deserts of Sidra and by Mauretania, also by the land of Ethiopia and the Trogodytes; but the biggest ones by India, as well as serpents which keep up a continual feud and warfare with them, the serpents also being of so large a size that they easily encircle the elephants in their coils, and fetter them with a twisted knot. In this duel both combatants die together, and the vanquished elephant in falling crushes with its weight the snake coiled around it . . . one difficulty that the serpent has is in climbing to such a height; consequently it keeps watch on the track worn by the elephant going to pasture and drops on him from a lofty tree. The elephant knows that he is badly handicapped in fighting against the snake's coils, and therefore seeks to rub it against trees or rocks. The snakes are on their guard against this, and consequently begin by shackling the elephants' steps with their tail. The elephants untie the knots with their trunk. But the snakes poke their heads right into the elephants' nostrils, hindering their breathing, and at the same time lacerating their tenderest parts; also when caught in the path of the elephants they rear up against them, going specially for their eyes: this is how it comes about that elephants are frequently found blind and exhausted with hunger and wasting misery . . . there is another account of this contest: that elephants are very cold-blooded, and consequently in very hot weather are specially sought after by snakes; and for that reason they submerge themselves in rivers and lie in wait for the elephants when drinking, and rising up coil round the trunk and imprint a bite inside the ear, because that place only cannot be protected by the trunk; and that the snakes are so large that they can hold the whole of an elephant's blood, and so they drink the elephants dry, and these when drained collapse in a heap and the serpents being intoxicated are crushed by them and die with them.'

Solinus (25.14), writing soon after AD 200, follows Pliny in the main, but explains that a snake would attack the rearmost elephant, so that when its legs became entangled and its pace slowed down, it was left behind by the herd. In hot weather the snake is very thirsty and attacks elephants when they are full of drink and their veins are full. After the fight, the spilt blood of both soaks into the ground and forms the pigment cinnabar. This information about cinnabar also comes from Pliny (*NH.* XXXIII, 116) who says that the Greeks gave the name of Indian cinnabar to the gore of a snake crushed by the weight of dying elephants when the blood of each animal gets mixed together. This substance, which is still called Dragon's blood, was really an exudation from an oriental plant named Dracaena or Pterocarpus.

The theme of a struggle between elephant and snake, which became very popular in the Middle Ages, had also entertained the Romans. Thus on a mosaic found at Carthage in 1965 an elephant is shown in the grip of a python, while earlier the poet Lucan, who seems to be fascinated by snakes and gives a long list of those that inhabit Africa, also believed that a snake could crush an elephant. This is perhaps more comprehensible in the light of the exaggerated reports of the length of some snakes. While in fact a normal maximum for a python is 30 ft, the one that plagued the army of Regulus in Africa was alleged to have been 120 ft. Aelian says that some snakes in Ethiopia, known as 'elephant-killers', reached 180 ft and, repeating Onesicritus, that in India an even longer one, measuring 140 cubits, was kept by a ruler. In fact the basis for this belief in the aggression of snakes seems very uncertain: thus Col. Williams writes, 'So far as I know, elephants don't worry about snakes, though the oozies believe that a number of elephant calves die of snake-bite. I have had this reported to me many times, but in no instance could I find any proof.']¹⁵³

'Ethiopia,' continues Pliny (35), 'produces elephants that rival those of India, being 30 ft high; the only surprising thing is what led Juba to believe them to be crested. The Ethiopian tribe in whose country they are chiefly bred are called the Asachaeans; it is stated that in coast districts belonging to this tribe the elephants link themselves four or five together into a sort of raft and holding up their heads to serve as sails are carried on the waves to the better pastures of Arabia.' [A nice item of elephant lore.]

### PLUTARCH AND ARETAEUS

Plutarch, who was roughly contemporary with the younger Pliny, included in his Essays (*Moralia*) a discussion *De Sollertia Animalium*, in which he debated whether water-animals were more intelligent than land-animals. He used similar sources to those drawn upon by Pliny and Aelian, but was somewhat more selective, and occasionally more critical. Thus he repeats (17.972) the story told by Juba about elephants who have fallen into pits being helped out by their fellows, but whereas Pliny merely recorded it (p. 214) Plutarch is not willing to accept its truth on the authority of King Juba. On the crossing of rivers he gives a different version (12.968) from Pliny: according to Pliny the young went first in order that the bed of the river might not be deepened by the weight of the larger beasts, but Plutarch says that the others waited to see how deep the river was from the possibility of the calves crossing. (According to Aelian, the youngsters swim across and the babies are carried by their mothers.) Plutarch records, without detail (32.981), that elephants avoid pigs, and also (10.966) that one tusk is kept sharper than the other. He tells (17.972), probably from Juba, how elephants pray to the gods, purifying themselves in the sea and worshipping the rising sun, raising their trunks like hands. Hence they are the animals best-beloved by the gods, as Ptolemy Philopator testifies: after his defeat of Antiochus (at Raphia) Ptolemy wished to honour the gods (the Sun, according to Aelian's version) and his sacrifice included four elephants. But in a dream he found that the god was angered by the sacrifice and so as an act

218

of propitiation he offered four elephants made of bronze in place of the sacrificed beasts. Plutarch's more anecdotal material includes the story that an elephant fell in love with a flower-seller at Alexandria and became a rival in her affections to Aristophanes of Byzantium, the chief librarian (cf. Pliny, VIII, 13 – above p. 212 – and Aelian, I, 38). On the authority of a philosopher, Hagnon of Tarsus, Plutarch tells (12.968) how an elephant in Syria, feeling that its keeper was stealing half its barley ration, carefully made two piles of it one day to make the thief aware that he knew. Another rascally keeper stole part of the ration and put stones under the remainder to make the pile look normal and deceive his master: the elephant took revenge by flinging with his trunk a mass of sand into the keeper's pot of porridge (cf. Aelian, VI, 52). Another story (12.968) told how boys in Rome used to annoy an elephant (one on exhibition?) by pricking its trunk with their styluses; one day the elephant seized a boy and lifted him up in his trunk, but when the spectators cried out the animal gently put the boy down, thinking that his fright was punishment enough. Finally, Plutarch twice refers to the skill with which the elephant of Porus picked out the javelins from its master's body (14.970; 20.974).

A certain Amyntianus, who dedicated a history of Alexander to the emperor Marcus Aurelius, also wrote a book *Concerning Elephants*. Unfortunately all we know about this is that according to a Scholiast on Pindar (*Ol.* III, 52) Amyntianus said that whereas Ethiopian and Libyan elephants, both male and female, have tusks (or horns, as some believe), the females of Indian elephants lack tusks. This correct piece of information makes the loss of the book the more regrettable. It might have been used by a medical writer of considerable distinction, named Aretaeus of Cappadocia, who lived about the same time and wrote works on medical matters in Ionic Greek. At the end of Book IV on the Causes of Diseases he has a chapter περὶ ἐλέφαντος, and a corresponding one at the end of Book VIII On Cures. Here ἐλέφας means not the animal but the disease elephantiasis.[154] However, he inserts a long passage about the animal, and his reason for so doing may best be given in his own statement: 'There are many things in common as to form, colour, size and mode of life between the disease Elephas and the wild beast the elephant; but neither does the disease resemble any other disease, nor the animal any other animal.' Then follows a description of how the elephant differs from all other beasts. 'In the first place he is the greatest and the thickest of animals; in size, he is as great as if you were to put one animal on top of another, like a tower; in bulk, he is as large as if you should place several other very large animals side by side. But neither in shape is he much like to any other. Then, as to colour, they are all intensely black, and that all over their whole body.' Other animals are varied in colour, 'but elephants alone are black, of dark skin, like to night and death. With regard to shape they have an unseemly head and face, of no marked form upon a small neck, so that the head appears to rest on the shoulders, and even then it is not very conspicuous. For the ears are large, broad, resembling wings, extending to the collar-bone and breast-bone; they conceal the neck together with the shoulders, like ships with their sails. The elephant has wonderfully white horns on a very dark body – others call them teeth – these alone are most white, such as is nothing else of even any other white animal: these are not above the forehead and temples, as is the nature of other horned animals, but in the mouth and upper jaw, not indeed quite straight but a little bent upwards, so that it might swallow in a straight direction, and lift a load in its flat teeth. Moreover the horns are large, the medium length being as much as about six feet, and some much larger, namely double that length. And the upper jaw from its lip has a long, ex-osseous, crooked and serpent-like protuberance; and there are two perforations at the extremity of this protuberance; and these by nature are perforated all the way to the lungs, so as to form a double tube, so that the animal uses this pipe as a nostril for respiration, and likewise for a hand; for it could take a cup if it please with this protuberance, and can grasp it round and hold it firmly, and none could take it by force from the animal, except another stronger elephant. And with this it also seeks its food; for neither does it live by eating flesh with its mouth and small teeth. For its feet being long, raise the animal considerably above the ground; but its neck also is small, and therefore it cannot browse on the earth with its mouth; and moreover the excrescence of the horns in front of the mouth prevents the mouth from touching the grass. Therefore it raises a great load with its protuberance; then as if with a binder having bound the same with it, he can convey it to his mouth; whence it has earlier been called *proboscis*, for it collects food in front of the animal. But neither is it able to drink from a lake or river with its mouth, for the same reason. But, if it is thirsty, it introduces into the water the extreme nostril of the proboscis, and then, as if inhaling, it draws in much water, instead of air; and when it has filled its nose, as it were a cup, it pours the same as a stream of water into its mouth, and then draws anew and discharges again, until it fills its belly, as it were a cargo ship. It has a rough and very thick skin, containing fissures with prominent edges, long channels, and other hollow clefts, some transverse, others oblique, very deep, in all respects like a furrowed field. Other animals have naturally hairs for a mane, but in the elephant this is mere down. There are also innumerable other differences between it and other animals; for, like man, it bends its leg backward at the knee; and, like woman, it has dugs at the armpits. But there is no necessity for me now to write concerning the animal, except in so far as there is any discrepancy between the animal and the disease, and in so far as the symptoms of the patient resemble the nature of the animal.'

In his subsequent description of the symptoms of the disease Aretaeus occasionally draws a parallel. Thus it is 'mighty in power . . . and filthy and dreadful to behold, in all respects like the wild animal, the elephant'. There are 'tumours prominent, not continuous with one another anywhere, but thick and rough, and the intermediate space cracked, like the skin of the elephant . . . the hairs of the whole body die prematurely'. A contraction of the eyelid is like that in lions and elephants. 'The nose, with black protuberances is rugged . . . teeth, not white indeed, but appearing to be so under a dark body; ears, red, black, contracted, resembling the elephant, so that they appear to have a greater size than usual . . . shrivelled all over the body with rough wrinkles, like wide deep fissures . . . and for this reason the disease had got the name of *elephas*.' The disease, though fatal, 'is long-lived, like the elephant'. The reader may be spared further gruesome symptoms, which are described at length in some three or four pages, since we are not directly here concerned with Greek medicine except to note that elephantiasis is a swollen condition of most of the parts of the body when the lymphatic system has contracted a diseased condition known as filiariasis, due to the infestation of the body by slender parasitic roundworms (*filiariae*).

So little is known about the personal history of Aretaeus that we can only speculate why he showed this unusual interest in the animal and to what extent he was familiar with the living beast. We do not know where he received his medical training, nor whether he was ever at Rome, although this has been suggested because once he prescribes some Italian wines (Falernian, Fundan and Surrentine) for his patients; but since he also mentions Greek wines, this may indicate only a 'universal' prescription rather than for personal patients in Italy. He has many vivid descriptive phrases, which seem original, although of course they might come from the lost work of Amyntianus. He does not involve himself in the debate whether tusks were horns or teeth, and he curiously harps on the blackness of elephants; could he perhaps possibly have seen only one, which happened to be particularly dark; if so, where? in the Circus at Rome, or somewhere in his native Asia Minor? Speculation is idle, but Aretaeus has provided an interesting side-line on how a skilled physician regarded elephants in the second century from a slightly different angle than the more conventional descriptions of Pliny and Aelian.

## AELIAN

Aelian taught rhetoric at Rome in the earlier part of the third century and among other writings compiled a work *De Natura Animalium*. This is no scientific treatise but a collection of material from other writers. Aelian curiously drew only upon Greek writers: at least he mentions no Roman authors. These include Juba, but Aelian may well have used many early authors by means of intermediaries rather than direct. The material is something of a hotchpotch without systematic arrangement, and is designed to entertain rather than instruct the reader. It contains many remarkable, if not miraculous, stories, with stress on the good qualities of animals. He claims to have written with diligence, love of truth, and real interest in his subject, while he anticipates criticism for his deliberate avoidance of a classificatory treatment. Here we may look at what he tells us about elephants, with the material arranged in a somewhat more orderly manner than it meets the reader of the book itself.

Aelian devotes one chapter to the anatomy and habits of the elephant (IV, 31): 'The elephant has what some call protruding teeth, others horns (cf. XI, 37: 'the elephant, I maintain, has horns, not teeth'). Each foot has five toes; their growth is just visible although they are not separate; and that is why he is ill-adapted for swimming. His hind legs are shorter than his forelegs; his paps are close to his armpits; he has a proboscis which is far more serviceable than a hand, and his tongue is short; his gall-bladder is said to be not near the liver but close to the intestines. I am informed that the duration of the elephant's pregnancy is two years, although others maintain that it is not so long, but only eighteen months. It bears one young as big as a one-year-old calf, which pulls at the dug with its mouth. When it is possessed with a desire to copulate and is burning with passion, it will dash at a wall and overturn it, will bend palm trees by butting its forehead against them, as rams do. It drinks water not when clear and pure but when it is dirtied and stirred up a little. But it sleeps standing upright, for it finds the act of lying down and of rising troublesome. The elephant reaches its prime at the age of sixty, although its life extends to two hundred years. But it cannot endure cold.' Aelian says that he is following accounts given by the Moors when he reports (xiv, 6) that 'the elephant is even said to possess two hearts and to think double: one heart is the source of anger, the other of gentleness'. He knows that one tusk tends to be more used than the other (vi, 56): 'one of their tusks they use as a weapon and keep sharpened; the other they use as a mattock, for with it they dig up roots and lever up and bend down trees'. On size he reports (xiii, 8) that 'Indian elephants are nine cubits high and five wide, and the largest are those they call Prasian; next to these one may reckon those from Taxila'. Aelian little realized the long ancestry of those from Taxila (p. 28). He also says (xvi, 18) that the elephants of Taprobane (Ceylon) are stronger, bigger and cleverer than those on the mainland; so the natives build large ships and transport their elephants to sell to the king of the Calingae. Further, the island is so big that the men living by the coast do not know, except by hearsay, how the elephants are hunted in the far distant centre of the island.

Regarding mating Aelian stresses (viii, 17) the continence of elephants who seek intercourse not from lust but through the desire to beget a family. This they do once in a lifetime and in the privacy of the forest. However, they can be jealous: to illustrate this Aelian tells a story (x, 1) which he obtained from the written account by a man who had some knowledge of hunting and obtained authority from the Roman emperor and set out to hunt elephants in Mauretania in the native manner. This suggests perhaps some official of the imperial herd at Ardea/Laurentum who was sent to keep up the supply, while it is interesting that he apparently left an account of his expedition. The story is that two young elephants were mat-

223

ing when a jealous older bull, the mate or lover of the young female, appeared and the two males fought with such violence that both damaged their tusks until they were separated by the hunters. Aelian then goes into a flight of poetic fancy and quotes the duel between Menelaus and Paris in the *Iliad* (III, 373) which Aphrodite broke up; thereafter, like Paris, the 'coward departed and slept with the adulteress'. This story embodies perfectly acceptable behaviour: Dr Sikes (65 f.) records that a single cow may accept several bulls in succession, and that a younger bull generally withdraws at the approach of a senior, but has been known to stay and fight. Describing the birth of an elephant Aelian records (VIII, 27) that the head emerges first and the baby is the size of the largest sucking-pig. Several small elephants follow a single mother. The mothers allow anyone to fondle the baby, since they know that no one would harm such a little creature. Later when they are hunted and are trapped in a pit they (apparently the youngsters) forget their spirit and readily take any food or water that is offered 'and if wine is poured into their trunks they do not refuse this loving-cup': more realistically one must imagine that even small elephants, when drunk, may be more easily caught than when sober. Aelian quotes Juba (IX, 58) who related that his father had inherited a very old elephant; that Ptolemy Philadelphus also had a very old African one; and that an Indian elephant which had belonged to Seleucus Nicator (who died in 281) survived until the supremacy of the Antiochi (a very vague phrase). In XVII, 7 he gives them a span of 200 or even 300 years. In the same chapter he quotes Aristotle on the quantity of food and drink that elephants need (see p. 46), while at VII, 6 he says that they feed on the bushy mastic tree, the tender leaves of the date palm and the more sappy shoots of other plants. When they are being tamed, they are given large loaves of bread, barley, dried figs, raisins, onions, garlic, much honey and bundles of mastic, palm and ivy leaves (X, 10). They instinctively avoid bad food: thus they do not enter a tract of land in India, named Phalacra, where eating the grass leads to loss of hair and horns (VIII, 15). When pierced by missiles, the elephant eats the flower of the olive or the actual oil and is then able to shake out the missiles and is well again (II, 18). Incidentally, unwounded elephants are said to pick out spears and javelins from their wounded comrades, with the skill of surgeons (VII, 45). In India the wounds of elephants are fomented with warm water and anointed with butter.

But if the wounds are deep, the Indians reduce the inflammation by applying pigs' flesh, hot and with the blood still in it. Ophthalmia is treated by frequent bathing with warm cows' milk. Other diseases are treated with dark wine, but if this fails, then nothing will save them (XIII, 7). Finally, we may note two uses of the body. Elephant fat, if rubbed on a man's body, is a remedy against the poisons of all savage creatures (I, 37), while the only parts of the body that are edible for man are the trunk, the lips of the mouth and the marrow of the tusks (X, 12). A modern parallel may be adduced: Col. Williams writes (*Elephant Bill*, 176), 'It was my Burman hunter's perquisite to have . . . the triangular tip of the trunk and the tip of the penis, also the big nerves out of the tusks, which are a native medicine for eye troubles, as well as a coveted aphrodisiac.'

On the movement of elephants Aelian has some remarks. Thus when they are unable to cross a ditch, the largest one drops into the gap and acts as a bridge; when the rest have crossed over on his back, they rescue him before moving on: this is done by one on the bank thrusting his foot forward for the trapped elephant to grasp with his trunk, while others throw undergrowth into the ditch (VIII, 15). In crossing rivers the young swim, the adults keep their trunks above water, and newly-born infants are carried on their mothers' tusks (VII, 15). Elephants, who grieve when transported from their own countries, have to be tricked on to ships by means of bridges covered with greenery to obscure the view of the sea (X, 17). On the march they go in single file and the leader, finding any grass that betrays the presence of man, pulls it up and gives it to the one behind to smell; it is then passed down the line to the rearmost elephant who then trumpets. At this signal they all turn aside to safer ground, always avoiding land that has been trodden by men [IX, 56; this is more reasonable than Pliny who suggests that the soil of the footprint was passed down the line: see p. 211].

The young show respect for the old. They give place to them in feeding and drinking; they never abandon the weak, even when being hunted; they help the old out of pits when they have fallen in; the females never desert their young; 'where, I should like to know, did an elephant ever belabour its sire with blows?' (VI, 61; VII, 15). The old in Mauretania were said to withdraw to a deep forest at the foot of the Atlas mountains, where they enjoyed a sanctuary and were regarded as under the care of certain gods and thus were not hunted by the natives. A story was told that a king sent three hundred picked men to acquire the tusks of some old beasts that had grown very big, but a pestilence fell on them and only one escaped: hence the love of the gods for the elephants was demonstrated (VII, 2). At a new moon elephants were said to pluck fresh branches and wave them gently to and fro in honour of the goddess, like the olive branches of suppliants (IV, 10). They also do obeisance to the rising sun, raising their trunks like hands: Aelian illustrates this (VII, 44) by the story of Ptolemy Philopator, which Plutarch had recounted (p. 218). When dying of wounds elephants throw up grass or dust to heaven, protesting to the gods the injustice of their fate, while an elephant will not pass by a dead elephant without casting a branch or some dust on the body (V, 49). This last statement was derived by Aelian from some 'Ethiopian histories (*logoi*), which are untainted by the pretentious plausibility of the Greeks'. In view of Aelian's preference for Greek as compared with Roman writers, this reference is intriguing. One would like to know more about these Ethiopian histories; it hardly seems likely that Aelian is referring to the North African Juba, who wrote in Greek. Some other habits or characteristics which Aelian notes are that elephants arouse themselves for fighting by lashing themselves with their trunks, and 'thus do not wait for the battle-song of a Tyrtaeus' (VI, 1). In the heat of summer they smear one another with mud, which is better than the shade from trees or a cave (IX, 56). In India when ordered to pull down a tree, they first shake and test its strength to see whether it is possible to overturn it or not (V, 55). The docility and intelligence of elephants is shown not least by their behaviour in the Circus: Aelian's contribution to this topic is mentioned below (p. 252).

Aelian also notes the relationship of the elephant to other animals. It fears rams and pigs, as witness Pyrrhus' experience (I, 38). In India pythons lie in wait for elephants, lurking in tree-tops with the front section of their bodies hanging down like ropes. As the elephant tries to pluck a branch the python strikes at its eyes, then entwines its neck and, holding on to the tree with the lower part of its body, it strangles the elephant (VI, 21). In Ethiopia also serpents are said to kill elephants (II, 21). Following Ctesias, Aelian records that the elephant is the only beast which the mantichora (man-eating tiger?) does not kill (IV, 21). Lions fear elephants in herds; Aelian adds that when stampeded by hunters, elephants do not scatter but bunch together, the young and most pugnacious animals outside, and in the middle the old and the mothers hiding their calves beneath them (VII, 36). The elephant and rhinoceros are enemies. Before battle the rhinoceros sharpens its horn on a rock and tries to get in under its opponent and rip open its belly, but if it is not quick enough the elephant crushes it, holding it fast with its trunk and hacking it to pieces with its tusks. The cause of the fight may be for possession of a feeding ground (XVII, 44), and in modern times in Africa the black rhinoceros has been the only serious competitor and rival to the elephant, especially where grassland habitats have been limited; in zoos, however, the two animals can live as neighbours. The Romans used to stage fights between them in the Circus (p. 22).

Aelian records that the Indians find it difficult to capture adult elephants, so they catch young ones in the swamps by rivers, where the elephant loves to pass much time. They then look after the youngsters like children, 'using soothing words, for the elephants understand the speech of the natives', and the baby elephants learn to obey (IV, 24). In another passage Aelian says that details of the trenches dug by trappers can be read about elsewhere: he concentrates on mother-love and tells how, when a youngster has fallen into a trench, the mother rushes with such speed and courage to its rescue that she may fall on it and crush it! (IX, 8). In another passage Aelian describes a hunt. Elephants have an instinctive apprehension of traps and turn back to fight their way out. The hunters assail them with spears, while if one falls an elephant seizes him, dashes him to the ground and tramples him to death. 'The animals attack, their ears in passion spread wide like sails, after the manner of ostriches which open their wings to flee or to attack. And the elephants bending their trunk inward and folding it beneath their tusks, like the ram of a ship driving along with a great surge, fall upon the men in a tremendous charge, overturning many and bellowing with a piercing shrill note like a trumpet'; the men are then reduced to pulp (VIII, 10). This splendid description rings true to life. First an elephant often makes a mock charge to test his opponent: he lifts his head and trunk and extends his great ears, thus increasing his apparent height and breadth. Then, as Dr Sikes tells (p. 282), 'if the enemy fails to retreat or responds by counter-aggression, the mock charge may turn to a serious attack. Then the trunk is thrown down and somewhat rolled under to one side, the head lowered and the tusks directed at the intruder. The elephant may scream or growl as it thrusts home the attack.' Aelian continues: 'sometimes an elephant in its forward rush overpasses a hunter and plants its knees upon the earth, and besides catches its tusks in a thicket or tree-root, and the hunter manages to escape while the elephant is trying to disengage its tusks.' A parallel incident is quoted by Dr Sikes: 'Carl Akeley, the famous hunter, was knocked to the ground and jabbed at with the tusks . . . which entered the ground either side of the victim's body and not only failed to pierce him but also prevented the now kneeling elephant from crushing him with the base of the trunk. Thinking the victim dead the elephant stood up, sniffed him over, and went away.' Aelian adds that the hunters try to frighten the animals by blowing trumpets, clashing spears on shields, lighting fires on the ground or waving fire in the air, or by hurling blazing javelins; thus they sometimes force the animals to fall back into the pit. He also tells how Libyan elephants, realizing that their tusks are the main objective, place those beasts that have mutilated tusks in the front line as a cover to the rest, perhaps trying to demonstrate to the hunters that they are risking their lives for an inadequate reward (VI, 56).

Apart from the tushes of infants, which are replaced by permanently growing tusks, elephants do not normally shed their tusks unless they have been injured or become diseased at the base. Aelian, who here says he is following the experts, believes that not only were the tusks of the female more valuable than those of the male (whereas in fact they are normally much smaller) but that in Mauretania the elephants dropped their tusks every ten years. To aid the process of shedding them the elephant would kneel and thrust its tusks deep into the ground until they were buried and then, when they were detached, it would cover the spot with soil which would soon be covered by vegetation. Hunters, however, had a trick to discover these hidden spots. They placed goat-skins filled with water at likely places, and watched there day and night; if there were tusks there, the water would empty out and the men would dig up the spoil, but if the skins remained full the hunters moved them to other possible spots (XIV, 5). Aelian describes how captured elephants are tamed by hunger, when tied up to trees; those that are particularly obstreperous are tamed only by prolonged starvation, by pleasant food or by means of goads. We have already seen the kind of food that was given to them (X, 10). If such blandishments fail, the Indians have recourse to music, especially a four-stringed instrument called the scindapsus; the elephant loves music and is thus tamed (XII, 44). Relevant to the burial and discovery of tusks, if not to Aelian's extraordinary 'water-divining' method, may be the fact that elephant 'cemeteries' do appear to exist; they could arise from elephants congregating around waterholes at times of great drought and many dying there, or else from death by fire when they are found in the open bush.

On war elephants Aelian records that those in India carry on their backs, either in a tower or on the back free from harness, as many as three armed men, two of whom hurl their weapons to left and right, with the third behind them, while a fourth holds the goad with which he controls the beast, like a helmsman or pilot (XIII, 9). He says that the king of India stages animal contests in which elephants fight to the death with their tusks (XV, 15) and he quotes Ctesias' attribution to the king of 100,000 elephants as an advance force, with 3,000 bringing up the rear to attack the walls; he also records Ctesias' personal observation of elephants uprooting date-palms (XVII, 29). He mentions among gifts brought to the Indian king trusses of hay and fodder for horses and elephants; if this is not fresh, the king punishes the Keepers of the Elephants, presumably for accepting inferior quality (XIII, 25). Finally, Aelian says that while tame elephants in herds drink water, fighting elephants drink wine made not from grapes but from rice or cane (XIII, 8).

Aelian records two anecdotes of elephants attracted by flowersellers. One is about the garland-maker in Alexandria (I, 38), already recounted by Plutarch. The other is about a woman at Antioch in Syria who daily offered an elephant a garland of flowers; after her death, the animal became inconsolable and savage (VII, 43). Elephants were said to love the scent of flowers. Aelian tells how they would pick flowers and place them in their trainer's basket and later refuse food until flowers had been brought to them which they would then arrange around their mangers, believing that the scent gave a flavour to their food (XIII, 8). Another anecdote tells how an Indian trainer had brought up from infancy a white elephant, which the Indian king demanded. The man fled with the beast to the desert and in the battle that ensued when the king's men caught up with him, he fell wounded from the animal's back. The elephant then stood over him, routed the soldiers, lifted his master up and carried him safely to its stable (III, 46). An example of an elephant punishing dishonesty (VI, 52) has already been quoted from Plutarch. Another elephant revealed a murder: a keeper murdered his wife in order to marry another woman and buried her near the elephant's manger. The elephant later dragged the new wife to where the body was buried and disinterred it 'such was the elephant's hatred of evil' (VIII, 17). Another elephant punished adultery: having caught the wife of its keeper in the very act, it drove one tusk through her and the other through her lover and left them exposed for the keeper to find. This occurred in India, but Aelian goes on to record a similar story from Rome in the time of Titus; this time the elephant threw a cloak over the bodies which he dramatically drew aside when the keeper arrived (XI, 15). Aelian also quotes a few historical examples: the elephant that saved Porus (VII, 37: cf. p. 71); the elephants and the pigs at Megara when besieged by Antigonus (XVI, 36: cf. p. 118); the rider rescued by his elephant at Argos (VIII, 41: cf. p. 114); how Nicaea, an elephant belonging to Antigonus Gonatas at the siege of Megara, was entrusted by the wife of the keeper with safeguarding her infant (she spoke to the animal in the Indian tongue, which elephants understand) and how it watched night and day over its charge, rocking the cradle and fanning away flies (XI, 14). Ptolemy Philadelphus was presented with a young elephant which understood the Greek language of the district where it had been brought up: 'Hitherto it was believed that elephants only understood the language spoken by Indians' (XI, 25; this may suggest that Ptolemy in training African elephants was still using Indian mahouts).

### PHILOSTRATUS AND OTHERS

Roughly a contemporary of Aelian, Philostratus was a sophist who gained the favour of the emperor Septimius Severus and his wife Julia Domna, and at her request wrote a life of Apollonius of Tyana. Apollonius was a sage who died about AD 100; he was a wandering teacher and was believed to possess miraculous powers. Philostratus sought to defend his reputation against charges of charlatanism and based his account more particularly upon memoirs written by Apollonius' friend Damas. We are not here concerned to distinguish fact from fiction, but only to see what Philostratus has to say about elephants when he recounts Apollonius' visit to

India. He tells how the travellers fell in with a boy of about thirteen years of age riding an elephant and guiding it only with his crook (*ancus*). The sage, struck by the contrast of the animal's bulky strength and the small boy, then expatiates on the elephant's intelligence and docility, reporting among other matters that it will allow its master to thrust his head into its wide-open jaws, 'as we have seen among the nomads' (II, 11). When the party reached the Indus they saw a herd of elephants crossing the river and were told that some were marsh elephants, others mountain, and a third kind belonging to the plains. They were used for war with ten to fifteen men in each tower, and they hurled weapons from their trunks, as from hands. 'The Indian elephants are as much bigger than those of Libya, as the latter are bigger than the horses of Nisa.' Other authorities say that elephants are long-lived, and Philostratus adds that Apollonius saw at Taxila the elephant named Ajax which had belonged to Porus and had been dedicated by Alexander to the Sun over 350 years earlier (II, 12, cf. 240: see p. 71).

Philostratus then (II, 13) quotes Juba as saying that the 'knights' of Libya used to fight one another on elephants, and one division of these had a tower engraved on their tusks, but the others nothing. When night had once interrupted a battle, Juba said, the defeated animals fled to the Atlas mountains and there he himself 400 years later caught one of them and found the stamp on the tusk still quite fresh. 'Juba is of the opinion,' continues Philostratus, 'that the tusks are horns, because they grow just where the temples are, and because they need no sharpening of any kind, and remain as they grew and do not, like teeth, fall out and then grow afresh. But I cannot accept this view; for horns, if not all, at any rate those of stags, do fall out and grow afresh, but the teeth, although in the case of men those which may fall out will in every case grow again (*sic*: Philostratus must surely have distinguished between milk and adult teeth), on the other hand there is not a single animal whose tusk or dog-tooth falls out naturally, nor in which, when it has fallen out, it will come again. For nature implants these tusks in their jaws for the sake of defence. And, moreover, a circular ridge is formed year by year at the base of the horns, as we see in the case of goats, sheep and oxen; but a tusk grows out quite smooth, and unless something breaks it, it always remains so, for it consists of a material as hard as stone. Moreover, the carrying of horns is confined to animals with cloven hooves, but this animal has five nails and the sole of his foot has many furrows in it, and not being confined by hooves, it seems to stand on a soft, flabby foot. And in the case of all animals that have horns, nature supplies cavernous bones and causes the horn to grow from outwards, whereas she makes the elephant tusk full and equally massive throughout; and when on a lathe you lay bare the interior, you find a very thin tube piercing the centre of it, as is the case with teeth. The tusks of the marsh elephants are dark, porous and difficult to work, because they are hollowed out into many cavities which offer difficulties to the craftsman's tool; but the tusks of the mountain kind, though smaller than these, are very white and not difficult to work; but best of all are the tusks of the elephants of the plain, for these are very large, very white, and so pleasant to turn and carve that the hand can shape them into whatever it likes.' Apollonius adds that the Indians regard the marsh beasts as stupid and lazy, those of the mountain wicked and treacherous, but those of the plain tractable and fond of learning tricks, as writing, dancing and swaying to the sound of the flute. It is interesting that Philostratus, unlike many writers, understands that elephants do not shed their tusks, and that he mentions the central tusk pulp or 'nerve' which contains tissue, nerves, veins and arteries.

When Apollonius saw a herd of some 30 elephants crossing the Indus, with the young ones being carried, held by the trunks of their elders on their tusks, he discoursed on parental love in animals (II, 14) and then went on to explain why the column was led by the smallest animals and increased in size until the biggest brought up the rear. The reasons were that the herd might be being pursued and thus the strongest animal would guard the rear. Secondly, it was a means of testing the depth of the river: if the smaller could cross, then all was well, while if the bigger and heavier went in first, they would disturb the bed and deepen the river (II, 15).

About this same period lived Heliodorus, the author of the *Aethiopica*, one of the Greek 'novels' or romances. He has a little to say about elephants in describing a fictional war between Persians and Ethiopians (IX, 18 ff.). A Persian invasion was defeated at the battle of Syene, where the Ethiopian king Hydaspes used elephants in his army, each with towers that contained six men who discharged their weapons from the front and two sides; after the victory the king entered Meroe on the elephant that he had ridden in battle. It is, of course, possible that a distorted memory of some historic event might lie behind Heliodorus' story. More interesting in regard to elephants is the romance of 'The Adventures of Leucippe and Cleitophon' by Achilles Tatius, who is now shown by papyrological evidence to have lived in the second century. In it a character said that the hippopotamus is, as it were, the elephant of Egypt and is second in strength only to the Indian elephant. When Cleitophon said that he had seen an elephant only in a picture, Charmides, who had seen a live one, proceeded to describe the animal. A ten-years pregnancy meant that the elephant was old when it was born and this explains its later great bulk. It lived long and had a jaw like the head of an ox, because it appears to have two horns, but these are in reality curved teeth. Between them grows a trunk, in appearance and size not unlike a trumpet. The beast uses this to eat, by bending it inwards to convey food to the mouth. But if it seizes anything too rich, it twists it up in a circle and lifts it up to offer to the master on its back. This rider is an Ethiopian whom the elephant fears and obeys, not least because of its master's iron axe. Charmides then said that he once saw an extraordinary sight: a Greek put his head in an elephant's jaw: the man said that he had given the elephant a fee for this because the beast's breath was only less sweet than the scents of India and was a sovereign remedy for headache. The elephant knows that it has this power of healing and will not open its mouth for nothing, but like a rascally doctor insists on its fee first; then it will keep it open as long as the man wants. The animal gets this delightful scent from the nature of its food, a flower called 'black rose'. This account by Achilles Tatius (IV, 4 ff.) is interesting as showing the rather vague ideas that were current about the animal. The 'black rose' is no doubt some form of cloves, while much later Cassiodorus commented (p. 234) on the elephant's breath as a cure for headaches in man.

As time went on, the sight of an elephant in the western Empire became increasingly rare and older errors about its characteristics revived. Thus St Ambrose, bishop of Milan in the later part of the fourth century, may well never have seen one. In a disquisition on 'Why God created some animals' necks long, and some short' (*Hexaemeron*, VI, v, 30 ff.), he observes that the elephant has a prominent trunk because, though taller than all other animals, it cannot bend to feed: thus it uses its trunk to collect food and to drink quantities of water. The neck is smaller than the body demands. The animal cannot bend its legs, because they have to be stiff like pillars to bear the weight of the body. The heel is slightly curved, but the rest of the foot is rigid from top to bottom. Hence the tame elephant is propped up with great beams for sleep. It leans on trees and rubs its ribs on them or relaxes in sleep; sometimes the trees are broken by their weight so that the animals fall and cannot get up again. Their backs cannot easily be penetrated by darts, and hunters for ivory cut through trees so that the beasts fall down. St Ambrose gives some examples of their usefulness in war (p. 205), says that they can live 300 years and that they use both trunk and feet in their work of destruction. Thus the bishop of Milan in the West had a very different view of elephants from the first-hand knowledge which his close contemporary, Ammianus Marcellinus, had been forced to gather in the east.

We find some of the same errors recurring about a century and a half later in the writings of the Roman senator Cassiodorus, who about AD 538 published under the title of *Variae* some letters and edicts which he had written for the Gothic kings. One of these (x, 30) is from King Theodahad to Honorius, the City Prefect, ordering the restoration of the bronze statues of some elephants on the Sacred Way at Rome: 'these animals, which in the flesh are accustomed to live for more than a millennium, seem in their bronze images to have suffered a very close decline' (the meaning would seem to be that they have collapsed after about 1,000 years, unless *proximum* means 'very recent' here). The gaping limbs are to be consolidated with iron clasps, and the sunken belly to be strengthened with a sustaining wall in order that this great marvel be not allowed shamefully to collapse in ruins. Cassiodorus then goes on to draw a parallel with living elephants which cannot get up when the trees on which they lean have been cut down, because their feet have no flexible joints but are rigid like columns. So they lie there, looking as dead and you might think that they were made of metal, with less strength than the tiniest ants. When helped up by man, they remember their benefactor and obey his orders. Cassiodorus comments on the use of the trunk, and the short neck which prevents the elephant taking food from the ground. Its breath is said to be a cure for headaches in man. If anyone refuses to give it what it asks for, it empties its bladder and such a flood follows that a river seems to have swept into the man's house. It remembers injuries. It has small eyes which it moves solemnly, so that you might think that you were looking at a king's countenance. Its skin is hard as bone, and so the Persians use the elephant for war. Thus, concludes Theodahad, it is very pleasant to have the form of the animal so that those who have never seen the living beast can picture what it is like. Honorius is not to allow the statues to perish, since it is consonant with the dignity of Rome that the skill of craftsmen should restore in that city that which bounteous nature is recognized throughout the different parts of the world to have produced.

Nearly 100 years later, in the early seventh century, Isidore, bishop of Seville, recorded that 'elephants are reluctant to breed, but when they bring forth their young, they drop them in the water or on some island because of the serpents, which are their enemies, and they are killed if they become entangled in their coils. Of Africa and India they were natives, but now India alone produces them.' This idea of early 'baptism' was soon taken over into medieval legend.

# CHAPTER IX

# IN WAR AND PEACE

### ORGANIZATION AND EQUIPMENT FOR WAR

When he first met elephants in the East Alexander had no previous experience of them and so he may well have taken over the organization used by the Indians, since he had to transport large numbers over great distances. Further, although he did not actually employ them in war, he incorporated them into his army for guard and ceremonial purposes. We have no detailed evidence for their military organization in the Hellenistic period apart from the account given by Asclepiodotus (and later repeated by an Aelian of the second century AD, who is probably a different writer from the natural historian). Asclepiodotus was not a military man but a Stoic philosopher. He was a pupil of either Panaetius or Poseidonius or of both, and therefore lived during the last century or so of the Roman Republic. He wrote a formal book on *Tactics* which deals with Greek and Macedonian warfare of earlier days and not with contemporary military practice. He thus used and preserved some older material, but does not seem unduly interested in his subject which he included in his works because no branch of learning should be outside the philosopher's range. Elephants, he tells us (Ch. XI), formed one of the three branches of the mounted force (cavalry and chariots being the other two) and the organization of a brigade of 64 elephants was as follows: a phalangarches commanded the phalanx of 64; then came a keratarchy of 32; an elephantarchy of 16; an ilarchy of eight; an epitherarchy of four; a therarchy of two; and a zoarchy of a single beast and man. A square of 64 elephants might be a possible formation for marching and easy for changing front, but it would be a terrifying sight if such a formation of eight broad and eight deep was ever used in battle. No doubt Asclepiodotus' description belongs more to the drill-book than the field, and an iliarchy of eight in single rank may well have been a normal unit in the battle-line. Arrian, in his book on *Tactics* written in the time of Hadrian, says (22.6) that it was not worth while giving the units and commands of elephants with their names, since their use had long ceased.

An elephant-corps was commanded by an Elephantarch (*magister elephantorum*). Some of these men are known by name, as Philip who commanded for Antiochus at Raphia and Magnesia, Eudemus for Eumenes at Gabiene, Nicanor for Demetrius Soter. The importance of these commanders was apparently appreciated by Roman audiences when Terence produced his *Eunuch* in 161 BC as earlier they had been by the Greek audiences of Menander, on whose work Terence's play was based: the braggart soldier, Thraso, plumes himself on the belief that everyone envied him 'especially the man who had charge of the king's Indian elephants. When he is more troublesome than usual, "Pray, Strato," I say, "are you made so fierce because you have command over wild beasts?"' (413 ff.).

Each elephant, as has been seen, had its own name; Ajax of Porus, Patroclus and Ajax of Antiochus, Nicon of Pyrrhus, and the Carthaginian Surus. When Carthage faced its final duel with Rome, and the population were roaming the streets in anguish at their betrayal, they not only either invoked or upbraided the gods but while some mournfully visited the empty arsenals and dockyards, others called their elephants by name, as though they were still there.[155] But if some elephants were widely known and appreciated, each individual beast was the special care of his *elephantagogos* or *elephantistes*, his *rector*, *magister* or *moderator*. The mahout or oozie is often likely to have known his beast from its childhood and indeed may have grown up with it, so that a very strong bond existed between rider and ridden. He usually sat on the beast's neck and guided it with voice or crook (ank, *harpe, cuspis*), and especially by pressure of his toes under the elephant's ears. The ank or hawkus, which is a rod with a hook projecting a little way down from the point, is often depicted in works of art, as on the Barcid silver coin from Spain with elephant and cloaked rider, or the silver dish in the Hermitage at Leningrad. As we have seen, the use of the word 'Indi' for the mahouts does not necessarily imply Indian nationality. The name probably spread as a generic term when Indian teachers were imported into Africa by the Ptolemies to train their native elephants, and then passed into Carthaginian usage.[156]

237

Fig. 20. Lamp in the form of
an elephant from south Russia
*Archäologischer Anzeiger*, 1912,
No. 13)

Fig. 21. Figure of elephant
from south Russia
(*Archäologischer Anzeiger*, 1912,
No. 28)

The purpose of an elephant in war was not only to destroy the
enemy but first to terrify him: so they were given splendid trappings, as well as receiving on occasion a ration of fermented wine
to stimulate their fury. Apart from the use of towers, which is discussed below, the purple trappings of Antigonus' beasts impressed
Eumenes' men, while the gold, silver and purple ornaments of
Antiochus' elephants at Magnesia were equally striking. Silver
*phalerae* also formed the reward which Antiochus gave to his elephant Patroclus for fording a river, 'and in these an elephant takes

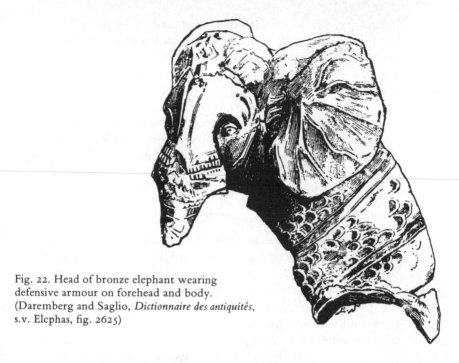

Fig. 22. Head of bronze elephant wearing
defensive armour on forehead and body.
(Daremberg and Saglio, *Dictionnaire des antiquités*,
s.v. Elephas, fig. 2625)

the greatest delight', wrote Pliny; it has even been suggested that
the two famous *phalerae* depicting elephants, now in the Hermitage
Museum, were actually used as decorations for the animals. Livy
refers to the daunting appearance of the head-pieces (*frontalia*) and
crests (*cristae*) of the elephants at Magnesia, while centuries later the
terrifying *cristae* of the Persian elephants at the battle in which the
emperor Julian was killed are noted by Ammianus. These crests
are likely to have been waving plumes, but the *frontalia* suggest
some form of defensive armour across the forehead. Heavier
armour seems to have been worn sometimes: thus Juba's elephants
are said to have been *loricati*, which suggests iron plates. *Frontalia*
and perhaps body armour are shown on a broken bronze statuette
in the Collection Greau (fig. 22). In Josephus' version of the story
of Eleazar (p. 156), his mistake arose because 'the tallest of the
elephants was armed with breastplates (θώραξι) like those of the
king' (unless here θώραξ is used for θωράκιον, meaning a tower).
But equipment was not merely defensive. Arrian (*Tact.* 2.4) says
that elephants' tusks were armed with sharp iron, which made
them keener and less liable to be broken off, while the poet Silius

Italicus (IX, 581–3) refers to spears fastened to the tusks. This practice is paralleled in more recent times: in *Portuguese Voyages 1498–1663* Mendes Pinto is quoted as writing, 'two hundred elephants armed with castles, and warlike *panoures*, which are certain swords that are fastened to their teeth when they fight'. Finally, an attack was made upon the enemy's hearing as well as his sight: beside the trumpeting of the beast, it often seems to have worn a clanging bell around its neck. Such bells are often depicted on both Indian and African elephants: thus, for instance, they appear on the Hermitage *phalerae* and on the Hannibalic coins issued in the Chiana Valley.[157]

## TOWERS

At times war-elephants carried only a mahout on the neck, at other times they had one or more armed soldiers on their backs, while yet again they had 'towers' or 'castles' ($\theta\omega\rho\acute{a}\kappa\iota\alpha$) containing warriors. It has often been said, though more often assumed than demonstrated, that towers were carried from the time of the battle between Porus and Alexander onwards, but this appears not to be true.[158] Apart from three passages the use of towers is not attested before at least 300 BC while the evidence for the battle of the Hydaspes suggests that they were not used. The decadrachm already discussed (p. 75) shows Porus riding bareback astride his elephant (and if kings did not have towers, commoners will not have been better treated), while descriptions of the fighting do not even suggest any fighting men on the backs: the animal alone, with its mahout, formed the weapon. Later accounts (e.g. Diodorus) compare the elephants themselves to towers but do not say they carried towers. On the painted funeral cortège of Alexander each elephant carried two riders, the mahout and one Macedonian soldier, but no tower (p. 76). 'The men on the elephants' at Camels' Fort were probably only mahouts, not soldiers (*anabatai*) and certainly not soldiers in towers. The same is true of Polyperchon's attack on Megalopolis, the great battles between Antigonus and Eumenes and the battle at Gaza. It is possible that soldiers may sometimes have been mounted on the elephants, but probably not frequently, since they would not find it easy to keep a firm seat if they could grip only with their bent legs (or perhaps they were helped by a rope passed around or along the beast's back). At any rate normally the elephant itself was the weapon used to neutralize the enemy cavalry, threaten his line or breach his walls. In pursuance of these tasks it might be given the support of light-armed troops who could protect the flanks of the individual beasts, since a flank attack was more threatening than a frontal assault which could be met by tusks and trunk. Not until the time of Pyrrhus' campaigns in the west were towers certainly used, and possibly, as recently suggested, he or his engineers should be given the credit for the invention: towers appear on the Villa Giulia plate, and again a few years later on the statuette and intaglio which celebrate Antiochus' Elephant Victory over the Galatians (pl. VII a, b).

The three pieces of seemingly contrary evidence hardly stand up to close examination. Diodorus (II, 17.8) mentions the towers of the elephants of the Indian king who opposed Semiramis (p. 35) in a passage which in general reproduces Ctesias, but it is uncertain whether he used Ctesias direct or via an intermediary or indeed to what extent he or his intermediary may have added items of information off their own bat; further, it seems (p. 35) that Ctesias himself said that there were two men on Semiramis' false elephants, but there is no mention of towers which it would be natural for her to have used if her opponent had them. In any case Greek practice need not have coincided with Indian, as indeed this passage suggests. Secondly, Paraetacene (p. 86 ff.). The main account in Diodorus, which derives from Hieronymus, makes no mention of towers or riders, though Plutarch does refer to towers in a general way (*Eumen.* 14.4; cf. below note 43). But this detail may come from the more picturesque Duris than the more sober Hieronymus and have been added at a time when towers were coming into use. Thirdly, Aelian (XII, 9) says 'a war-elephant in what is called the tower (θωράκιον), or even, I assure you, on its bare back, free of harness carries as many as three armed men . . .' two in front (thus a lacuna should be filled) 'who hurl their weapons to left and right, and a third behind them, while a fourth holds the goad with which he controls the beast'. According to Strabo (XV, 1.52) in a passage derived from Megasthenes, 'the elephant carries four persons, the driver and three bowmen'. If, with Müller but not with Jacoby, the passage of Aelian is thought to have a common origin in Megasthenes with the Strabo passage, then we should have Megasthenes speaking of towers. But apart from the uncertainty of origin, even if Aelian does derive from Megasthenes, the mention of towers could well be an addition by Aelian himself on the basis of its frequent mention by Hellenistic writers whom he knew. Evidence roughly contemporary with Megasthenes confirms riders but not towers: a clay figure from Taxila of the Maurya period shows traces of four people mounted on an elephant. Further, the *Arthacastra*, which is attributed to Kautilya, a minister of Chandragupta, and contains some material which goes back to the original version, deals very fully with the equipment and use of elephants, but makes no mention of anything like a tower. Thus although the matter is not without some uncertainty, it seems extremely unlikely that towers were used in Hellenistic (or Indian) armies until well into the third century BC.[159]

The evidence for possible use of towers by the Carthaginians suggests that they did not follow the example of Pyrrhus.[160] On the Barcid coinage the elephants are depicted bare-backed or with only a mahout, and on Hannibal's coin from the Chiana valley the elephant, whose bell suggests that it is a war-elephant, is also bare-backed. One reason why the Carthaginians did not use towers may be that their elephants, unlike the larger Indians, were not big or strong enough for such an armament without loss of mobility or endurance; further, towers were less necessary if their elephants did not have to face endorsed enemy elephants. True, Ptolemy's African elephants at Raphia did have towers, but he had to use them because he could not have sent unprotected elephants into battle against fully equipped ones without the mahouts being skewered by enemy *sarissae*. But what Ptolemy was forced to do is not evidence for what the Carthaginians did. There is no specific reference to the use of towers in the descriptions of battles in the First Punic War or in the Mercenaries Revolt. Thus, for instance, when in 255 the Romans faced Xanthippus, Polybius' reference to 'the men on the elephants' refers merely to the mahouts (or less probably to soldiers as well), while he twice emphasizes the strength or force (βία) of the elephants themselves in crushing the unfortunate Roman ranks (I, 34). At Metaurus Polybius says that six elephants 'together with their men' were killed, while four, deserted by their Indoi, were captured (XI, 1); this might indicate that the 'men' were different from the 'Indians' (though not necessarily), but it certainly does not suggest towers. True, later sources do refer to turreted elephants: thus Silius Italicus, IV, 599; IX, 239 f., 577 f.; Lucretius, V, 1300 f.; and the *Suda*, s.v. θωράκιον of which the source is not known and only very doubtfully could be attributed to Polybius.

But such late usages can scarcely outweigh the general impression given by Polybius, and so on balance it is safer to believe that the Carthaginians in their earlier use of elephants did not encumber them with towers.

When Livy says (XXVIII, 14.4) that at Ilipa the Punic line 'presented from a distance the appearance of forts', he is speaking of the animals themselves, not of towers on their backs, but nevertheless some archaeological evidence does suggest that towers were carried on occasion during the Hannibalic War. This evidence has already been described (p. 170 ff.). It comprises the tiny silver coins, showing endorsed elephants, the phiale from Cales and the terracotta figure from Pompeii. These three items seem to belong to the period of the Hannibalic War, but they need not suggest that Hannibal used towers in the formal battles of the war. Their use could have been confined to parades in order to impress his Italian allies and to the more static fighting in Campania when towers might have been of service when elephants were used against fortified positions.

That North African elephants not only could at need carry towers but actually did is shown by the events of the campaign of Thapsus in 46 BC (p. 197 ff.) when the elephants of Juba and Scipio are described as *turriti* by the author of the *Bellum Africum* (30.2; 41.2; 86.1); whether by his specific use of this epithet he wishes to denote unusual practice or not can hardly be determined. In any case this would not provide evidence for third-century Punic practice, especially in regard to elephants which had to march long distances: the Thapsus fighting, like that in Campania earlier, was limited in geographical area and to relatively flat country. But if the Carthaginians had made little use of towers in the battle-line, other Hellenistic powers had turned to them more readily: thus early in his career Antiochus III had employed them at Raphia and then again much later against the Romans at Magnesia, where according to Livy (XXXVII, 40) each tower contained four armed men; however, Florus remarks (II, 8) that these were 'elephanti immensae magnitudinis'. The Seleucids continued the practice when they had an opportunity to use elephants; thus in 162 those led by Lysias against the Jews had wooden turrets.

These towers scarcely each contained 32 soldiers, as the unemended text of Maccabees records (p. 188 f.), while the ten to 16 men which Philostratus (II, 6) attributes to a tower may also safely be dismissed, at any rate for normal practice: two or three seems a more likely number. Aelian (XIII, 9) and Pliny (VIII, 22) speak of three soldiers, while three dots, presumably human heads, appear above the tower on the tiny Hannibalic coin. In the towers portrayed on the plates in the Villa Giulia and Hermitage two men are found in each tower. These men would be archers, javelin-throwers or spearmen, and were presumably chosen for their shooting skills, together with their agility and perhaps smallness of stature: the lighter and nimbler they were, the better. Four monuments in particular reproduce many details of the towers: the Villa Giulia and Hermitage plates, and the Myrina and Pompeii statuettes (pls VIIa, b, Xa, XII).[161] In all four the tower is crenellated, while on the outside at the top are fixed two shields in the Myrina example and one in the Pompeian. The Villa Giulia elephant has a fine reddish saddle-cloth, while that of the Hermitage animal is embroidered with a dragon which though Greek in style foreshadows the Sassanid dragons; the cloth of the Myrina elephant is plainer and much longer, reaching down nearly to the animal's feet. The construction of the towers themselves can only be surmised. They would presumably be made of light wooden frameworks, fenced round with light material, such as wicker-work; although the Hermitage example appears pretty solid a close examination of the Villa Giulia tower suggests a number of parallel lines running down from top to bottom, which could indicate some form of light slatting. The shields were hung out as further protection, while wet skins might well have been used against attacks by fire. The rear section of the tower must either have contained a door or opening or have been built lower than the rest to allow the men to get in and out, while presumably they got up by climbing a rope or rope-ladder attached to the tower: an elephant might have been trained to lift its mahout on to its neck, but it could hardly have placed the whole crew in position. Inside the tower there might have been a low shelf on to which the men could step when actually engaging the enemy, while standing on the bottom level of the tower for protection at other moments. No doubt the weight and height of the towers were graded to the immediate objectives, and towers designed for use against city walls would be more strongly constructed. The tower was fastened to the elephant's back by means of ropes or chains which passed around its body, in the front, middle and backside.

Fig. 23. Engraved gem of elephant with low platform and soldiers. (Daremberg and Saglio, *Dictionnaire des antiquités*, s.v. Elephas, fig. 2624)

Finally, there is an interesting device shown on an engraved gem in the Cabinet de France: this is an open platform, with two soldiers standing on it and in the act of hurling their weapons (fig. 23).[162] This flat platform is fastened to the elephant by two attachments which depend vertically from its two ends: it even suggests that a rectangular hollow framework might have been fitted around the whole body. The elephant is here lifting up an enemy in its trunk, which is slightly reminiscent of the Gaul who is being crushed in the Myrina statuette, but this should not influence us in trying to determine whether the elephant is an Indian or African. It would seem to be an African because the ear is fairly big and the back is fairly flat: perhaps the use of a platform instead of a tower is a concession to the smaller race. Furthermore, this interesting little monument opens up the possibility that when fighting-men *were* placed on the back of an elephant without the protection of a tower, they may at times, although the literary sources do not mention this, have had the support of a simple platform instead of having to rely on the strength of their leg muscles, as King Porus apparently had done, or to cling with one hand to a rope, thereby cramping their offensive potential.

### TACTICS

We may now look summarily at some of the tactical uses of elephants which we have already seen in more detail in various battles. Some elephants might be kept in reserve if they were too numerous to deploy in a single line, as Seleucus will have done at Ipsus if he had 400: the interception of Demetrius' cavalry may well have been carried out by some of Seleucus' elephants that had been kept behind his line (p. 98). Equally, if elephants were very few, they could be held in reserve and then launched at a critical moment, as by Nobilior at Numantia (p. 190) or placed where they could inflict the greatest terror, as by Antiochus against the Galatians (p. 122). The normal position was a single line of elephants in front of either part or the whole of the main battle-line, and not too near the front line in order that they might have some room to retreat if necessary and to give the infantry time to open up the line to let them through. At the Hydaspes Porus placed all his elephants in front of the greater part of his infantry, not on his wings (p. 68). At Paraetacene and Gabiene both sides placed their elephants along the whole of their fronts, including the wings where the cavalry was stationed; tactical hopes, however, dictated a heavier concentration in some parts of the whole line than in others, while on one wing the elephants projected in a curving line beyond the cavalry (p. 87 ff.). The disposition at Magnesia, where some were placed at intervals *in* the line, between sections of infantry, seems to have been unusual (p. 180 f.). Or they might be placed on the wings only, either when they had to face enemy elephants as at Raphia (p. 139 ff.) or only enemy cavalry as at Ilipa (p. 167); at Thermopylae Antiochus puts his small force on one flank only in a defensive position (p. 180). When in line the distance between the individual animals would naturally vary according to number and location, but 100 feet may have been a normal space, and half or less than that on occasion. When the intervals were large, units of men were placed between them; perhaps each elephant had its escort of light-armed archers, slingers or javelin-men. Thus at Gaza Demetrius put 1,500 men among 30 elephants (p. 95), that is 50 per beast; this is a more reasonable figure than the escort of 1,000 infantry and 500 cavalry which Lysias is said in *Maccabees* to have assigned to each of his 32 elephants (p. 188). This practice may have been fairly normal (cf. the 'usual guard', *cum adsueto praesidio*, mentioned at Thermopylae): special men may have undergone training with individual elephants for their mutual benefit, and such groupings would help to keep the elephants isolated from each other and from other units of the army, and this might give greater security. Such light-armed troops, which could be properly controlled, would be more effective than a screen of light-armed men drawn up in front of the elephants, since these might fall back and confuse the animals, as happened to Hanno at Agrigentum (p. 149).

The detailed use of elephants in battle has been amply illustrated already. Terror was their primary weapon, and its effect runs like a red thread through the history of elephant-warfare, terror inflicted on men and horses; elephants were especially useful against men who faced them for the first time and against horses untrained to meet them. If they faced other elephants, individual duels ensued, but if not they thundered down on phalanx or legion. The opposing side developed all kinds of methods of trying to cope with them until the genius of Scipio Africanus reached the neatest solution: to neutralize them by leaving lanes in his battle-line along which they could be forced to the rear (p. 168 f.). Careful training of the individual and of the horses was the first need. Personal courage was no doubt essential, and we hear of many brave exploits: Ptolemy I, armed with a *sarissa*, facing the leading enemy elephant (p. 79); Eleazar gaining his everlasting name (p. 182); the veteran of the Fifth Legion at Thapsus hacking the elephant's trunk (p. 197). The author of *Bellum Africum* describes how Scipio made his new elephants battle-worthy before Thapsus and how, in order to train his men, Caesar procured some elephants from Italy and put them through a crash course of instruction (p. 196 f.). An elephant, which is most vulnerable in trunk and feet, can be killed by one man: a Gaetulian killed one at Pompey's Games, as allegedly Commodus and Caracalla did so much later (p. 251 f.); but arenas offered easier conditions than did the battle-field. Horses too could be familiarized with the smell and habits of elephants, although not always by the use of a model beast such as Perseus (and Semiramis) are said to have done (p. 184); Caesar used live beasts for such training at Thapsus (p. 196).

In the actual attack the obvious aim was to try to isolate and surround individual beasts, threatening them from flank and rear. For this special weapons might be devised, such as the scimitars and axes used by Alexander's men at the Hydaspes (p. 70). Light-armed troops might advance on foot or on horse (Vegetius, III, 24) or be placed in the gaps between the maniples, as at the Ibera (p. 166). Slingers who could aim at mahout as well as elephant, were also used, as by Caesar against Juba at Thapsus (p. 195). For the period of the Sassanid wars we hear of cataphracts, that is men armoured with iron spikes which prevented the elephants seizing them with their trunks (Vegetius, III, 24). More elaborate methods included the use of the iron-pointed beams, mounted on waggons, which the Romans are said to have used against Pyrrhus at Ausculum (p. 108). Vegetius, writing in the early fifth century AD, apparently is thinking of this battle when he describes how the Romans yoked two armoured horses to a chariot, in which were *clibanarii* (a late Latin word for heavily-armed soldiers) who aimed *sarissas* (*conti* in Vegetius' day) against the elephants; the men were protected by their armour from the arrows of the archers on the elephants, and their speed saved them from direct onrushes by the beasts. Vegetius describes another weapon, which is first attested on Trajan's Column early in the second century AD: the *carroballista*, which was an arrow-firing catapult, mounted on a vehicle drawn by a pair of horses or mules; such machines were stationed behind the line and with their more powerful arrows inflicted greater wounds on the beasts. Fire was a valuable weapon. The waggons at Ausculum also had projecting poles fitted with fire-bearing grapnels. Blazing arrows could be used, while two special fire-bearing missiles were developed: the *malleolus* and the *falarica*. Noise also might be a deterrent: thus Polybius (xv, 12.2) records that at Zama some of the elephants took fright and turned tail at the shrill sound of the Roman trumpets and bugles, and the same happened to Juba's untrained elephants at Thapsus (Florus, II, 67). A less conventional deterrent was the use of pigs, as against Pyrrhus (p. 113 f.) or at the siege of Edessa (p. 205). More mechanical devices were also tried. Ditches might be useful, and before Thapsus Scipio sent a reconnaissance party to see if Caesar had dug any (p. 196), but time would not always allow for trenching nor would the direction of attack always be known beforehand. Moveable barriers included the nail-studded frames used by Polyperchon at Megalopolis (p. 83) and the iron-spiked 'mine-field' laid by Ptolemy at Gaza (p. 95). But despite the great ingenuity spent on these various devices, in a pitched battle the solution of Scipio Africanus was the simplest, and possibly Metellus had it in mind at the battle of the Muthul (p. 193), when he placed slingers and archers between the maniples perhaps with the intention of trying to force Jugurtha's elephants between the lines of the legionaries.

Apart from their primary use in pitched battles and from occasional deviations, such as when Perdiccas used his elephants as a barrier in the Nile to break the force of the water (p. 79 f.), elephants were employed to attack camps and towns: they had been famed as 'overthrowers of walls' since the days of Ctesias (p. 34). Thus

Hanno's 100 elephants had stormed the camp of the rebel mercenaries at Utica (p. 152 f.), Hannibal's beasts broke into the Roman lines at Capua (p. 162 f.), and in the Third Punic War Aemilianus had used Gulussa's elephants to storm the Punic camp at Nepheris (p. 178). Attacks on cities might not always be successful, as Polyperchon found out at Megalopolis (p. 83) and Pyrrhus at Argos (p. 117 f.), while elephants proved of only limited value to Antiochus III in his threat against Larissa (p. 179 f.) and to Nobilior against Numantia (p. 190). Elephants were used with very varied results in many of the sieges of the later Persian wars (p. 202 ff.), but whatever their impact on city walls and the defenders, no doubt remains about their impact on the morale of the Romans: the shaken nerves of Ammianus testify to that. But even though at times they might recoil upon their employers, they often provided valuable physical help at sieges. Thus they could thwart sorties by the besiegers, as at Capua. They could raise men up to the level of battlements either for observation or attack, and they could be fitted with specially high towers. Thus they might prefigure the later use by Indians of elephants which carried small pieces of artillery. Then they must surely have been used in helping to move the various heavy siege-weapons which the Persians used at, for instance, the siege of Amida (p. 203). At close quarters an elephant could, as Aristotle observed, 'batter down a wall with its big tusks' (p. 48), while it could pull up palisades with its trunk: thus at Camels' Fort (p. 79) they 'tore up the palisades and threw down the parapets' (Diodorus, XVIII, 34.2).

Elephants were a two-edged weapon, *genus anceps* in Livy's phrase (XXVII, 14) and κοινοὶ πολέμιοι, 'common enemies', in Appian's (*Hisp.* 46). Liable at all times to be panicked, perhaps by a sudden noise or movement, they naturally became especially unruly when wounded or when their mahouts were killed. We do not know to what extent mahouts were regularly equipped with the means to put them out of action: silence reigns for nearly 600 years between the references to their mallet and chisel at Metaurus and their knives in Julian's campaigns (pp. 165; 204), but spiking your own guns must always be a second-best. No doubt most commanders who used elephants would say 'first time lucky' but after that a gamble. Yet we must remember that, despite the uncertainty and despite the great expense and labour of feeding and transporting fodder, many states continued to employ them, while a hard-headed general like Seleucus thought that a large elephant-corps was worth more than control of North-west India. The Romans in the main may have taken a different view, but the last word may be given to Vegetius, a Roman who was writing when late Roman armies had to face elephants once again after the lapse of several centuries: 'By the great bulk of their bodies, the terror inspired by their trumpeting, and the strangeness of their shape, elephants in battle throw into confusion both men and horses' (elefanti in proeliis magnitudine corporum, barritus horrore, formae ipsius novitate homines equosque conturbant).

THE GAMES

Whereas the Greeks used elephants mainly for war, the Romans used them mainly for public spectacle.[163] The first occasion was when Manius Curius displayed at his triumph in 275 the Indian elephants that he had captured from Pyrrhus, while twenty-five years later Metellus exhibited the Africans which he had taken from the Carthaginians at Panormus; it is uncertain whether these were merely displayed in the Circus or made to fight (p. 111; 152). Animal-fights (*venationes*), like the bloody battles of the gladiators, became popular in Rome, but at some relatively early date a resolution of the Senate forbade the importation of African beasts, perhaps in order to prevent ambitious magistrates gaining undue popularity by lavish displays, perhaps even because they might be somewhat dangerous to house and liable to escape. However, this prohibition was repealed by a tribune, Cn. Aufidius, whose measure allowed *Africanae* (primarily lions and leopards probably) to be imported for use in the Circus Maximus. The date is uncertain, but Aufidius may well have been the tribune of 170, since in the very next year the aediles exhibited 63 leopards, 40 bears and some elephants. Perhaps the elephants got off lightly and were there chiefly for show, since Pliny reports Fenestella as saying that elephants first fought in the Circus in the year 99 BC, and that they were first pitted against bulls twenty years later in the aedileship of the two Luculli (pl. XVIIb). More is known about the famous, or rather infamous, Games given by Pompey in 55 BC on an unprecedentedly lavish scale to celebrate the opening of his theatre. The world was ransacked for animals, and as Pompey himself had hunted elephants in Africa he was likely to see to their presence; they numbered

20 and appeared in the Circus on the last day of the Games, where no less than 600 lions were massacred (on an earlier occasion Sulla, despite his friendship with Bocchus, had raised only 100). According to Seneca the elephants, only 18 in number, fought against criminals in mimic battle, but Pliny says that their opponents were Gaetulians from Africa armed with javelins. He describes how one animal in particular put up a magnificent fight: wounded in its feet, it crawled against the hordes of its enemies on its knees, snatching their shields and throwing them into the air; the spectators were delighted by the curving flight of the falling shields (or perhaps, because they fell in a circle around the beast), as if they were thrown by a trained juggler and not by an infuriated animal. Another elephant was killed by a single javelin which struck it just under the eye. But not all went well for Pompey. The elephants in a mass tried to break through the iron fence that kept them in and frightened the spectators. Then the doomed beasts, by their piteous trumpetings and waving their trunks in the air as if betrayed (the story went that their mahouts had guaranteed their safety before they embarked from Africa), so moved the crowd that it burst into tears and rising up in a body cursed Pompey. Cicero, who was himself present at these Games and recorded his reactions in a letter to a friend, does not dramatize the episode to the same extent as Pliny did, but he does say that the crowd, although greatly impressed, showed no pleasure. This feeling of compassion, so unusual in a Roman mob, was intensified in the humane Cicero who thought the Games magnificent, but vulgar and ostentatious, and wrote, 'what pleasure can it possibly be to a man of culture, when either a puny human being is mangled by a most powerful beast [incidentally, Seneca was more concerned about the fate of the men than of the elephants] or a splendid beast is transfixed with a hunting-spear . . . the result was a certain compassion and a kind of feeling that the huge beast has a fellowship with the human race' (esse quamdam illi beluae cum genere humano societatem).[164]

The next great spectacle at Rome was at Caesar's triumph in 46 BC where elephants were among the exhibits. Whereas Dio says that men fought from the backs of 40 elephants, and Appian refers to a fight of elephants, 20 a side, Pliny records an engagement of 20 elephants against 500 infantry, followed by another between elephants, with castles on their backs and three men on each beast, against 500 infantry and apparently 20 horsemen. Suetonius says that the turning posts (*metae*) of the arena were removed at each end of the Circus and 'camps' were built for the opposing sides. Pliny adds that subsequently under the emperors Claudius and Nero combats between elephants and men single-handed became the crowning achievement of a gladiator's career – and no doubt often the last. Contests continued under later emperors but few details survive. Thus coins issued in 149 display an elephant and allude to Games given the previous year to celebrate the tenth year of the reign of Antoninus Pius. Whereas Marcus Aurelius disliked the cruelty of the Games, his son Commodus went to the other extreme and himself performed in the arena, like a Roman Hercules, on one occasion killing three elephants. Elephants are mentioned among the Circus beasts under the Severi, Gordian III and Aurelian. Thereafter we have less evidence for the Games and almost none for the part played by elephants in them, but the mosaics, especially those of Piazza Armerina, show that the trade in African elephants continued briskly at the end of the third century. A century after that the letters of Symmachus reveal what efforts he made to get a good collection of animals for the Games of 393 and 401, but there is no evidence that the *Libycae ferae* which he obtained included elephants. Similarly, about this time the poet Claudian expatiates upon the exertions of Stilicho to procure noble animals to celebrate his consulship: lions and leopards came from Libya, and also huge ivory tusks for the tablets that are to carry the consul's name, but elephants are not mentioned. Further, India supplied tusks, but though eager to send the beasts themselves as a spectacle, she feared that their vast weight would retard the ships. Thus apparently trade in the live animals was drying up.[165]

There is fortunately a lighter side to this tale of slaughter: elephants were also trained with very great skill to do tricks in the Circus, while some may have been kept purely for display. At least this is suggested by the story that Augustus, when presented with a petition by a frightened suitor, pleasantly told the man that he was holding it out 'like a penny (*as*) to an elephant': the animal seems to have been taught to accept the 'entrance money' at an exhibition. Aelian was greatly impressed by the elephant's docility and ability to learn and particularly to respond to music by dancing or marching in time. He records that at a show given by Germanicus, perhaps in AD 12, some elephants which had been born and carefully trained in Italy, put on an amazing act. They entered the arena on both sides in two groups of six, wearing the flowered garments of dancers; they formed into a line, wheeled in circles and performed various movements at their teacher's order, keeping time in a rhythmic dance; at one time they sprinkled flowers delicately on the floor. But what really sent the spectators wild with delight was when six males and six females came on in pairs, suitably dressed, and took their places at a rich banquet which had been laid out: they used their trunks, as hands, to take their food with great delicacy and drank from bowls placed in front of each; the act ended in more slapdash fashion when they started squirting each other or their attendant with water, though 'in fun, not by way of insult'. Pliny, perhaps referring to another occasion, tells how elephants picked their way among crowded guests, reclining on couches; they planted their steps carefully and apparently took their places among the guests. Pliny says that it was common for them to hurl weapons in the air and to play together in a war-dance. They learnt to walk on tight-ropes (surely this means two parallel ropes); and once four walked on ropes, carrying a litter in which a female elephant pretended to be in labour. They could not only climb up sloping ropes, but at a festival given by Nero in 59 an elephant, with a rider on its back, even came down a rope from the highest gallery of the theatre. Seneca tells how they walked on tight-ropes and would kneel down at the word of command from a tiny Ethiopian boy, while Pliny tells how one animal, much beaten because of its slowness in learning, was once found at night practising all by itself.[166]

The need to keep the arenas supplied was met by a trade about which not very much is known. It was probably controlled for the emperor by his *procurator ad elephantos* who will have acted through commercial companies. Some of these had offices at Ostia in porticoes around a large square (Foro delle Corporazioni). Many of the mosaic pavements of these offices survive and indicate the trade of each company (pl. XVIII). Office no. 28 depicts an African elephant, while no. 14 shows another and is inscribed STAT(IO) SABRATENSIUM (the office of Sabrata in Tripolitania).[167] Another Tripolitanian city, Lepcis Magna, also has monuments relating to its interest in the export trade: part of a marble elephant, which once graced a main road, has been found (pl. XIXa). An inscription records the dedication, to one of the city's deities, of a pair of tusks of a 'Lucanian cow', thus showing that the elephant's old nickname was still used in the third century AD. Another inscription records that a loyal citizen once presented Lepcis with four live elephants (*feras dentatas quattuor vivas*), presumably for show in the local Games.[168] Elephants in the act of being embarked for transportation are shown in mosaics in Carthage, in a house at Veii and on the 'Great Hunt' mosaic at Piazza Armerina (pl. XIXb). Owners of the houses to which the mosaics belonged probably had some connection with the trade in elephants: at any rate the owner of the great villa at Piazza Armerina in Sicily, the stepping-stone between North Africa and Italy, seems likely to have been connected with the importation of animals for the arenas in Italy. To what extent elephants were imported from India is uncertain, but the trade does not seem likely to have been very extensive. Apart from the great distances involved, the author of the *Periplus of the Erythraean Sea*, who wrote in the first century AD when commercial contacts between Italy and India were frequent, does not mention the export of any animals by sea from any Indian port.[169] Some elephants no doubt arrived by the long overland route. In earlier days Lucretius indicated that Indian elephants were seldom seen in Rome, and the white elephant which Augustus may have received from Siam was a rarity indeed.[170]

PROCESSIONS AND RELIGION

The funeral cortège which brought the body of Alexander to Alexandria was decorated with the figures of elephants, but was not apparently led by live beasts (p. 76). However, Alexander, in the guise of Zeus Ammon, in a chariot drawn by Indian elephants, is depicted on a coin of Cyrene (pl. XVc): this clearly refers to his triumphant return from the East and it may even reflect a historical procession staged by Ptolemy I in his honour. There is, however, no doubt about the famous procession arranged by Ptolemy II in the 270s where not only was the mythical victorious return of the god Dionysus from India on an elephant's back shown in statuary, but the figure of Alexander appeared in an elephant-drawn chariot, and other elephants graced this splendid pageant (p. 124). In much later times, especially in the second part of the second century AD, the legend of Dionysus' triumphant return from the East, which was intimately associated with the historical return of Alexander, provided a popular theme for sculptured sarcophagi where the god was shown in a chariot drawn by elephants or even on elephant-back; since Dionysiac processions symbolically reflected the joy of victory over death, the presence of elephants which were believed to be favourites of the Sun-god gave further point to the triumph of light over darkness (pl. XXa).

It was about the period of Ptolemy's great Procession that elephants were first seen by the Romans, and before long they made occasional appearances in the Circus, but they were not used in religious procession until the time of the Empire. Their private use, if rare, had not been banned: thus Domitius had ridden about southern Gaul on one to celebrate his victory of 121 (p. 192). Julius Caesar had been escorted home by elephants (p. 197) and Cornificius had ridden out to dinner (p. 200). True, Pompey's attempt to enter Rome in a chariot drawn by elephants had failed, but for physical rather than political reasons (p. 193). There is no record that Augustus tried to follow these precedents, but a coin issued in 18 BC shows him standing in an elephant-biga, while another issue depicts another such biga resting on an arch which stands on an aqueduct and celebrates his repair of the main roads of Italy. This latter scene clearly reproduces a statuary group, as presumably does the coinage of 18 BC. Augustus also dedicated four obsidian statues of elephants in the Temple of Concord. However, after his death when Augustus had been enrolled among the Divi, a coin of Tiberius shows a statue of his deified predecessor on a throne in an elephant-quadriga.[171] This links on to the old Roman tradition of the *pompa circensis* (pl. XXIV, f).

The formal triumphal procession of a victorious general goes back to the earliest days of Roman history; the Circus procession also goes back a long way. Public Games, which had a religious background, were opened with a grand procession which started from the Capitol and wound its way down to the Circus Maximus which it entered and marched around. It might be led by the presiding magistrate or later by the emperor himself in a horse-drawn biga or quadriga, followed by citizens and the competitors in the games. Then came priests and statues of gods in chariots (*tensae*) drawn by horses or mules or in litters (*ferculae*). When the Senate decreed that an ivory statue of Julius Caesar might be carried in such processions, the line between gods and men was wearing rather thin, and the chariot of Divus Augustus on the Tiberius coin takes the honour one stage further with the use of elephants in place

Fig. 24. Circus procession shown on a sculptured sarcophagus. (Daremberg and Saglio *Dictionnaires des antiquités*, s.v. Circus, fig. 1528)

of horses. A rather crude sculptured sarcophagus of later date shows part of such a pompa with an elephant-quadriga preceded by two men in togas (fig. 24). Caligala gave this honour to celebrate the birthday of his dead sister Drusilla. Augustus' chariot was paraded under Claudius, who also accorded this honour to the memory of his grandmother Livia, the wife of Augustus. Under Nero coins of AD 55 show two figures (Divus Augustus and Claudius?) in an elephant-quadriga, but in 59 a similar procession somewhat miscarried when the elephants refused to go any further than the seats of the senators in the Circus. Similar honours were paid posthumously to Vespasian and Julia, daughter of Titus. Domitian displayed a golden statue of himself in each of two elephant-drawn chariots on at least one triumphal arch in Rome. Deceased members of the imperial family continued to be commemorated on the coinage in this way: Nerva, Marciana, the two Faustinae, Pius, Verus (pl. XXIVg). Marcus and Pertinax; they ceased during the third century. However, on the Greek coinage of Alexandria Domitian and Hadrian had appeared even during their lifetimes, as did Caracalla and Gallienus on coins of Asia Minor. By this time, at least according to the *Historia Augusta*, living emperors were appearing in elephant-chariots in Rome: Caracalla (in imitation of Alexander the Great), Elegabalus, Severus Alexander and Gordian III. Two gold medallions (pl. XXIVh) show Diocletian and Maximian entering on their consulships of 287 in an elephant-quadriga, while on a coin of 310 Maxentius is similarly depicted: these may possibly re-

256

present real processions, though they could be merely symbolic, as a medallion struck in 326 to celebrate Constantine's twenty years of rule almost certainly was (here the somewhat grotesque elephants were drawn by a die-cutter who had probably never seen one, since they were minted at Treves – even St Ambrose a little later at Milan had curious ideas about elephants: p. 233 f.). Finally, an ivory diptych shows an imperial apotheosis and an emperor's effigy in a shrine on a car drawn by elephants; this work is possibly as late as the fifth century, but it has also been assigned to the fourth, and to Julian in particular, thus emphasizing old pagan beliefs and rituals (pl. XXb).

The honour of an elephant-biga in the *pompa circensis*, which was apparently first granted to Divus Augustus, is recorded in an epigram by Philip of Thessalonica: 'No longer does the great-tusked elephant, with tower on back and ready to fight phalanxes, charge unchecked into battle; but in fear it has yielded its thick neck to the yoke and draws the chariot of divine Caesar (*Kaisaros Ouraniou*). The wild beast knows the delight of peace; throwing off the gear of war, it conducts instead the father of good order (*eunomia*).' The epigram has often been connected with a specific historical event, namely Caligula's honouring of Drusilla and the dedication of a temple to Augustus at the end of A D 37. However, in view of the coin issued by Tiberius late in his reign, showing the statue of Augustus in the elephant-biga, probably he rather than Caligula should be credited with the institution of this honour to Augustus.[172] The use of elephants in place of horses no doubt magnified the honour simply because of the impressiveness of the animals, but there was probably another element present. The elephant was regarded as a 'pious' animal that worshipped the sun and moon, as Juba, who lived at this time, recorded.[173] Further, in the East, as Aristotle noted (p. 48, n. 34), elephants were taught to kneel in adoration before kings and, adds Pliny, to offer them crowns. Obviously this did not happen with elephants harnessed in *bigae*, but it did occur somewhat later with Domitian's more open acceptance of divinity: an epigram of Martial (*de spect.* XVII) records that an elephant, after fighting a bull in the arena, of its own accord adored the emperor:

> 'quod pius et supplex elephas te, Caesar, adorat
>     hic modo qui tauro tam metuendus erat,

non facit hoc iussus, nulloque docente magistro;
crede mihi, nostrum sentit et ille deum.'

But not too much should be read into a passing episode devised by an obsequious trainer (whose touch behind the ear, rather than some direct guidance from heaven, will have caused the beast to kneel) although some of the more philosophically minded spectators may have ruminated on the relations of animals and gods and if they had read their Pliny they might even recall that elephants were said to kneel in worship before kings. It was not until over 100 years later that a Roman emperor apparently first rode in an elephant-chariot: Dio Cassius (LXXVII, 7.4) records that Caracalla 'took about with him many elephants in imitation of Alexander, or rather of Dionysus', and he will presumably have been driven rather than merely escorted or have ridden himself. An inscription from Banasa in Mauretania records an edict of Caracalla of AD 216 in which he remitted some taxes and expressed his confidence that the officials would do their duty, including in 'the forests themselves which nourish celestial animals' (silvis quoque ipsis caelestium fertilibus animalium). These animals are almost certainly elephants in which Caracalla took an especial interest, if only because he was involved in a Parthian war and wished to be regarded as a new Alexander. The precise significance of 'celestial' is not easy to pin down, but it probably reflected the idea of the piety of elephants and the favour of heaven and also emphasized the superhuman, if not supernatural, character of the emperor who favoured these animals and used them as a symbol of his eternal authority.[174]

Elephants clearly had gained an aura of sanctity, or at least of religiosity, in the eyes of many, but equally their symbolic significance must have varied for different people at different times and places, so that it is difficult to try to analyse these somewhat nebulous ideas too closely. Many factors had contributed to this symbolic aspect: their association with life and light (statues were often worked into candelabra),[175] and with victory over death and the link with the god Dionysus, their supposed worship of the sun, their longevity (coins of Philip I show an elephant and the inscription 'Aeternitas Augusti'), the increasing imperial patronage that they enjoyed at a time when the person of the emperor was becoming more involved in worship, their use in religious ceremonies, first drawing statues of the Divi, then living emperors. Thus, whereas Cicero, disgusted at the slaughter in the Circus, had felt that a bond of fellowship (*societas*) existed between the elephant and the human race, in later times the elephant had come to be associated with the gods, or at any rate with vague religious feelings which were wrapped up with the majesty of the emperor.

This feeling passed over from the pagan to the Christian world, at least as exemplified in two splendid stories told in the Church History, written in Syriac, by John of Ephesus in the sixth century about the elephants in Constantinople.[176] Some elephants to whom the God of the Christians had granted victory over their foes in the East lived for some time in the city. Whenever they passed by a church the leader turned to the East, bowed its head and trunk and prayed; it then raised its trunk aloft and made the sign of the Cross and passed on. All the others followed suit. John claims that he himself had often seen this happening and gives thanks that irrational beasts were led to a knowledge of Christianity to the shame of the rational who disregarded it. The second occurrence was at the time of the Games: the elephants entered, with their riders, stood in the middle of the Circus opposite the emperor, bowed, as well as their nature allowed, and prayed; each then made the sign of the Cross with its trunk over against the emperor to the astonishment of all present. After receiving presents from the emperor they withdrew. If John had lived after the seventeenth century he might with Milton have rejoiced that in Paradise

> 'the unwieldy elephant
> To make them mirth us'd all his might, and wreathed
> His lithe proboscis'

or have echoed the words of Thomas Ken, 'Praise Him, all creatures here below'.

# APPENDIX: IVORY

The history of ivory in the ancient world would require a book to itself, and even a sketch would exceed the scope of the present volume as well as the competence of its author. However, since many must have regarded the sole function of the elephant to be the production of ivory and in view of its great importance in the fields of art and commerce, a few words on this topic may be appended: they owe much to the work of an expert in this field, Dr R. D. Barnett.[177]

Ivory was highly prized and skilfully worked in Minoan and Mycenaean times. Traces of the raw material, of the workshops and of numerous worked objects attest its widespread use as a luxury object among the people that could afford it. In Crete four elephant tusks were found in the east of the island in the palace at Zacro which was destroyed about 1450 BC, while at Cnossus the shop of an ivory worker of about the same date provides fragments of large ivory statuettes. These were made of separate pieces, joined together by pins and dowels, while some were covered with gold leaf and thus were forerunners of the chryselephantine (gold and ivory) statues which the Athenians so much admired in the fifth century; round caskets carved in relief from sections of tusks also formed part of the stock in trade.[178] Mycenae has produced a carved elephant tusk, while of its ivories perhaps none is more famous than the figures of two goddesses with a child. In this early period ivories had a very wide range, the impulse emanating from the East. They are found in Palestine (e.g. at Megiddo), North Syria (e.g. at Ras Shamra), Cyprus, Rhodes, Delos and Attica, and are mainly luxury articles, as toilet-boxes, combs, mirrors, plaques for the decoration of furniture, seals and statuettes. Some must have been dispersed by trade, but others were doubtless the handiwork of travelling craftsmen from Phoenicia and Syria who settled, at least temporarily, in various centres where their specialized skill may have led to the formation of closed guilds of workers.

After the Mycenaean period comes a lull until the ninth or eighth centuries when contact between Greece and the East was re-established. The famous Nimrud ivories exemplify the Oriental pieces which stimulated early Greek artists to copy and excel their models. These ivories represent at least three traditions in Western Asia: the schools of Phoenicia (cf. the ivory house of King Ahab at Samaria which Amos denounced), North Syria, and Anatolia. The two first influenced Rhodes, Crete, Samos, Sparta and Athens, while the Anatolian tradition passed through Phrygia and Lydia to Ionia and Corinth.[179] Some influences penetrated even farther west to Etruria, not to mention Spain, or eastwards to South Russia and India, and south to the Sudan.

The sources of supply were, of course, the natural habitats of the elephants. The Phoenicians at first could draw on the local Syrian herds (p. 29 f.), but as these began to die out they had to turn to the East. Hiram of Tyre seems to have co-operated with Solomon of Judah about 1000 BC in getting ivory from India (Ophis), together with apes and peacocks (1 Kings, 10.22). Ezekiel (27.15) shows that by the sixth century the Phoenicians were importing ivory from Dedan (North Arabia) where in turn it must have come from India or Ethiopia and Somalia. Of similar date are ivories found at Bahrein. Part of a tusk used in an ivory throne at Nimrud shows that the tusk, when whole, must have had a very large diameter and thus suggests an African origin. The Egyptians obtained their ivory from Syria, where in early days Pharaohs had hunted, and from the South, namely the Sudan and Somalia (p. 27). The Persian king Darius proudly tells in an inscription how craftsmen and materials had been brought from the ends of the earth to decorate his palace at Susa: these included 'the ivory which was brought from Kush (Ethiopia), from India and from Arachosia (Afghanistan)'. Herodotus tells how in his own day the Ethiopians still sent 20 great elephant tusks every third year to the Persian court (p. 32). The Greeks, who had drawn lavishly on Oriental sources, found this supply decreasing in the seventh century and apparently turned to Libya where, according to the comic poet Hermippus in the later fifth century, they found an adequate supply (p. 32): this will mean probably North Africa rather than the area south of Egypt. The author (pseudo-Scylax) of a *Periplus* of *c.* 350 BC describes the island of Cerne on the west coast of Africa (which Hanno had already mentioned: p. 33) where Phoenician merchants traded with the Ethiopians: one of the items they sought was elephant tusks. Tusks thus formed an element in Punic trade. Some were used locally, but the ivories of Carthage and the west in general were artistically inferior to the earlier work of the East; others may have been pased on to the Greek world by Phoenicians acting merely as middlemen. In Hellenistic times contacts with India increased and this source of supply became more readily accessible to the western world, while the exploitation of the South by the Ptolemies made more African ivory available.

With the Roman Empire the demand for ivory exceeded all bounds. The main depot for the African trade was Adulis, while Indian supplies came both overland and, increasingly after the discovery and use of the monsoon, by sea, the harbours in India being Barygaza, Musiris and Nelcynda on the western coast and Dosarene (Orissa) on the east. Roman greed led to a shortage of African ivory in Pliny's day (VIII, 7), though the Indian supply was maintained. The fact that a merchant named Dioscorus adventured (early second century?) as far south as Cape Delgado in Portuguese East Africa may suggest the need to probe further afield. But in the third century when Rome's direct trade with India declined, the African supply was renewed, but in the following century Avienius refers to the supply from India still. However, while the demands of the Circus as well as for ivory led to the gradual decrease of elephants in North Africa in the fourth century and their virtual disappearance by the seventh (p. 31), the supply from Eritrea and Somalia increased: in the sixth century Cosmas implies that African ivory was supplanting Indian, since Ethiopian tusks were even being exported to India; he also says that the small tusks of the elephants of Ceylon were no longer being used in commerce.[180]

Further discussion of the uses to which ivory was put would take us too far from elephants, except that we might note that its employment in statues, often of deities, gave it some religious as well as regal associations: it decorated both temple and palace. Tusks were often dedicated in temples and carried in triumphal processions, while the resemblance of ivory to human flesh made it a suitable substance for exposed parts of statues of gods and men. Legend recorded that the gods gave Pelops of Phrygia an artificial ivory shoulder; the ivory statue by the Phrygian king of Cyprus, Pygmalion, even came to life; and Penelope in the Odyssey recalled that lying dreams issued forth from a gate of ivory. In early Italy worked ivory is found in the rich tombs of Etruria and Praeneste and was the privilege of the ruling class. Under Etruscan influence the kings, and later the magistrates of early Rome adopted it for their insignia of office, their sceptres and curule chairs. Apart from that it would be little used in the frugal days of the early Republic, but when eastern luxuries began to flood into Rome from the second century, ivory was among them, and Cicero can speak of 'houses of marble that glitter with ivory and gold' (*marmoreis tectis ebore et auro fulgentibus*). The blatant extravagancies of the Empire increased the demand. Caligula gave his horse an ivory stable, while Seneca possessed 500 tripod-tables with ivory legs. 'In literature alone,' wrote E. H. Warmington, 'we find it used for statues, chairs, beds, sceptres, hilts, scabbards, chariots, carriages, tablets, book-covers, table-legs, doors, flutes, lyres, combs, brooches, pins, scrappers, boxes, bird-cages, floors and so on.'[181] Finally, it made its appearance in the splendid diptychs of the early Byzantine period and in the ritual of the Christian church. To pander to these demands of luxury, not to mention of Circus and war, serious inroads were made upon the elephant population of the ancient world, resulting in the total disappearance of two groups, the Syrian and North African. Today the future of the elephant is in the balance: let us hope that this noble beast, which Cicero regarded as in some way man's ally (*socius*), survives all attacks from man's greed or neglect and does not disappear completely from the face of this earth which would be a poorer place without it.

# NOTES

Abbreviations

| | |
|---|---|
| *Bull Corresp. Hellen.* | Bulletin de Correspondance Hellénique |
| *CAH* | Cambridge Ancient History |
| *Class. Quart.* | Classical Quarterly |
| Jacoby, *FGrH.* | F. Jacoby, *Die Fragmente der Griechischen Historiker* |
| *Journ. Hellen. Stud.* | Journal of Hellenic Studies |
| *Journ. Rom. Stud.* | Journal of Roman Studies |
| *Num. Chron.* | Numismatic Chronicle |
| *OGIS* | Dittenberger, *Orientis Graecae Inscriptiones Selectae* |
| *PW* | Pauly-Wissowa, *Real-Encyclopädie d. klassischen Altertumswissenschaft* |
| Walbank, *Polybius* | F. W. Walbank, *A Historical Commentary on Polybius* (1957 f.) |

1 Much of the information in this chapter I owe to two books: R. Carrington, *Elephants* (1958) and Sylvia K. Sikes, *The Natural History of the African Elephant* (1971). The former is an entertaining but reliable account for the general reader, the latter a scientific work, of which the more technical aspects are enlivened by exciting examples of elephant behaviour, many culled from the author's own experience. Further, it contains a detailed index and an impressive bibliography of over 1,500 items. In view of this I have not attempted to document this section of this book, but refer the reader to these works. See also A. Jeannin, *L'Éléphant d'Afrique* (1947). I have not come across any very recent monograph on the

Indian elephant: see L. C. Miall and F. Greenwood, *The Anatomy of the Indian Elephant* (1878); P. E. P. Deraniyagala, *Elephas Maximus, the Elephant of Ceylon, I* (National Museums of Ceylon, Colombo, 1951). H. F. Osborn's *Proboscidea*, 2 vols (1936–42) deals with all elephants, extinct as well as living; his classification is regarded as too complicated. Much, of course, may be learnt about elephant behaviour from books such as J. H. Williams, *Elephant Bill* (1950).

2 See A. Jeannin, *L'-Éléphant d'Afrique* (1947), 19, 174.

3 That Juvenal thought that an essential difference existed between the elephants of Morocco and those of Ethiopia is deduced by some scholars from his

famous passage about Hannibal, where he refers to Africa as a land 'beaten by the Moorish sea and stretching to the steaming Nile, and then, again, to the tribes of Aethiopia and a new race of elephants' (X, 148 ff., as translated by G. C. Ramsay in the Loeb edition). 'Africa Mauro/ percussa oceano Niloque admota tepenti, / rursus ad Aethiopum populos aliosque elephantos.'

But the use of *alius* in *aliosque elephantos* may not indicate a difference in kind or identity but simply 'another group of', i.e. separate but not different. Further, it is to be noted that some MSS give *altosque*, and it may not be irrelevant that a poet of the Augustan period, C. Rabirius, had used the epithet of elephants: *elephans altus*.

4 See L. Balout, *Préhistoire de l'Afrique du Nord* (1955), esp. 97 ff. (with table of prehistoric elephants). G. R. Vaufrey, *L'Art rupestre nord-africain* (Arch. de l'I.L.P. Mem. no. 20 (1939), pp. 22, 30, 90). Plate VI shows an elephant with a very marked nuchal hump: this is probably not a special physical characteristic of a separate race, but shows the close observation of the artist, since when elephants are standing in certain positions the hump is accentuated, as shown by photographs of modern elephants given by S. K. Sikes, *op. cit.* pl. 97 and 114b.

5 See H. A. Winkler, *Rock-drawings of Southern Upper Egypt*, I (1938), II (1939), especially plates xxi, 2; xxvii, 2 and 3, lvi, 1, lvii, 1. These are African elephants (although lvi, 1 looks rather more Indian. S. R. K. Glanville, *Journal of Egyptian Archaeology*, 1926, shows (pl. 13, 1, 2) a vase in the form of an elephant with broken tusks in which he sees a tamed animal (pl. VIa). An elephant inscribed on ivory in the Carnarvon collection is placed alongside an object which has been interpreted (somewhat boldly perhaps) as part of a corral: *J. Egyptian Arch.*, 1918, pl. 1, 2; 4, 1. See also for Libya, P. Graziosi, *L'arte rupreste della Libya* II (1941).

6 For the inscription see J. H. Breasted, *Ancient Records of Egypt* (1906), I, n. 510 note b; its last line 'Four men brought him . . .' may also refer to the elephant mentioned.

7 See J. H. Breasted, *Ancient Records of Egypt*, II, no. 125 (very fragmentary: it should be assigned to Thutmose I, not II) and no. 588 (for Amenemhab).

8 See N. de G. Davies, *The Tomb of Rekh-me-re at Thebes* (1943), pl. 23; R. D. Barnett, *Palestine Exploration Quarterly*, 1939, pl. 1.

9 On the Indus civilization see J. Marshall (ed.), *Mohenjo-Daro and the Indus civilization* (1931), with many illustrations of elephants; Sir Mortimer Wheeler, *The Indus civilization*[3] (1968).

10 See A. Berriedale Keith, *Cambridge History of India*, I (ed. E. J. Rapson, 1935), 81, 127.

11 See B. Brentjes, 'Der Elefant im Alten Orient', *Klio*, 1961, 12 ff., with references.

12 See A. T. Olmstead, *History of Assyria* (1923), 63 (Tiglathpileser), 95 (Assurnasirpal), 142 (Shalmaneser. The elephant is here said to be African), 224 (Hittite tribute), 306 (Hezekiah. The Biblical account in *II Kings* xvii, esp. 14–15, in listing the tribute does not mention the elephant-skins which occur in Sennacherib's list). For Tiglathpilesar and Assurnasirpal see also Luckenbill, *Ancient Records*, I, 247; 520. For the new Assurnasirpal inscription see D. J. Wiseman, *Iraq*, 1952, 24 ff., esp. 31. E. D. van Buren, *Clay Figurines of Babylonia and Assyria* (1930), 168 and fig. 220, refers to the cast of an elephant with small head, dabs for eyes, a long trunk, a little tail, slight indication

of tusks and traces of the legs of a rider; this he dates to *c.* 400 BC, but it may be Hellenistic: see B. Brentjes, *op. cit.* 18. For Bethsham see A. Rowe, *The Four Canaanite Temples of Bethsham* (1940) and Brentjes, *op. cit.*, 18 f. The latter discusses Syrian elephants, 14 ff.

13 See L. Woolley, *A Forgotten Kingdom* (1953), 74.

14 See R. D. Barnett, *Palestine Exploration Quarterly*, 1939, 4 ff.; D. Harden, *The Phoenicians* (1962), 156, 184 ff., 206 ff.; J. Gray, *The Canaanites* (1964), 168 ff., 181 ff., 226 ff.

15 Some references may be given. Pillars of Heracles: Aristotle, *De Caelo*, II, 14.15; Pliny, *NH*, v, 18; Aelian, vII, 2, x, 1; Solinus, xxv. Mauretania: Strabo, xvII, 3.4; 7; 8; Pliny, *NH*, v, 5; 15; 18, vIII, 2; 32. Numidia: Appian, *Libyc.* 9; Frontinus, *Strat.* Iv, 7.18; Plutarch, *Pompey* 12. Between the Lesser Syrtes and the Garamantes: Pliny, *NH*, v, 26. Themistius *Orat.* x, p. 166 (Dindorf), cf. xII, 2.16.

The use of the word 'Libyan' (African) in ancient writers *might* cause confusion, since 'Libya' was in early days regarded as the area west of the Nile, while the district to the east (including Ethiopia and Eritrea) was strictly part of Asia. But since the first African elephants known to the Greeks were those of North Africa (i.e. Libyan), no doubt Libyan was applied to all elephants in what we call Africa. Some geographers soon shifted the boundary to the Red Sea, perhaps as early as Ephorus in the fourth century (cf. F. W. Walbank, *Comm. Polybius*, I, 368). But even if some writers, like Polybius, adhered to the earlier division of the continents, Polybius is obviously using Libyan as a generic term when he refers, e.g. to Libyan elephants in connection with the battle of Raphia (v, 84.5); these animals came in fact from Ethiopia, where the Ptolemies had hunted them for many decades.

CHAPTER II—

**16** In old editions of Liddell and Scott the Greek word *elephas* ( ἐλέφας ) was derived from the Sanscrit *ibha*, meaning an elephant, to which the Arabic article *al* had been prefixed. A somewhat more likely derivation is the Hebrew or Phoenician *aleph*, meaning an ox (cf. the Roman use of 'Lucanian oxen'). R. D. Barrett (*Journ. Hellen. Stud.* 1948, 6) believes that the decipherment of the Hittite hieroglyphs has provided the true etymology: an inscription from North Syria gives the word *ulubadas*, meaning a bull; this form lacks an unwritten nasal and should be *ulubandas*. Horace (*Epod.* 12.1) uses the (Indian?) word *barrus* for an elephant; cf. *barrire*, to trumpet, and *bar(r)itus*, trumpeting of an elephant (Apul. *Fl.* 17). According to the *Historia Augusta* (*Aelius* 2.3) the Moorish word for an elephant was *caesai* (cf. Latin *Caesar*). In Egyptian (cf. Thutmose III inscription, p. 27) it is called 'Hand',

as in the Rigveda: see p. 28. **17** For Hanno, see Müller, *Geographici Graeci Minores* (1855), I, 1 ff. Cf. E. H. Warmington, *Greek Geography* (1934), 72 ff. **18** Ctesias. Text in Jacoby, *FGrH* C 688 (1958). Edition by R. Henry, 1947. Discussion of his historical value by A. Momigliano, *Quarto Contributo alla storia degli studi classici* (1969), 181 ff. **19** See D. M. Balme, Aristotle's *De Partibus Animalium*, *I* (1972), 69. **20** The middle period (345/4–342) is supported by H. D. P. Lee ('Place-names and the date of Aristotle's biological works', *Class. Quart.* 1948, 61 ff.), with additions, e.g. on elephants, later. He thus rejects the view of W. W. Jaeger (*Aristotle* Eng. transl. 330) that the *Hist. Animal.* was late. **21** *The Alexander-historians*. For the fragments see Jacoby. *FGrH*, IIB, pp. 618–828. Translation in C. A. Robinson, *The History of Alexander the Great, I* (1953). See further, L. Pearson, *The Lost Histories of Alexander the Great* (1960). *Onesicritus and Nearchus*: fragments in Jacoby, *FGrH*, nos. 134 and 133. See T. S. Brown, *Onesicritus* (1949) and art. in *PW* by H. Strasburger. **22** Aulus Gellius, IX, 4.1–3. **23** On relation of Onesicritus and Nearchus, see L. Pearson, *op. cit.*, 127. **24** Jacoby, *op. cit.* p. 474, tries to save Onesicritus' reputation on the length of gestation by supposing a textual error of ten for two years. **25** Tigers. See J. H. Wil-

liams, *Elephant Bill* (1950), 68, 98. He describes how two elephants, the mother and an 'auntie' protect the calf, while the tiger tries to stampede first one and then the other. **26** Fragments of Megasthenes in Jacoby, *FGrH*, III C. no. 715. **27** For Agatharchides see Müller, *Geographici Graeci Minores*, I, 111 ff.; Jacoby, *FGrH*, n. 86 (but excluding *On the Red Sea*); for a full discussion and appreciation of his value see P. Fraser, *Ptolemaic Alexandria* (1972), esp. 539 ff. **28** Polybius, v, 84. Pliny, *NH*, VIII, 9. **29** W. W. Tarn (*Class. Quart.* 1926, 98 ff.) assigned the remark in Diodorus II, 16.4 to Ctesias. Jacoby's comments are not very clear (*FGrH* IIB, p. 474); with Tarn, he regards the remark as erroneous in fact but believes that Ctesias' responsibility for it '*ist möglich, aber nicht nachweisbar*'. He then adds: '*falsch Tarn, der Diod. II. 16.4 und 35.4 auf Ktesias statt auf Megasthenes zurückfuhrt*'. But while he does include Diod. 35.4 among the fragments of Megasthenes, Jacoby does not include 16.4 and he does, of course, include Onesicritus' belief (in fact the above comments arise from Jacoby's observations on Onesicritus, not on Ctesias).

If then the author of the idea is not Ctesias but Onesicritus, the question arises as to whether his remark is merely his own speculation, based on the assumption that everything in India was larger than in Africa or whether it derives from greater information, which might have some bearing on the date when he wrote. Now from about 280 BC Ptolemy was beginning to send large-scale hunting expeditions to Ethiopia, and these presumably were preceded by some reconnaissance and smaller probes. Thus in the early years of the third century more was becoming known about the elephant of central Africa, and so it is just possible that Onesicritus might have been stimulated by such reports to make his observation; this hypothesis would require that he wrote his book late in life and might offer a supplementary argument (though a very frail one) to those scholars who believe the book to be late (cf. p. 52 above).

**30** H. Delbrück, *Geschichte der Kriegkunst*, I (1920), 252. E. Bevan, *Egypt under the Ptolemaic Dynasty* (1927), 176. W. W. Tarn, 'Polybius and a Literary Commonplace', *Clas. Quart.* 1926, 98 ff.; cf. *Hellenistic and Military Developments* (1928), 99.

**31** Sir William Gowers, 'African Elephants and Ancient Authors', *African Affairs*, 1948, 173 ff.

**32** Tarn apparently did not reveal his reaction to Gowers' article in his published work, apart from quoting it in a footnote in the third edition of his *Hellenistic Civilization* (ed. by G. T. Griffith, 1952), 62, without comment, which might imply approval. However, perhaps it may be permissible to

refer to his correspondence with Gowers which the latter kindly showed me: in a letter dated 6.11.1946 Tarn wrote, 'You have certainly cleared Polybius.' But though apparently abandoning his early view about the relative size of the two races of elephant, Tarn still fought a rearguard action: in a letter to me dated 12.6.1950 he wrote in connection with Carthaginian elephants, 'Gowers says that the Forest elephants whom the Belgians tame are very sensitive to noise and easily frightened'; Tarn then cites some examples of the efficiency of Carthaginian elephants (as those of Xanthippus smashing through Regulus' battle-line, or those that stormed the camp of the Mercenaries) and concludes, 'the Carthaginian elephants were not Sir William Gowers' Forest elephants, whatever they were, but a different species, and quite as efficient in war as any Indians.' This invention of another race of elephants in North-west Africa seems an entirely unnecessary hypothesis, devised as it is merely to obviate the fact that the Forest elephant (as indeed the Bush also) was sensitive to sudden sounds. Modern elephants have been trained successfully despite such a possible weak spot, so there seems no reason why the ancient Forest ones should not also have responded to training: an ancient battle may have been rather a noisy affair, but the elephants could have been given

preliminary battle indoctrination: indeed, with bells round their necks on occasion and trumpeting with rage, they themselves made a considerable contribution to the din. And in any case it was *Indian* elephants of Pyrrhus that were said to have been frightened by the sudden grunting of swine (see p. 113 f.). Thus we may now surely accept both the reliability (from the point of view of the ancients) of the *cliché* and the fact that Ptolemies and Carthaginians drew upon the Forest race.

CHAPTER III—

**33** G. T. Griffith, 'Alexander's generalship at Gaugamela', *Journ. Hellen. Stud.* 1947, 77 ff., and E. W. Marsden, *The Campaign of Gaugamela* (1964) virtually ignore the elephants. See W. W. Tarn, *Alexander the Great* (1948), I, 47 and cf. II, 189.

**34** According to Polyaenus (IV, 3.22) at the subsequent battle against Porus Alexander did use elephants, which he placed on his left wing. This must be rejected in view of (a) the silence of all the other authorities, and (b) the difficulty Alexander would have experienced in getting any elephants across the river in the confusion of the night crossing.

**35** The main sources for the battle at the Hydaspes are Arrian, *Anab.* V, 8–18; Plutarch, *Alexander*, 60; Diodorus, XVIII, 87–88; Curtius, VIII, 13–14; Polyaenus, IV, 3.22. Arrian's account, though not without many difficulties, is the most satisfactory record: his main source was Ptolemy, Alexander's general who fought in the battle. Detailed problems are discussed by Kromayer-Veith, *Antike Schlachtfelder* IV, 385 ff. (1929, cf. Veith, *Klio*, 1908, 131 ff.); W. W. Tarn, *Alexander the Great* (1948), II, 190 ff., and J. R. Hamilton (on the cavalry action) *Journ. Hellen. Stud.* 1956, 26 ff. General accounts of the battle are given by Bury-Meiggs, *Hist. of Greece* (1951), 802 ff.; N. G. L. Hammond, *Hist. of Greece* (1959), 628 ff.; J. F. G. Fuller, *The Generalship of Alexander the Great* (1958), 180 ff.; P. Green, *Alexander the Great* (1970), 207 ff.

For the topography see Sir Aurel Stein, *Geographical Journal*, lxxx, July, 1932, 31 ff., and *Archaeological Reconnaissances in N. W. India* (1937), 1 ff.

A full account of the battle and its problems would be out of place in this book: attention is primarily concentrated on the issues affecting the elephants.

**36** The numbers of Porus' forces in the battle are given variously. Arrian gives 30,000 infantry, 4,000 cavalry, 300 chariots and 200 elephants. Curtius gives the same number of infantry and chariots, but 85 elephants. Plutarch gives only 20,000 infantry and 2,000 cavalry. Diodorus' figures are 50,000 infantry, 3,000 cavalry, over 1,000 chariots and 130 elephants. Confusion may have arisen from the fact that Porus did not take all his infantry and elephants, but left some as a covering force in his rear against Craterus. Arrian's authority should generally be preferred, but although it is not normally good practice to pick out from a variety of sources what seems to the historian to be most likely, it may perhaps be suggested here that Porus had 20,000 infantry (and 4,000 cavalry and 300 chariots) in the battle, the remainder of Arrian's 30,000 infantry having been left behind.

But what of the elephants? Here complications arise. According to Arrian, Porus drew them up in front, at a distance from each other of about a hundred feet. Since Arrian implies a single line of 200 elephants, a total distance of some four miles would be involved. This seems excessive, although we cannot calculate the precise length of the lines behind the elephants, since there are too many uncertain factors, such as the number of infantry and the depth to which they were massed. Polyaenus, on the other hand, says that the elephants were posted at 50 feet apart. (Later, at the battle of Magnesia, Antiochus' elephants seem to have been about 50 or less feet apart). We are justified in reducing Arrian's total of 200 beasts, if only because he himself says that Porus had left a few behind. It is tempting to turn to Diodorus' 130, but in fact we must remain uncertain.

**37** See L. Renou, *La civilisation de l'Inde ancienne* *d'apres les textes Sanscrits* (1950), 175; R. K. Mookerji, *Chandragupta Maurya* (1966), 178: both references are given by P. Goukowsky, *Bull. Corresp. Hellen.* 1972, n. 54.

**38** Arrian (VI, 2.2) luckily gives the number as about 200: otherwise we could scarcely have said more than that Alexander *could* have between 200 and 300. There are too many ambiguities in the scattered references to his acquisition of elephants and we do not know that he always took his latest addition along with him. Thus he had 27 at Susa (15 from Gaugamela and 12 sent to him at Susa); but when he advanced eastwards did he take them with him or leave them at Susa? The number captured at Ora seems to be under 30 while he rounded up 13. If he kept all together, his total might be some 60. Then Taxiles had promised him 25 and later sent 30; does this mean 55 or 30? Allowing 30 and the 56 he received at Taxila, the total would rise to 144 and then with the 80 captured at the Hydaspes to 224. Abisares sent at least 30 (and possibly 40 or even 70 in all). Thus when Alexander began his return journey he could have had at least 250 (and possibly nearly 300). If all the presents he received and captures he made have been recorded in the sources, it looks as if he may well have left his original 27 behind in Susa.

**38**A On these coins (two in the British Museum, and one in New York) see C. Seltman, *Greek Coins*[2]

(1955), 213, and pl. xlix, nos. 6 & 7; *Brit. Museum Quarterly*, 1926, 36, pl. 18b; P. Goukowsky, 'Le roi Poros, son elephant et quelques autres' *Bulletin Corresp. Hellen.* 1971, 473 ff.

Goukowsky believes the weapon to be an ankus and discerns a bell hanging from the neck. He draws attention to an elephant depicted on a relief of Mathura (1st cent. BC, his fig. 5) and also to the accuracy shown in depicting the beards and hair in top-knots of the two riders; he compares these and other details with the figure depicted on the throne of Xerxes at Persepolis which is generally thought to be an Indian from the Punjab.

It is held by some that these coins were minted after, rather than before, Alexander's death.

The suggestion of a direct struggle between the two kings is, of course, fictitious: the coin is merely symbolic. But such a single combat is alleged, on the authority of Lucian (*Quomod. Hist. Conscrib.* 12), to have been described in the works of Aristobulus, one of the Greek technicians in Alexander's army. This flattery did not please Alexander: according to Lucian's tale, Aristobulus read this account to Alexander as they were sailing down the Hydaspes; whereupon Alexander snatched the book and threw it into the river, remarking, 'You ought to be thrown overboard yourself, Aristobulus, for fighting duels and killing elephants with a single javelin on my behalf.' It is uncertain whether this anecdote really goes back to Aristobulus' own work: cf. Jacoby, *FGrH* n. 139 T 4 and *Komment.* p. 509 f.

A recent attempt has been made by S. Settis (*Parola del Passato*, 1968, 55 ff.) to link the Alexander-Porus coin with the *Curculio* of Plautus. In that play a signet-ring has an important role in the development of the plot which culminates in a 'recognition' scene which is based on various characters identifying the ring. The scene engraved on the ring was 'a bucklered warrior cutting an elephant in half with his blade' (clupeatus elephantum ubi machaera dissicit; line 424). P. Grimal saw in this a reference to the 'elephant victory' over the Galatians (*Mélanges . . . à A. Piganiol*, III (1966), 1731 ff.) but this has been rejected (surely rightly) by Settis. Settis himself argues that the background should be sought in Alexander and Porus and the coin in particular, while he finds echoes of Alexander in Therapontigonus, the braggart soldier who had conquered vast numbers of peoples and had just returned from India ('*ex India*', line 439). Not all his arguments are very convincing, but it is perhaps easier to believe that in Plautus (and his Greek original) there was some parody of Alexander than to link the scene on the signet-ring so directly with the Porus coin. Settis' article contains very full bibliographical material.

*If* a reference to Alexander be accepted and if the *Curculio* is one of Plautus' later plays (i.e. after 189 BC), then perhaps Settis' argument might be taken a stage further than he goes: whereas the Greek play used by Plautus may have alluded to Alexander, Plautus himself may have wanted his audience to recognize an oblique sarcastic reference to Scipio Africanus and the defeat of Antiochus. Such criticism of Scipio would agree with the belief of Tenney Frank (*Anatolian Studies Presented to W. H. Buckler*, 85 ff.) that in his later years Plautus became critical of Scipio and poked fun at his achievements (e.g. in the *Bacchides, Truculentus* and *Trinummus*). This view in general is, of course, possible, but it must be regarded with caution: cf. Scullard, *Roman Politics²* (1973), 254. Yet the reference to the elephant admittedly would fit very neatly into the theory, since Scipio's defeat of Hannibal's elephants at Zama must still have been fresh in the mind of Plautus' audience, which recently had also very likely been reminded of the great Punic elephant Surus (p. 174). Alternatively, since there is no indication of the date of the production of *Curculio*, one could turn the argument round and suggest that if the reference does suggest Scipio, then the date of the play will have been after 188. But seeking contemporary references in ancient plays is hazardous work.

**39** The funeral carriage is

described in detail by Diodorus, XVIII, 26–27, probably following Hieronymus of Cardia, an historian of the period from Alexander's death to at least 272 BC (cf. Athenaeus, V, 206e). For a bibliography on the carriage see Goukowsky, *op. cit.* n. 38ª above.

**40** The main surviving source for the period 323–301 BC is Diodorus, XVIII–XX. His narrative is full and in the main reliable since it is largely derived from Hieronymus of Cardia. The latter not only wrote an account of the period but had taken an active part in many major events. He had supported his fellow-countryman Eumenes in his struggles against Perdiccas and Antigonus, but after Eumenes' death following the battle of Gabiene he served Antigonus for many years and was present at the battle of Ipsus in 301; in fact he survived until about 250 when he was serving Antigonus' grandson, Antigonus Gonatas. A second major source for the period was Arrian's *History of the Events after Alexander* (τὰ μετὰ Ἀλέξανδρον), but only a few extracts survive: see Flavius Arrianus, II (ed. A. G. Roos, 1968), 253 ff., and Jacoby, *FGrH*, n. 156, frgs. 1–11. Plutarch's *Lives* of *Eumenes* and *Demetrius* also depend partly on Hieronymus but partly on other material. Nepos also wrote a Life of Eumenes. Justin, XIII–XV, with Trogus, *Prologues*, is brief. Appian, Strabo, Pausanias and others add a few details.

On Hieronymus see T. S. Brown, *American Historical Review* 1947, 684 ff. On Eumenes and the sources for his life see the brief paper by H. D. Westlake, *Essays on the Greek Historians* (1969), 313 ff.

General histories of the period are W. W. Tarn, *Cambridge Ancient History* VI (1927), ch. XV; M. Cary, *A Hist. of the Greek World*² (1963); *Histoire grecque*, IV, Pt I, by G. Glotz, P. Roussel, R. Cohen; the part dealing with 323–301 (pp. 257 ff.), by Roussel, is well documented and is fuller than the corresponding part of E. Will, *Histoire politique du monde hellenistique*, I (1966), which, although more up-to-date, has been deliberately shortened by the author at some points in view of Roussel's treatment.

**41** Arrian, τὰ μετὰ Ἀλέξανδρον frg. I, 43 (= Jacoby, frg. 11.43). There is no corresponding passage in Diodorus, since there is a large lacuna after XVIII, 39.

**42** At this point Diodorus (XVIII, 50.3) in summing up the forces of Antigonus attributes to him 30 elephants. This must be an error. Arrian (see n. 41 above) had assigned 70 to him, while later at the battle of Paraetacene in 317 he had 65 (Diod. XIX, 27.1). True, he used only 30 in the battle at Orcynia (Diod. XVIII, 40.7), as we have seen, but these did not represent his total force. In fact the error of 30 in XVIII, 50.3, probably arises from mistaken recollection of this passage. Kromayer-Veith, *Antike Schlachtfelder* IV

(1929), 407, suggest that a copyist, who knew nothing of the original figure of 70 (which they believe occurred only in Arrian) and who had read 30 so far in Diodorus, did not understand the figure 70 and altered it to 30.

**43** For the battle of Paraetacene Diodorus, XIX, 26–34, is the chief, and virtually the only, source. Difficulties in his account have been exaggerated by many modern writers; on the whole it makes very good sense. See above all the discussion by Kromayer and Kahnes in Kromayer-Veith, *Antike Schlachtfelder*, IV (1929), 393–424 (they refer to Blatt 8 of the *Griechische Abteilung* of their *Schlachtenatlas*, but although this was obviously drafted it has unfortunately not been published, I believe). They deal effectively with criticisms by H. Delbrück, *Geschichte der Kriegkunst*³, 20, and other writers.

Plutarch gives no real account of the battle, but does mention (*Eumenes*, xiv.4) towers and purple trappings on the elephants; this reference to towers is almost certainly wrong: see p. 241. One point not discussed above is that Diodorus, XIX, 29.7, says that the battle-line of Antigonus started to move forward obliquely, with the right wing in advance and the left wing held back. The apparent difficulty is that the left wing engaged the enemy first, and the right wing last. However, this preliminary alignment needed not have been kept up for long: indeed the

268

holding back of his left wing might have been an attempt by Antigonus to deceive Eumenes and to lead him to expect the *first* blow on *his* left, whereas in fact Antigonus delivered it on Eumenes' right.

**44** For the battle of Gabiene see Diodorus, XIX, 40–44. Difficulties in this account are well discussed by Kromayer and Kahnes, *op. cit.* n. 43 above, pp. 425–434.

**45** On the battle at Gaza see Diodorus, XIX, 80–84. For discussion see Kromayer-Veith, *op. cit.*, IV, 435 ff.

**46** W. W. Tarn, who originally accepted 480 elephants at Ipsus (*CAH*, VI, 504), changed his mind after a detailed examination of the Indian evidence for the generic use of 500: see *Journ. Hellen. Stud.* 1940, 84 ff. He argued that the tradition that the treaty named 500 elephants was derived by Strabo not from Hieronymus but from Megasthenes. Hieronymus (as reflected in Diodorus) was more interested in Antigonus than in Seleucus, whose activities from 311 to 302 he neglected to record, while Megasthenes was actually sent later by Seleucus as an ambassador to Chandragupta. Megasthenes would thus know about the treaty but his information may have come from an Indian informant who did not know the precise number but, knowing it was large, naturally expressed it as 500. But a difficulty arises: as Tarn agrees, both Diodorus and Plutarch go back to Hieronymus for their account of Seleucus' forces and in part for the battle itself, but Tarn would except the elephant numbers: 'The numbers 400 and 480 cannot possibly be derived from a common source; we have therefore to proceed on the basis that *neither* figure is from Hieronymus, and that the number he gave is unknown. (I take it to be a sound rule that if two texts, derived from a common source, give, on one matter, conflicting accounts, then what the common source gave on that matter is, in the absence of evidence *aliunde*, unknown)' (p. 87). In sum, we should accept that the real number, which was given by Hieronymus, is unknown and that all references to 500 derive from the treaty as recorded by Megasthenes. Tarn's detailed arguments as to how the figures 480 and 400 arose are even more speculative. He suggests that an author, possibly Duris, applied to the 500 a scale of losses of one-fifth, which he knew had been suffered by 20 elephants which were hurriedly marched across Asia to Antiochus in 277–75 BC; thus there would be 400 for Ipsus. But if Duris, or anybody else, felt that the 500 was too large why should he try to correct it by this arbitrary calculation and not simply have given Hieronymus' figure if that was lower; while if Hieronymus had given 500, would Duris have questioned his authority? As to the actual number at Ipsus Tarn suggests that since later Antiochus III got from the Maurya Sophagasenos sufficient elephants to bring his force up to 150, he was following the precedent of Seleucus, who then had 150 and (with a wastage of 20) 130 at Ipsus itself.

The ground would be partly cleared if we could suppose a textual corruption in Plutarch's *Eumenes* and there read 500 for 400: since 480 could be equated with 500 minus some 20 not actually used in the battle, we should then be left only with the problem of the reliability of the 500. But perhaps such a supposition is unjustified. In any case, the question would still remain whether we must reject the 500, not because of any supposed contradiction in the sources, but on the ground that it is out of scale with what we know of other elephant-forces (e.g. Porus' 200) and the problem of what happened to so large a number later. It would make matters easier if we could follow Tarn in believing that Hieronymus' figure is lost, but it is not very easy to believe that the figure of 480 in Diodorus, XX, 113, is not derived from him, since Diodorus is often contradictory in the numbers which he gives and is perhaps unlikely to have corrected Hieronymus' figure from his recollection of what Megasthenes had said. On the other hand, we cannot be certain that Diodorus used Hieronymus direct rather than through an intermediary and the latter of course might have made the change. No clear solution can be suggested, but a feeling persists that 500 should be viewed with caution.

**47** W. W. Tarn (*Journ. Hellen. Stud.* 1940, 87, n. 41) raises the possibility that Seleucus might have laid a trap: 'his cavalry may have had orders to fly, which, as they were unbroken, would inevitably draw Demetrius on and enable the elephants, who were waiting for this, to intervene'. Although Plutarch does suggest that the cavalry engagement was fought in earnest and that Demetrius routed his opponents, Tarn's hypothesis cannot be ruled out.

**48** Lysimachus presumably had no elephants before Ipsus: Geyer (*PW*, *s.v.* Lysimachus, col. 10) rightly suggests that the reference to the elephants of Antigonus and Lysimachus at Ipsus in a fragment of Diodorus (XXI, 1.2) is a slip due to the epitomator. After the battle Seleucus and Lysimachus divided much territory in Asia Minor between themselves, but since (so far as I know) there is no reference to Lysimachus having any elephants in the immediate future, it may be supposed that Seleucus took all or most of those captured from Antigonus (if, in view of his own large numbers, he did concede some to Lysimachus, they seem to have left no mark in history).

**49** Cf. W. W. Tarn, *Antigonus Gonatas* (1913), 286, n. 29.

CHAPTER IV—

**50** The chief surviving source for Pyrrhus is Plutarch's *Life of Pyrrhus*. This draws on a variety of sources, including Hieronymus of Cardia. The latter in turn appears to have made use of Pyrrhus' own *Memoirs*. For his battles in Italy, with which we are here primarily concerned, there is thus the substratum of a reliable tradition, although it has been added to from various other sources, some of which are less reliable. The Roman annalistic tradition is represented in Livy's Epitome, Frontinus, Orosius, Dionysius of Halicarnassus, Dio Cassius and the Epitome by Zonaras, and others. It emphasizes the role of Pyrrhus' elephants more than do the Greek writers to whom at this time the animals were more familiar (cf. Lévêque, *op. cit. infra*, 55).

For a full discussion of the sources and of Pyrrhus' career see especially P. Lévêque, *Pyrrhos* (1957). Cf. also the much briefer treatment in G. N. Cross, *Epirus* (1932).

**51** For Heraclea the most important sources are Plutarch, *Pyrrhus*, 16–17; Dionysius, XIX, 12; Zonaras, VIII, 3. The hypercriticism of K. J. Beloch (*Griechische Geschichte*, IV, ii, 474 f.) seems unjustified, while De Sanctis (*Storia dei Romani*, II, 393 ff.) reconstructs perhaps more than is necessary. See especially P. Lévêque, *op. cit.*, 322 ff.
**52** For Ausculum see especially Plutarch, *Pyrrhus*, 21; Dionysius, XX, 1–3;

Zonaras, VII, 5, 1–7. Greatest regard should be accorded to Plutarch, since his account derives from Hieronymus, but unfortunately it is much shortened. Much in the other sources derives from the Roman tradition, which was composed later in time than the early Greek writers and is in part self-justificatory. Some modern scholars would reject a very great deal of it, but much care is needed: even Lévêque (*op. cit.*), who would reject most, admits that the description of Pyrrhus' battle-line which Dionysius gives in detail, derived from Hieronymus and perhaps ultimately even from Pyrrhus' own *Memoirs*, but he rejects the description of the Roman battle-line as a late Roman annalistic reconstruction. But Pyrrhus surely knew the order in which the four legions faced him. Also we should hesitate before rejecting all that is recorded by Dionysius and Zonaras about the Roman method of dealing with Pyrrhus' elephants. However, for the general course of the battle Plutarch's account must be given priority, though at the same time its very brevity should allow the acceptance of other evidence if this does not contradict it.

There is a great volume of modern literature on the battle, but since we are concerned primarily with only one aspect of it, it will be sufficient here merely to cite the comprehensive work of Lévêque, *Pyrrhos*, 375 ff., whose reconstruction I would follow in many but not in all points. Nor would it be appropriate here to enter into many of the very detailed problems involved. On the topography E. T. Salmon (*Papers Brit. School Rome*, 1932, 44 ff.) argues that the river involved is the Carapella and that the battle was fought north of Ausculum (and south of Herdonia), while Lévêque follows those who believe it to be the Aufidus (Ofanto). One objection to the latter view is that the site would be nearer to Venusia than to Ausculum, so that it might be expected to have been known as the battle of Venusia; however, the Aufidus seems to suit the more rugged picture given by Plutarch.

**53** Orosius (IV, 1.10) refers the incident to the battle of Heraclea and names the man Minucius, but Numicius should be preferred (cf. F. Münzer, *PW*, *s.v.* Numicius, n. 2). A Numicius was consul in 469 and another was tribune in 320. Numisius is a more common name of a different family (although from the same root).

**54** Pyrrhus takes his elephants to Sicily: Appian, *Samm.* 11.6; Diodorus, XXII, 8.2. He leads them against the Carthaginians: Diod., XXII, 10.2. He loses two against the Mamertines: Plut. *Pyrrhus*, 24.2.

**55** The general tradition that the battle was fought near Beneventum should probably be preferred to the variant that it was near Paestum in the Campi Arusini (cf. Orosius, IV, 2.3).

The main sources for the battle are Plutarch, *Pyrrhus*, 25; Dionysius, XX, 11–12: Zonaras, VIII, 6.6. For full discussion see Lévêque, *op. cit.* 516 ff. On p. 523 he raises the question whether the part played by the elephants depends on the Greek or the Roman annalistic strands in the tradition (he decides on untrustworthy Roman writers).

**56** See Lévêque, *op. cit.* 523 n. 1 and J. H. Williams, *Elephant Bill*.

**57** J. D. Beazley, *Etruscan Vase-Painting*, 215; Gowers and Scullard, *Num. Chron.* 1950, 273 n. 9. A second copy of the plate from Capena has been found at Aleria in Corsica: see J. Jehasee, *Mélanges Carcopino* (1966), 547 ff., and *Roma medio repubblicana* (Rome, 1973, Catalogue of Exhibition of the Capitoline Museums, 1973), p. 67 and pl. ix. This plate is artistically inferior to the Capena example and the border is different, but the representation of the elephants is said to be the same. There are, however, slight differences; the tip of the trunk of the calf elephant can be seen in front of its mother's hind leg, and the calf itself appears to have a tusk. This tusk is drawn parallel to the trunk: thus (unlike the tusks of the mother) it is physically incorrect, while its position is curiously like that of the tusk of the elephant on the Aes Signatum (p. XIVb) which also seems to depict one of Pyrrhus' elephants. For another mother and calf see pl. IXb and below n. 161.

**58** G. Nenci, 'Un prodigio dei signa nella battaglia di Ausculum', *Rivista di Filologia* 1955, 391 ff., has an ingenious but far-fetched solution. He refers to Festus' statement (267. 5 ff. L) that the standard of the Fifth Legion was a *porcus* and argues that the story in Aelian arose from confusion with this pig. He believes that legend attributed the Roman success to a *prodigium* of the theriomorphic *signum*, which could have manifested divine power by emitting sounds which frightened the elephants, and he even sees this reflected in a fragment of Ennius, 'iam cata signa ferae sonitum dare voce parabant' (where he reads *ferae* for *fere*), i.e. 'the sagacious *signa* prepared to emit with their animal voice a sound'. However, apart from the difficulty of a Fifth Legion, a *porcina vox* as a prodigy may surely seem to many to be more difficult to accept than the presence of a live animal.

There is an interesting scene on a gem of 'an elephant drawing a car, driven by a pig(?)'. If the small figure standing in the car is a pig, and elephants were known to be afraid of pigs, then even more point would be given to this comic scene. Such humorous little scenes seem to have been popular: another gem shows an elephant emerging from a snail-shell, and a third an elephant coming out of a conch-shell and ridden by a rabbit. See H. B. Walters, *Catalogue of the Engraved Gems and Cameos, Greek, Etruscan and Roman, in the*

Brit. Museum (1926), nos. 2339, 2340, 2341.

Two fables were told about the elephant's supposed fear of small animals. In one the elephant told the lion that he constantly flapped his ears because 'if a gnat gets into my ear, I am a dead elephant' (C. Halm, *Fabulae Aesopicae Collectae* (1852), 261). In the other (Halm, *ibid.* 183) when the elephant and camel were contending for the kingship of the animals, the ape said that neither was fit to rule: the camel because it lacked a proper sense of anger, the elephant 'because he was afraid of pigs and could not defend his subjects against an attack from that quarter'. In a lyric poem by Mesomedes in the time of Hadrian a gnat and an elephant exchange pleasantries: see E. Heitsch, *Die Griechischen Dichterfragmente der römischen Kaiserzeit* (1961), 31.

**59** A. Alfoldi, *Early Rome and the Latins* (1964), 272, believes that the elephant stood for Pyrrhus and the sow for the Latins, being the sow with the thirty piglets which led Aeneas, ancestor of the Latins, to Alba Longa, i.e. it was a badge of the Latins. But there seems no reason why the Romans should choose a symbol of the Latins to commemorate their clash with Pyrrhus; later in the Social War they were represented by a wolf on the coinage. Interpretations of the two bars has often been fanciful. See T. Thomsen, *Early Roman Coinage*, III, 143 ff. and 225 ff., for a sober estimate.

**60** I owe to Dr G. Nuttall a reference to a remarkable saying in the *Talmud* (Baba Metzia, fol. 38b): 'Perhaps you are from Pumbeditha, where they draw an elephant through a needle's eye'. E. Klostermann (*Handbuch zu Neu. Testament*, II, i (1919) in commenting on Mark 10.25 translates this 'rabbinisches Sprichwort' as 'bist du vielleicht von Pumbeditha (d.h. ein Schildbürger), wo man einen Elephanten durch ein Nadelöhr fuhren will?'. A Schildbürger and a man of Pumbeditha appear to have gained the reputation for being simpletons (cf. a man of Gotham). Pumbeditha was a centre of Rabbinic studies in Babylonia, and some of its adherents indulged in very wild speculation. The relation of this saying to the words of Jesus ('It is easier for a camel to go through the eye of a needle, than for a rich man to enter into the kingdom of God') naturally depends upon the date of the former. If it is post-Christian, one can only speculate on its background. Since Pumbeditha is in Babylon, where elephants would be known from Sassanid use in the third century AD onwards, could it be that a Rabbi, wishing to make the saying as ludicrous as possible, substituted for a camel the largest beast that *he* knew?

The phrase occurs once again in the *Talmud, Berakoth*, 55b (I. Epstein, *The Talmud*, p. 342) in relation to dreams, which concern only normal thoughts and possible imagery: 'an elephant is never shown going through the eye of a needle' (because man never thinks of such things). *Berakoth* 56a (p. 350) adds that in dreams 'elephants are of good omen if saddled, of bad omen if not saddled'. *Menahoth* (69a, p. 408) raises a question which one can hardly think was a frequent practical problem: 'what is the law if an elephant swallowed an osier basket and passed it out with its excrement?' *Shabbath* 77b, p. 366, refers to an elephant's fear of a mosquito (presumably that the insect might get into its trunk?), while the *Mishnah* (N. Danby (1933), 38) says that 'the wild ass is reckoned a kind of wild animal, and the elephant and ape a kind of wild animal; and with any of them a man may draw or plough or drive'. Such references, which unfortunately cannot be dated, suggest that the elephant was not unknown in Babylonia and indeed that it may have been used for transport (cf. 'draw' and 'saddled').

CHAPTER V—

**61** See Memnon, Jacoby, *FGrH*, n. 434, fr. 8.8. Justin XXIV, 5.6.

**62** See W. W. Tarn, *Journ. Hellen. Stud.* 1926, 155 ff., and M. Cary, *History of the Greek World, 323–146 BC*² (1951), 387 ff.

**63** If elephants were effective in war only between the ages of 20 and 60, we may assume an attrition rate of some 25% every ten years.

**64** Sidney Smith, *Baby-*

lonian Historical Texts (1924), 156. The situation that faced Antiochus in Asia Minor was more complicated than indicated in the text, and other reconstructions of the chronological development of his relations with Ptolemy are possible: see e.g. E. Will, Histoire politique du monde Hellénistique (1966), 121 f. See also note 65.

**65** On the Myrina terracotta and the gem see P. Bienkowski, Les Celtes dans les arts mineurs greco-romains (1928), ch. v. In the gardens at Bomarzo are several Cinquecento statues of animals. One of an elephant is so similar to the Myrina terracotta that it has been suggested that a copy of the terracotta may have been found in this corner of Etruria and have inspired the later sculptor: see S. Settis, Bolletino d'Arte, 1966, 19 ff.

On the 'elephant victory' see now B. Bar-Kochva, Proceedings of the Cambridge Philological Society, 1973, 1 ff., who finds, as I have done, more reliable material in Lucian's account than do many historians. He also believes that Smith's dating of the Babylonian Chronicle is wrong and that the reference (and therefore the battle) belong to 272 (p. 5, n. 7). He also refers to his forthcoming book on The Seleucid Army: this will obviously be relevant to the history of elephant-warfare.

**66** See P. M. Fraser, Ptolemaic Alexandria (1972), 180 f.

**67** See Fraser, op. cit., 231 ff. The date is uncertain, but lies between 279/78 (W. W. Tarn, Journ. Hellen. Stud. 1933, 59 ff.) and 271/70 (W. Otto, Zeit d. 6 Ptolemaers, 82, n. 6).

**68** See also Gowers and Scullard, Num. Chronicle, 1950, 273 ff. Regarding the epithet ἀληθινοί, the text of Athenaeus could be corrupt: ἀληθινῶς, applied to the figure of Alexander, would suit very well apart from the fact it is separated from the word χρυσοῦς by ἐφέρετο.

**69** See especially P. L. Shinnie, Meroe (1967), 94, 100 f., 111, 127, 128, 146 and plates 20 and 71, and figs. 27 and 48, especially the former.

**70** The ancient evidence for the exploration and hunting expeditions sent to the Red Sea coast of Africa is somewhat scattered. It is collected and discussed by P. M. Fraser, Ptolemaic Alexandria (1972), I, 175 ff., and II, 299 ff., to which reference should be made for details (including topographical matters). The sources include, beside inscriptions and papyri, Agatharchides, 53 ff. (C. Müller, Geographici Graeci Minores, I); Diodorus, III, 25 ff.; Strabo, XVI, 769 ff.; Pliny, NH, VI, 165 ff., XXXVII, 24. Cf. Naville, The Store-City of Pithom⁴ (1903), 18 ff. For the elephant-hunts see briefly, M. Cary and E. H. Warmington, The Ancient Explorers (1929), 67 ff.; E. Bevan, A History of Egypt under the Ptolemaic Dynasty (1927), 175 ff.

**71** See a report by Capt. K. Caldwell, of the Kenya Game Department, summarized in The Times

newspaper of 9th April, 1927.

**72** Papyri Petrie, II, 40 = Wilcken, Chrestomathie, 452.

**73** St Jerome, Comment. on Daniel, xi.5 (=Jacoby, FGrH, n. 260 (=Porphyry), 42, cf. 43 for Euergetes' war. This derives from Porphyry, but on his possible sources see Jacoby, IID, p. 877 f. Appian claims that his figures for the resources of Ptolemy Philadelphus derive from 'the royal register' (βασιλικαὶ ἀναγραφαί); they include 200,000 infantry. Despite the alleged source, they inspire no confidence.

**74** See Dittenberger, OGIS, 54.

**75** On the extent of Ptolemy's invasion of Seleucid territory see M. Cary, Hist. of Greek World, 323–146 BC, 399.

**76** For a detailed collection and assessment of the evidence for all these hunting expeditions see P. Fraser, Ptolemaic Alexandria (1972), I, 178 f., II, 305 ff.

**77** Fraser, op. cit., I, 179.

**78** See G. T. Griffith, The Mercenaries of the Hellenistic World (1935), 119.

**79** See Papyr. Elephantine 28 (=Wilcken, Chrestomathie, 451). On this and the papyrus about fish see C. Préaux, L'Économie royale des Lagides (1939), 36.

**80** For Molon's revolt see Polybius, V, 43 ff. (53–4 for the battle).

**81** The chief source for Raphia is Polybius, V, 65 (Ptolemaic army) and 79–86 (battle). His source is unknown: it could be Zeno of Rhodes, a contemporary of Polybius (cf. A. Momigliano, *Aegyptus*, 1929, 189), but in view of the general clarity of Polybius' account of the battle and his criticism of Zeno's lack of clarity in his description of the battle of Panium this is perhaps not very likely. On Zeno and Polybius' criticism of him, see above p. 145. For details of Polybius' account of the battle, see Walbank, *Polybius*, I, 489 ff. and 607 ff. One debatable point is the strength of Ptolemy's phalanx. Polybius mentions both a phalanx of 25,000 and a phalanx of Egyptians of 20,000, and he includes both these in his grand total of 70,000 infantry. But since a phalanx of 45,000 would presumably have had no trouble in dealing at once with an enemy phalanx of only 20,000, it is generally believed that there was only one Ptolemaic phalanx of 25,000 men of whom 20,000 were Egyptians: see M. Cary, *Hist. of Greek World, 323–146 BC*, 405, and cf. Walbank, p. 590. (P. Chantraine, *Revue Phil.* 1951, 292 ff., and E. Will, *Hist. pol. du monde hellen.*, II, 30, still prefer the larger figure).

**82** On the Pithom stele, see E. Bevan, *Hist. of Egypt under the Ptolemaic Dynasty* (1927), 388 ff.; W. Otto, *Abh. Bayer Akad.* xxxiv/1 (1928). On the error in Polybius' numbers see Gowers and Scullard, *Num. Chron.* 1950, 277n. 22 (possible transposition in the MSS) and Walbank, *Poly*, I, 615 (P.'s own error).

**83** See E. Lewis, *Aloysius Horn*, 109.

CHAPTER VI—

**84** Panormus (?) coin: *Sylloge Num. Graec.*, Denmark, *Sicily*, pl. 4/172. Mr G. K. Jenkins of the British Museum tells me that there are now some grounds to believe that this coin comes from Pergamum. It remains a great puzzle. Agathocles coin: e.g. Seltman *Greek Coins²* (1955), 246 and pl. lx, 5; anecdote about owls, Diodorus, xx, 11.3. Juba, apud Philostratus, *Vita Apollon.* II, 13.

**85** Stables: Appian, *Lib.* 95. The 300 are more likely to have included some cavalry stables and perhaps even storerooms than to have been all reserved for elephants.

**86** See Polybius, I, 18.8 (numbers); 19.11 (capture). Diodorus, xxIII, 8.1, following Philinus, gives the original number as 60, while Orosius, IV, 7.5, puts it at 30, with 11 captured.

**87** Polybius, I, 29 ff. The Livian tradition, preserved in Orosius (IV, 8.16) and Eutropius (II, 21.3), says (probably with exaggeration) that 18 elephants were captured.

**88** On Regulus' campaign, see Polybius, I, 30–36.

**89** Polybius, I, 40. Freedom for prisoners: Zonaras, VIII, 14: Eutropius, II, 24. The total number captured is given variously: 142 or 140 (Pliny, *NH*, VIII, 16 f.); nearly 140 (Polybius); 138 (Dionysius Hal. II, 66); 130 (Frontinus, *Strat.* II, 5.4; Eutropius, II, 24, giving 26 captured and the rest rounded up); 104 (Orosius, IV, 9.15, giving 26 killed and 104 captured);

100 (Florus, I, 18.28): 60 (Diodorus, xxIII, 21, captured and sent to Rome).

**90** Among the coins which later members of the Metellan family issued in order to commemorate their ancestor's victory at Panormus are the following:

(1) Sydenham, *Roman Republican Coinage*, n. 480: *obv.* Roma, *rev.* Macedonian shield, with elephant's head in centre, M. Metellus Q.F. This coin commemorated both Panormus and Metellus Macedonicus' victory in the Fourth Macedonian War. It was issued late in the period 150–125 (Crawford, *Rom. Rep. Coin Hoards*. Table X), perhaps by the later consul of 115. A 'restored' issue (Syd. 719) with *obv.* of Apollo and same *rev.* is dated by Crawford *c.* 82 BC.

(2) Syd. 496: Roma/Pax in biga, below an elephant's head with bell attached. 497 corresponding bronze, *rev.* prow, elephant's head. Anonymous. Crawford: fairly late in period 150–125 and issued probably by L. Caecilius Metellus, consul 117.

(3) Syd. 485: Roma/Jupiter in biga of elephants. C. Metellus. 486: bronze, *ren.* prow with elephant's head above. Very late in 150–125 (Crawford). Moneyer possibly the consul of 113.

(4) Syd. 750: Pietas/elephant walking, with bell on neck. Q. Caecilius Metellus Pius (consul 80). Crawford Table XII, a little before 79 BC.

(5) Syd. 1046: Jupiter/elephant walking. Q.

Metellus Pius Scipio, Imp. This belongs to 47 and the Thapsus campaign, as does 1051 : Head of Africa, with elephant head-dress.

A similar depiction of Africa appears on three issues of rare gold coins: (a) Syd. 1028 of Pompeius Magnus Proconsul, which Crawford (p. 40) would date between Sulla and Caesar. (b) Syd. 1153 of L. Cestius and C. Norbanus of 43 BC. (c) Syd. 1355 of Q. Cornuficius of 42 BC.

(6) To return to the Metelli we have, beside the Roman issues mentioned above, a most interesting tetradrachm from Gortyn in Crete (Head, *Historia Numorum*, 467). The *obv.* shows the head of Roma (named) in a winged helmet, adorned with an elephant's head; *rev.* Ephesian Artemis, with a bee and an elephant's head in the field, and a laurel wreath. This coin must have been struck at Gortyn after the reduction of Crete by Q. Caecilius Metellus, consul in 69 BC, who in 67 resisted Pompey's attempt to oust him and then organized the island as a Roman province.

**91** On the battle of the Tagus, see Polybius, III, 14; Livy, XXI, 5, 8 ff. Both writers probably drew upon a common source (perhaps Silenus who accompanied Hannibal), Livy using Coelius Antipater as an intermediary. For a discussion of minor differences, see Walbank, *Polybius*, I, 316. For some topographical speculations (e.g. another Tagus in the province of Valencia), see N. Primitivo Gomez,

*Guerras de Anibal preparatorias del sitio de Saguntum* (Valencia, 1951), 37 ff.
**92** See E. S. G. Robinson: 'Punic Coins of Spain' in *Essays in Roman Coinage presented to Harold Mattingly* (ed. R. A. G. Carson and C. H. V. Sutherland, 1956), 34 ff. For the assignment of the second series to Hamilcar Barca, despite recent finds in Sicily, see H. H. Scullard, *Scipio Africanus* (1970), 252 f. For the Lascuta coin, see pl. XXIIa and A. Vives, *La Moneda Hispanica* (1924), pl. xcii, nos. 2–5.
**93** Of the immense literature on these two topics it will here be sufficient to refer to Walbank, *Polybius*, I, and Sir Dennis Procter, *Hannibal's March in History* (1971). Both provide sane and lucid discussions of the problems.

On the Rhone crossing, see Polybius, III, 42 ff. (46 for the elephants); Livy, XXI, 26 ff. (28. 5–12 for elephants). The place of the crossing has been hotly debated, the issue being whether it was made at or near Beaucaire-Tarascon (cf. Walbank) or else considerably further up stream (cf. Procter).
**94** On the crossing of the Alps, see especially Polybius, III, 49 ff.; Livy, XXI, 31 ff. For modern views, see Walbank and Procter, *op. cit.* (n. 93). For a rejection of the views of Sir Gavin De Beer: *Alps and Elephants* (1955) and *Hannibal* (1969), see Walbank, *Journ. Rom. Stud.* 1956, 37 ff. For a light-hearted account of the party that led an Indian elephant over Hannibal's route over the

Alps (crossing by Mt Cenis, although Col. Clapier was considered the more probable) in 1959, see J. Hoyte, *Trunk Road for Hannibal* (1960). *Inter alia* it showed that the elephant was not affected by altitude.
**95** On the battle of the Trebia, see Polybius, III, 60–74; Livy, XXI, 39–56 (Appian, *Han.* 5 ff. and Zonaras, VIII, 23 f., add little that is reliable). The basic study is Kromayer-Veith, *Antike Schlachtfelder*, III, i, 47–103 (cf. *Schlachten Atlas, Röm. Abt*, i, Blatt 3). Polybius' account derives mainly from a pro-Carthaginian source (probably Silenus). Livy follows the same account closely, though via Coelius Antipater, from whom he may have added some details. The part played by Hannibal's elephants is exaggerated in Livy, probably through both confusion and patriotism: the essence of his acount, however, can be reconciled with that by Polybius, if it is recognized that he has added details some of which are inconsistent with the main account. On this see Kromayer-Veith, *op. cit.* p. 71, n. 2.
**96** Uncertainty about the position of the elephants arises from the use of the word 'wings', which could refer either to the real wings, i.e. the cavalry who flanked the infantry line, or else the flanks of the infantry. Livy may well have thought of them as being on the outside of the cavalry (see XXI, 55.2 and 55.7, with the reading *divisos* and not *diversos*), while Appian puts them in

front of the cavalry. But Polybius (together with Livy, 55.9: et elephanti iam in mediam peditum aciem sese tulerant) clearly places them in front of the flanks of the infantry. See Kromayer-Veith, *op. cit.* and Walbank, p. 408. According to Livy (a) the elephants on the wings caused the Roman cavalry to panic and (b) the elephants charged the central Roman line but were driven back towards their own line by skirmishers who showered them with darts, made them turn back and then wounded them in the soft skin under the tail; to avert disaster Hannibal then ordered them to be driven against the extreme Roman left of Celtic mercenaries whom they routed. These two versions could of course be reconciled if it were supposed that Hannibal had divided his elephants into two sections and that Polybius had not recorded (a). In that case Livy's version of (b), which only in part follows Polybius, must have been elaborated to honour Roman valour or be due simply to his misunderstanding of his source. But it would be safer to rely on Polybius alone.

**97** See Livy, XXIII, 13.7 and 32.5 (Mago); 18.6 (Casilinum); 41.10 (Bomilcar); 43.5 and 46.4 (Nola and Marcellus; cf. Plut. *Marcell.* 12.3). De Sanctis rejects the elephants at Casilinum and a major victory by Marcellus, but accepts the arrival of the reinforcements: *Storia dei Romani*, III, ii, 237 n. 52; 255 n. 47.

**98** See Livy, XXVI, 5–6.8 (first account); 6.9–13 (second account); Appian, *Han.* 41–42; Polybius, IX, 3. Cf. De Sanctis, *Stor. dei Rom.* III, ii, 301 n. 158 and p. 339. Walbank (*Polybius*, II, 118 f.) rejects the suggestion by A. Klotz, that the first account in Livy comes from Coelius and the second from Valerius. Appian gives an acount which is similar to the second by Livy, except that he places it in the camp of Fulvius Flaccus not at Capua but when later Flaccus was pursuing Hannibal on his march to Rome. However, the idea that Q. Fulvius left Capua to follow Hannibal, although given by Livy (XXVI, 8.9 ff.), must be rejected in view of Polybius' contradictory version. Some confusion may have arisen from the activities of two Fulvii: Q. Fulvius Flaccus, *cos.* of 212, who continued at Capua in 211, and Cn. Fulvius Centumalus, *cos.* of 211. Confusion may also have arisen about the attack on the Roman 'camp'; although the main camp may have been threatened, much of the fighting may have been around the ditches and palisades which formed the double lines of investment drawn by the Romans around the city.

**99** There can now be no reasonable doubt that these coins must be assigned to this period: see H. Mattingly and E. G. S. Robinson, *Proc. Brit. Academy*, 1933, 10 ff.

**100** The route followed by Hannibal is much debated. Polybius (IX, 5) is somewhat vague: through Samnium and over the Anio. Livy (XXVI, 9 f.), on the other hand, sends him by the direct route along the Via Latina, but he also records (11.10 ff.) the route given by Coelius, which corresponds in general with Polybius, namely Via Alba, Amiternum, Teate, and Lucus Feroniae, a little way north of Rome. Both Polybius and Coelius probably derive their accounts from the pro-Carthaginian historian Silenus, who accompanied Hannibal on part of his campaigns. Livy's source assumed that Hannibal took the most direct route, possibly being confused by two towns named Sulmo. See E. T. Salmon, *Phoenix*, 1957, 159 ff., and Walbank, *Polybius*, II, 121 ff. The longer route receives support from recently discovered traces of destruction, dating to this period, at Lucus Feroniae, and now also perhaps by the elephants at Alba.

On the elephants see F. De Visscher, 'Une histoire d'elephants', *L'Antiquité classique*, 1960, 51 ff.

**101** See Livy, XXVII, 2.6; and Plutarch, *Marcellus*, 24 (210 BC); Livy, 14.6–14, and Plut. 24, 25 (209); Livy, 42.7 (207 BC).

**102** On the battle of the Metaurus, see especially Polybius, XI, 1–3; Livy, XXVII, 46–49. Livy's account differs from Polybius in some details, e.g. he places Ligurians in the centre of the Carthaginian line, with the elephants in front of them. On this and the elephants, see Kromayer-Veith, *Antike Schlachtfelder*, III, i, 465, n. 1. In general, see Walbank, *Polybius*, ii, 267 ff.

**103** See Livy, XXIV, 35.3 (214 BC); XXV, 41.7 (Agrigentum); XXVI, 21.9 (ovation).

**104** See Livy XXIII, 29.14 (Ibera); 49.11 (Iliturgi); XXIV, 42.3.8. Cf. Scullard, *Scipio Africanus* (1970), 252 n. 30.

**105** For Baecula, see Pol., X, 38–39; Livy, XXVII, 18. Livy on the elephants: 18.18 (in battle), 19.1 (withdrawal). Livy could be saved from contradiction but at the expense of straining the Latin: he might have meant that the enemy would not have attacked over such ground if the enemy had stood firm (which they did not) and if the elephants had been placed in front of them (which was not done). On the battle in general, see Scullard, *Scipio* (1930, ch. 4, and (1970), ch. 3, and Walbank, *Polybius*, II, 245 ff.

**106** On Ilipa, see Pol., XI, 20–24; Livy, XXVIII, 13–15. Livy, 15.5 refers to the elephants rushing to the centre, but no doubt their stampede was widespread. In general, see Scullard and Walbank, *op. cit.*, above n. 105.

**107** Livy, XXX, 18. Livy's account of the battle is not dissimilar from one fought in Spain in 205 (XXIX, 2), but which is the original account is uncertain.

**108** See Appian, *Libyca*, 9.

**109** On Zama see Polybius, XV, 5–15 (on elephants, 9. 7–10; 12. 1–5); Livy, XXX, 29–35 (elephants, 33. 1–4. 13–16; 35.

3, losses). The other authorities add little except some romantic inventions, such as that Scipio personally wounded the leading elephant and later fought a duel with Hannibal (Appian, *Lib.*, 43–44). For discussion of detail, see Scullard and Walbank, *op. cit.*, n. 105 above. For some difficulties about the elephants, see Scullard, *Scipio* (1930), 239, n. 1.

**110** According to Polybius (XV, 18.4) the Carthaginians had to give up all their elephants; Livy (XXX, 37.3), Appian, *Lib.* 54 and Dio, XVII, 57.82 add that they were not to train any more (thus Livy: *neque domarent alios*). Elephants given to Masinissa or sent to Rome: Zonaras, IX, 14. Scipio's triumph: Appian, *Lib.* 66 for the elephants (this account is over-elaborated, but this detail is reasonable enough). For shorter accounts, see Polybius, XVI, 23; Livy, XXX, 45.

**111** On all the coinage discussed in this section, see Scullard, 'Hannibal's Elephants', *Num. Chron.* 1949, 158 ff., Sir William Gowers and Scullard, *ibid.* 1950, 271 ff.; Robinson, 'Carthaginian and other South Italian Coinages of the Second Punic War', *ibid.* 1964, 37 ff.; R. Thomsen, *Early Roman Coinage*, 1–111 (1957–1961), especially 1, 157 f., II, 111 ff., where the older literature and numismatic problems are discussed in more detail than can be done here.

**112** See Robinson, *op. cit.* 42.

**113** For the fact that one Velecha overstrike is on a Roman rather than a Mamertine coin see Thomsen, *op. cit.* 1, 138, n. 29. For the surrender of Volcei see Livy, XXVII, 14.2.

**114** See Robinson, *op. cit.* 47 f. and Livy, XXVII, 21.6–7; 22.13; 24; 38.6. An examination of all known specimens of this series in an attempt to find an overstrike would be valuable for dating purposes. The suggestion by F. P. Rosati in *Studi Annibalici* (1964), 176, that these coins do not necessarily belong to the Val di Chiana should be rejected. A hurried inspection some years ago showed that they are found in the museums at Cortona, Chiusi and (naturally) Florence in some numbers, but not in Perugia.

**115** See *Class. Rev.* 1953, 140 ff.

**116** See N. J. De Witt, *Class. Philology*, 1941, 189 f.

**117** On these two vessels, see Pagenstecher, *Die calenishe Reliefkeramik*, 49; A. J. Reinach, *Monuments Piot*, 1913, 193 (Cales), 194 (Pompeii); P. Bienkowski, *Les Celtes dans les arts mineurs greco-romains* (1928), 143 (Cales), 142 (Pompeii); Scullard, *Num. Chron.* 1950, 281 f. Bienkowski had misgivings about linking the Cales vessel with Antiochus I. On the negro driver, see Sir John Beazley, *Etruscan Vase-Painting*, 212.

The indifference of some artists to the distinction between African and Indian elephants is well illustrated by a representation of one of the most famous African elephants kept in captivity, namely Jumbo, the pride of the London zoo from 1865 until 1882 when amid widespread national dismay it was sold to Barnum in America. Carrington, *Elephants*, pl. 19a, reproduces an excellent photo of it and also the cover of a music-sheet of 1882 which contained the song 'Why part with Jumbo?'. On this latter sheet the elephant has a good African ear, but its back, on which an assortment of children are riding, is shown rounded and convex like that of an Indian.

CHAPTER VII—

**118** See Livy, XXXII, 27.2 (198 BC), XXXVI, 4.8 (191 BC), XLII, 62.2 (171 BC), Appian, *Hisp.* 46 (153 BC), Appian, *Lib.* 71–72 (150 BC; Aemilianus), *id.* 126 (Gulussa), Appian, *Hisp.* 67 (142 BC; Fabius), 89 (134 BC, Aemilianus).
**119** Masinissa's help: Livy, XXXIII, 27.2. Elephants at Cynoscephalae: Polybius, XVIII, 23.7; 25.5–7; Livy (dependant on Polybius), XXXIII, 8.3; 9.6 According to Livy under the terms of the treaty with Philip he was to have no elephants (XXXIII, 30.6) while Valerius Antias added (Livy, XXXIII, 30.10) that his elephants were handed over to Attalus of Pergamum. These, and some other clauses, derive from a bad annalistic source and, in view of their absence in Polybius' account (XVIII, 44), they should be rejected, and the view maintained that Philip in fact never had any elephants.

278

See De Sanctis, *Storia dei Romani*, IV, i, 96, n. 185: Walbank, *Philip V* (1940), 180, n. 1.
**120** Livy, XXXV, 43.6 (Antiochus' six elephants). Livy, XXXVI, 4.9 (Masinissa's offer); 10.8 (Larissa); 14.1 (Acilius has fifteen elephants); 18.4 (elephants at Thermopylae); 19.4–6 (in the battle).
**121** The Romans' march through Thrace was facilitated by Philip of Macedon, thanks to the good relations that Scipio Africanus had established with him. Unlike the return journey, when the Romans suffered severe attacks from Thracian tribes, the outward journey was in general peaceful (Livy, XXXVIII, 7.16; 33), but Livy retrospectively refers to an incident on it which he found in the annalist Claudius Quadrigarius (XXXVIII, 41.11–14), which he had perhaps not read when he wrote book XXXVII. Its historical value can hardly be judged, but it is not improbable in itself. Claudius recounted that the Romans sent out a reconnoitring party of 400 Numidian cavalry and a few elephants under the Numidian Muttines. It was attacked by large numbers of Thracians, but Muttines' son broke through their centre and a little later attacked their rear while they were held on the front by a line with the elephants in the centre and the cavalry on the wings. The reference to 'a few elephants' accords with the fact that the Romans had only 16 at the later battle of Magnesia.

**122** On Magnesia see Livy, XXXVII, 37–44: Appian, *Syr.* 30–36. Livy's account is essentially reliable since it derives from Polybius' description of the battle, now lost. See in detail Kromayer-Veith, *Antike Schlachtfelder*, II, 154–219. I *Maccabees*, 8.6, attributes 120 elephants to Antiochus in the battle, but since it also wrongly says that he was captured alive, the number of elephants should not be accepted as against Livy's smaller figure.

On the triumph of L. Scipio: Livy, XXXVII, 59.3. On the treaty of Apamea: Polybius, XXI, 45.12; Livy, XXXVIII, 38.8 and (gift to Eumenes) 39.6.
**123** Livy, XLII, 29.8 (elephants promised); 35.6 (Commissioners); 62.2 (22 elephants); 65.12 (Phalanna).
**124** Livy, XLIII, 6.13 (Masinissa's promise); XLIV, 5 (mountain passage); Polybius, XXVIII, 12–13 (Polybius with Philippus). On Philippus' precise route over Mt Olympus see W. K. Pritchett, *Studies in Ancient Greek Topography*, II (1969), 170 ff., who writes, 'In that saddle of Mount Analipsis which carries the path leading from the valley of Karia to the western edge of Lake Nezero, there is on the Nezero side a long series of stepping-stones large enough to have supported the feet of elephants. These are shown in plate 158. I have seen nothing like them anywhere in Greece.' Whatever the explanation, Pritchett seems to have no doubt

about Livy's account of the construction of the collapsing platforms (though a sceptic might argue that it arose from the stepping-stones). **125** Elephants at Pydna, Livy, XLIV, 41.3–5. Pydna in general: Livy, XLIV, 42; Plutarch, *Aemilius Paullus*, 16–23. Livy depends largely on Polybius whose account is mainly lost. See full discussion in Kromayer-Veith, *Antike Schlachtfelder*, II, 294–348, and Pritchett, *op. cit.* 145 ff. for the topography. Anti-elephant corps: Zonaras, IX, 22; Polyaenus, IV, 21. Diodorus, XXXI, 8.12, apud Syncellum p. 511 (tusks). Valerius Maximus, II, 7.13 (deserters). **126** For Daphne see Polybius, XXX, 25 (XXXI, 3). **127** I *Maccabees*, 6, 34–46. Josephus (*Ant.. Iud.* XII, 9.4 = 371), whose account follows *Maccabees* very closely, adds the information that Lysias' force had to advance through a narrow pass, where his elephants had to march in single file; also that the towers during the battle contained archers. **128** Josephus, *Ant. Iud.* XIII, 4 (esp. 8–9 = 117, 120). **129** Josephus, *Ant. Iud.* XIII, 5.3 (144). **130** For older views see G. F. Hill, *Greek Historical Coins* (1906), 140 f. For this new suggestion see H. B. Mattingly, *Num. Chron.* 1969, 329 f. (reviewing M. Thompson, *The Agrinion Hoard*). **131** See Appian, *Hisp.* 46. For Nobilior's camp on the Gran Atalaya near Renieblas (camp III of several partly superimposed

camps) see A. Schulten, *Numantia*, IV, and more briefly, *Geschichte von Numantia* (1933), 41 ff. For the loom-weight see *Numantia*, IV, 90. See also H. Simon, *Roms Kriege in Spanien, 154–133 v. Chr.* (1962), 25 ff. **132** See Appian, *Lib.* 71, 72 (Aemilianus in Africa); Valerius Max., IX, 3.7 (Metellus); Appian, *Hisp.* 67 (Servilianus); *ib.* 87 (Jugurtha). **133** The elephants are mentioned by Florus, I, 37, and Orosius, V, 13. Domitius' elephant, Suetonius, *Nero*, 2. **134** See Sallust, *Bellum Iugurthinum*, 29.6 (Bestia); 40.1 (Mamilius); 49.1 (Bomilcar); 52. 5–53.5 (battle); 62.5 (negotiations). **135** See Plutarch, *Pompey*, 11–12 (Africa), 14.4 (entry to Rome). **136** See Caesar, *Bell. Gall.* v, 18. Polyaenus, VIII, 23.5. C. E. Stevens, *History Today*, Sept. 1959, 626 ff. E. A. Sydenham, *Roman Republican Coinage* (1952), 167, n. 1006 (dated *c.* 54–51 BC); M. H. Crawford, *Roman Republican Coin Hoards* (1969), Table XIV (49 BC). Caesar = elephant in Moorish, *Hist. Augusta, Aelius* 2.3. **137** Juba's 60 elephants: Caesar, *Bellum Civile*, II, 40. His coinage: J. Mazzard, *Corpus Nummorum Numidiae Mauretaniaeque* (1955), 49 ff., nos. 90 and 92 for elephants; n. 89 has Africa wearing an elephant-scalp head-dress. The king's portrait (e.g. n. 84) shows him well bearded. **138** Juba's elephants: 120

reported (*Bell. Afr.* 1 and 19); 30 left at Ruspina (ib. 25.2); 30 others (30.2); 64 at Thapsus (86.2); Appian, *Bell. Civ.* II, 96 gives Scipio and Juba 60, probably due to confusion. Metellus' African coinage: Sydenham *op. cit.*, 175 ff.: n. 1046, elephant walking; n. 1051, head of Africa, wearing elephant-scalp. **139** For the operations in Africa see especially *Bellum Africum*. Modern accounts: Kromayer-Veith, *Antike Schlachtfelder*, III, 717–907: S. Gsell, *Hist. de l'Afrique du Nord*, VIII, 1–155; T. Rice Holmes, *The Roman Republic*, III (1923), 95 ff., 236 ff. Photo of field of Thapsus, Kromayer-Veith, p. 842. *Bell. Afr.* 25 (Juba leaves 30 elephants); 27 (training by Scipio); 30 (battle-line); 35 (spies); 41 (battle-line); 48 (Juba's return); 59 and 70 (battle-array); 72 (training by Caesar; cf. Dio Cassius, lxiii, 3.4); 81, 83, 84 (Thapsus, cf. Appian. *Bell. Civ.* II, 96: Fifth Legion adopts elephant as badge); 86 (threat to Thapsus). **140** Caesar's escort: Dio Cassius, XLIII, 22.1; Suetonius, *Iul.* 37, says he was escorted thus up to the Capitol: this is much less probable. Games: Suet., *Iul.* 79; Dio, XLIII, 23.3. Octavian's elephants: Cic. *Phil. V*, 17, 46; Dio Cassius, XLV, 13.4. **141** Didius Julianus: Herodian, II, 11.19; Dio Cassius, LXXIV, 16.2–3. Caracalla: Dio, LXXVIII, 7.4. **142** Procurator: Dessau, *ILS*, 1578. Juvenal, XII, 102 ff. Aelian, II, 11. The reference to Rutulian forests is to Ardea, the chief city of the Rutuli: it is near Laurentum. There are several references which connect Tibur (Tivoli) with ivory and perhaps elephants; its sulphur was thought to whiten teeth. Thus Martial alludes to this three times:

Dum Tiburtinis albescere solibus audit
antiqui dentis fusca Lycoris ebur,
venit in Herculeos colles
(VII, 13. Cf. IV, 62) ('hearing that, under Tibur's suns, the ivory of an old tusk grows white, dusky Lycoris came to the hills of Hercules', i.e. of Tibur, where Hercules was worshipped).

Martial also refers to a toga, which was given to him, as whiter than 'the ivory that gleams white on Tibur's mount' ('et Tiburtino monte quod albet ebur'. VIII, 28.12). So too Propertius writes (IV, 7.81): 'et numquam Herculeo numine pallet ebur'. These references might of course be only to the ivory trade and ivory working, but a line in Silius Italicus, *Pun.* XIII, 229 introduces a fresh note: 'quale micat semperque novum est quod Tiburis aura/pascit ebur' ('like the ivory, ever bright and new, which the air of Tibur feeds'). The use of *pascit* suggested to Armandi (*Hist. milit. des elephants*, 540 ff.) living elephants rather than dead ivory, and he hazarded the guess that Tibur might have been a centre for imperial elephants, perhaps even sick elephants.

**143** Cornificius: Dio Cassius, XLIX, 7.6. Hadrian:

*Historia Augusta, Hadr.* 17. Aurelian: *Hist. Aug., Aurel.* 5.5.

One is reminded of later imperial gifts at times when elephants were extremely rare in the West. Thus Haroun-el-Raschid, the Caliph of Baghdad, sent an elephant to Charlemagne which excited great interest when after many adventures it arrived at Aix-la-Chapelle in 802, conducted by the Jew Isaac. Frederick II brought back an elephant from the Holy Land in 1229, and a few years later in 1254 St Louis (IX) brought another from Syria which he presented to Henry III of England who kept it for some years in the Tower of London, again exciting much interest. It is curious that an illustrated MS (Parker 16, Corpus Christi College, Cambridge) which is alleged to depict this beast shows an *African* elephant. See G. C. Druce, *Archaeological Journal* 1919, 1 ff. This article is a most valuable discussion of the elephant in medieval legend and art, including bestiaries. Emmanuel of Portugal in 1514 sent from India to Pope Leo X an elephant named *Hanno*, which inspired much poetic composition in Rome. Henry IV of France passed on to Elizabeth I of England one which he had received from India. The appearance of an elephant in Europe was still a great rarity in the seventeenth century. See P. Armandi, *Hist. Milit. des Elephants* (1843), 528 ff.

**144** *Hist. Aug., Sev. Alex.* 55–56; Herodian, VI, 4–5.

**145** *Hist. Aug., Gord.* 26, 27, 33.

**146** Theodoret, *Hist. Eccles.* II, 30. Julian, *Orat.* II, 64 ff.

**147** Ammianus, XXIV, 6.8 (Ctesiphon); XXV, 1.4 (knives); 3.4 (light-armed attack); 3.11 (crests); 6.2–3 (some killed); 7.1 (Shapur's loss). Zosimus, III, 30.2.

**148** See the French translation of the Armenian version of Faustus in Müller, *Fragmenta Historicorum Romanorum*, V, Faustus, IV, 22. For earlier uses of elephants, I, 8; also IV, 21; 23; 57. Ambrose, *Hexamer.* VI, 5. Pacatus, *Panegyr. Lat.* II, 22.5.

**149** Amida: Procopius, I, 7; Zacharias Mitylene, VII, 3; Joshua Stylites, LIII. Edessa: Procopius, VIII, 14.35 (pig). Archaeopolis, Procop., VIII, 13.4–5; 14.8; 14.32. VIII, 17.9.11 (many used against Lazi). In *Buildings* II, 1.11 Procopius describes how elephants were like movable towers which could be brought to bear at critical points of an attack and allow missiles to be shot down at the heads of the Romans within a city. Barrier in river: Agathias, III, 20.5. Cf. III, 26.8 for another encounter in which elephants helped the Persians, and III, 27 for an elephant which was wounded in the eye by a spear and did much damage (AD 556).

**150** Melitene: Theophylactus Simocatta, III, 10; 11; 14. Gift to the Khagan: Theophylact., I, 3. Sargana: Theophyl., V, 10.ii. who says that Bahram put his elephants, Indian beasts, like a bulwark in front of his cavalry, and placed his bravest men on them, 'nor did each lack the help of such beasts'. (οὐκ ἠμοίρει δὲ καὶ τὸ ἑκάτερον τούτων δὴ τῶν συμμαχων θηρίων). 'Each' must mean 'each side', i.e. Romans and Persians. Though it is tempting to take it to refer to each part of the Persian army and not to the Romans as well, this does not appear to be the meaning of the Greek (I am grateful to Professor and Dr A. Cameron for confirming this view: two wings are mentioned in v, 10.5, but not here, while the ἑκάτεραι δυνάμεις in v, 10.7, who looked at each other must be Romans and Persians). Whether Theophylactus is right in thus attributing elephants to the Romans is another matter.

**151** Taq-i-Bustan reliefs, R. Ghirshman, *Iran, Parthians and Sassanians* (1962), 194–199, pl. 236; comment, p. 199. Embassy to Ethiopia: fragment from book of Nonnosus, preserved by Photius, in Müller, *Frag. Hist. Graec.* IV, 180 and Jacoby, *FGrH*, n. 180, 673, frg. 165. (For another embassy, in 531, led by a Julian, see John Malalas, XVIII, 457, cf. Theophanes, *Chronogr.* p. 244, 16, but with wrong date): Julian was received by the king who was standing in a chariot, drawn by four elephants.

CHAPTER VIII—

**152** On Juba see Jacoby, *FGrH*, n. 275 and Commentary, p. 317 ff.; S. Gsell, *Histoire de l'Afrique du Nord*, VIII, 206–276. Coin: J. Mazard, *Corpus*

*Nummorum Numidiae Mauretaniaeque* (1955), n. 276. The references to Juba's topics are, respectively: Pliny, *NH*, VIII, 7; Polux, v, 88; Aelian, IX, 58; Pliny, VIII, 24–25; Aelian, XIV, 5; Pliny, VIII, 15; *ibid.* 24; 28; 15; 13–14; 13; 2.

**153** Mosaic: J. M. C. Toynbee, *Animals in Roman Life and Art* (1973), 25. Lucan, IX, 700 ff. Aelian, II, 21, (Ethiopia), XVI, 39 (India). Williams, *Elephant Bill*, 146.

**154** The translation of Aretaeus is based on that by F. Adams, *Aretaeus the Cappadocian* (1855), which contains text and translation, with a few changes made in the light of the text by C. Hude (1923; *Corpus Medicorum Graecorum*). A commentary in Latin was written *c.* 1662 by a Parisian physician named Peter Petit, and was printed in the edition of Aretaeus produced by H. Boerhaave at Leiden in 1735 and again by Kuehn in 1828. It excited the admiration of F. Adams who refers to 'the most ingenious and judicious labours of the kind which have ever been expended on an ancient author'. Thus for instance Petit provides a long discussion of the horns versus teeth issue, and concludes 'verumtamen non dissimulabo, mihi eorum opinionem magis placere, qui arma illa elephantorum, necque plane esse dentes, neque cornua censent, sed naturam mediam'. On the disease Lucretius (VI, 1114), pointing out that each climate has its

own dangers, writes: est elephas morbus qui propter flumina Nili gignitur Aegypto in media neque praeterea usquam.

CHAPTER IX—

**155** Appian, *Lib.*, 92. It is interesting to note what J. H. Williams says about the names of Burmese elephants (*Elephant Bill*, 81): 'the name given to a calf sticks to it for life, but it never knows its name, as a dog does; for the oozies do not usually call their elephants by name. The real reason why they are christened is so that men can talk about them to each other'.

**156** P. Goukowsky, *Bull. Corresp. Hellen.* 1972, 483, n. 36, points out that neither Arrian in his *Anabasis* nor Diodorus in book 17 (Alexander) uses Ἰνδός in the sense of mahout or cornac, but this usage, which is common in Polybius, Appian and others, appears in Diodorus, book 18.

**157** Wine: Aelian, XIII, 8: I *Maccab.* 6; III *Maccab.* 4. Eumenes: Plutarch, *Eumenes*, 14. Patroclus: Pliny, *NH*, VIII, 5.12. Hermitage phalerae, P. Goukowsky, *op. cit.* 492, n. 70. *Cristae*: Livy, XXXVII, 40.4: Ammianus, XXV, 3.11; *Catalogue de la Collection Greau*, n. 118; *Gazette des Beaux-Arts*, 1855, 171; Daremberg-Saglio, *Dict.* s.v. Elephas, fig. 2625. Eleazar: Josephus, *Ant. Iud.* XII, 4.373. On Silius, see E. L. B. Meurig Davis, *Class. Quart.* 1951, 153 ff., to whom I owe the reference to Pinto, which is in the edition by C. D. Ley (Everyman Library), 218.

**158** For a very full and useful discussion see P. Goukowsky, *op. cit.* note 156 above.

**159** See further Goukowsky, *op. cit.*, 475 n. 11; 12 (Semiramis); 484, n. 41 (Eumenes); 488 f. (Megasthenes and the *Arthacastra*).

It is interesting to see to what uses Indian elephants were put at this period as detailed in the *Arthacastra* (x, 4): 'marching in front; marching where there are no roads, places of shelter or landing places along rivers; protecting the flanks; crossing the rivers; penetrating into places rendered inaccessible by bushes and shrubs; breaking through the phalanx of the enemy's army; setting fire to the enemy's camp and quenching in one's own; capable of achieving victory without the help of other limbs of the army; restoring the broken phalanx and breaking through that of the enemy forces; protection against danger; trampling down the enemy forces; terrorizing the army; inspiring terror, giving an imposing appearance to the army; capturing the enemy's soldiers and releasing one's own; destruction of ramparts, gates, towers and rooms over them; and carrying treasures'.

**160** See also H. H. Scullard, *Numism. Chron.* 1949, 4 f.

**161** These and other representations of elephants with towers are discussed by P. Bienkowski, *Les Celtes dans les arts mineurs*

*greco-romains* (1928), ch. v, and are briefly listed by J. Beazley, *Etruscan Vase-Painting* (1947), 212. (Cf. above, p. 176 f., n. 117.) To these must now be added two other representations:

(a) Two terracotta statuettes from the Sanctuary of Apollo at Veii, depicting a mother elephant and calf: see pl. IXb and M. Santangelo, *Bolletino d'Arte* 1952, 157 and fig. 37. They appear to belong to the third or second century BC. The adult carries a tower, but this is broken and any rider or men in the tower are lost. Santangelo thinks that the small ears and tusks indicate an Asiatic elephant, but the ears and tusks are broken, while the little one's back certainly looks African. So too the clay of the back of the adult could have been built up by the artist to hold the tower rather than intended to indicate a convex formation. It is thus not easy to decide on the race. They could therefore belong to either Pyrrhus or Hannibal, I am inclined to the latter and African beasts. If Pyrrhic, was the artist perhaps influenced by knowledge of the theme of the Capena plate which he used in statuary, or did he draw his inspiration from live animals?

(b) A silver-gilt phalera (perhaps the decoration for a horse) found in a hoard on Sark in the Channel Islands early in the 18th century and now lost. It contained 13 phalerae. The original drawings survive,

and one shows an elephant with an empty tower; the animal's body has a crisscross pattern, thus attempting to show the nature of the hide. Though the ears are large, it is presumably an Indian, and may be compared with the turreted elephants on the Hermitage phalerae. The phalera may also be compared with one in the Bibliothèque Nationale, Paris, which shows the facing head of an elephant with large ears and foreshortened trunk; the beast is being attacked by dogs. The hoard belongs to the first century BC and its origin is eastern European: perhaps it belonged to a Thracian horseman and fell into the hands of a Gaul as the spoils of war. For all this see D. F. Allen, *Archaeologia* ciii (1971), 1 ff. (esp. 11, 19).

For another mother and calf, though not war-elephants, see a painting at Pompeii, where the mother is clasping her baby in her trunk: S. Reinach, *Repertoire des peintures gr. et rom.* (1922), 367, 9 and above fig. 2.

**162** See Daremberg-Saglio, *Dict.* s.v. Elephas, fig. 2624 (p. 540).

**163** For fuller treatment of the material in this and much of the next section, and for further references to the ancient evidence see J. M. C. Toynbee, *Animals in Roman Life and Art* (1973), 39 ff. and the corresponding Notes.

**164** Aufidius: Pliny, VIII, 64. 169 BC: Livy, XLIV, 18.8. Fenestella; Pliny, VIII, 19. A new inscription shows that Claudius Pulcher, aedile in 99, had links with Cyrene: hence probably the source of the elephants (E. Rawson, *Historia* 1973, 230). Pompey's Games: Cicero, *ad fam.* VII, 1.3; Pliny, VIII, 7; Dio Cassius, XXXIX, 38, 2–4; Seneca *de brevit. vit.* 13.6.

**165** Julius Caesar: Dio, XLIII, 23.3; Appian, *Bell. Civ.* II, 102; Pliny, VIII, 22; Suetonius *Div. Iul.* 39.3. Pius: *Hist. Aug., Ant.,* 10.8. Commodus: Herodian, I, 15: Dio, LXXIII, 10.3. Severus: Dio, LXXXVII, I. Caracalla: Dio, LXXVIII, 6.2. Elegabalus: Dio, LXXX, 9.2. Gordian: *Hist. Aug., Gord.* 33.1. Aurelian: *Hist. Aug., Aurel.* 33.4. Claudian, *De cons. Stilichonis,* III, 333 ff., esp. 345 ff.

**166** Augustus: Suetonius, *Div. Iul.* 53.2. Aelian, II, 11. Pliny, VIII, 2–3. Seneca, *Epist.* 85.41. Nero, II (cf. Dio, LXI, 17). Practising: Pliny, VIII, 3.6, Plut. *de sollert. anim.* 12. In connection with the elephant in labour we might here note the extraordinary statement of Tatian (*Adv. Graecos* p. 34.26) that Niceratus had made a sculpture of Glaucippe and the elephant to which she had given birth. With this may be linked the fact that, according to Pliny, VII, 34, among the statues with which Pompey had adorned his theatre in Rome was that of Alcippe, who gave birth to an elephant. These two references seem to apply to the same statue, that from Pergamum having been taken to Rome; it was presumably of a woman with a small elephant

which was wrongly thought to have been her child. See S. Settis, *Bolletino d'Arte* 1966, 20.

**167** See R. Meiggs, *Roman Ostia* (1960), 283 and pl. xxiiia; G. Becatti, *Scavi di Ostia,* IV (1961), 66 ff.

**168** *Africa Italiana,* 1940, 67 ff.; J. M. Reynolds and J. B. Ward-Perkins, *The Inscriptions of Roman Tripolitania* (1952), 92, 159.

An inscription from Sala, on the west coast of Mauretania near modern Rabat, records how the local Senate honoured Sulpicius Rufus, the prefect, for many services, including the fact that he had procured for the citizens 'free access to the forests and fields' ('liberam copiam silvarum et agrorum praebuisse'). Now Pliny (*NH,* V, 5) said that Sala was 'on the very edge of the desert and beset by herds of elephants' ('solitudinibus vicinum elephantorumque gregibus infestum'). Thus Carcopino has very reasonably linked the inscription with the ivory trade (*Le Maroc antique* (1943), 200 ff. for the inscription, and p. 230 for the ivory). Many of the leading citizens will have been engaged in this trade and united to thank Rufus for some help he gave in protecting the hunters.

**169** Cf. E. H. Warmington, *The Commerce between the Roman Empire and India* (1928), 146.

**170** Horace, *Epist.* II, 1.196: cf. Florus, II, 34.

**171** For detailed reference to the numismatic evidence in this section see J. M. C. Toynbee, *op. cit.* n. 163 above. Temple of

Concord; Pliny, *NH,* XXXVI, 196.

**172** *Anthologia Palatina,* IX, 285. Discussed by C. Cichorius, *Römische Studien* (1922), 344 ff., and O. Weinreich, *Studien zu Martial* (1928), 78 ff. The latter follows the former in assigning the poem to the time of Caligula, but both have overlooked the Tiberius coin. If, as they think, the poem was written for a specific occasion, namely the introduction of this new method of honouring Augustus, then the poem should be dated a few years earlier since the Tiberian coins belong to AD 34–37.

**173** See Pliny, *NH,* VIII, I; Aelian, IV, 10; VII, 44; Plut. *de solert. animal* 18.2; Dio Cassius XXXIX, 38, and above pp. 209, 218, 235 f. A. Passerini, *Athenaeum* 1933, 142 ff., argued that the story of elephants worshipping the moon in Pliny and Aelian derived from Juba, but that Dio recorded an older and contradictory account of their behaviour (and thus stories of their religiosity would have been known in Rome before Juba's time). A. Momigliano, however (*ibid.* 267 f.) shows that Dio was slightly mistaken and does not represent an older tradition. The story of elephants worshipping the sun also probably comes from Juba (as Jacoby, fr. 53): Juba is probably referring to the eastern (Indian) connection with the sun and adding a Mauretanian connection with the moon; an origin in Alexandria and Egypt seems less probable.

283

174 See especially J. Guey, *Revue des études anciennes* 1947, 248 ff., for the inscription and discussion of the implications of *caelestis*.

175 For a candelabrum upheld by three African elephants from Pompeii, see *Papers Brit. Schol. Rome* 1950, pl. v.2.

176 John of Ephesus, quoted by O. Weinreich, *Studien zu Martial* (1928), 84 f. I am grateful to Professor A. Cameron for drawing my attention to this passage.

177 See R. D. Barnett, 'Phoenician and Syrian Ivory Carving', *Palestine Exploration Quarterly*, 1939, 4 ff., 'Early Greek and Oriental Ivories' *Journ. Hellen. Stud.* 1948, 1 ff., *B.M. Catalogue of the Nimrud Ivories* (1957) esp. 173 ff., and for the technique of ivory working, *A History of Technology*, i

(1954), 663 ff. See also D. Harden, *The Phoenicians* (1962), 184 ff. (the East), 206 ff. (the West). H. Kantor, *Amer. Journ. Tech.* 1947, 85 ff. For attempts to distinguish between ancient African and Indian ivory see T. K. Penniman, *Pictures of Ivory*, etc. (*Occ. Pap. Techn.* Pitt Rivers Mus. no. 5, 1952).

178 See S. Hood, *The Home of the Heroes* (1967), 99 f.

179 See Barnett, *Journ. Hellen. Stud.*, 1948.

180 Avien(i)us, *Descriptio Orbis Terrae*, 1315: pars Indi procurat semina dentis/atque ebur invigilat. Cosmas, xi, 449 C–D. See E. H. Warmington, *The Commerce between the Roman Empire and India* (1928), 162 ff. (with full references) for these fluctuations in trade.

181 Cicero (*In Verr.* ii, 4.102) tells of some tusks of

astonishing size in the temple of Juno in Malta: these were plundered by an admiral of Masinissa and presented to the king, but when the latter learnt their origin he sent them back, inscribed in Punic with the statement that he had received them without knowing their source. Cicero also refers to a great quantity of other ivory in the temple, together with many objects of art, including some ivory figures of Victory of ancient and exquisite workmanship. Cf. Pliny, *NH*, viii, 31; Lucian, *dea Syr.* 16. Ivory gate: *Odyss.* xix, 562. Marble houses: Cicero, *Paradox.* l, 3.13. Caligula: Sueton. *Gaius*, 55. Seneca: Dio Cassius, lxi, 10.3. E. H. Warmington, *op. cit.* n. 180 above, p. 163.

# SELECTIVE INDEX

James, St, of Nisibis, 202
Jehu, 29
Jerusalem, 186
Jesus Christ, n.60
Jews, 186–88
John of Ephesus, 259, n.176
Jovian, 204
Juba I, 195f.; II, 147, 208f., 212, 231
Judas Maccabaeus, 186f.
Jugurtha, 192ff.
Julian, 202f.
Jumbo, n.117
Juvenal, 161, 199, n.3, 142

Kaward (Cobades), 205
Khagan of the Avars, 206

Larissa, 179f.
Lascuta, 156
Laurentum, 199
Lazi, 205
Leo X, n.143
Lepcis Magna, 263f.
Libya, definition, n.15
Lichas, 135f.
Licinius, see Crassus
Lilybaeum, 110
Livius Salinator, 164f.
Locri, 162
Loxodonta, 17
Lucan, 217
Lucanian oxen, 104, 243
Lucian, 122
Lucretius, 254, n.154
Lysias, 18ff., 243
Lysimachus, 68, 77, 95, 98, 99f., n.48

Maccabees, 186ff., 244
Magnesia, 180f., 243
Mago, 159f., 162, 167f.
Mammoth, 14
Maranga, 204
Marcellus, Claudius, 162, 164, 165, 172
Marcius, see Philippus
Martial, 257, n.142
Martichora, 34
Matho, 153
Mauretania, 30, 148, 216
Maurice, 206
Mauritania, 25
Maxentius, 256, n.26
Maximian, 256
Mecca, 206
Megalopolis, 83
Megara, 114
Megasthenes, 55–59, 83
Megiddo, 30
Megreb, 26
Meleager, 78

Meles, 171
Melitene, 206
Memphis, 79, 133
Meroe, 120, 232
Mesomedes, n.58
Metaurus, 164f., 242, n.102
Metellus, L., 151f.; Q. Macedonicus, 191; Q. Numidicus, 193; Q. Scipio, 195ff.; coins of, 152, n.90
Micipsa, 178, 191
Minoans, 30, 260
Mishnah, n.60
Mnesitheus, 51f.
Moeris, Lake, 13
Moeritherium, 13, 15
Mohenjo-Daro, 28
Molon, 138
Mucianus, 210
Munda, 166
Musaw-warat, 126
Musri, 29
Muthul, 193
Muttines, n.121
Mycenae, 30, 260
Myrina, statuette, 123, 244, n.65

Narses, 206
Nearchus, 53ff., 74, n.23
Negro, 172f., 177
Nero, 252, 253, 256
Nerva, 256
Nicaea, elephant, 113
Nicanor, 179, 188
Niceratus, n.166
Nicon, elephant, 118, 230
Nile valley, 26f., battles in 79f.
Nimrud, 30, 261
Nisibis, 201, 202
Nobilior, Q. Fulvius, 178, 190
Nonnosus, 207
Nora, 85
Nubia, 27
Numantia, 190f.
Numicius, 109f., n.53
Numidia, 148
Numistro, 164

Octavian, 198
Octavius, Cn. 188
Olympias, 84
Olympus, Mt., 182f.
Onesicritus, 50, 52f., 54, 60, n.23
Ora, 65
Orcynia, 82
Ostia, 253

Pacas, 204
Pacatas, 205
Panium, 144f.

Panormus, 151
Paraetacene, 86–90, 241, n.43
Patroclus, elephant, 212
Paullus, L. Aemilius, 184, 185
Peitholaus, 135, 137
Pelusium, 79
Perdiccas, 68, 77–80
Perseus, 178, 182ff.
Pertinax, 256
Peucestas, 92
Phasis, 206
Philip, V, 144, 178f.: III, see Arridaeus; of Thessalonica, 257, n.172; Roman emperor, 202
Philippus, Marcius, 182f., n.124
Philon, 126
Philostratus, 230–32
Philotera, 126
Phoxidas, 140f.
Piazza Armerina, 252, 254
Pigs, 113ff., 205, 215, n.58
Piraeus, 83
Pithom stele, 128, 142, n.82
Pithom, 88, 91f.
Plato, 36
Plautus, 175, n.38a
Pliny, 209–18
Plutarch, 218f.
Polybius, 218f. and passim
Polyperchon, 83f.
Pompa circensis, 255f.
Pompe at Alexandria, 124f.
Pompeii, statuette, 177, 244, n.117
Pompey, 193, 250f.
Popillius, 185
Porus, 66–71, 75f., 240, n.36
Prasii, 72, 203
Proboscidea, 13ff.
Procurator ad elephantos, n.142
Propertius, n.142
Ptolemais, 128
Ptolemy, Ceraunus, 99f., 120; I, 68, 77–81, 95; II Philadelphus, 99, 123ff., 133, 148, 230; III Euergetes, 133ff.; IV Philopator, 135f., 137–45, 188; V Epiphanes, 137, 144; VI Philometor, 189
Pumbeditha, n.60
Pydna, 84, 184, n.128
Pyrrhus, 100–119
Pythangelus, 135
Pytheas of Boura, 123

Rabirius, C., n.3
Raphia, 139–43, 242, n.81
Regulus, Atilius, 150f.
Rekhmire, 28, 30

287

Rhone, 156ff., n.93
Rigveda, 28

Sabata, 253
Sala, n.168
Sangala, 72
Sargana, 206
Sark, phalera, n.161
Sassanids, 200–207
Satyrus, 120
Scipio, Lucius, 180f.; Publius, 157, 159, 166; P. Africanus, 166–70, n.38a, n.180; P. Aemilianus, 138, 191f. See also Metellus
Scopas, 137
Seleucus, I, 68, 77, 95–100; II, 121, 133ff.; IV, 181
Semiramis, 35f., 241
Sempronius, Ti., 159
Seneca, 173
Sennacherib, 29
Serpents, 216f.
Sesostris, 27
Severus Alexander, 201, 256
Shalmaneser, 27, n.12
Shapur, I, 201; II, 202ff.
Simmias, 59, 135
Simonides of Magnesia, 22f.
Solinus, 31, 217
Solomon, 261

Somalia, 26, 27
Sophagesenus, 144
Sparta, 117f.
Spendius, 153
Sulpicius, see Galba
Surus, 174ff.
Susa, 74
Symmachus, 252
Syracuse, 165
Syrian elephants, 27, 28ff.

Tacfarinas, 208
Tagus battle, 155, n.91
Talmud, n.60
Taprobane, see Ceylon
Tarentum, 102f.
Taxila, 66, 242
Taxiles, 65f.
Terence, 237
Thames, 194
Thapsus, 197, 243, n.139
Themistius, 31
Theodahad, 234f
Theodotus of Rhodes, 122
Thermopylae, 180
Thutmose, 27f. n.7
Tibur, n.142
Tiger, 34, 53, 54, n.25
Tiglath-Pileser, 29, n.12
Towers, 35, 75, 104f., 109, 118, 143, 170, 180, 187, 196, 199,

202, 229, 240–45
Trebia, 159ff., n.95, 96
Trogodytes, 59, 126, 128, 134, 216
Tryphon, 189

Ursicinus, 203
Uzitta, 196

Valerius Laevinus, 103f.
Varus, 194f.
Vedas, the, 28
Vegetius, 250
Veii, statuettes, n.161
Velecha (Volcei), 172, n.113
Verus, 256
Vespasian, 256
Villa Giulia plate, 105, 113, 241, 244
Volcei, see Velecha

Xanthippus, 150

Year of the Elephant, 206

Zama, 168f., n.109, 110
Zeno of Rhodes, 145, n.81
Zoos, ancient: Alexandria, 133; Assyria, 29; China, 28; Dastagerd, 206; Egypt, 28

288